The End of
the American Century

The End
of the
American Century

Hidden Agendas of the Cold War

JEFFREY ROBINSON

SIMON & SCHUSTER
A VIACOM COMPANY

First published in Great Britain by Random Century Group Ltd, 1992
Revised and updated paperback edition published by
Simon & Schuster Ltd, 1997
A Viacom Company

Simon & Schuster Ltd
West Garden Place
Kendal Street
London W2 2AQ

Simon & Schuster Australia
Sydney

A CIP catalogue record for this book is available
from the British Library

ISBN 0-684-81774-8

Typeset in Plantin by
Palimpsest Book Production Limited, Polmont, Stirlingshire
Printed and bound in Finland by
WSOY – Book Printing Division

This book is for Joshua Seth
who also changed the world
with love
papa

Contents

Acknowledgements

There will always be dreamers.

Because certain dreamers have been skillful enough or determined enough or simply lucky enough to see at least some of their dreams come true, the Smithsonian Institute in Washington, DC, has become a living monument to man's dreams. And nowhere are they more vividly displayed than at the Smithsonian's National Air and Space Museum.

When the collection was housed at the famous Castle, they had a few rockets outside, too tall to fit under the roof, lined up like some sort of used ballistic missile lot. You'd walk in from the Mall, weaving your way around ICBMs, before stepping indoors to see the rest of the collection. In those days, there seemed to be a lot on view. But it probably wasn't all that much because, if memory serves, you could see everything in about 20 minutes. You spent most of the time looking up at the ceiling where important planes dangled on wires, as if frozen in midflight.

That's where they hung the Wright brothers' dream.

Orville and Wilbur Wright ran a bicycle shop in Kitty Hawk, North Carolina, in the days when only birds flew. In December 1903, their motorized plane managed to get off the ground and stay that way for 120 feet. It wasn't much. The entire flight could have taken place inside the cabin of a 747 jumbo jet.

Next to that was Charles Lindbergh's dream.

The *Spirit of St Louis* was the single engine, high-wing plane that took him solo across the Atlantic. It had a cowling so huge and instruments piled so high onto the panel in front of a tiny seat that he couldn't see straight ahead unless he leaned out of the window on the flimsy doors that kept him inside the plane. For 33½ hours, he bounced around, strapped into a canvas seat, with his knees crammed up against the forward panel, a yoke coming up between his legs. Although there were times when he managed to climb as high as

10,000 feet, there were also times when he was no more than 10 feet above the waves.

He took off from Roosevelt Field on Long Island, headed across the corner landmass of North America, passed Greenland, somehow found Shannon, Ireland, came down to the Channel and hugged the northern coast of France until he found the Seine and Paris. He was $25,000 richer for the stunt, and a hero too. Although, like so many heroes, he became a hero largely because he lived to tell the story.

In the years that followed, more planes were strung from the ceiling. More missiles joined the collection. And before too long there wasn't any room in that wing of the Castle, so they built a new place, a block down on Independence Avenue. Of course they put the Wright brothers' plane in the main hall. And Lindbergh's plane too. Next to them is Chuck Yaeger's Bell X-1, the first plane to break the sound barrier, and the Bell X-15, which once broke the world's manned altitude record. They also put missiles in there too – American missiles and Russian missiles – and space capsules. They filled the museum with as much hardware as they could collect, honoring the achievement of dreamers who, since Daedalus, longed to leave the bounds of earth. Everything on display is the genuine article. Except for one piece. There is only one replica in the collection. And it too hangs from the ceiling on wires in the main hall.

It's a simple, round, highly polished steel ball, with four antennae sticking out of it. It was produced in a factory not far from Moscow where, ever since 1957, a series of these replicas has been made and given as gifts by the Russians, to display in museums as a reminder of one of the most spectacular achievements in the history of man.

But it almost didn't happen. And when it did, at least at first, very few people realized how significant it would be.

It was left to dreamers to believe that a simple, round, highly polished steel ball, with four antennae sticking out of it, could change the world.

This is the story of that.

The complexity of this story required extensive research in the United States, Europe and the Soviet Union. I am extremely grateful for the cooperation I received in the United States at the National Archives. In particular, my thanks to John Taylor, Milton Gustafson, Will Mahoney, Sue McDonough, Cathy NiCastro and Richard von Dornhoff.

Through the Freedom of Information Act I was able to petition documents, a large number of them never before seen, from the following agencies: the State Department, the Central Intelligence Agency, the National Security Council, the Secret Service, the FBI, the National Security Agency, the United States Information Agency, the Defence Intelligence Agency, the National Science Foundation, the National Aeronautics and Space Administration, and the Defense Department, which includes the Departments of the Army, Navy and Air Force, plus the offices of the Joint Chiefs of Staff.

I owe a special debt of gratitude to the Dwight D. Eisenhower Presidential Library in Abilene, Kansas, and acknowledge my appreciation to the various staff members who were so generous to me there. Materials were received from the Harry S. Truman, John F. Kennedy and Lyndon B. Johnson Presidential Libraries. I also called upon Richard Nixon's Vice-Presidential papers stored in Liguna Niguel, California, and the John Foster Dulles papers at Princeton University. The Eisenhower Administration Oral History Project is housed at Columbia University in New York where the administrator, Ronald Grele, was most kind to help me rummage through as many files as I needed.

In addition to all of the people who so kindly submitted to personal interviews and correspondence – acknowledged in the bibliography – my sincerest thanks go to the staff of the Library of Congress, who were absolutely wonderful; Leroy Doig III, historian for the US Naval Weapons Center, China Lake, California; Jeffrey Richelson of the National Security Archives, Washington, DC; Major Kirk Shippers, United States Army Missile Command, Redstone Arsenal, Huntsville, Alabama; Dr Dean Allard, Director of Naval History, Washington, DC; and Mrs Doris Hunter, Alabama Space and Rocket Center, Huntsville, Alabama.

Also to Emily McKay, the *Huntsville Times*; Huburt Auburn, the *Cleveland Plain Dealer*; Debbie Reid, the *Halifax Mail Star*; Linda Henderson, the *Providence Rhode Island Journal*; John Clark, Richmond Newspapers; Theresa Redderson, the *Seattle Times*; Steven Gibb and Ann Findlay, the *Star Phoenix*; Judy Zipp, *San Antonio Express-News*; Mary Dedinsky, *Chicago Daily News*; Jack Reber, *San Diego Tribune*; Jeanette Curby, *San Antonio Light*; Amanda Valpy, *Toronto Globe and Mail*; Kay Pettit, Missouri State Historical Society; Judy Sall, *Dallas Morning News*; Debra Maneau, *New Orleans Times-Picayune*; Diane Hunter, the *Atlanta Constitution*; Norma Harris, *Vancouver Columbian*; Susan Whiteman, *Schenectady Gazette*; and Joanne Santino, *Jersey City Journal*.

In the United Kingdom I am grateful to the staff of the Public

Record Office and the British Library, although both are infuriating places to work in. They are understaffed, underequipped, have ridiculously inefficient photocopying facilities and are open at hours which appear more convenient to staff members than anyone attempting to do research there.

I received kind assistance from the Cabinet Office, the Foreign Office, the press office at No. 10 Downing Street, the Imperial War Museum, the City of Westminister Public Library system, author Peter Hennessey, and translator Kate Simms.

My many thanks, yet again, to Liz Paton, who copy-edited the manuscript. She's the best. And to Fred Halliday, Professor of International Relations at The London School of Economics and Political Science, for his having gone through it with his scholarly eye, adding his expertise to the text.

In the Soviet Union, I must begin by expressing my thanks to the office of then Foreign Minister Edvard Shevardnadze, and in particular to George Ogonov, who helped steer me through the bureaucratic maze. Sergei Shilov, then assigned to the Embassy of the USSR in London, was my initial contact and he couldn't have been more helpful in arranging further contacts. I received a warm welcome from both the Writers' Union and the Russian Pen Center, which touched me and for which I am enormously grateful. I also wish to say thank you to Sergei Boora and Vladimir Looskanov at *Moscow News* who were very kind, as were members of the staff of what used to be called the Lenin Library, the Communist Party Archives, the Korolev Museum, and the museum to space flight. I also wish to thank members of the staff of the then President, Mikhail Gorbachev, who helped cut through some red tape.

There are a few people whose enormous kindness, generosity, guidance and help on this project I wish to acknowledge separately and with my utmost thanks: Irina and Vladimir Stabnikov, Andrei Podzolka, my fearless interpreter who kept saying, 'You can't ask questions like that,' and kept translating when I did, and, as usual, there is La Benayoun. *Mille merci.*

All dates given in context with the Soviet Union are new calendar dates. Because Russian is written in Cyrillic, you often find variations in name and place spellings. To avoid confusion, I have simply endeavored to use whatever spelling seems to be the most popular.

*   *   *

I wish to add one minor note on research.

One of the joys of a project like this is getting neck deep in all the loose ends which, you hope, will somehow tie together to become a story. You find a thread and follow it – as if it were a clue that leads to other clues – like when we were kids and played detective.

In the case of this project, my research has been divided into four categories, with my emphasis on source material placed in descending order.

(1) *Primary human sources*. That is, interviews and correspondence with the people who were there at the time. I honestly believe that I have tracked down everyone still alive who was involved with this story. Unfortunately, not all of them could be helpful, even when they wanted to be. Age and health were a factor. But in those few cases where someone couldn't help, they were kind enough to point me in the direction of other people who could.

(2) *Primary historical sources*. That is, those documents obtained through Presidential Libraries and the Freedom of Information Act in the United States, the Public Record Office in England, various ministries in France and a myriad of sources, public and private, in the USSR. I include in this category transcripts from several Oral History Programs, such as the Eisenhower Project at Colombia University and the John Foster Dulles papers at Princeton.

(3) *Primary written sources*. That is, autobiographies. Many of the important players and some of the minor characters involved in this story have at some point put pen to paper, giving their version of the events. But that, by definition, presents a problem. Autobiographies are all too often about ego pampering. After all, it's not unheard of to read the same story written by someone else, only to discover that the two versions do not agree – especially when it comes to attributing credit for success and blame for failure. Truth is not always an ingredient of autobiography. Furthermore, because some countries, like England, maintain an Official Secrets Act, there are times when the truth cannot be told at the time of the writing. Therefore, important details are either left out, glossed over, or sometimes, changed to suit a political persuasion. Autobiographical sources tend to be most interesting when dealing with personal opinions and observations. It's not crucial to learn from Harold Macmillan that John Foster Dulles doodled constantly, but it's one

of those little facts that make the character of Dulles that much more human. It's also a safe bet that, had Dulles lived long enough to write his own autobiography, he wouldn't have mentioned it.

(4) *Secondary written sources.* That is, newspaper, magazine, radio, television and film reports of the era. Included here too are books. In this particular case, I've discounted anything for which a source is not satisfactorily referenced. In the case of material that is both relevant and well sourced, I've tried to go back to the original sources to verify both the accuracy and context of the information.

Now, it must be said that research in the United States is particularly easy. I have never once been asked why I wanted certain information. Nor have I ever been asked who I was, or what I intended to do with the information. The fact that I was interested in finding out something was usually enough to gain entrance. This is especially true when dealing with the Freedom of Information Act (FOIA). I've said it before and do not hesitate to say it again: the Freedom of Information Act is tremendous testimony to the complete openness that is a basic requirement for a democratic society.

Skeptics who have never used the FOIA insinuate that government moles do their best to bury embarrassing material, forever keeping such things from the public view. It's nonsense. In fact, quite the opposite is true. The men and women who work in the various FOIA offices of government agencies, in addition to the men and women who work at the National Archives, the Library of Congress and the Presidential libraries, are almost all more than anxious to help researchers find whatever might exist about their specific subject. I have never once encountered any form of interference or any inclination towards obfuscation. It may take time to locate what you want. And there is always the possibility that what you're looking for doesn't exist. But if it does exist and you're willing to take the time, the people working in those offices are paid to help you find it. Once you do find something, you are usually welcome to it. Power outlets for laptop computers are more and more commonplace and photocopiers are almost always readily available. At the National Archives, for instance, you buy a card with a magnetic stripe which serves as a credit card in the photocopying machine. Yes, there are certain copyright restrictions that must be observed. But restrictions are minimal and you can almost always get copies of whatever you want. Making research easier still, libraries and archives are usually open from very early morning until late at night and, often, on weekends.

This is not the case for research in Europe.

I don't know what it is about the European mentality, but I've found it almost the norm to run head first into hordes of suspicious bureaucrats who do whatever they feel they must to keep you from getting the information you want. The simple fact that in Great Britain all government papers are locked away for a minimum of 30 years supports that contention. Why? There is no acceptable reason. Not in a democracy, anyway.

I firmly believe the papers of a government belong to the people and, at the same time, that the public has a right to know what has been and is being done in their name. That is written into US law by the FOIA. It is specifically written out of British law by the 30-year rule and the Official Secrets Act.

The British system is not only undemocratic, it is also open to the most ludicrous sorts of abuse.

Some years ago I was researching an odd criminal case that took place in Britain during the late 1920s and early 1930s. An American fraudster had come to London, fleeced unwitting investors of several million pounds, and fled back to the States when the police caught onto him. By the time I requested the Home and Foreign Office files from the Public Record Office, more than 50 years had elapsed and everyone involved was long dead. The case was interesting because the British failure to extradite the man from the States to stand charges in Britain resulted in a change of the US-UK extradition treaty. But when I looked through the Home Office files, all sorts of papers were missing. The PRO informed me that the matter was still closed. I asked to whom I might appeal and was told I could always write to the Home Office but the chances of getting any joy were almost nil. That proved to be the case. I not only wrote to the Home Office but managed to locate a woman there who claimed to be in charge of such appeals. She admitted on the phone that her job was basically to turn them down. Refusing to let me see those documents made no sense whatsoever. Nor did she ever come forth with a reason. The files were closed and they would stay closed until someone decided to open them. Who was that someone? She said, the Home Secretary. I tried appealing over her head to him, but my request to him was rerouted back to her and steadfastly refused. I returned to the PRO, where, by this time, the Foreign Office files had been located. Not only were they open, but they contained copies of the very same Home Office papers that were being withheld.

A mature democracy trusts its own people, is accountable to its own people. Under the FOIA, an agency withholding information must tell you what they are withholding and why, and then you can appeal to have it. If you run out of appeals with the agency, you can go into the Federal courts and let a judge decide. Yes it takes time and yes it can be expensive, but access to documents cannot be denied to you simply because someone decides, 'National Security.' You don't have to prove they are not sensitive; the burden of proof is on the government to convince a judge that the documents truly meet 'National Security' criteria. If the government can't prove that, you get the papers.

Frankly, it's sinful that there's no Freedom of Information Act, similar to the American statutes, in Great Britain. Believe it or not, during the two years I was researching this story, it was actually easier to get important material from the Soviets than it was from the British. A window was created by *glasnost* and *perestroika*, which meant that secret files were no longer secret and you could see them just for the asking. When the cash crunch came in mid-1991, that window closed. The Russians became instant capitalists and started selling the information. But it still meant you could have it if you could find it, and no one spoke about any 30-year rules.

Research in the USSR was not, however, without its peculiar problems. Many people were still afraid to talk. *Glasnost*, for many people – especially the older generation – is a difficult concept to understand. I found, for example, former diplomats delighted to talk to me about their tours of duty in the West during the 1950s, but the moment I mentioned security, the KGB, intelligence gathering or the like, they clammed up. Conversation stopped dead. Although, amusingly, when the words 'intelligence gathering' were mentioned, they almost to a man gave me the same answer, word for word, 'I was never aware of anything about that.'

Next, there was great confusion about what documents, papers and records actually existed and what should be shown. To begin with, absolutely everybody wants to know why you want to see anything. So you meet with officials and tell them what you want and why you want it and after much talking they decide that you'll need ministerial permission before they can grant you access to the files, which may or may not exist – at least that's their story – depending on how suspicious they are. It's quite a mountain to climb, even though I'm told it's easier these days than it was, say, ten years ago. Thanks to friends with friends in high places, I was shown hundreds of documents. Yet, even with friends who had friends in high places pulling for me, when I asked for photocopies, the usual answer was, that can't be done. Why not? Because it can't be done! In one case, having located certain newspaper cuttings from the 1950s, I was informed that all newspaper cuttings in the Soviet Union over ten years old are classified. Figure that one out! Obviously the people at *Pravda* and *Izvestia* and the *Moscow News* never heard of that edict and their files were most helpfully opened to me.

Another problem is that much of the documentation that does exist in the USSR, be it newspaper accounts or in book form, is unreliable. You cannot immediately discount the official version of events on the odd chance that it may (a) be the truth and/or (b) lead you on to someone or something else. But because the Soviets have, since the Revolution, done whatever has been necessary to keep the system pure, their 'historians' have therefore recreated events to suit ideology rather than the truth. *Glasnost* has gone some way towards changing that, but the starting point is far too late for my purposes.

Just as seriously, documents from the Khrushchev era are scarce. They either don't exist because they've been purged, or they never existed to begin with – believe it or not, much of the business of government in those days was conducted orally – or, simply, no one knows where to find it. Again, it has only been since the Gorbachev era that any serious emphasis has been placed on maintaining papers and documents. It remains to be seen whether the New Russia will ever shed 75 years of tradition and open all its doors. One hopes. But then, one has the same hopes for Great Britain, too.

Prologue

It happened on Saturday, 5 October 1957, at 1:28 a.m. local time, at Baikonour, the brand-new top secret rocket base hidden in the desolate center of the Soviet Union near Tyuratam in the middle of the Kazakhstan steppes.

First there was a colossal roar that shook the ground.

Then there was a massive burst of flames that lit up the pitch-black sky.

The gigantic missile began to move, hesitated for one split second – almost as if it was hanging in mid-air – then lurched upward, forcing its way into the cold and windy night.

Less than 150 yards away, directly in front of the burning launch site, seventeen men in a cramped underground bunker jostled for position to get a better view of the television monitors piled onto a bank of desks shoved up against a badly painted light-green wall. Three other men watched the missile through converted submarine periscopes that poked out of the low, reinforced concrete ceiling just above their heads.

When the rocket's flames disappeared, everybody turned to the flickering radar screens that tracked it for another few minutes. But with each pulsating sweep of the radar's arm, the white blip moved further away from the center, until it just fell off the screen.

Now there was nothing left to do but wait.

Those men in the command post and four other men, packed into a tiny radio van some 700 yards away, stayed where they were. Some of them talked. Most of them smoked. A few shut their eyes and tried to sleep because they'd been awake now for 60 hours. Fatigue showed clearly on faces that already looked deathly ill in the glow of oscilloscopes and radar screens and the light from the black and white television monitors.

There was only enough room in the bunker for one person to pace

I

the floor and the man who claimed that privilege was the stocky, dark-haired, 50-year-old, somewhat bad-tempered Sergei Korolev. He never stopped moving. The others knew enough to stay out of his way. And so they waited.

It was 101 minutes later when they all heard it.

At exactly 3:09 a.m. their radio monitors crackled with a high-pitched 'Beep . . . beep . . . beep . . . beep . . . beep . . . beep.'

Everyone started to scream.

The men in the bunker and the men in the radio van shouted and whooped in triumph. They congratulated Korolev and they congratulated themselves. They hugged and they kissed and a few of them started to sing. High on his success, Korolev turned to embrace the man standing directly behind him, Vasily Rabikov, First Deputy Minister for Heavy Industries and head of the ad hoc State Commission charged with overseeing the launch.

Rabikov held on to Korolev's shoulders with both hands. He was shouting, 'You did it, you did it.' Korolev kept saying, 'Yes, yes, yes.' Rabikov wondered, 'Should we make the call now?' Korolev shook his head. 'Not yet.' A single orbit of the earth was indeed a phenomenal achievement, but no one knew if the thing would stay up there. 'Not yet,' Korolev repeated over the noise, 'not yet.' And for the next 96 minutes, the men in the bunker and the men in the radio van smoked and talked and waited again.

Then, at 4:45 a.m., right on cue, it was there. 'Beep . . . beep . . . beep . . . beep . . .'

For the second time, the room exploded with shouts and cheers.

'Now,' Korolev hollered to Rabikov and pointed to the phone. 'You can call now.'

A triumphant Rabikov screamed that everyone in the bunker must be silent. It took several minutes before they calmed down enough that he could give the operator the number he wanted in Moscow. And it was several more minutes before his call went through.

The man who answered the phone 1600 miles and three time zones away did not say hello. He simply said, 'Ustinov.'

Rabikov told his boss, Marshal Dimitry Ustinov, that the rocket had been successfully launched, that Korolev's satellite was in orbit, that it had already made two trips around the earth and that the radio transmitter was working perfectly.

The Minister for Heavy Industries said that was good news and asked

Rabikov to congratulate Korolev. He put the phone down, and picked it up straight away to dial the First Secretary.

It was just before 2 a.m. Moscow time when a phone started ringing in the two-story house at No. 21 Leninskiya, in the leadership compound on Lenin Hill, near the university, overlooking the Moscow River.

Nikita Khrushchev was fast asleep in the master bedroom on the top floor. He'd returned to Moscow just two days before, after a full month's holiday in the Crimea. The phone didn't wake him there.

But it often did in Moscow.

Throwing a bathrobe on his small, round frame – worried that the ringing would wake his wife in her room or his children and their children in the other rooms downstairs – he marched into the oak-paneled study that adjoined his bedroom. On the big red wooden desk in front of the window, there were four telephones: one without a dial to reach the guard outside, a simple black one for local calls, another black one for long-distance calls, and a large white one – a special line reserved for the most senior members of the government.

It was the large white one ringing.

He grabbed the receiver. 'Hallo,' he said gruffly.

Ustinov greeted him. 'Nikita Sergeivich.'

Khrushchev asked what he wanted.

'I am calling with the exciting news that everything has gone well at Tyuratam. The launch of the rocket has been successful. The artificial earth satellite has been deployed. It is in orbit, circling the earth and the radio signal can be heard very clearly.'

'Oh,' Khrushchev mumbled, then shook his head. 'Frankly, I never thought it would work.'

With that he hung up, padded into his bedroom and went straight back to sleep.

PART I

The Best of Times –
The Worst of Times

*America cannot be responsible for the good behavior of the entire world.
But America is responsible, to herself as well as to history, for the world-
environment in which she lives. Nothing can so vitally affect America's
environment as America's own influence on it, and therefore if America's
environment is unfavorable to the growth of American life, then America has
nobody to blame so deeply as she must blame herself.*

Henry Luce, *The American Century*

Chapter One

Opening Moves

The heavy folder of perfectly typed, wide-margined pages which landed on Harry Truman's desk late on an autumn afternoon in 1946 spelled out, in no uncertain terms, what many people in the country instinctively and so deeply feared – that the United States and the Soviet Union were on an irreconcilable course towards war.

The words 'Top Secret' were prominently stamped at the head and foot of every page. The indication that this was 'Copy No. 1 of 10' appeared on the front of the report, just above the title, 'American Relations with the Soviet Union.'

Truman hastily thumbed the first few pages before glancing at his watch.

His Special Counsel, a 39-year-old attorney and fellow Missourian named Clark Clifford, had spent the past six months consulting with the cabinet, senior military commanders and the nation's highest-ranking intelligence officers to compile what the 33rd President expected to be the most up-to-date and accurate assessment of the nation's fate.

This wasn't something he wanted to rush through. But he saw that if he started reading it now he'd be late for dinner. So he carried it back to his private apartments on the second floor of the west side of the White House and later that evening got into bed with it. He usually read himself to sleep every night, preferring biographies and books about the troubles of some previous President to anything like official documents.

This was different. He was mesmerized by Clifford's revelations, and stayed up most of the night, until he finished it.

Early the next morning he rang Clifford at home to ask how many copies had been made. Clifford reminded him there were ten. All right, Truman ordered, get the other nine and bring them to me in the Oval Office right away. A few hours later, Clifford piled them onto a table in front of the President. Staring at the stack of copies, Truman said the report was so red hot it would have to be kept under lock and key. No one else was to see it. 'If this should come out now it could have an exceedingly unfortunate impact on our efforts to try to develop some relationship with the Soviet Union.'

So all ten copies were abruptly locked away in a White House safe.

Nine months old, this had already been one hell of a year.

On 9 February, Josef Stalin addressed a Communist Party rally held in Moscow's Bolshoi Theatre, announced an ambitious five-year plan for armament production to 'protect the USSR against any eventuality,' and, in the same breath, officially abandoned his former allies. Denouncing coexistence with the West, he spelled out his intention to spur on a world revolution for the proletariat, declared capitalism the cause of World War II and condemned the capitalist world – specifically the United States – for standing in the way of this goal.

American reaction to the speech was severe. Most critically, Supreme Court Justice William Douglas labeled it, 'The declaration of World War III.'

A week or so later, Igor Gouzenko, a code clerk at the Soviet Embassy in Ottawa defected to the Canadians and subsequently blew the whistle on a far-flung network of atomic spies. He helped to unmask Klaus Fuchs in England and the Greenglass-Sobel-Gold-Rosenberg network in the United States. That, in turn, helped to reinforce the Soviet's image as the enemy.

On 5 March, Winston Churchill stamped the term 'Iron Curtain' into the history of the modern era. These days it's often accepted that Churchill coined the expression. Not true. He lifted it from several people, beginning with H. G. Wells, who used it in a 1904 short story, *The Food of the Gods*. The phrase next appeared at the outset of WWI when the Queen of Belgium referred to the German division of Europe, and again at the end of WWII, in reference to the Soviet division of Europe, this time used by Nazi propaganda minister Joseph Goebbels. Not long afterwards, Britain's *Sunday Empire News* headlined a story, 'An Iron Curtain Across Europe.' Yet it took Churchill to put it into the vernacular in these early 'sound bite' days.

It was in Fulton, Missouri, during a commencement address at the otherwise obscure Westminster College, where he said, 'From Stettin in the Baltic to Trieste in the Adriatic, an iron curtain has descended across the continent.' Proclaiming the Communists a growing peril to

Christian civilization, he alleged that, while they did not want war, they did indeed want the fruits of war. He insisted that the way to stop the Russians was with the only thing they respected, a show of strength, and emphasized his staunch belief that to preserve peace, the United States and Great Britain must form a permanent military alliance centered around America's atomic monopoly.

Some Americans felt Churchill was being deliberately belligerent, that he saw danger where no real danger existed. Harry Truman, among them, discreetly distanced himself from such rhetoric. But Stalin likened Churchill to Hitler and openly accused him of plotting against the Soviet Union's right to exist by calling for war.

It was journalist Herbert Bayard Swope who then coined the phrase 'Cold War.' He put it into a speech written for financier Bernard Baruch, although Baruch thought it too strong and didn't bother with it until the following year. Newspaper columnist Walter Lippmann turned it into a popular term when he used it as the title of his bestselling book on American-Soviet relations.

Unbeknownst to the general public, and underlying this sense of unease, was a 5500-word, top secret telegram from America's *chargé d'affaires* in Moscow to Secretary of State George C. Marshall. Dated 22 February, 1946 – just 13 days after Stalin's speech – it was written by George Frost Kennan, a 42-year-old Princeton graduate, career foreign service officer and expert on Russian matters.

In what is commonly referred to today as 'The Long Telegram,' Kennan was trying to remind his superiors that the post-war Soviet regime was exactly the same as the pre-war Soviet regime, that postwar Stalin was still Stalin of the purges. He stressed that any American dreams of worthwhile collaboration with the Soviets were fanciful, illustrated how the Communists saw the capitalist world beset with internal conflicts and explained why they believed these conflicts could never be solved by peaceful means. Conveying Stalin's thoughts, he portrayed a Soviet leadership who preached, 'Everything must be done to advance relative strength of USSR as factor in international society. Conversely, no opportunity must be missed to reduce strength and influence, collectively as well as individually, of capitalist powers.'

Kennan steadfastly maintained that, hand-in-hand with the Kremlin's neurotic view of world affairs, came a traditional and instinctive sense of insecurity. 'They have always feared foreign penetration, feared direct contact between Western world and their own, feared what would

9

happen if Russians learned truth about world without or if foreigners learned truth about world within. And they have learned to seek security only in patient but deadly struggle for total destruction rival power, never in compacts and compromises with it.'

Furthermore, he observed, Soviet power, unlike the power held by Hitler and the Nazis, was neither schematic nor adventuristic. 'It does not work by fixed plans. It does not take unnecessary risks. Impervious to logic of reason, it is highly sensitive to logic of force. For this reason it can easily withdraw, and usually does, when strong resistance is encountered at any point. Thus, if the adversary has sufficient force and makes clear his readiness to use it, he rarely has to.'

Likening the Russians to a toy car that moves along a prescribed path, 'wound up and headed in a given direction, stopping only when it meets some answerable force,' he hoped to compel Marshall and the others to come to terms with a basic fact of Soviet life: The USSR was 'committed fanatically to the belief that with the United States there can be no permanent *modus vivendi*, that it is desirable and necessary that the internal harmony of our society can be disrupted, our traditional way of life be destroyed, the internal authority of our state be broken, if Soviet power is to be secure.'

Marshall was so impressed with Kennan's report, he circulated it throughout the State Department. An equally impressed Secretary of the Navy, James Forrestal, made certain it became required reading at the Pentagon. Unquestionably, Truman also saw it.

Now here was Clark Clifford underscoring Kennan's thesis by reporting that Stalin was steering the Russians on a course designed eventually to lead to world domination.

'Soviet leaders,' Clifford wrote, 'believe that a conflict is inevitable between the USSR and capitalistic states, and their duty is to prepare the Soviet Union for this conflict. The aim of current Soviet policy is to prepare for the ultimate conflict by increasing Soviet power as rapidly as possible and by weakening all nations who may be considered hostile.'

Clifford pointed out that the Soviets broke, or at least 'reinterpreted' to their own advantage, every one of the agreements signed at Teheran, Yalta and Berlin. He noted, they were forever improving their military position, had just constructed air bases in northeastern Siberia from which they could attack the United States, and were in the midst of building a huge submarine fleet for commerce raiding. At the same time, they were actively involved in both subversive movements and espionage on US soil.

He cautioned that any sudden or unexpected moves by the Soviet Union might, if America did not fully understand the methods of the Kremlin, lead to a showdown of force. And, if that happened, the West would probably be unprepared. 'The United States must assume that the USSR may at any time embark on a course of expansion effected by open warfare and therefore must maintain sufficient strength to restrain the Soviet Union.'

Throughout the year, the Russians had grown adept at testing American mettle by openly confronting US foreign policy in Germany, Iran and Turkey. At one point, Truman feared the Russians might even try to make a stand in France. The situation there was chaotic and the local Communist Party seemed poised to seize control of the government. To prevent the Russians from moving in with the French Communists, Truman secretly ordered his Army commanders in Germany to prepare for the invasion and occupation of France. When that confrontation was averted, he thought he might somehow be able to buy the Soviets out of Eastern Europe. Truman offered them a $1 billion loan together with membership in the World Bank and the International Monetary Fund. But Stalin saw the bribe for what it was, and flatly rejected it. He also turned down American proposals to eliminate the spread of atomic weapons when the United Nations formed its Atomic Energy Commission.

At the end of WWII, Truman had naively disbanded the Office of Strategic Services (OSS) because he'd believed that political manipulation, paramilitary operations and psychological warfare did not constitute tolerable behavior for a government during peace time. He didn't have any intelligence experience and obviously didn't have much interest in the field either, because now – for little reason other than keeping the more hawkish members of his cabinet at bay, those members who contended Pearl Harbor could never have happened if America had been more active in the intelligence field – he agreed to form the National Intelligence Authority (NIA) and, under it, the Central Intelligence Group (CIG).

On 24 January, 1946, he called Fleet Admiral William Leahy and Rear Admiral Sydney Souers into his office to give them their orders. Leahy would set policy at the NIA, Souers would carry it out through the

CIG. To make everything official, after handing each man a black hat, black coat and wooden dagger, Truman proclaimed, 'By virtue of the authority vested in me as Top Dog, I require and charge Front Admiral Leahy and Rear Admiral Souers to receive and accept the vestments and appurtenances of their respective positions, namely as personal snooper and as director of centralized snooping.'

It's little wonder that anyone ever bothered to take the NIA and CIG more seriously than the President, and credit to both Leahy and Souers that they were able to function at all. Without the weight of the Oval Office strongly behind them, they still somehow convinced the State Department to establish a 'special section' at the US Embassy in Moscow, which turned it into a listening post. The British quickly followed suit, and the following year a treaty was signed between the United States, Britain, Canada and Australia to pool specific types of intelligence information. Electronic spying was still in its infancy so the emphasis had to be placed on a systematic perusal of the Soviet press. Selected embassy staff became zealous readers, not only of *Pravda* and *Izvestia*, but of every technical journal and trade paper they could get their hands on. Press reports were supplemented by whatever direct contacts could be established with Soviet citizens, although Leahy and Souers both stressed that such contacts not only were to be considered dangerous, they were also highly unreliable.

In the short term, there seemed little Truman could do to cool Stalin's increasingly confrontational behavior. With 'Uncle Joe's' grip on Soviet foreign policy as firm as it was ever going to be, the United States and the Soviet Union had long since stopped speaking to each other and were now speaking past each other. Americans were starting to see themselves as the final defenders of the free world, while the Soviets were thinking that they were the ultimate defenders of socialism. That November, the American people showed their concern by giving control of Congress to the Republicans, bringing to Washington men like Richard Nixon and Joseph McCarthy, who would soon make significant contributions to the growing tension.

By the end of 1946, the stage was fully set.

The British had spent much of the past 100 years pompously trying to civilize the world. The Empire had just about evaporated and the Commonwealth was reduced, for all intents and purposes, to nothing more than a seating plan for Coronations and royal weddings. The

Soviets were intent on liberating the workers of the world. America intended to conquer the world with Hershey bars, nylon stockings and Tupperware. The struggle against Communism was therefore based on more than just physical survival. It had, at its very essence, America's capitalistic heritage and ideals.

A renewed sense of Pan-Arab nationalism swept through the Middle East at the same time that Israel championed statehood, putting an end to what little credibility the British still had in that part of the world. There was turmoil in Africa and unrest in India, which created genuine fears around Whitehall that the sub-continent could swing to the Communists and the realization that there was nothing anybody could do about it. The United Kingdom, Harold Macmillan later wrote, was well on its way to confirming its place as one of the world's eminent second-class powers, soon to be joined by post-war France and a rebuilt Germany.

As it happened, Britannia's rule of the waves was officially declared dead on Friday morning, 21 February, 1947. The British Ambassador to Washington, Lord Inverchapel, rang the State Department to announce a letter – referred to as 'a blue piece of paper' – which he needed to deliver urgently to George Marshall. The Under Secretary of State, Dean Acheson, explained that his boss was out of town and wondered if it could wait until Monday. Inverchapel said it could not and that the British Embassy's First Secretary was bringing it over right away. The note, which was titled, 'Crisis and Imminent Possibility of Collapse,' formally urged the United States to send $200 million to a Greek coalition government so that it could defend itself from a possible Communist take-over. It was necessary, Inverchapel explained, because his government could no longer afford to meet that commitment. He went on to state that the Turks needed money too and, much to his own embarrassment, that Britain was seeking help as well.

Under the umbrella of the Truman Doctrine, the President offered the Greeks and the Turks economic and military aid, in addition to promising support to any country willing to resist Communist intervention. But dealing with the United Kingdom was not as straightforward. At first Truman felt that the $40 billion in Lend-Lease and the additional $3.75 billion he'd loaned Britain only seven months before should have been enough to pay off any obligations America might have. His stance softened when he learned the UK was paralyzed and that the economy was about to collapse. Industries were shut, unemployment was at a record high and agriculture was in such a sorry state that food rationing had surpassed wartime levels.

Under Secretary of State Will Clayton had seen the problem first hand during a six-week tour of Europe and returned to Washington with the brief outline of a solution. He explained the plan to Dean Acheson, who took it to Truman. On 8 May, Acheson revealed the basics of it at a speech on the campus of Delta State Teachers College in Cleveland, Mississippi. After recounting how the margins of survival had been so narrow over the past winter that the peoples of northern Europe had been faced with extinction, Acheson said, 'It is one of the principal aims of foreign policy today to use our economic and financial resources to widen those margins. It is necessary if we are to preserve our own freedoms and our own democratic institutions. It is necessary for our own national security.' That became the blueprint for the European Recovery Plan, remembered these days as the Marshall Plan. It turned out to be one of the most brilliant successes in the history of international relations. America fed Great Britain and 15 other countries and single-handedly restored the economic health of Western Europe.

But it was not all for the sake of charity.

There had been talk around Washington early in Truman's first term that the best way to check the spread of Communism was to 'book-end' it, to create bulwarks on each side of the Soviet Union. That argument was justified in 1948 when the Russians showed their hand by blockading Berlin. A deliberate decision was made to politically, economically and militarily strengthen West Germany and Japan. The Marshall Plan fit handily into the wider scope of this agenda.

Superimposing that over continued concern for the revelations in Clifford's report, Truman set about reorganizing the national defense structure, bringing the Army, Navy and newly born Air Force together under the Department of Defense. Realizing his mistake with the NIA/CIG, he convinced Congress to pass the National Security Act, which provided for the creation of a secret intelligence agency that would not be subject to the usual congressional reviews. On paper, the Act entrusted his newborn Central Intelligence Agency with a basic overt mission, that being the collection of intelligence. However, Truman staffed the CIA with former OSS men, such as Allen Dulles, and somehow never seemed to notice that one clause of the Act also authorized the agency to conduct, 'Other functions and duties related to intelligence.' The top men at the CIA immediately took that to mean they were also in the covert mission business, which included all of the political manipulation, paramilitary operations and psychological warfare they could find. The Agency opened its doors in July 1947, using borrowed offices all over Washington, employing literally a handful of people. By October 1957, the CIA payroll numbered more than 15,000.

Kennan, who'd been brought back to Washington to head up the State Department's policy planning staff, now expounded on his earlier thesis. Writing under the anonymous byline 'X' in the much-respected quarterly magazine *Foreign Affairs*, his 'Sources of Soviet Conduct' defined Communism as one of the world's great religions. He said it was as indestructible as Islam and that it came complete with doctrine, rites and historic goals. Like Islam, it would take hold in societies weakened by people seeking change. Once that happened, it could never be completely eliminated. However, he considered, Communism could be 'contained.'

Truman was so smitten with the idea that containment quickly became a key theme in his defense policy. Yet by deliberately conceding to the Soviets their present borders, and then trying to confine Communism to those borders, he did not eliminate the possibility of war. Containment, in fact, heightened it. The CIA was reporting back to the President that, while it was unlikely the Kremlin would intentionally go to war to gain its ends within the next decade, no one could rule out circumstances which might compel the Russians to act violently.

'In this respect,' the CIA anticipated, 'the situation will remain critical. . . . Moreover, there is constant danger of war through accident or miscalculation.'

Several factors seemed to be leading up to that possibility.

In February 1948, Stalin took Czechoslovakia with a Communist coup. Three months later he cut off land access to Berlin, requiring a monumental air lift to keep the American, British and French zones of the city alive.

A beleaguered Harry Truman now flirted with the idea of standing aside. Astonishingly – not once but twice – he offered his place on the Democrat's 1948 presidential ticket to General Dwight David Eisenhower. If Ike would accept the party's nomination, Truman said, he would acquiesce and move down a notch, going onto the ticket as Eisenhower's Vice-President.

Having hit the national bestseller lists in 1948 with his well-written memoirs, *Crusade in Europe*, Eisenhower was such an attractive person-ality that both parties wanted to nominate him. Truman didn't have the slightest idea if Eisenhower was a Republican or a Democrat. In fact, no one knew what his personal politics were. All that really mattered was that Ike was a genuine folk hero and probably could have won an election on either ticket. Although there's always been some speculation that he turned down Truman's offers because he suspected that, with Truman as his running mate, he might just lose, in the end he refused because he strongly believed soldiers should not immerse themselves in politics. He even told a reporter, 'I cannot conceive of any circumstance that could drag out of me permission to consider me for any political post from dog catcher to Grand High Supreme King of the Universe.'

That November, Truman faced Thomas Dewey in what turned out to be one of the most dramatic elections in history. The President went to bed on election night in Kansas City convinced he'd been defeated. The Republican Governor of New York woke up the next morning, was shown the *Chicago Daily Tribune*'s banner headline, 'Dewey Defeats Truman,' and then had to be informed that, in fact, he might not have won the Presidency. Just before noon, it was confirmed that Truman had been returned to office.

The new term began with Truman moving out of the White House while it was completely renovated. He lived and worked in the very cramped three-story Blair House, an official guest residence diagonally across Pennsylvania Avenue that looked more like No. 10 Downing Street than it did a presidential mansion. Still, the single most important problem facing him continued to be how to deal with a hostile Soviet Union.

As the next step in the 'book-end' policy, Truman oversaw the formulation of a military counter-weight to the Russian forces in Europe which eventually became the North Atlantic Treaty Organization. By increasing American presence on Japanese soil, Truman thought – mistakenly – he could reduce American aid to the Chinese Nationalist regime under Chiang Kai-shek. That miscalculation brought about the fall of mainland China to Mao Tse-tung.

Even more menacing, on 23 September, 1949, Truman announced that the Soviets had successfully tested an atomic bomb. It came as a great shock, especially since many people who were supposed to know about these things were saying the Russians had not yet amassed either the know-how or the fissionable materials necessary to create an atomic explosion. It was especially prophetic that almost four years to the day before Truman's announcement, George Kennan had warned about the dangers of just such an occurrence. Having witnessed first hand the Russians' particularly keen interest in the bombs that destroyed Hiroshima and Nagasaki, he'd cautioned in September 1945 that atomic secrets must never make their way into Russian hands. 'There is nothing, I repeat nothing, in the history of the Soviet regime which could justify us in assuming that the men who are now in power in Russia, or even those who have chances of assuming power within the foreseeable future, would hesitate for a moment to apply this power against us if by doing so they thought it would materially improve their own power position in the world . . . To assume that Soviet leaders would be restrained by scruples of gratitude or humanitarianism would be to fly in the face of overwhelming contrary evidence on a matter vital to the future of our country.'

Russian success was put down to invaluable assistance from captured German scientists and a masterful spy network operating in North America. Truman argued that the Russians had been working on the weapon for years, having made an all-out effort at Stalin's insistence. But the country took little solace in any of the various explanations. Not only was Truman now seen as the man responsible for the loss of China, but just like that, he'd also forfeited America's atomic monopoly.

When the National Security Council went to work on the new state of the world, they came up with some horrifying conclusions. Their report, known as NSC-68, was based not on what the Russians might do, but on what they could do. It began by taking two points for granted: First, that the Americans and the Soviets now dominated the world; and second, that the USSR was enslaved by a fanaticism that sought to impose its absolute authority over the rest of the world.

It was transparent to the men who drafted NSC-68 that, based on both Soviet theory and practice, the Kremlin sought to bring the free world under its domination by fighting and winning the Cold War. 'The Kremlin is inescapably militant because it possesses and is possessed by a world-wide revolutionary movement, because it is the inheritor of Russian imperialism, and because it is a totalitarian dictatorship.'

In the minds of the Soviet leaders, they wrote, 'achievement of this design requires the dynamic extension of their authority and the ultimate elimination of any effective opposition to their authority.'

From what was known of Soviet capabilities, the report surmised:

(1) the Russians could overrun most of Europe, threaten oil supplies in the Middle East and consolidate their gains in the Far East;
(2) they could attack England by air and successfully control both the Atlantic and Pacific shipping routes;
(3) they could use atomic weapons against selected targets, which would include Canada and the United States.

Four courses of action therefore seemed open to the United States. It could:

(1) do nothing, which meant maintaining the status quo;
(2) launch a preventive surprise attack on the USSR to stop any further expansion;
(3) withdraw behind Fortress America;
(4) create a massive military to meet any Soviet challenge anywhere on earth.

In the end it was obvious that the United States, as leaders of the free world, had no choice but to impose order around the world.

It was NSC-68 that made America the global policeman.

The key to peace, came the theory, lay in possessing such enormous military power that any attack against the United States would be unthinkable. Therefore, rebuilding the American military was an immediate requirement. The report concluded that there was no future in any further negotiations with the Soviets at this time because they were clearly not going to change their policies. At the same time, America would now have to develop the 'ultimate' hydrogen weapons to offset Russia's atomic bomb. Finally, the nation would have to fund a hugely powerful conventional force so that, if and when a conflict erupted, atomic weapons would be unnecessary.

The man behind NSC-68, Dean Acheson, had by this time succeeded George Marshall as Secretary of State. That America's Soviet experts – George Kennan and the future Ambassador to the USSR Charles 'Chip' Bohlen – were disagreeing with much of the report's wording and many of the NSC's conclusions, seemed irrelevant. Acheson had convinced Truman that the Russians were coming and that containment meant meeting their force with superior force wherever American interests were threatened.

Not that Acheson and the NSC had a monopoly on paranoia. Word around the Pentagon was, now that the Russians have atomic weapons they are obviously planning to use them. And, if they use them wisely, in a surprise attack during a very specific window of opportunity, Soviet forces could conquer the United States.

While NSC-68 was still being written, the Joint Chiefs of Staff – seriously alarmed by the fact that Russia had the bomb – ordered their Joint Intelligence Committee (JIC) to study the implications of atomic weapons in the USSR. The top secret 60-page answer, submitted on 23 February 1950, was even more shocking than Clark Clifford's 1946 report to the President.

According to the JIC, the Soviets wouldn't deliberately venture into any military action which might involve them in an open war, *unless* they feared that the Western powers were ready to attack, or they considered that other methods of attaining their objectives had failed, or they felt at any time that it was to their advantage to start a war. Except – and here the report qualified that concession – 'until such time as the Soviet regime considers that it possesses an adequate military capability, atomic as well as conventional, as compared with the United States and its allies.'

In other words, the JIC anticipated, once the Russians had sufficient strike power they would launch a surprise attack against the United States and its allies.

'With the progressive increase in Soviet atomic capability, the attitude of the Kremlin will become more truculent, thus increasing the risk of war.' The report persisted, 'Unless the United States suffers such a devastating economic collapse that it becomes unable to oppose effectively the Soviet Union, military conflict between the Soviet Union and the United States and its allies is not only inevitable but essential to the realization of the Soviet ultimate objective.'

Much of how and when this would take place rested with the Soviet leaders themselves. If they considered that all other means and methods of obtaining their objective of world domination had failed, they would probably attack the United States and its allies at the earliest opportune moment. The committee also reasoned that the probability of a surprise attack against the United States and/or its allies would increase as the Russian atomic stockpile increased. As part of their game plan, the Soviets would continue to stir up mass opinion in the West for disarmament and against the use of atomic weapons in the event of war. They might even be willing to sign an international agreement outlawing the use of atomic weapons. But, based on past performance, it was evident that the USSR would not hesitate to violate any agreement, especially if it gave them an advantage over the Western powers who would clearly abide by the agreement.

Not only was the Continental United States vulnerable to air and guided missile attack, the JIC discovered, but the Soviet atomic bomb also threatened the United Kingdom, which would have to be the main launching base for Allied air operations against the USSR. It was vital that the British resist the Russians. But if the Marshall Plan failed, Great Britain might turn its back on America. Because of their extreme vulnerability to atomic attack, a British government might also become somewhat reluctant to support the United States in a proposal which could somehow provoke the USSR into using armed force. Therefore, the JIC wrote, 'It must be considered possible that the United Kingdom, because of its extreme vulnerability, could be detached from alignment with the United States.'

Intelligence reports uncovered that the Soviets could produce 24 bombs a year but had a uranium stockpile for 150. The TU-4 – their equivalent of the B-29 bomber – was capable of carrying 10,000 pounds of bombs 2150 nautical miles on a two-way mission or 3960 nautical miles on a one-way mission. Great Britain was easily within range. So was Canada. So too was a good portion of the United States. A horde of Russian bombers coming on the northern run from Siberian bases could, on one-way missions, reach every important industrial, urban and government control center in the US. To manage that, the Russians would have to be willing to sacrifice airplanes and crews. And the JIC was convinced they wouldn't think twice about paying such a price.

The Soviets were also developing their guided missile capability, and within a few years would have at least 51 submarines which could bring atomic bombs inside US waters to threaten both coasts.

To achieve their objective, the JIC concluded, it wouldn't be necessary for the Russians to have as many bombs as the Americans, just enough to inflict critical damage. Based on an assumption that the Soviets, in order to destroy the United States in a surprise attack, would have to deliver 60% of their A-bombs on target, the 'Doomsday scenario' looked like this:

Putting 10–50 bombs on target required a stockpile of 16–83 bombs, which, according to intelligence estimates of Soviet atomic bomb production, the Russians would have between January 1951 and mid-1952. But with those numbers, even if they hit the major political and population centers – Washington DC, New York, Los Angeles, San Francisco, possibly London and possibly Ottawa – plus the major retaliatory targets such as Strategic Air Command bases and major US Navy installations like the ones at Norfolk, Virginia and San Diego, California – it would not be enough to win the war. Mobilization would be seriously hampered and the neutralization of key ports would greatly delay an American response. Yet it would not be fatal.

To deliver 50–125 bombs, they'd need to produce 90–200, which they would manage between January 1953 and mid-1954. Now they could expand their targets to include all major North American cities and selected industrial facilities. Still, the backbone of the American and Canadian capacity for war production would not be broken. If they also targeted London, Glasgow, Birmingham, Manchester, Liverpool, Sheffield, Belfast, Bristol, Newcastle, Cardiff, Coventry, Derby, Preston and Hull, they would, in the words of the JIC, 'create a profound and awe-inspiring impression.'

But again, it would not be enough to win the war.

It would be when the Soviets could successfully deliver 200 bombs – meaning they'd need to produce 300 – that the attack would be decisive. And the Russians would have produced that many bombs sometime after January 1955.

For the handful of men who controlled America's destiny, World War III was just five years away.

Chapter Two

The Soviet Challenge

Red Square hasn't changed much since the days when Vladimir Ilyich Lenin walked to his office at the Kremlin from his rooms across the street in the building which is now the National Hotel.

The large cobblestones were put there sometime in the 17th or 18th centuries, as the huge expanse east of the Kremlin's walls developed into the commercial center of Moscow. It's doubtful that the painted white lines which once, famously, divided the square into columns for parading troops, passing rocket launchers and dancing school children bearing banners were there in Lenin's days, even though the square has been the site of manifestations, demonstrations, proclamations, markets and public repression since the 16th century. Ivan the Terrible challenged the people there, Czars were proclaimed there and at times Czars were deposed there. Peter I carried out mass executions there and Lenin's forces massed there in November 1917 to launch their final assault on the Kremlin. Nazi war prisoners were paraded there at the end of World War II. What was left of the victorious Soviet army were reviewed there as well. And year after year, all those big, noisy, traditional May Day parades happened there too.

The Kremlin is better lit now than it was in Lenin's day. Huge spotlights around Red Square illuminate the majestic Italian-designed walled fortress all night long. The doors to the GUM department store – with a splendid glass ceiling and birds flying around inside – are shut on Red Square because someone arbitrarily decided the main entrance must be around the corner. St Basil's Cathedral has probably been painted a few times since Lenin's day, but still looks like a joke wedding cake. The red-brick building on the north side of the square was the original site of Moscow University and is now the Historical Museum. Exhibits there include Lenin's Rolls-Royce and the bullet-ridden shirt he wore during an assassination attempt in 1918.

You usually find a *marroshnia* vendor somewhere on Red Square, ice cream being one of the best things that Russia has to offer. And every now and then someone is bound to slink up to ask if you want to exchange money, need a taxi, care to buy some sort of souvenir, or if you have ever considered selling the shirt off your back. None of that is likely to have been there in Lenin's day.

Yet the single most dramatic difference is the mausoleum on the west side of Red Square. It was built in October 1930 in red, grey and black granite to be Lenin's tomb. For a while it was Stalin's tomb too, which must have troubled Lenin's spirit because Stalin would not have been his choice of roommate, and anyway, Lenin had asked to be buried next to his mother in his old home town.

When he died in 1924, Lenin's body was brought from Gorky and put in a ramshackle wooden structure on the square. When that looked like it was about ready to collapse, a sturdier one was built. New embalming techniques were developed so that the great leader's remains could stay on view for future generations to worship. But those new techniques weren't good enough, so Stalin approved this stone vault – in the style of an Aztec stepped-pyramid – and ordered the creation of a special embalming laboratory inside the mausoleum to keep Lenin in shape. When the Germans threatened in 1941, the Communist leadership hustled the body out of Moscow, hiding it in the Urals until April 1945 when Stalin decreed it was safe enough to bring it back. In the meantime, the Russians camouflaged the mausoleum to protect it from the Luftwaffe.

Indirect lighting and special temperature conditions were devised to protect what was left of Lenin. At least he was protected as long as there was something left to Communism. For 67 years, from his death until those few fateful nights in August 1991, the mausoleum and the glass-topped coffin inside it were the focal point of world Communism, much like the Vatican is the focal point of world Catholicism. In fact, the way Soviet society was structured – at least the agnostic society that Russia used to be – religion was the state and the state was religion, and Lenin was the Messiah.

Because no one ever had to bank on his resurrection, his brain was taken out from between his ears and sent to the Institute of the Brain, which Stalin specifically created to prove that Lenin – and the men who pioneered Communism with him, who naturally included Stalin – were far beyond normal genius status and therefore represented some kind of mental master race. Lenin's brain was stored in Room No. 19 of the Institute, which used to be permanently guarded by the KGB, at least in the days when there still was a KGB. Spanning three decades, approximately 30,000 slivers of Lenin's brain – thinly sliced, like the way a great deli does cold cuts – were studied. Work on Lenin stopped at about the time Stalin's brain was brought to the Institute and pickled for the same purpose. Other brains in the collection once belonged to composer Peter Ilyich Tchaikovsky, poet Vladimir Mayakovsky, writer Maxim Gorky and film director Sergei Eisenstein. A recent addition is the brain of the dissident physicist Andrei Sakharov.

In the old days, it took hours to get in to see Lenin. You'd queue with the pilgrims, shuffling solemnly past his Red Army guards, just to get a five-second glance. At least the official story always had it that what you saw was the real thing. There are however some Russians who'll lead you to believe that what you were seeing was nothing more than sculpted wax – which is what he looked like anyway after all this time – that his body decayed years ago and was secretly disposed of. There are others who swear they were walking past the bier one day when Lenin's ear fell off. Whether the ears on his head were melted on or glued on or nailed in place – whether they're his or somebody else's – hardly matters now. The fact is, he's gone too. And so has the system he created.

Lenin walked the earth to show the working classes the route to social freedom and, having done that, what remains is one re-embalmable corpse, and enough quotes – sometimes real, often imagined and now out of date – to have fit any occasion. Lenin said this. And Lenin said that. And the world according to Lenin dictates there is only one way, ours, and we shall triumph.

The man who became Pope to Lenin's Holy See was Josef Stalin.

At the time of Lenin's death, Communism was little more than an ideal in the minds of a few enthusiasts. The Union of Soviet Socialist Republics was not yet formed. Russia was a backward, rural land mass. It was Stalin who converted it into an international power. It took him a few years, but he ultimately eliminated his adversaries on the left – men like the internationalist Leon Trotsky – and eliminated his adversaries on the right – men like the early Bolshevik theorist Nikolai Bukharin – and by 1929 he was not only the undisputed leader of the Party, he was the absolute ruler, the new Czar of this empire.

He seized land and crops from the *kulaks* or middle-class farmers, deported some five million of them as 'bourgeois residue,' exported the stolen grain to raise capital and began a massive industrialization program. When any opposition arose to his tyranny – as it did among the peasants during the famine of 1932, or at the beginning of 1934 when Leningrad's Party leader Sergei Kirov spoke out against him – he settled his scores swiftly and effectively. He liquidated Kirov and used the assassination as a pretext to arrest virtually all the Party's major figures on the grounds that they were saboteurs. From 1936 to 1938, Stalin's purges saw prominent people arrested for, charged with and convicted of preposterous crimes. Nearly 80% of the Central Committee members elected in 1934 had been shot by 1939 and 60% of the delegates who'd attended that 17th Party Congress were in prison. He unleashed the secret police on the population and countless millions were sacrificed. At the same time, Stalin's cult of personality fostered such adulation of him that, by the time the purges ended, his dictatorship was incontrovertible.

Understanding egomania as only another egomaniac can, Stalin feared Hitler enough to sign a non-aggression pact with him in 1939. When the Germans invaded western Poland, Stalin sent his troops to occupy the eastern part of that country, then attacked Finland. But Hitler turned on Stalin and invaded the Soviet Union in June 1941. That created the bizarre situation of sending Stalin into the Roosevelt – Churchill camp. They dealt with him because they had no choice, although he is said to have impressed them with his day-to-day handling of the Soviet war effort. He'd stay up all night to move his armies across Europe and supposedly had a tremendous grasp of detail. Without any doubt he turned out to be a very competent negotiator, matching Churchill and Roosevelt, then Churchill and Truman, as the allied leaders carved up what was left of Europe.

Despite the ill-informed opinions of otherwise well-informed men such as General Walter Bedell Smith, who served as US Ambassador to the Soviet Union from 1946 to 1949 and claimed that Stalin was neither an absolute dictator, nor a prisoner of the Politburo – 'His position, I would say, is more that of chairman of the board with the decisive vote' – the truth of the matter was anything but. Under Stalin, the Politburo virtually ceased to exist. He ruled with unconditional autocracy, couching his reign in military terms – problems were 'attacked,' solutions were part of the 'campaign,' failures necessitated 'retreat' – and, at least from the end of WWII, Soviet foreign policy was whatever Stalin said it was.

At the apex of his power for the last eight years of his life, Stalin unleashed a new wave of oppression. Paranoia reigned. Arrests once again swept the country. Concentration camps and psychiatric wards filled up. True to character, he turned on his former allies and some of his closest associates. In January 1953 he announced that he'd uncovered a plot to murder half a dozen of the country's most important military men, including the Minister of War. Standing accused were nine physicians working in the Kremlin, six of whom just happened to be Jewish. He labeled them enemies of the state and implicated American and British intelligence, the world Zionist movement and the Joint Distribution Agency. It was a well thought out ploy. As long as Nazi Germany was the enemy, he couldn't use Jews to serve his purpose. With the Nazis gone, he could exploit the caricature of the Jew as a cosmopolitan, claiming proof positive that capitalist agents were everywhere.

A second great purge was waiting in the wings.

That's when Stalin dropped dead.

He'd been Chairman of the Council of Ministers, head of the Politburo and First Secretary of the Central Committee of the Communist Party. Because no other jobs in the country mattered and because he trusted no one, he'd never groomed an heir. His death on 5 March 1953 left the Soviet Union without an obvious leader.

Although Stalin's illness was not immediately announced to the Russian public, word of it reached the British Embassy in Moscow on 3 March. After making inquiries, Ambassador Sir Alvary Gascoigne sent a telegram to Anthony Eden at the Foreign Office noting the critical state of Stalin's health and suggesting possible successors. He wrote that the logical choice was Vyacheslav Molotov, Foreign Minister since 1939. Next in line would be Georgi Malenkov, 'the most influential of the younger generation. Although he cannot match Molotov when it comes to either executive or international experience.' Gascoigne also suggested that the Minister of the Armed Forces, Nikolai Bulganin, 'should not be ignored as a possibility.'

Within a few hours, Malenkov had managed to cut himself a deal with Molotov and Lavrenty Beria, Stalin's much feared 'bloody right hand,' a man who'd risen through the Party ranks from informer to State Security chief. In exchange for their endorsement, Malenkov merged the Ministry of Internal Affairs (MVD) with the Ministry of State Security (MGB), putting Beria in charge there, while Molotov continued as Foreign Minister and First Deputy Premier.

Malenkov at 52 was two years younger than Beria and 11 years younger than Molotov. Short, stout and waxen, he was a man with an elementary sense of humor who dressed in drab gray suits. A late-comer to the Party – he joined in 1920 – he'd been one of the leaders of the Great Purge, which not only endeared him to Stalin, it also sharply honed his survival skills. Hardly the sort of man who'd stop short at outright lying, he quickly pulled off a fairly neat trick by directing *Pravda* to print a photo which showed him standing alone with Stalin and Mao Tse-tung. The message was that Stalin had long ago chosen Malenkov to be his heir. However, when that particular photo was taken in early February 1950, an entire group of people surrounded Stalin and Mao, with Malenkov no less than three places from Mao. Malenkov had ordered someone to airbrush everyone else out of the picture, then cut it down, bringing the three men shoulder to shoulder. Gascoigne described him as shrewd and quick. 'He looks self-confident and ruthless. He speaks well. He had a middle-class upbringing which he conceals by wearing rather untidy party clothes.' He said Malenkov appeared to be much more accessible than Stalin had been in recent years and considerably less dictatorial.

At least on the surface, Malenkov seemed to enjoy excellent relations with the man he'd kept on as Foreign Minister. Molotov had a slight lisp, wore gold-rimmed glasses and looked like he should have been a high school calculus teacher. One of Stalin's earliest supporters, he was a stubborn man with a tendency towards groveling in Stalin's presence. He was born with the name Scriabin but changed it for the Revolution to 'Hammer.' Lenin once referred to him as 'the best filing clerk in Russia.' Winston Churchill described him as 'a man of outstanding ability and cold-blooded ruthlessness.' While Harold Macmillan was struck by the strange duality of his character: 'In spite of his reputation for a hard, negative, brutal attitude, when one saw him alone there appeared an unexpected attractiveness and even softness.' Nikita Khrushchev, on the other hand, would later write that Molotov was 'just plain thick.' He was, if nothing else, a very strange man. During the war he'd been invited to stay at the White House by Franklin Roosevelt and, as the visit was to be a secret, he was listed as Mr Brown. Typical of so many Russians who leave home for extended periods of time – even today – Molotov traveled with the two things he knew he'd miss most, that famous Russian black bread and spicy Russian sausage. On arrival at the White House, a valet had taken his bags up to the Lincoln Bedroom and, as was the custom, began unpacking for the guest. The valet was the one who found the bread and sausage. He also discovered, among Molotov's belongings, a loaded pistol.

The weakest link in the chain was Beria. Having come from a Georgian middle-class background, he owed everything to Stalin. He'd ingratiated himself first as one of the dictator's biographers, then through the sheer perversity and zeal with which he carried out Stalin's orders. Responsible for countless murders during the purges, he was swiftly promoted to head the state security system, allowing him to profit from the distrust and suspicion that surrounded everyone close to Stalin. The day after the United States dropped its first atomic bomb on Japan, it was Beria whom Stalin assigned to manage the Soviet version of the Manhattan Project, which culminated in the successful atomic bomb test of 1949. Unlike the others, Beria owed everything to Stalin and had no real alliances with his successors. Once Stalin was gone, Beria was without protection.

As such insecurity had surrounded these men for so long, no one seemed willing to stake his life on open opposition to either the ruling triumvirate or any one member of it. Although on the eve of Stalin's death, Nikita Khrushchev went as far as anyone dared, hoping to bring about a different result. The 5'3" long-time Ukrainian Communist Party boss took the risk of confiding in Nikolai Bulganin, 'If Beria takes power, he'll exterminate us all in order to start at zero.' Bulganin encouraged Khrushchev to test the waters with Molotov. But Beria was long since off the mark and had already negotiated with Malenkov.

Because Malenkov knew these men and knew the way their minds worked, he understood just how precarious their support was. Stalin had increased the Politburo from 14 to 36, renaming it the Presidium of the Central Committee. Malenkov immediately put it back the way it had been – 10 regular members plus 4 non-voting candidates – thus diminishing his exposure to possible opposition from outside his immediate circle.

The speed with which the three men acted was a deliberate move to impress the people with their solidarity at a moment of national uncertainty. Malenkov, Molotov and Beria couldn't afford to let anyone suspect that control at the top had weakened. They even issued a statement to say they'd assumed power to ensure uninterrupted direction of the state and Party and to prevent any disorder or panic. Left unsaid was the need to show their Eastern bloc allies and the West that the Party was still in control. But then, lacking Stalin's authority, they were not taking any risks. The three ruled collectively, dividing the real power among themselves by simplifying the chain of command and taking more direct control over the administration. There was little left for the seven men who joined them on the Presidium: Klement Voroshilov (Stalin's 72-year-old Defense Minister who was named Chairman), Khrushchev, Bulganin, Lazar Kaganovich, Anastas Mikoyan, Maxim Saburov and Mikhail Pervukhin.

Placing the older, more senior Molotov behind Malenkov seemed curious enough. But Khrushchev's promotion struck Ambassador Gascoigne as the biggest surprise. He described Khrushchev as 'a somewhat enigmatic figure of obvious ability and his future should certainly be watched.' Interestingly enough, also tipped by Gascoigne for watching was someone called Leonid Brezhnev, 'a party-politico with a rather unsavoury record. He seems to specialize in cleaning up any branch of the party apparatus which is not functioning correctly.'

To ensure support for themselves, Malenkov restored to favor the ever popular hero of World War II, Marshal Grigory Zhukov, naming him Deputy Defense Minister. The three men running the country then granted an amnesty on a huge scale, canceling the sentences of anyone who'd been jailed for five years or less. The Kremlin doctors were released, suggesting that the 'new look' Russians were prepared to safeguard civil liberties. They announced a wave of price reductions to lessen financial burdens on the masses, and offered some bread crumbs as initiatives towards detente – they eased some of the restrictions on Berlin, used their influence with the North Koreans to encourage the release of wounded prisoners of war and approved Dag Hammarskjöld as the compromise candidate for Secretary-General of the United Nations.

Malenkov sent word to the West that he did not relish the prospect of war because the last war had been horrendously costly for the Soviets and he believed that the next one would be even worse. Sometime during the summer of 1953, Malenkov is said to have reinforced that view by confiding in an East German comrade that he desperately needed to avoid war with the United States because if it came the Soviets would be the losers. He emphasized that this was not simply his opinion, but also the consensus of his military commanders.

At the National Security Council meeting on 11 March, called to discuss the effects of Stalin's death, CIA Director Allen Dulles noted that Stalin, while ruthless and determined to spread Soviet power, had never allowed his ambitions to lead him into reckless courses of action in his foreign policy. Nevertheless, Dulles warned, 'It would be unsafe to assume that the new Soviet regime will have Stalin's skill in avoiding general war.' Especially since Malenkov was still singing all the usual songs: That it was the United States and not the Soviet Union that was the main threat to peace, that America needed continued world tension in order to avoid serious economic trouble, that America had profited rather than suffered from two wars.

Churchill tried in vain to argue that particular point with the Soviet Ambassador to the United Kingdom, Yakov Malik, late one December afternoon in 1953, over a very long pre-Christmas lunch at the Prime Minister's official country residence, Chequers.

Made hearty with drinks and treacle pudding, Malik contended, 'Some people in America, realizing the difficulty of dispensing their production surplus, thought that they could only retain a healthy economic system by retaining warlike preparation. The American Government and people have aggressive intentions and ought to thank God for Russia since they are able to ascribe all the evil things that happened in the world to the Soviet Union.'

Puffing on a cigar, Churchill insisted that simply wasn't so.

If not, Malik wondered, 'Why is America spending so much on armaments? With Canada to the north and Mexico to the south, the Atlantic Ocean to the east and the Pacific to the west, they have nothing to fear in the way of aggression. These armaments are evidently not therefore for defense but for offensive purposes.'

'America,' Churchill tried to explain, 'has arrived at the summit of power and only wants to do what is right. Neither Russia nor anyone else has anything to fear from American aggression. I do not myself believe that war is at all probable for the next 25 years. It is too horrible to contemplate what it would be if it came.'

There Malik agreed, emphasizing that the Soviets wanted nothing more than to abide by the Potsdam Agreement and never had anything but peaceful intentions. 'It is only Americans who have distrusted our ideas and brought about this fear of war.'

Churchill saw what the Russian was driving at and cautioned him, 'There is no chance of splitting the English-speaking world, though we use our common language to argue about a lot of things.'

Within a week, the Soviet Ambassador was telling people Churchill had confessed to him that one of the main reasons for making his 'Iron

Curtain' speech was to prevent the Americans and the Soviets from becoming too close.

The Soviets were clearly uneasy about the new Republican administration in Washington and needed to come up with a more subtle approach to their relations with the West. As Gascoigne summarized for the Foreign Office, there were no grounds to believe that anything substantial had changed where the ultimate objectives of Soviet foreign policy were concerned: 'Stalin's successors were selected by him during and after the Great Purges, they have been closely associated with him for many years and there has been no evidence to suggest that they have disagreed with his basic policies.'

He felt the more subtle approach was calculated to split the various Western alliances, especially to divide the United States from Great Britain, and to lull the West into a sense of security. Such tactics, he cautioned, might well prove more dangerous to Western cohesion and to the military and economic strength of the West than the bludgeoning xenophobia displayed by Stalin since 1946.

What he didn't know was that the man best equipped to exploit this more subtle approach was already plotting his take-over.

Nikita Sergeivich Khrushchev was born into a strict religious family in the village of Kalinovka, in the rural Kursk region, nor far from the Ukraine border, in April 1894. Because rags to riches stories apparently appeal even to hardline Communists, he always made sure that everyone knew he was born in a mud hut. It was presumably something he saw as vital to his image, much like Abe Lincoln and his fabled log cabin. Anyway, his father was a carpenter by trade, whose biggest dream in life was to own a horse. It went unfulfilled.

At the age of 15, Khrushchev joined his father working in a coal mine, although he soon left to learn the metal fitter's trade and spent the next six years in local generator plants employed by a French mining company. He was 24 when he discovered the Bolsheviks and fought for them in the Civil War. Afterwards, they sent him to a technical college for miners – 'The Cambridge of Russia's disinherited,' he liked to call it. When he finished there, he began courses in metallurgy at the Moscow Industrial Academy, a school that produced several prominent members of the Party's Central Committee. However, Khrushchev left without a diploma, returning to the Ukraine where he started working his way up the political ladder. In 1932 Stalin named him Second Secretary of the

Moscow City Party Committee, under Kaganovich. The following year he was promoted to Second Secretary of the Moscow Regional Party, again under Kaganovich, where his claim to fame was to have overseen the construction of the first branch of Moscow's subway line. To do that, Khrushchev had to order the destruction of certain old buildings. But the morning the wrecking cranes arrived, so did a group of protesters who wanted the buildings saved. When Khrushchev explained this to Stalin, his boss couldn't see what the difficulty was. The crowds, Khrushchev reminded him, came to protest every day. Stalin merely shrugged, 'So, tear the buildings down at night.'

He was appointed to the Central Committee of the Communist Party in 1935 and soon took Kaganovich's place as First Secretary on both Moscow boards, where he remained throughout the purges of the party apparatus. In 1938 he returned to the Ukraine, now as First Secretary of the Communist Party there, gaining a reputation as an agricultural expert. Although it now emerges, at least in certain diplomatic circles, that he was quietly referred to as 'the Butcher of the Ukraine' for the zeal with which he followed Stalin's orders.

On a personal level, Khrushchev was a man who enjoyed going to the theatre and adored films, especially documentaries about science or agriculture. He worked long hours, had a fairly raw sense of humor and didn't much care to spend time alone. He needed to have people around him. He was not, however, either a close confidant or a notably intimate chum of Stalin's. He saw Stalin whenever Stalin called for him but didn't actively court his attention the way others did. On one occasion, he arrived at Stalin's dacha earlier than his appointment and was shown into the dining room that Stalin also used as an office. Khrushchev spotted smoke coming from behind the curtains and pulled them back to find Stalin standing there with a cigarette in his mouth, as surprised to see Khrushchev as Khrushchev was to see him. 'Everyone in the world says I have an iron will,' Stalin told him, 'but it's very hard for me to quit smoking.'

By emphasizing his own technical achievements, Khrushchev avoided getting trapped in the considerably more seductive game of obvious political ambition. That not only spared him from the purges, but won him a seat on the Politburo. After the war Stalin brought him back to Moscow, again to head the Regional Committee.

Throughout those years, Stalin's relentless grip on all aspects of Soviet life had critically diminished the role of the Party. He made decisions alone, or at best after private consultations with a few very close hench-men. It was in direct contradiction to the way the Russians had defined their one-party state, where power derived from a Communist Party Congress and meetings of the Central Committee between Congresses. 'Without me,' Stalin used to tell Khrushchev, 'you will all perish. The will of Lenin has mixed us all up.' And then he would admonish, 'You'll see, when I'm gone the imperialistic powers will wring your necks like chickens.'

Now that Stalin was dead, and even though Malenkov's personal authority was considerably less than Stalin's, no one in the new collective leadership foresaw the rebirth of the Party. Nor does it appear as if anyone in the Party genuinely considered Khrushchev capable of ever becoming a major player in the struggle for Soviet leadership. He might have been hardworking, but even his closest allies acknowledged he was little more than an ordinary man, uninspiring, weak in political theory and often crude. He was, for the most part, considered to be the kind of man who would always faithfully follow.

For several of Khrushchev's associates, that turned out to be a catastrophic error of judgement.

An ambitious man with ideas of his own, he was crafty enough to go about getting what he wanted in a plodding and patient way. He knew very well that any serious move towards power on his part would be at the expense of the power held by Beria. But going up against Beria, especially now that the MVD and the MGB had been merged, was unquestionably a risky undertaking. If nothing else, Beria had ten divisions of MVD troops in and around Moscow. He also controlled the border police, the guards protecting the Kremlin and the important members of the government, plus the State Security men who, under Stalin, had long since infiltrated every office and every department of the government.

Knowing how universally detested Beria was, Khrushchev believed that his position inside the MVD was not as strong as Beria himself made it out to be. He'd purged the top echelons and reorganized the power structure. Khrushchev was willing to bet that if push came to shove, a substantial number of senior MVD officers – men made so insecure by Beria that they feared for their own lives – would gladly give him up. It was a considerable gamble. If he lost, it would be fatal. He also needed fellow conspirators in the Central Committee, but recruiting them was an equally precarious game. You never knew whom to trust. You never knew who might be listening.

First he turned to his old cohort Nikolai Bulganin and they came to a meeting of the minds. Bolstered by that support, Khrushchev approached Marshal Zhukov, who admitted he too was worried about Beria. Proceeding now with extreme caution – Beria's informers were everywhere – he waited a full three months, until June, to take a private meeting with Malenkov.

His timing was good. Malenkov had begun to feel that Beria was using the MVD more and more to further his own ambitions, which lay outside the collective leadership. So together they plotted Beria's arrest. Malenkov enlisted Voroshilov while Khrushchev tried to enlist Mikoyan but never managed to gain his wholehearted support. Luckily, everyone kept quiet and Beria never suspected a thing.

In July, a joint meeting of the Central Committee and the Presidium was called. Legend has it that Khrushchev came to the meeting with a gun in his pocket. Zhukov was waiting in an ante-room with armed soldiers. Beria strolled in, took his place and was immediately charged with several crimes, including spying for the British during World War I. An astonished Beria listened as Khrushchev claimed that he was not a Communist but a careerist and that there was no longer any place for him in the Party. Beria vigorously protested. Malenkov proposed that he be relieved of all his duties in both the Party and the state. Only Mikoyan rose to suggest that Beria deserved less harsh treatment. His pleas fell on deaf ears.

Malenkov pushed a button which rang a bell signalling Zhukov. Soldiers rushed into the room. Beria made a sudden move for his handkerchief. Thinking he might have a gun, Khrushchev kicked him. The soldiers grabbed Beria and took him to Zhukov, who ordered Beria held outside Moscow, beyond the reach of his own troops. Within hours, Beria's close allies in the MVD were arrested, as were many of the MVD commanders. At the same time, Beria's Kremlin guards were replaced by men loyal to Zhukov. Arrests continued throughout the country, and at all levels of government. Anyone suspected of being loyal to Beria was seized.

The vacant seat on the ruling triumvirate was still warm when Khrushchev claimed it as his own.

A formal trial took place at the end of the year. Beria was accused of conspiracy, espionage based on associations with foreign intelligence services and terrorist murders. He sat in the dock with six of his aides. The tribunal, convened under the auspices of a 1934 law which forbade the defendants any right to counsel or appeal, was of course a sham. After six days, Beria and his henchmen were sentenced to death and, because terrorism had been part of the charge, they were summarily executed. But then Khrushchev, Bulganin, Malenkov, Molotov and the men with them merely did to Beria what he would have done to them had the roles been reversed.

In September 1953, Malenkov decided to relinquish his post as First Secretary of the Communist Party in order to devote himself full time to being Premier. Again, the Party didn't mean terribly much. As agricultural matters were still such a major concern, he appointed Khrushchev in his place. It seemed like a harmless enough thing to do, especially as Khrushchev, in this new role, had no authority whatsoever over Malenkov.

At least, that's the way Malenkov saw it.

One of the greatest ironies of the Soviet Communist system was that collective leadership – so fundamental a theme to Communist doctrine – never turned out to be the accepted procedure. A single leader always emerged. And the Communist Party network, as it branched out across the country, was now reporting to Nikita Khrushchev.

Believing that his main task was to restore the influence of the Party, he aimed to return to the Central Committee the power which Stalin had taken away. Slowly, and almost imperceptibly, over the next few months he started replacing Malenkov's men in the Party hierarchy with men loyal to him. He also set about making several significant changes in the country. For example, he opened the Kremlin to the public. Designated a security zone by Stalin, which meant that even photographs of the Kremlin were prohibited by law, Khrushchev allowed anyone in for the simple purchase of a tour ticket. He also changed the government's working hours. Because Stalin chose to stay up all night and sleep during the day, anyone whose job depended directly on him soon found themselves up all night as well. It wasn't long before most of the government was working at night and, like Stalin, sleeping until noon. Khrushchev put an end to that with a decree that government offices would operate from 9 a.m. to 6 p.m. These days it may not seem like a difficult decision to make, but after so many years of doing it backwards, the change affected just about everyone in the country. It was a major alteration to Soviet society and did not come easily. Khrushchev actually had to order inspections of offices to assure compliance. But those inspections didn't take place at 9 a.m. to see if

35

people were coming in to work. In typical Soviet fashion, they happened at the end of the day to make certain everyone left on time.

The recently installed First Secretary of the Communist Party of the Union of Soviet Socialist Republics got up on the morning of 17 April 1954, and reminded his wife that he wasn't going to celebrate his 60th birthday. Nina Petrovna had lived with him long enough to have expected that – it was the same story every year – so she told him not to worry, that nothing was planned. Of course, his children wished him happy birthday but that, he insisted, would be the end of that. He didn't enjoy big family parties and, most of all, he disliked his own birthday.

He took his usual early morning walk around the grounds of the house, singing obscure Ukrainian folk songs to himself, loudly and badly. He inspected the vegetables planted in the garden at the very rear of the property and also listened to the birds in the woods, enjoying their songs in the brisk spring morning. After breakfast, his driver took him to his office. At 12:30, he lunched as he did every day with the other members of the Presidium. Afterwards, the driver brought Khrushchev back to Lenin Hall to take a hot bath. There didn't seem to be any rhyme or reason for bathing at that time of the day, except that it was an old habit and Khrushchev enjoyed it. He returned to his office for the afternoon, coming home at around 8 p.m., in time to change into one of his favorite embroidered short-sleeved Ukrainian shirts before dinner. That's when, to his chagrin, some black ZILs and several black Chaika automobiles unexpectedly arrived at his front door. Malenkov, Molotov, Voroshilov, Mikoyan and Bulganin had all come to wish him a happy birthday.

Reluctantly he sat them down at his huge dining-room table – it could seat two dozen if everyone squeezed together – and told one of the servants to bring cognac and food. The others were in dark suits and, because the bareness of his short, stubby arms made him feel uncomfortable, Khrushchev suggested they take off their jackets. But none of them did.

They often made him feel socially uncomfortable like that. It was typical of their intellectually superior attitude towards him. However, as the evening wore on and the vodka bottles emptied, he began to relax a little. He started telling jokes and making rude puns. The ruder he got, the more uneasy the others became with his characteristically unsophisticated behavior. After a time it was clear they wanted to leave.

Oddly, none of them made a move. They stayed at his table celebrating his birthday until Nina Petrovna whispered, 'Let them leave.'

Once they were gone, he took his tape recorder onto the veranda, plugged it in and put on the tape he'd made of birds singing. He loved to set it up in the middle of some shrubs and listen as the local birds answered the calls of the birds on tape. Then he took his usual evening walk around the grounds of the house before going to bed.

In the seven months that he'd been First Secretary, he'd managed to ease Malenkov's people out of the most important Party posts and install his own. Perhaps they did think of him as uneducated and unsophisticated. But he saw that none of them took their jackets off to relax with him and none of them left his table until he said they could. Not even Malenkov.

For Nikita Khrushchev, this had been a quietly eventful day. And it was about to become an even more eventful year.

He began touring the country, making speeches, appearing at fêtes, compaigning at a time when there was nothing obvious to campaign for. He traveled right across the USSR, inspecting collectives, meeting in back rooms with the local Party bosses and visiting factories. At one near Moscow he gave the factory director an electronic watch that an American visitor had given to him. He told the man to copy it and produce watches of that quality. Before long, they were doing just that. The story was repeated at razor factories and cigarette lighter factories. He carefully courted Western technology and helped to establish factories that would produce goods the Soviets hadn't yet seen, such as synthetic furs.

Malenkov stayed in Moscow while Khrushchev cast his lot with the people. Little by little Malenkov's power base eroded. After a time, even the Army abandoned him.

In August, against the advice of the others, Khrushchev put forth a plan to turn much of arid Kazakhstan into farmland. His 'Virgin Lands Campaign' encompassed some 90 million acres, more than all the farmable land in England, France and Spain put together. He would ship 120,000 tractors there, mobilize half a million volunteers through the Young Communist Party and eventually bring in a record harvest.

Despite Malenkov's hold on the media, *Pravda* recognized the Party apparatus and the Central Committee as more important than the Council of Ministers. Khrushchev then traveled to China, dealing with Mao – First Secretary to First Secretary – leaving Malenkov at home to brood. Khrushchev now began issuing decrees, signed by him as First Secretary, without even asking Malenkov's permission. By the first week of February 1955, Malenkov was defeated. The Supreme Soviet met and replaced Malenkov as Prime Minister with Khrushchev's handpicked choice, Nikolai Bulganin. By the time Khrushchev celebrated his 61st birthday, he was in charge. But only just. So he focused his sights on the two men with whom he shared power. Malenkov and Molotov were not only standing in his way, they were fair game.

Chapter Three

The American Century

A largely empty continent, lush and graced with natural resources, no nation in history was ever more ripe for economic growth on such an unimaginable scale as America was by 1 January 1900.

The Puritan ethic that had wrapped itself around the eastern seaboard throughout the 18th century spent the next 100 years rolling through the Great Plains and across the Rockies to the Pacific. The men, women and children who made that trek carried with them a native belief in the first law of nature – survival of the fittest – and a unique spirit of free enterprise.

Eli Whitney's cotton gin and Cyrus McCormick's reaper freed workers on the farms so they could move into factories where they built machines to build other machines. By the end of the 19th century, with railroads networking the continent, young America had overtaken Britain in its output of coal and iron and in the consumption of raw cotton. Electricity lit up the cities and machines worked even faster.

Some 76 million people lived in America when William McKinley was President, the first electric omnibus was put to work in New York, the world's first book of stamps was invented and Wall Street worried about a 'prosperity panic.' Hawaii became a US territory, the replaceable razor became a reality and so did vacuum cleaners. Kodak invented the Brownie Camera and Coca Cola was exported for the first time to Britain. So were department stores, when Gordon Selfridge opened his 'American Store' on Oxford Street in London. The United States Automobile Club decided traffic was getting so congested that signs should be posted on street corners, and Louis Armstrong was born. When McKinley got assassinated, 'Rough Rider' Teddy Roosevelt took over and for the next seven years the country walked softly but always carried a big stick, proving in the process that not many people argue with nations carrying big sticks.

You could get arrested in St Louis for spitting, in New York for flirting and, if you were a woman, just about anywhere for smoking in public. When Booker T. Washington, the educator son of a Virginia slave, dined at the White House, newspapers declared it a major advance in race relations because no black man had ever dined there before, at least not one who came in through the front door. Walter Reed beat yellow fever, Thomas Alva Edison invented a battery and the Panama Canal project was taken over from the French for $40 million. Henry Ford proved that assembly lines were the future and Kit Carson starred in the first ever genuine western. The Wright brothers flew an airplane, William Kellogg formed a company to exploit something called toasted corn flakes, which he'd invented as a therapy for mental patients, and an American woman won at Wimbledon.

The country was fast becoming a 'melting pot,' the term having been coined by Israel Zangwill in a book with that title. He wrote, 'America is God's crucible, the great melting pot where the races of Europe are melting and reforming.'

An earthquake devastated San Francisco, but a black man named Jack Johnson became Heavyweight Champion of the World, a Red Indian named Jim Thorpe became the hero of the 1912 Olympics and a millionaire oil man named John Davison Rockefeller became the world's first billionaire.

The United States skillfully managed to avoid World War I until 1917, a full three years after the assassination of Archduke Ferdinand at Sarajevo started the whole thing. When it became inevitable that the fight would have to be joined, both the Senate and the House overwhelmingly passed a declaration of war and on 6 April, Woodrow Wilson signed it because 'The world must be made safe for democracy.'

It was also good for business.

For ship builders, aircraft engine manufacturers and the armament industry it was boom time. The US was now the world's most important producer of steel and automobiles, and was already supplying half the globe's food exports. The country didn't have much of a standing army at the beginning of the war but conscription brought in the recruits and, before the Kaiser could whistle 'Over There,' the Yanks were coming with 4.7 million fresh, well-fed, well-dressed, well-armed, inexperienced fighting men. Nineteen months later, when the so-called 'war to end all wars' ultimately ended, Europe was ravaged, Russia had succumbed to the Bolsheviks and more than 10 million people were dead. In between, the moving picture business was ruled essential to the war effort, baseball was ruled non-essential to the war effort, John Fitzgerald Kennedy was born, George Gershwin wrote 'Swanee,' Sinclair Lewis wrote *Main Street*, and women got the vote.

Metro-Goldwyn merged with Mayer and the Fairbanks-Pickford-Griffiths-Chaplin foursome became United Artists. Marilyn Monroe was born, as were Allen Ginsburg, Andy Warhol and Mickey Mouse. So too were the *Reader's Digest*, shopping malls and commercial radio. Hemlines rose, stunt men went over Niagara Falls in barrels, Chicago banned short skirts and bare arms, Americans owned 61% of the world's telephones and Hemingway ran with the bulls in Pamplona. Charles Lindbergh flew to Paris, Richard Byrd flew over the North Pole and Amelia Earhart flew to Wales. The world's first motel opened in California, Babe Ruth hit 60 home runs, the talkies got invented and so did color television.

For the entire decade that became known as the roaring twenties, dancers marathoned and the stock market roared, at least until 24 October 1929, when the roar turned into a blood-curdling scream.

Mr Birdseye figured out how to freeze peas, Greyhound created a national bus service and Fats Waller sang 'Ain't Misbehavin''.'

The 'Star Spangled Banner' was officially proclaimed to be the national anthem, the world's tallest building was opened in New York, Prohibition ended and everybody started playing a game called Monopoly. An American divorcee cost Edward VIII his throne, the world's longest suspension bridge connected San Francisco with Marin County, Elvis was born, Margaret Mitchell wrote *Gone with the Wind*, and John Wayne starred in *Stagecoach*. Nylon toothbrushes went on sale for the first time and so did a comic book called *Superman*.

That's when war broke out in Europe again.

Roosevelt declared America would be neutral, Congress passed the 'Cash and Carry' bill, which ended the arms embargo, and the first orders from Britain and France were worth over $1 billion. Ships got built and planes got built and, when Lend-Lease came along, the administration committed $50 billion to bolstering the Allied defenses. Business went from good to great until 7 December 1941, when it became better than ever. The United States knuckled down to liberate Europe and to clear the Pacific and, even though this time it took four years, before the summer of 1945 ended, Mussolini was hanging by his feet, Hitler was dead in his bunker and the Rising Sun was set.

The boys came home to the GI Bill, which sent them to school and guaranteed mortgages so they could purchase tract houses built by a Henry J. Kaiser and William J. Levitt. For nothing down they got two bedrooms with prefabricated walls, a fully equipped kitchen, a fireplace and a built-in television set they could watch from the table while having dinner.

There were more than 140 million people living in the country – nearly twice as many as there'd been at the beginning of the century. Up and down every Main Street in every one of the 48 states, there was a car in every garage – or if there wasn't a garage there was at least a car-port – dungarees on every kid and a shiny new bicycle under every kid. Almost everybody in the country owned a radio and almost everybody who owned a radio also had indoor plumbing. Jackie Robinson joined the Brooklyn Dodgers, Alfred Kinsey wrote about sex, the marriage rate doubled, the baby boom was in full swing and Americans knew that undefeated America could do anything.

Americans knew, nothing could stop them now.

On 25 June 1950, the North Koreans invaded South Korea and America went to war again. With Chinese troops coming in to help the North Koreans and Truman's inability to contain the war, then stop it, Americans became even more convinced than they already were that normal relations with any Communist regime were impossible.

Dwight Eisenhower was swept into office on a wave of hope for the future. He was going to end the war in Korea, beat the Communists at their own game and protect Europe because, if Europe fell, the very roots of American democracy would be endangered. We liked Ike because he was a war hero and because he would keep us safe from the Russians. We liked Ike because he epitomized everything America thought about itself in 1952. And, in 1952, America liked itself a lot.

We'd marched smartly into the second half of the century with unprecedented power and prestige. We saw our national conscience as a role model for the rest of the world and believed that, given the chance, other nations would follow in America's footsteps to freedom. The country must, Henry Luce had written, 'accept whole-heartedly our duty and our opportunity as the most powerful and vital nation in the world and in consequence to exert upon the world the full impact of our influence, for such purposes as we see fit and by such means as we see fit.' If that meant killing some North Korean Communists, well, that was just too bad. We would take our rightful place as the elder brother of nations in the brotherhood of man.

After all, this was the American century.

With only ten weeks to put a cabinet together, the President-elect turned his campaign headquarters – Suite 615 of the Commodore Hotel at 42nd Street and Lexington Avenue, next to Grand Central Station – into the White House-in-waiting. He spread out, moved in additional staff and went to work.

For John Foster Dulles, the man who would come to symbolize much of America's hard line in the Cold War, it was an easy drive down Park Avenue from 72 East 91st Street, his townhouse off Central Park. He'd had to wait three weeks once the election was over before Eisenhower asked him to be Secretary of State. Now, in late November, he arrived at the Commodore early every morning and stayed late into the evening helping Eisenhower make ready to assume office.

A tall, large-framed, clumsy man – Churchill once described him as 'the only case I know of a bull who carries his own china closet with him' – he loved good wines, good food and good cigars. He wore expensive clothes, but didn't wear them well, and there was always a rumpled look about him. When gout caught up with him, he stopped wearing garters, which meant he was forever bending down to pull up his socks. He looked as if he would have bad breath – and did. An old-school diplomat who could negotiate, at least to some degree, in French, Dulles managed to come across as being a lot more cultured than he really was. He had no interest whatsoever in music or art and, when it came to literature, he confined himself to detective stories.

Eisenhower and Dulles had never been close. They'd first met towards the end of the war but didn't have much of an acquaintance until 1949. Ike was President of Columbia University and Dulles, who was running for the Senate at the time, hoped to get Eisenhower's endorsement. He'd invited the Eisenhowers to dinner and spent most of the meal talking about world affairs. Before the evening was over, Eisenhower suggested Dulles write a book. The next time they met, several months later, Eisenhower mentioned again, 'You really should write that book.' Dulles retorted, 'I have.'

He'd sat down the very next morning with a team of secretaries to dictate *War or Peace*, which was published in 1950. Dulles used the book to argue that, while Truman's policy of containment had saved Western

Europe, Greece, Turkey and Iran, it had clearly failed to save Eastern Europe or China. Accordingly, he felt boundaries, like those drawn by NATO, offered the Communists immunity to aggression as long as they stayed on their side. Such boundaries also implied America's acceptance of a world divided between Capitalism and Communism.

Seeing the struggle against Communism as a moral obligation – 'Soviet Communism,' he wrote, 'starts with an atheistic, Godless premise. Everything else flows from that' – Dulles outlined the great weaknesses that always go with despotism: an underlying distrust, suspicion within the top leadership, a lack of mobility due to limited delegation of authority. But, he cautioned, 'They are weaknesses that are fatal only under pressure. If there is no pressure, purges can occur, organizational wounds can be healed at leisure and the despotism can go on.' So he advocated pressure to force the rigid, top-heavy and overextended structure of Communist rule into a state of collapse.

The book was an ideological success and boosted Dulles' visibility as a pundit in international affairs. He and Eisenhower maintained some contact over the next two years, but it wasn't until Eisenhower seemed almost certain to win the Republican nomination that Dulles decided, if he was ever going to be Secretary of State, this might be his last chance.

Born in Washington, DC, in February 1888 and raised in upstate New York, he was the grandson of one former Secretary of State – John W. Foster served under Benjamin Harrison – and the nephew of another – Robert Lansing served under Woodrow Wilson. Educated at Princeton, the Sorbonne and George Washington University Law School, he attended the 1907 Hague Peace Conference as a French translator for the Chinese delegation. After being admitted to the New York Bar in 1911, he joined Sullivan and Cromwell, an important Wall Street law firm. Fifteen years later, he was not only senior partner, he was generally considered the highest-paid corporate lawyer in the country.

Never one to conceal his dyed-in-the-wool Republican tendencies, he once tried to hire the young New York City prosecutor Thomas Dewey. When Dewey wouldn't come to work for Sullivan and Cromwell, Dulles in a sense went to work for Dewey. He helped Dewey get elected Governor in 1943 and became a moving force the next year when Dewey ran for President against Franklin Roosevelt. Uniquely talented at walking the fine line of bi-partisan politics, Republican President Woodrow Wilson invited Dulles to serve as a legal counsel at the World War I peace conference, while Democrat Roosevelt made Dulles a delegate to the United Nations meeting in San Francisco in 1945. Three years later Truman, also a Democrat, appointed him to be George Marshall's deputy at the opening of the UN in Paris. Dulles backed Dewey again later that year to run against Truman, confident that Dewey would name him Secretary of State. But the Truman victory queered that. Instead, when New York Senator Robert Wagner left Washington for health reasons in 1949, Dewey appointed Dulles to fulfill a four-month term until a special election could be called. It was the only time in his life Dulles ever held elected public office. Herbert Lehman, the popular former Governor of New York, stood for the Democrats, Eisenhower remained uncommitted, hiding behind his military status, and Dulles was soundly beaten.

But his national reputation as an authority on world affairs continued to grow. In 1952, a *Saturday Review* magazine poll asked which living Americans would make the best President. Eisenhower came first. Robert Taft, the Republican Senator from Ohio and eldest son of former President William Taft, was second. Estes Kefauver, the Democratic Senator from Tennessee, was third. And John Foster Dulles was fourth. Behind them were a whole slew of well-known people, including Eleanor Roosevelt.

When Taft, who was one of Dulles' oldest friends, then sought his support for the Republican nomination, Dulles waited until he could see a clear winner, abandoned bi-partisanship politics, abandoned Taft, abandoned Dewey with what slim prospects he had for a third nomination and sided with Eisenhower.

His support was welcomed. But while Dulles might have been his most logical choice for Secretary of State, Eisenhower saw him as one of several possibilities. Henry Cabot Lodge was in the running and so was Ike's pal, former Assistant Secretary of War and High Commissioner for Germany, John J. McCloy. *Time* magazine publisher Henry Luce thought he might be in with a chance and, by total coincidence, Eisenhower's face was featured on *Time's* cover four times in nearly as many issues. Each faction of the party lobbied for their own man. Even Churchill's Foreign Secretary Anthony Eden reportedly added his two pence worth in May 1952 by advising Eisenhower, 'anyone else but Dulles.' Eden later denied it but Eisenhower insisted it was absolutely true.

In the end Dulles won out, not simply because he had substantial party weight behind him – which he did, leaving some critics to believe that the Republican Party forced its right-wing man on the more liberal President – but also because Eisenhower recognized his technical competence in the diplomatic field. What niggling doubts Ike had about Dulles were down to the man's personality. It didn't take long before he observed that his Secretary of State was 'not particularly persuasive in presentation and, at times, seems to have a curious lack of understanding as to how his words and manner may affect another personality.' That was Eisenhower's polite way of saying that the naturally pedantic Dulles could, at times, bore the hell out of him.

Because Dulles was such an unusual and often difficult type of person – as it were, an acquired taste – more than once over the course of Eisenhower's administration the President found it necessary to defend his Secretary of State. 'Foster's a bit sticky at first,' he'd say, 'but he has a heart of gold when you know him. You have to get to know Foster. He's all right when you get to know him.'

Eden never thought so, but Harold Macmillan found Dulles more gracious than he'd expected. 'With all his faults – his agonisingly slow speech, his unwillingness to look you straight in the face, his deviousness of method – there was something engaging about him if you could once penetrate the surface.'

The real problem, as Macmillan saw it, was that Eisenhower was completely under Dulles' influence. 'Except on very rare occasions of supreme importance it was no good appealing to the President over the head of the Secretary of State.'

It's perfectly true that, until Eisenhower, no President of the United States had ever delegated as much authority over the nation's foreign policy. But then, no President before Eisenhower ever had John Foster Dulles as Secretary of State, a man not merely willing to assume that responsibility but anxious to do so. Dulles had, after all, spent his life preparing to be Secretary of State. Yet it wasn't until late that November in the Commodore Hotel that Eisenhower began to see how right his judgement had been in choosing Dulles.

A hotel bellhop arrived at the suite one morning with a five-page telegram. A secretary took it and immediately passed it to Eisenhower, who read it and just as quickly showed it to Dulles. It was from the nationalist Iranian Prime Minister Muhammad Mossadeq, inquiring what attitude the new administration would take towards his country.

The two men were flabbergasted.

Firstly, the telegram was unclassified. It had been sent over ordinary Western Union wires and anybody could have seen it. Secondly, it was highly irregular for a government to communicate this way, outside of established State Department channels. Thirdly, it was all the more irregular because Eisenhower did not yet speak for the United States government.

When he and Dulles talked about it, they concluded that the telegram warranted a reply. So later that afternoon, Dulles sat down to draft one. He was just about finished when a secretary gave him a long handwritten memo from Eisenhower. It read, 'I had a free hour so I tried my hand at an answer.' Without any way of foreseeing the future – that Mossadeq would be overthrown by Eisenhower's CIA, which would then reinstall the Shah on the Peacock Throne – Dulles studied Ike's drafted response. Because it so closely mirrored his own thinking, he told Eisenhower, you don't need a Secretary of State, this is a perfect answer.

Eisenhower – who at least in the beginning often appeared restlessly uneasy in Dulles' presence – could bask for a few minutes in the self-delusion that his own intellect was in the same league with Dulles. While Dulles could see that establishing his influence over Eisenhower would not be particularly difficult.

Every American President, with the exception of George Washington, has lived at 1600 Pennsylvania Avenue. However, fewer than half of them have worked in the Oval Office.

The Executive Mansion – as it was then called – was designed in 1792 by a 30-year-old Irish-born architect named James Hoban. Thomas Jefferson attached a pair of terraces to the ends of the building when he lived there but, in 1814, the British burned the place and most of the original structure had to be rebuilt. A semi-circular portico was added to the south side in 1829 and a rectangular portico was added to the north side three years later. Except for a solarium installed on the third floor, the mansion remained pretty much the way Hoban had envisioned it, until 1902. In those days the President's office was on the second floor. So were his private rooms. Teddy Roosevelt, who was trying to govern the country while raising a rather boisterous family, convinced Congress he needed more space. What he really needed was to keep his kids out of his hair. The result was a total refurbishment of the East Gallery – the largest room, traditionally used for State receptions – and construction of the low-slung, white-brick Executive Office wing on the west side.

47

For his own office, Roosevelt chose a copy of the oval library on the second floor, which had been the President's study and is now part of the private quarters.

A good-sized room, but not nearly as large as most people imagine it to be, the thing about the Oval Office is that, because there are no corners, there's no place to fix your eyes, no way to keep your own optical balance, except by homing in on one very imposing piece of furniture – the President's desk – and, of course, the man behind it.

Roosevelt did that on purpose.

He was also the man who officially renamed the place the White House.

In those days the grounds were open to the public and the surrounding lawn was a popular picnic spot. For the next several administrations, so they say, tourists visiting the White House when the President was out of town were shown into the Oval Office where they could have their picture taken sitting at his desk. Those days were long gone by the time Harry Truman moved in. He only lived there during his first term because, by 1948, the Army Corps of Engineers had deemed the building structurally unsound. Part of the second floor was caving in, the roof had become a hazard and, when the engineers looked closely, they found some charred beams, remnants of the British burning. The President moved to Blair House and the White House was gutted, its structure entirely replaced with steel framing before the rooms were restored.

The private apartment did not have its own formal dining room or its own kitchen – Jackie Kennedy added those – so Eisenhower took to barbecuing in the solarium. Of course there were offices, meeting rooms, a communications center, a situation room, garages, cloak rooms, washrooms, several staff cafeterias, and a subterranean escape route for the President should the building ever come under attack. These days the White House is a fortress and the President is virtually a prisoner in his own home. There are guards everywhere, heavily armed with automatic weapons and backed up by the world's most advanced security devices, guaranteeing that no one can get anywhere near the mansion on foot or in a car without alarms going off. There is also a battery of surface to air missiles stashed somewhere on the roof just in case someone tries to get close in a plane, blimp, balloon or hang-glider. Security wasn't anything like that in Eisenhower's day.

There's a swimming pool – Franklin Roosevelt put it in – plus a bowling alley, a projection room for movies, a clinic for medical attention and a barber shop. The furniture when Eisenhower lived there was mostly pretty awful, mediocre hotel-quality reproductions mixed in with standard government issue. It had been passed down from one administration to another ever since the 21st President, Chester A. Arthur – whose place in history has risen to the obscurity he so richly deserves – sold the antiques. Again, it would take Jackie Kennedy to restock the house with important furniture.

Yet Eisenhower was the first fully air-conditioned, fully fire-proofed, extra-television-socketed President. He was also the first to use the White House's south lawn as a helicopter pad. However, his most memorable contribution to the place, alas no longer there, was the putting green he had installed in the Rose Garden, a patch of lawn just off the terrace beyond the French doors in the Oval Office, directly behind the President's desk.

He would live in the house for eight years, the longest he'd lived anywhere up to that time under one roof. In fact, until he bought his farm in Gettysburg, Pennsylvania, he and his wife Mamie had never owned a home of their own. Ever since his graduation from West Point in 1915, they'd lived in government quarters, moving from one Army base to the next. On the other hand, thanks to the Army, Eisenhower was the first President in the 20th century to have spent considerable time living outside the United States. In addition to his years in Europe, he'd been four in the Philippines and three in Panama. He not only brought to the White House a perspective on the world and America's place in it that most of his predecessors didn't have, he also had a wide array of relationships with the men already in power. He'd met Stalin, was friends with Churchill, was admired by de Gaulle and had long since been on a first-name basis with Eden and Macmillan. What's more, he'd been in and out of Washington for much of his adult life and understood how the capital functioned. As General MacArthur's congressional liasion in the 1930s, he knew his way around the Hill. And, while he'd never had a warm personal relationship with either Roosevelt or Truman, he'd served both of them and had an intimate knowledge of how the Presidency worked.

Eisenhower refused to be seduced by politics in 1948, so the Republicans spent the next four years indulging in flattery, blatantly courting him until he changed his mind. They were shrewd enough to play up to Ike's deep sense of patriotism and duty, and somehow got him to believe their slightly illogical stance that, should he not run in 1952,

America's two-party system was forever doomed. That argument, when superimposed over the war in Korea, the Soviet success in developing an atomic bomb and what Eisenhower himself once referred to as 'the monolithic mass of Communist Imperialism,' was sufficient enough to get him onto the campaign stumps.

He was an easy candidate to sell to the people, a smiling, amiable man who'd risen from humble beginnings in Texas and Kansas to achieve international fame – infinitely more marketable than the Democrats' urbane, egg-headed Governor of Illinois, Adlai Stevenson.

Once Ike was installed behind that big desk in the Oval Office, he ran it the only way he knew to run anything, like a soldier. In that respect he was an experienced administrator. He delegated well and didn't cut people's legs from under them. He told them what he wanted them to do and then let them do it. But, like so many soldiers, there were times when he simply wasn't prepared for civilian life and many of the faults of his Presidency derived from the military side of his character. When a General issues an order, he depends on it being carried out immediately. When a President wants something done, he has to hope that, by the time his wishes seep all the way down through the bureaucratic maze with its various special interest groups, someone might eventually act on it. He's got to watch it at every step, or at least have someone protecting his interests at every step, otherwise it's almost guaranteed to get lost.

At the same time, the cocooned nature of the Army had somewhat protected him from the press. As President, not only was he more exposed, he was a much bigger target and was inclined, justifiably or not, to be somewhat suspicious of newspapermen. One day early on, while going over a statement with his press secretary, James Hagerty, he explained how he wanted Hagerty to handle a certain point. Hagerty winced, 'If I go into the press conference and say what you want me to say, I'd get hell.' Eisenhower patted Hagerty on the back. 'Better you than me.'

David Brinkley, who covered the White House in those days for NBC, often observed Eisenhower's folksiness first hand. When the President ad-libbed, Brinkley recalled in his *Memoires*, sentences 'bounced around like Dodgem cars at a carnival' winding up in the middle of nowhere with no one sure how he got there or what he'd said. One story, then circulating through the White House, had it that when a particularly difficult issue was on the agenda, and Hagerty was worried about it, Eisenhower would advise his staff, 'Send the press in to me and I'll confuse them.'

The small town, down-to-earth image that helped propel him into the White House was not something anybody could have manufactured. But now as President, when his speech writers tried to play on it, feeding him lists of synthetic down-to-earth phrases, he rightly complained, 'I'm folksy enough as it is without you making it worse.'

That he was. Televised coverage of the Presidency was still in its infancy, yet his better instincts told him he needed some polish for the cameras. Eisenhower wasn't the first television President – John Kennedy was that – but the medium's obvious importance prompted him to hire actor Robert Montgomery to be his TV coach. His performances were practiced as Montgomery helped him learn to show just enough General, just enough President and just enough corn-fed Ike. Away from the cameras, he had a very commanding presence, was clearly the man in charge and there was deference to him all along the line. Yet every now and then he'd refer to himself as 'the old dodo.' When he first met George Humphrey, the man who would be his Treasury Secretary, and noticed that Humphrey was going bald – as he was – the first thing Ike said to him, even before hallo, was, 'I see you comb your hair the way I do.' He was used to ceremony but not always very comfortable with pomp. After taking office, he found that he enjoyed the presidential retreat in the Maryland mountains, but felt 'Shangri-La' – as Franklin Roosevelt had named the place – was 'just a little too fancy for a Kansas farm boy.' So he renamed it Camp David, after his grandson.

Literally within hours of his victory over Stevenson, newspaper editorials and broadcast commentaries across the country were urging the new President to meet with the Soviets as soon as possible.

As the war in Korea began winding down, the nation's editors felt it was time to deal with Stalin. However, Eisenhower appeared reluctant to do so, in spite of his pronounced insistence that he would go anywhere in the world to meet with anyone as long as it would help promote a greater solidarity between nations and further the cause of freedom. He'd pledged during the election campaign to go to Korea, and he did. That trip resulted in the North-South Korean Armistice which, as one observer put it, 'was a poor substitute for victory but a tolerable substitute for war.' Talking to the Russians was different. Already under Dulles' potent influence, Eisenhower said he'd meet with the Soviets only if there was a good chance that such an encounter would produce some sort of positive result, something that would be acceptable to the peoples of the West. Sensing an opportunity to score a few propaganda points, Stalin suggested that perhaps he and Eisenhower should indeed get together.

They'd already met once, in August 1945, when the Russians invited Eisenhower to Moscow, welcomed him as an ally and a hero, and bestowed upon him the unique honor of being the first foreign dignitary ever to review a parade from the top of Lenin's Tomb. Stalin had great respect for Eisenhower, to the point that he was perhaps the only General on the Western side Stalin would have liked to have had in the Red Army. Of course, long before he got there, Eisenhower had heard all the usual stories about Stalin. Like the one where Churchill supposedly passed some secret news to Stalin but two days later had to confide in the Russian dictator, 'I'm a bit worried about the information I gave you. It's so confidential.' Stalin is said to have reassured the Prime Minister, 'Don't worry, the interpreter has already been shot.'

Yet Eisenhower was not prepared to find a human being so totally devoid of humor. At one point, while thousands of Soviet gymnasts were performing below them in Red Square, Stalin turned to him and said solemnly and with great pride, 'This develops the war spirit. Your country ought to do more of this.' Later that evening, at a private showing of a film which glorified Marshal Zhukov's campaign to take Berlin, Eisenhower asked his interpreter to tell the nearby Zhukov, 'If he ever loses his job in the Soviet Union, he can surely get one in Hollywood.' Zhukov laughed but Stalin didn't understand. He told Eisenhower rather flatly, 'Marshal Zhukov will never be without a job in the Soviet Union.'

The prospect of a second Stalin meeting could not have filled Eisenhower with much delight, although with mounting pressure in the press to arrange such a meeting, it might eventually have taken place had Stalin's death not ended such speculation forever.

Meeting Stalin's successors, in particular Malenkov, was a very different matter. Eisenhower viewed Malenkov as someone who was both less fearful and less suspicious than Stalin, especially in his attitude toward the West. Winston Churchill felt Malenkov was someone the West could talk to and suggested to Eisenhower in May 1953 that the two of them arrange a summit with the Russians. But Eisenhower was not in favor of the idea. Neither was Dulles. Despite continuing pressure from the media, which have always viewed summits as good events to cover, Eisenhower begged off. His much-quoted excuse became, 'Actual deeds, giving some indication of a Communist readiness to negotiate constructively, will have to be produced before I would agree to such a meeting.'

As it turned out, it would be two years before the President decided that the Soviets were ready.

Nevertheless, because Britain was America's primary ally – and as much out of friendship for an aging Winston Churchill as out of pity for him – Eisenhower agreed to attend a compromise meeting with the British and French Prime Ministers at Bermuda in June. But then Eden took ill and Churchill suffered a minor stroke and the meeting had to be pushed back to December.

The warmth that Eisenhower and Churchill felt for each other understandably manifested itself in the 'special relationship' that Britain and America sometimes share. They'd first met in Washington at the very beginning of the war. Churchill was there to see Roosevelt and the President invited Eisenhower and General Mark Clark to come by one morning to meet him. Whenever Churchill was 'in residence' at the White House, he opted for the Queen's Bedroom, preferring that suite to the more famous but much less cheerful Lincoln Bedroom – which wasn't his bedroom but the Cabinet Room where he signed the Emancipation Proclamation – just across the hall on the second floor. Eisenhower and Clark were ushered into the small sitting room and asked to wait a moment while the valet informed the Prime Minister that his guests had arrived. The valet returned a moment later to escort the men into the large rose and white room where Churchill, still in bed, was propped up on a bunch of pillows, reading a stack of papers. Undaunted by strangers, Churchill explained that he always did a morning stint of reading before going to work. Eisenhower later said, 'I liked him from that moment on.' The feeling was clearly mutual. Churchill later told Eisenhower, 'The reason I like you so much is because you ain't no glory-hopper.'

They addressed each other as 'Dear Friend' and peppered official communications with little personal touches. While making arrangements for the meeting in Bermuda, Churchill reminded Eisenhower, 'I am bringing my paint box with me as I cannot take you on at golf. They say the water is 67 degrees which is too cold for me.' Eisenhower responded in tone, feeling as close to Churchill as he was to anyone, especially in these first years of his administration when Churchill still had some of his vigor. Within a year of the meeting in

53

Bermuda, as Churchill's health and mental state visibly diminished, Eisenhower began acting less like an intimate equal and more like a much admiring son.

Eisenhower had plainly seen this coming. As President-elect, just three weeks before taking office, he observed privately that Churchill was 'quite definitely showing the effects of the passing years. He has fixed in his mind a certain international relationship he is trying to establish – possibly it would be better to say an atmosphere he is trying to create. This is that Britain and the British Commonwealth are not to be treated as other nations would be treated by the United States in our complicated foreign problems. On the contrary, he most earnestly hopes and contends that those countries shall enjoy a relationship which will recognize the special place of partnership they occupied with us during World War II . . . In the present international complexities, any hope of establishing such a relationship is completely fatuous.'

Now that Stalin was gone, the old warrior was evidently making one last-ditch effort to find an end to the Cold War. The prospect of a Nobel Peace Prize did not elude him. But like a great baritone whose voice has forever left him, this was a farewell performance filled with sadness, frustration and delusion. Eisenhower and Dulles understood, and so unofficial American policy became 'humor Churchill,' especially on marginal issues he felt strongly about. Behind the scenes they put pressure on Eden to win important issues. Where Churchill was accorded a great deal of sentimental consideration by the men around Eisenhower, no one believed for a minute that his Foreign Secretary warranted the same treatment.

Eden was not everyone's cup of tea.

A tall, handsome, at times charismatic man, he'd first entered the House of Commons in 1923 at the age of 26 and had been appointed Foreign Secretary nine years later. He'd resigned from the government in 1938 in disagreement with Neville Chamberlain's handling of Hitler and Mussolini, but had returned to the Foreign Office two years later under Churchill's premiership. He'd stayed there throughout the war, had gone into opposition with Churchill in 1945, and had come back as Foreign Secretary for the third time in 1951. He and Foster Dulles had met in 1942 when Dulles had come to London as chairman of a religious commission. Eden had found Dulles 'uninstructed.' And their relationship went downhill from there.

It's true that Dulles was a vain man, but his vanity was intellectual. He was highly opinionated, and the type of man who believed he'd earned a right to his opinions. Eden's vanity was personal. It was evident in the way he dressed and the way he comported himself in that laid-back, British upper-class manner. Dulles thought it affected. He might have displeased Eden by always calling him 'Antny' but that's the way he spoke. On the other hand, being constantly called 'My dear,' the way Eden referred to everyone, got straight up Dulles' nose. Their inability to get on would become a factor in the Cold War.

Making matters even worse, Eden had known Eisenhower almost as long as Churchill had. As Churchill's heir apparent since 1940, he seemed to feel that his relationship with the American President should be as open as Churchill's. Eisenhower didn't necessarily agree and never showed Eden the same warmth he had for Churchill.

Then again, Churchill didn't always treat Eden very well either. Among other things, he was growing increasingly suspicious that after all these years Eden wasn't up to the Premiership. Once with Dean Acheson in the room, Churchill remarked about the way the two Foreign Ministers were dressed, praising Acheson's cultured taste, admonishing Eden, 'That's the way you're supposed to look.' Later, an aging Churchill showed an almost sadistic glee in dangling his impending retirement in front of Eden's face, telling him it would happen soon, then snatching it away at the last minute by refusing to retire. The two might have been in total agreement on certain foreign policy matters, but, as 1953 wore on, Eden became more and more the butt of Churchill's maliciousness and only made matters worse by occasionally allowing his impatience to show.

Where the Americans were concerned, Eden had his own agenda. Like Churchill, he too was trapped inside a sort of imperial time-warp, trying to preserve Britain's role as a great power. In the middle of 1952 he warned the cabinet that, if Britain relaxed its grip on the outside world, the nation would sink to the level of a second-class power. He wanted the United States to help maintain Britain's position and surmised, 'The more gradually and inconspicuously we can transfer the real burdens from our own to American shoulders, the less damage we shall do to our position and influence in the world.'

A year later, Lord Salisbury, as Acting Foreign Secretary for the convalescing Eden, dispatched a secret document to the cabinet, outlining the differences he saw in British and American policies towards the Soviet Union. He felt that the Americans under Truman had chosen to let events behind the Iron Curtain develop further before embarking on any high-level talks. Now, he wrote, there was a new, more dangerous American tendency, rooted in the Republican election campaign and exemplified by John Foster Dulles, who saw the situation behind the Iron Curtain as already very shaky and was trying to promote the early liberation of the satellite countries.

Salisbury urged his government 'to resist American pressure for new initiatives of this kind. A policy of pinpricks is calculated to exasperate the Russians and is most unlikely to help the unhappy peoples of the occupied countries. The last thing we want to do is bait the Russians and satellite governments into taking violent measures . . . We must of course keep the spirit of freedom alive in Eastern Europe but we should also counsel prudence and restraint.'

He acknowledged the danger of a highly armed Russia. After all, the Soviets had not disarmed after the war, choosing instead to spend the years since 1945 successfully modernizing their armed forces. They'd now reached the point where they rivaled the armies of the West in quality and outstripped them in number. Salisbury concluded, while it was always possible that Stalin's successors might ease up on the pace of military production, 'We must thus count on being faced by a clearly powerful military threat. It would be a mistake to suppose that, if the Soviet Government made some adjustments in their external policy, they would automatically go over to a policy of disarmament. It follows that, even if a detente in relationships could be produced as a result of a four-power meeting, it would still be necessary for the Western Powers to maintain a policy of collective defence and rearmament. In this view, we should be supported by the United States.'

At least in theory, Eisenhower agreed. He and Churchill were joined at the hip when it came to their cynical view of Soviet ambitions. Churchill was forever insisting that, since the end of the war, nationalism was on the march and the world Communist movement was intent on causing dissension wherever it could. Eisenhower was equally unequivocal in furthering the theme that Moscow was leading 'misguided people' to believe they could count on Communism to achieve their nationalistic aims. They agreed word for word that the Soviets were constantly trying to undermine existing relationships in their aim of world dominance. But Eisenhower did not feel that the US and Great Britain should be seen by the rest of the world as a twosome whose goal was to compel adherence to their own views.

In Bermuda, the two old allies lunched privately without upsetting the French, although it was much to the discomfort of Dulles and Eden. Among the topics they discussed between themselves were atomic weapons. Churchill wanted to know if Eisenhower intended to use the A-bomb in Korea should the Communist Chinese come to the aid of the North Koreans. Eisenhower said if need be he would, explaining that the bomb was not something new and terrible, the way Churchill saw it, but only the latest improvement in military hardware. That alarmed Churchill. Eisenhower insisted there was no distinction to be made between atomic weapons and so-called conventional weapons because all weapons eventually come to be considered conventional. Eisenhower also tried to impress on his old friend that, to Americans, 'Liberty is more precious than good government.' They also explored together the idea of storing American atomic bombs in Great Britain. The plan was that those weapons would remain in US custody, but could be made instantly available to the British should war break out. The idea personally appealed to Churchill, who staunchly maintained that the best way to keep peace in the free world was through a solidly unified British-American stance on the major issues. But nothing of that sort would happen until the Russians forced it to happen in October 1957.

Ironically, while this was the first time Eisenhower ever appeared at an international conference in a political role, it was one of Churchill's last appearances. Yet, even at 79, he continually showed signs of the earlier flair which had made him famous. He constantly impressed those members of the Eisenhower party who'd never met him with his most dramatic and personal command of the English language, skillfully relying on what Eisenhower's press secretary James Hagerty described as 'typical British understatement.' But all was not well. His hearing had become a serious problem. The story told about him in those days is of the time he was walking through one of the long hallways of the House of Commons and 50 yards behind him were two fellow MPs. One of them said to the other, 'There goes Winston. Isn't he a tremendous figure of what Britain used to be.' At which Churchill called back to them, 'Yes, and they also say he is hard of hearing.' Just how hard of hearing he was at Bermuda is not clear, although he showed up with a kind of loudspeaker system that served as a hearing aid, which must have been a difficult thing for Churchill's vanity. Whenever the discussion got hot, especially when he disagreed with the French delegation, he'd take out the ear plug and deliberately turn off the machine.

One of the stated objectives of the meeting was to demonstrate to the world – and in particular to the Soviets – that the three powers were acting together. But this was easier said than done, especially with the French government in a state of flux. Making matters worse, Churchill's impatience with the French was a constant worry. He treated President Joseph Laniel and Foreign Minister Georges Bidault with complete and utter disdain. Meeting around a large table at the Mid Ocean Club, it was as if Churchill was going out of his way to insult the French. One afternoon, with Laniel absent due to illness – he might have been genuinely ill, though there's good reason to suspect he was merely sick of Churchill – the Prime Minister's valet dutifully arrived carrying one brandy and water on a silver tray, which he placed directly in front of his boss. Churchill was about to drink it when he looked at Ike. Immediately he told his valet to bring a drink for the President of the United States. When a second brandy and water arrived, Churchill raised his glass to offer a toast. A slightly bemused Eisenhower reminded Churchill that Bidault didn't have anything to drink. Oh . . . there was a long pause . . . all right, and Churchill begrudgingly told his valet, please bring a third one.

Churchill's contempt for the French became even more evident as the days passed. Laniel remained in bed for most of the conference, leaving Bidault to explain that he couldn't speak for Laniel, with whom he was constantly arguing anyway. Behind their backs, Churchill referred to them as 'bloody Frogs,' and stipulated that Eisenhower deal with them. He wanted the French called to their duty, insisting that they be spoken to harshly, 'But not by me.' When Eisenhower wondered why not, Churchill confessed, 'Because I hope to spend a portion of my declining years in the South of France.'

With the French government in a continuous state of disarray, it wasn't necessarily clear to Churchill why Eisenhower had asked them to come along. The reason was, of course, because Eisenhower and Dulles needed a subtle way to show the British that their status vis-à-vis the United States was not what it had been during World War II.

So much had changed in just four years.

In 1949, the US Senate had considered Britain the keystone of America's North Atlantic defense strategy. The Joint Chiefs of Staff had come to the conclusion that the US could not successfully defend Germany, so they drew the line at the English Channel, marking the UK as the last line of defense, a must-hold position against a Soviet invasion of the Rhineland. British military planners agreed that the Continent was expendable as long as America was willing to defend Britain. It was the domino theory of Europe. Then came the Soviet atomic bomb test, NSC-68 and the war in Korea. With the signing of the NATO treaty, American planners decided that the loss of Europe was not a pre-drawn conclusion and new strategic boundaries were drawn. But again, the burden to defend those boundaries fell on the United States.

Churchill put forth the view that since Stalin's death there was a 'new look' to Soviet policy. At the end of the war, he said, the Soviets must have thought they had only to press forward in order to carry Communism, and Soviet imperialism, to the shores of the Atlantic. Now that Stalin's regime was over, the men who had taken his place might have seen an opportunity to reconsider their situation. 'They must have recognized,' he said, 'that if they persevered in their earlier policy they'd face a tremendous struggle.' The Allies, therefore, must be mindful, 'First, that we should be put off our guard. And second, that we should exclude altogether the possibility that there might have been a real change.' He advocated a two-fold policy towards the Soviets: a show of strength and the hand of friendship. 'I am particularly anxious that no opportunity should be lost to improve contacts between the Western peoples and the Soviet Union.'

Eisenhower wasn't nearly as enthusiastic. He worried about this 'new look,' and suggested they had to consider carefully if this was 'a new dress or the old dress with a new patch on it.' In any case, he didn't want anyone to be under the illusion that the woman wearing it had changed her profession. America, therefore, intended to prevent her from plying her trade on the main avenues and relegate her to the back streets. 'For myself, I do not believe that there has been any significant change in the basic policy and design of the Soviet Union to destroy the capitalistic system and the free world by force, lies and corruption.'

That Churchill might or might not agree was a moot point. For Eisenhower and Dulles, it was more important that Churchill and the men who would follow him understood that there was now a 'new look' Washington. As far as they were concerned, the British Empire was dead. The days of great influence were over. Britain's role had been reduced to that of an aircraft carrier, a staging point for American planes on bombing raids to Moscow. If Churchill wouldn't accept it – or, more likely, couldn't bring himself to accept it – that was just too bad. Eisenhower saw Britain's ultimate choice coming down to either joining a United States of Europe or becoming the 49th state. Regardless of how anyone in London might try to fool themselves, no one was going to fool Eisenhower or Dulles. Britain would be welcomed as an ally, but this was not like it was in World War II.

The disparate importance of the United States and the United Kingdom was masked for a time by Ike's fondness for Churchill. But it was about to become very evident as focus shifted away from wartime friendships to the business of standing up to the Soviets.

No matter how Eden and Macmillan might want to fool themselves, this was no longer an equal partnership.

Chapter Four

Drawing the Boundaries

Josef Stalin was utterly convinced that America intended to invade the Soviet Union.

It was his worst nightmare.

He spent most of the final dozen years of his life holed up in his dacha at Volnyskoy, a secure property of several small buildings – servants' quarters, garages and guard shacks – and an old rambling house that was his, where the roof was painted green so that it would blend in with the surrounding pine trees should planes ever come to bomb it. Wooden floors were covered in dark-red carpets, supposedly so that no one in the house could hear him walking through the halls. The furniture was old and heavy and unstylish. He lived mainly in the dining room, with its walls covered in dark wooden paneling. He ate his meals at the big table there, worked at his desk there and met with people there, staying up all night to run the country. Then, when morning came, he'd retire to his small, austere bedroom down the hall to sleep for much of the day.

He lived surrounded by servants who hardly if ever left the property and bodyguards who'd been with him for years. Whenever he got lonely, Stalin would insist that his Politburo come to see him and on those nights he'd force them to suffer interminable suppers where he would lecture to them, droning on while they all got drunk. Then he'd play records on his old Victrola – he loved to listen to martial music – and make them dance with each other. They all hated those nights, but no one more than Khrushchev who was especially embarrassed by them because he didn't know how to dance.

For those last seven years of his life, a virtual recluse at Volnyskoy, Josef Stalin literally trembled at the thought of going to war with the West. He knew that should it happen – and he seriously expected it was about to happen – the Soviets would be defeated. His generals assured him that he held the advantage in conventional forces, which was true, because the Red Army far outnumbered whatever ground forces the Western allies could muster. But no matter what they said, no matter how hard they tried to placate him, he knew the Red Army wouldn't survive because he also knew he was fatally outgunned by America's atomic arsenal.

At the start of the Cold War, Stalin imagined he could meet force with force by moving planes into Eastern Europe. But his Air Force didn't have the range to reach America. The United States, however, put B-29s within range of Soviet territory. Convinced they were armed with atomic bombs, Stalin called for a crash program to match the US and develop what he termed 'absolute arms.' That same year, 1947, he took an interest in missiles. He was briefed on the theory behind them and their capabilities, became enthusiastic about them and passed his exuberance on to the Politburo. 'Do you realize the tremendous strategic importance of machines of this sort?' Without waiting for anyone to answer, he assured them, 'They could be an effective strait-jacket for that very noisy shopkeeper Harry Truman. We must go ahead with it, Comrades. The creation of the transatlantic rocket is of extreme importance to us.'

In fact, Stalin became so obsessed with the American menace that the traditional Russian mania for secrecy, especially where the military has always been concerned, overshadowed almost everything that went on around him. Not only did he designate military bases as highly restricted areas, he zoned off entire cities because he deemed them strategically sensitive. He insisted on categorical secrecy, refusing to permit any unnecessary discussions about weapons or the military. The first rule of survival became, if you weren't told, you weren't meant to know and you'd better not ask. One of his most trusted bodyguards was forever going from room to room, taking papers out of the trash, ripping them up or burning them so that no information of any kind ever left the house. And God help anybody who spoke about nuclear research. On those occasions when someone even casually broached such a taboo subject, Stalin instantly suspected him of being a Western spy who needed answers for his 'real masters,' and arrests followed.

Apprehension that the West would one day launch an attack against the USSR didn't die with Stalin. According to Nikita Khrushchev, many Russians continued for years to live in a world 'where war was expected to break out at any minute.'

The fear was so real for so long that it came to be ingrained in the Soviet psyche. And just because America and Britain categorically denied any intention to do so, that wasn't reason enough for the Soviets to believe they wouldn't. What no one in the Kremlin knew for certain was that their apprehensions were well founded, that in denying their designs to invade Russia, the Americans and the British were lying through their teeth.

As early as July 1945, the Joint Chiefs of Staff (JCS) advocated a first-strike policy against the USSR. Meeting in a stuffy windowless room in the Pentagon on a hot summer morning, with the battle for Europe over and the atomic bombs being made ready for the final raids on Hiroshima and Nagasaki, four men made a decision that would have profound ramifications for the next 40 years.

General George C. Marshall, then the Army's Chief of Staff, sat next to General Henry 'Hap' Arnold, commander of the Army Air Corps. Across the table Admiral Ernest King, Chief of Naval Operations, sat next to Admiral William Leahy, whose title was Chairman of the Combined Staff. Having already come to the conclusion that the Russians would be the enemy next time, they drafted a top secret statement advocating that America should abandon its defensive position and consider launching an all-out attack against the Soviet Union. No dates were set and no conditions for the attack were established. But the fact that these men were now promoting such a scheme was a major shift in American military planning. That set the wheels in motion. Within three months they formally advised the President, 'We cannot afford, through any misguided and perilous idea of avoiding an aggressive attitude, to permit the first blow to be struck against us.' Under those circumstances, they said, they were ordering their forces to make 'all preparations to strike the first blow, if necessary.'

Truman accepted their recommendations and in October 1945 asked General Eisenhower to draw up a complete set of plans for an attack on and for the occupation of the USSR. Eisenhower drafted Operation Totality as a conventional war. Coinciding with that, Hap Arnold and the Joint Intelligence Committe formulated an assessment called 'Strategic Vulnerability of the USSR to a Limited Air Attack.' They targeted 20 Soviet cities, assumed they could deploy 20–30 atomic bombs, and studied their chances of destroying Russia in an unprovoked, surprise attack. In 1946, the Pentagon's top strategic planners integrated Totality with the Hap Arnold study and formed Operation Pincher. Their notion was that no fewer than 50 atomic bombs should be delivered in a 'prompt strategic air offensive whose purpose is to destroy the Soviet war making ability.' Strikes would be launched from bases in the UK – which brought the British into the plan as collaborators – North Africa, Italy, Egypt, northwestern India and possibly western China. Primary targets would be Moscow, the oil production facilities at Baku and industrial centers in the Urals. The initial air strike would be followed by a land and sea invasion through Poland, the Balkans and the Middle East.

A US-British all-out attack on the Soviet Union was not only feasible, it was outlined and ready to go as soon as the President of the United States and the Prime Minister of Great Britain agreed the time was right.

For the next two years, the plans and codes for Pincher sat locked in safes at the Pentagon and the White House. In 1948, during the Berlin blockade, Truman asked that they be revised. The result was Operation Broiler, an advanced first-strike scenario, and Operation Bushwhacker, an updated strategy for the occupation of the Soviet Union. The following year, coinciding with the announcement of the Soviet atomic bomb, Truman approved the National Security Council's top secret directive NSC-57, which formalized the plans for nuclear weapons to be used in a first-strike, 'preventative' attack.

Summarizing their case against the Soviets, the Joint Chiefs of Staff wanted it made perfectly clear that the use of force against the Communists was the only reasonable way to avoid the inevitable use of force by the Communists. 'There can be no peace or mutual tolerance, at least until an ideal [Communist] society has been achieved. Progress towards this goal is of necessity resisted by the vested interests in the 'dying' [Capitalist] social order. Moreover, the exploited masses cannot be expected to see the light. The goal can never be reached by persuasion and democratic processes. Force must be used to overcome the resistance of the capitalists and the inertia of the masses. Progress can be achieved only by violent revolution conducted by the militant minority who do see the vision. In its own interest, as well as that of the world revolution, the USSR must provide a secure base and strong support for the revolution in other countries. In turn, all Communists throughout the world must serve and defend the USSR, since its preservation is essential to the world revolution.'

But that was not necessarily the way the Soviets understood the situation.

Their version had it that the West started the Cold War. Some

Russians, Nikita Khrushchev among them, went so far as to name Winston Churchill as the man mainly responsible for it. Witness, they said, the Fulton speech. Here was a man who so bitterly hated Communism he devoted his entire life to preventing it from spreading into the West. They believed he was forever trying to corral socialism in behind his 'Iron Curtain,' so that he could then set about to destroy it.

According to Khrushchev, John Foster Dulles merely picked up where Churchill left off. To further his case, he alleged that, while the Western allies formed NATO in 1949, it wasn't until 1955 that the Soviets and their allies countered with the Warsaw Pact. It was, Khrushchev insisted, strictly a preparation for the defense of the socialist world. For instance, anti-aircraft batteries had been set up all over Moscow, with live ammunition at the ready, for the moment when the capitalist countries, notably the United States, would attack. During Stalin's final years, Khrushchev used to point out, the United States not only had the atomic bomb, but maintained a powerful Air Force as its primary delivery system. In contrast, the Soviets had only just perfected an atomic mechanism and possessed a negligible number of finished bombs. Under Stalin the Russians had no means of delivering those weapons. Khrushchev always argued that in those days the Russians had neither long-range bombers capable of reaching the United States, nor long-range rockets. He said the best they could muster were short-range rockets, capable perhaps of terrorizing Europe, but nothing that could threaten US soil. Such an imbalance weighed heavily on Stalin, which Khrushchev claimed, was the principal reason why Stalin wanted to avoid being dragged into a war with the US. However, within a year or so of Stalin's death, there were significant changes to the Soviet arsenal.

Forty years after the event, *Pravda* published the 'inside story' of the American threat, featuring a top secret map of the USSR that US intelligence had supposedly drawn to show the primary targets of a planned surprise attack. Once again, the villains of the Cold War were Winston Churchill, Harry Truman, John Foster Dulles and Dwight Eisenhower. The gist of the article was that the Soviets had constantly sought peaceful coexistence while the West, especially the US and the UK, had constantly sought confrontation and were forever planning World War III.

For the Soviets, a first strike by the United States and Britain was not only a logical strategy, but a definite possibility. They'd lost 15–20 million people during World War II and were suffering a great sense of national depression. The country was in a state of total dilapidation as more than one-third of it had virtually been destroyed. At the same time, America had emerged from the war very strong. As the Russians often remind visitors, not a single town in the United States suffered as much as a broken window at the hands of the Nazis.

No sooner was the war over than nuclear weapons appeared. The atomic bombs that were dropped on Hiroshima and Nagasaki were seen by the Russians as direct threats. They argued that America could have won the war without the A-bomb, but chose to use it because Harry Truman wanted to send the Soviets a message. In 1946, Truman threatened a young Soviet diplomat, Andrei Gromyko, that if the Russians didn't pull out of Iran, he'd use the weapons again. And when an American plane was shot down by the Soviets over Yugoslavia, Truman sent six B-29s to overfly the country in a similar sort of menace.

The strength of the North Atlantic Treaty Organization, they went on, was not based in London, Paris or Bonn. Nor was it ever intended that it should be. NATO was designed to appear as if it gave Britain, France and Germany a strong voice in the defense of Europe, but was quite evidently and entirely an American operation. Furthermore, it depended almost exclusively on Washington keeping the Europeans convinced that World War III would be fought on German and French soil and in the skies above Britain. Once the battle lines were drawn, the reinforcement of Europe was a perfectly reasonable conclusion. At the same time, the Russians insisted, America managed to convince the Canadians that the threat to North America would come from over the Pole. It was the shortest, most direct route for the massive Soviet bomber fleet strategically and purposely based in the remote eastern USSR. To defend against that, the Canadians agreed to allow the US Air Force to build a series of 'Distant Early Warning' radar stations along the Arctic Circle of northern Canada. Backed up by fighter bases and guided missile stations, the DEW-Line defense system became America's way of protecting itself. Not only would Russian bombers be seen – and it was hoped shot out of the skies – before they could reach Washington or New York, but just as well, they'd be blown up over Canada.

Through NATO, the Russian argument followed on, America thought it could dictate its will not merely to the British, French and Germans, but in particular to the Soviets. Consequently, the Russians had no choice but to follow America's lead and expand their own military strength to defend the motherland.

Once again, the Soviets blamed the West.

The way they saw it, if the Cold War had drawn the lines which divided the world into camps, then ideology was the reason. And who, they asked, put ideology into the history books? Not the Soviet Union. Lenin's first words were 'peace and cooperation.' Ideology, they asserted, had been allowed to cause confrontation. It had found its way into diplomacy and international relations. The Soviets said they always viewed the Russian Revolution as a free choice by the people, which is why so many people in the Soviet Union since 1985 found it totally comprehensible that Mikhail Gorbachev should defend the right of free choice. Lenin, they used to teach, wasn't an advocate of world revolution, a fact the Americans and the British conveniently forgot. They stressed it was Trotsky and the left wing that wanted world dominance, and even then it was only a response to the challenge made by the West. When the West denounced the free choice of the Russian people and the West mobilized all its forces to crush Russia, the leftists saw their only possibility of survival in fighting the capitalistic threat.

Just as John Foster Dulles had predicted in 1950, the world had drawn boundaries around two camps.

By the middle of 1954, Churchill was preaching that friendly relationships with the Soviets were not in fact contradictory to forming the strongest combination possible against Soviet aggression. 'On the contrary,' he said, 'it may well be true that the Russians can only be friends and live decently with those who are as strong or stronger than they are themselves.'

Dulles was horrified. He thought it should be perfectly clear to everyone that the Soviets would do anything they could, say anything they had to, in order to effect the withdrawal of all US troops from Europe and see the West abandon NATO. He worried about anything that might cause the West to let down its guard and take the pressure off the Russians.

But then, Churchill's days in power were coming to an end.

The inevitable happened on 6 April, 1955. The old man was finally shoved aside and Robert Anthony Eden was granted permission by the Queen to form a government.

Within a month of moving into No. 10, Eden called a general election, which the Tories won with a majority larger than that of Churchill's 1951 victory.

As Foreign Secretary, Eden had been forced to channel official communications with Eisenhower through John Foster Dulles. Now, as Prime Minister, he could deal with the President face to face. It cut Dulles out of the equation, which suited Anthony Eden just fine.

On 8 April, Eisenhower cabled Eden, 'I cannot tell you how delighted I am that my old friend Winston has been succeeded by an equally valued friend in an office in which friendliness and genuine readiness to cooperate can mean so much to my own country.'

Eden's response was just as warm. 'I am sure that you can have no doubt of the sincere admiration I have felt for so many years for the service you have rendered not only to your country but to the world . . . You will know that I will do everything I can to help the course of the relations between our two countries run smoothly. In the many anxious problems which face me here, nothing gives me more pleasure than to know that our common friendship will help us to find the joint solutions we seek.'

Over the next four months, the tone of their correspondence remained much the same. After Eden visited the United States and stayed with the Eisenhowers at the White House, he wrote, 'I feel that our friendship is closer than it has ever been. I value that immensely.'

But the friendship wasn't to last. Gamal Abdel Nasser, Nikita Khrushchev and especially John Foster Dulles would see to that.

The year 1955 was a definite turning point in the Cold War.

The Soviet Union's first intercontinental bomber became operational, giving the Russians the capability of carrying an atomic bomb to the United States. This meant America and Russia had reached the point where, in the case of an all-out war, each could simultaneously annihilate the other. For the first time in the history of the world, incalculable penalties would have to be paid by anyone who committed serious errors in the game of international foreign relations.

A new term also came into the vocabulary: the bomber gap.

Allen Dulles at the CIA had been asked by the Defense Department to find out just how many bombers the Soviets could muster now and how many they would have over the next few years. The Agency responded with a set of figures, but it was not the number of bombers the Russians were actually producing, it was, misleadingly, the number of bombers the Russians were capable of producing. Senator Stewart Symington, a Democrat from Missouri, picked up on those figures, claimed they proved a superior Soviet bomber fleet, and clubbed the administration over the head for being weak on defense. As the first Secretary of the Air Force in 1947, he was well known in military circles for having successfully championed a showdown with the Navy over funding for the B-36 bomber. Campaigning on a platform that the growing Soviet military threat required a forceful American response, he won his Senate seat in 1952. He not only rallied the upper house with accusations that Eisenhower was allowing the bomber gap to develop, he soon carried it a step further, cautioning that the Soviets would certainly develop ICBM capability long before the US because the administration was being so stingy with research and development funding.

'If we are attacked tomorrow,' he warned, 'and do not have the capacity to retaliate with instant total devastation, we shall go down in defeat and freedom will perish from the earth.'

His crusade was destined to bring him such prominence that in 1956 the Senate Armed Services Committee would put him at the head of a sub-committee on the Air Force. He would then hold three months of public hearings on American defense posture, with the express intention of awakening the country to the fact that the US was behind the Soviets in both military development and military might. Much of it turns out to have been political posturing, as Symington had ambitions of his own and did in fact launch a bid for the presidential nomination in 1960. But in 1955, the idea of a bomber gap hit at the very heart of the nation's security and, against Eisenhower's wishes, the Defense Department handed the Air Force almost $1 billion to buy more B-52s.

Eisenhower resisted Symington because he didn't believe in the bomber gap. After so many years in the Army he'd grown especially skeptical of intelligence 'estimates,' having witnessed first hand the lengths the services would go to, to boost their budgets. Yet reports coming back to him seemed to substantiate Symington's case. In the spring of 1955, American diplomats invited to the Soviet Air Force's annual Aviation Day disclosed that the Russians had shown a large number of their latest long-range bombers, including the TU-16 Badger – roughly the Russian equivalent of the B-47 – and the M-4 Bison. At one point, nine Bisons flew by in formation. Symington and the US Air Force now projected that the Soviets would have at least 500 heavy bombers in their fleet by the mid-1960s. The following year, USAF

Chief of Staff Nathan Twining and Commander of the Strategic Air Command Curtis LeMay were among the guests at Red Air Force Day. Now the Soviets wheeled out their TU-20, the first production model of their Bear bomber, an early alternative to America's B-52. It was capable of carrying two nuclear bombs for a range of 8000 nautical miles, more than enough to reach New York and Washington. There was also a flyby of 10 Bisons, followed by a second pass of 18 Bisons. Twining and LeMay were suitably impressed, although at a reception later in Moscow, Marshal Zhukov let it slip to Twining – quite obviously on purpose – 'US estimates of the production of Soviet aircraft and submarines were much too high.'

Publicly refuting the bomber gap was a near-impossible chore for Eisenhower. It wasn't until the U-2 began flying that he had a reliable source of information with which to make a case, but then he couldn't use that information without compromising the source. The U-2 divulged that the Russians had only a limited number of long-range bombers and that actual bomber production was nowhere near the levels bandied about by the Air Force and Symington. It also turns out that the nine Bisons which overflew Moscow on Aviation Day 1955 were the only airworthy Bisons in the country that day, and that the next year they showed only 18, not 28. With the clear intention of impressing their American guests, the ten planes making the first pass hurried back to join with eight more to come around a second time.

The truth of the matter is that, by 1956, the Soviets had enough planes to defend themselves, but they did not possess a sufficient atomic arsenal to be absolutely certain that a surprise attack against the United States would destroy America's major population centers. On the other hand, they had enough muscle to worry Washington, London, Paris and Bonn and they were willing to gamble that, as long as the Allies were worried, it was enough to prevent a first strike against them.

As the term 'peaceful coexistence' crawled into the vernacular, there was the hopeful interpretation in the West that it meant the Soviets might be willing to abandon their steadfast opposition to coexistence with capitalism. But Khrushchev saw it differently. He welcomed peaceful coexistence in the commercial and cultural sense because those didn't pose a threat. On the contrary, they made him look like a reformer. However, when it came to political and military considerations, he intended to remain confrontational. Where Soviet foreign policy was concerned, Khrushchev was going to move in any direction where there was a vacuum and a lack of resistance.

Being an optimist at heart, Eisenhower began thinking it might be time to meet with the Soviets. John Foster Dulles wasn't so sure. But during Anthony Eden's general election campaign of May 1955 he'd picked up Churchill's earlier theme and had announced that as Prime Minister he intended to meet with the Soviets. The French were willing, the Russians accepted and a 'Big Four' summit was organized in Geneva for July. To prepare for it, Dulles grit his teeth and arranged to meet privately on 10 May with Britain's new Foreign Minister Harold Macmillan. They chose the neutral turf of the Palais Chaillot in Paris.

Eden hardly had to warn Macmillan what to expect, as his views of Dulles were well known around Whitehall. Eden never bothered to hide his distaste for Americans, especially Americans like Foster Dulles, who exhibited how little they apparently knew about Europe and Europeans.

Nor did Macmillan have to be reminded how Eden and Dulles had got on each other's nerves the year before at the Foreign Ministers' Conference in Geneva. Eden had assumed what Dulles considered to be an anti-American stance and Dulles flew into a rage. In turn, Eden had become so fed up with Dulles, as Evelyn Shuckburgh wrote in his diary on 30 April, that he 'almost resents seeing him.' The following day Shuckburgh observed, 'Both are behaving rather like prima donnas. Dulles is said to be irritated by the imprecision of A.E.'s mind.' Twenty-four hours later Shuckburgh quoted a spiteful Eden as saying that the Americans 'want to run the world.' At one point Eden had gone so far around the bend about the Americans that he actually suggested to Molotov, who happily agreed, that all the ills of the world were caused by them.

That Eden and Dulles simply could not stay on the same wave length for very long was perhaps due to the fact that Dulles' character was too complex for Eden. After all, Eden was a man who, according to Churchill, was totally incapable of differentiating great points and small points.

A calmer, more collected Macmillan was intent on seeing that his relations with the Secretary of State were maintained on a reasonable footing. As it turned out, these two got along considerably better than had Dulles and Eden. Noting that Dulles doodled incessantly – and at times disconcertingly stuffed himself with hard-boiled eggs just when somebody was trying to make an important point – Macmillan was stunned with Dulles' almost encyclopedic knowledge and his occasional bursts of remarkable revelation. 'This strange man had moments of vision,' he wrote later, but qualified that to note, he often relapsed into the obscure, was usually over-legalistic and was at times downright devious.

Macmillan was also occasionally caught off balance by Dulles. One afternoon at the Palais Chaillot, out of the blue, Dulles wondered what Macmillan thought about the possibility of Richard Nixon coming to the summit instead of Eisenhower. Believing that Dulles was joking – something Dulles hardly ever did – Macmillan told him the story of the woman who was in mourning for her two sons. 'What happened?' asked the woman's friend. She answered, 'One of my boys went down with the *Titanic*. The other became Vice-President of the United States. Neither of them was ever heard of again.' Dulles listened to the story, obviously unamused. 'Poor Nixon wouldn't like that.' So the matter was dropped and, as planned, Eisenhower came to the summit.

Had Dulles been given the final say, the summit would never have taken place. He had grave doubts about sitting down to talk with the Soviets. To begin with, he felt the meeting would appear to be a concession to their rulers, turning them into moral and social equals of the Western leaders. That would be a considerable gain for them. Next, he worried that for eight years the Western allies had been held together largely by a cement compound of fear and a sense of moral superiority. He now saw that fear diminishing and the lines of demarcation becoming blurred. His view was that the free world could not afford to relax its vigilance or substantially alter its program for collective security, especially when 'the strength sought has never been excessive and the unity sought has never been aggressive.'

He was convinced that, in accepting to come to Geneva and talk peace, the Soviet leaders were merely applying the classic Communist maneuver known as 'zig-zag.' He reminded Eisenhower that they would 'resort to tactics or retreat in order to buy off a powerful enemy and gain a respite,' and warned, 'We must not be caught by such a maneuver.'

A weighty US delegation arrived at Geneva, led by a smiling Eisenhower and a brooding Dulles. Eden and Macmillan, with their advisors, made up the British side. Premier Edgar Faure, his Foreign Secretary Antoine Pinay and their staff accounted for the French. But the allied team paled in comparison with the legions which comprised the

Soviet delegation. Taking over an entire hotel, much to the indignation of the guests whom they rather unceremoniously displaced, the Russian front line consisted of Chairman of the Council of Ministers Bulganin, Foreign Minister Molotov, Deputy Foreign Minister Gromyko, Defense Minister Marshal Zhukov and, for the first time in Western limelight, Communist Party Chief Khrushchev.

The weather was hot and sunny. Crowds lined the streets. The press corps was everywhere. The police were everywhere. Helicopters circled overhead. And the Russians bathed luxuriously in the publicity of their first major international 'media event' since World War II. They moved between their hotel and the Palais des Nations – the old League of Nations building – in large open touring cars, making themselves the most visible of the four delegations. Bulganin and Khrushchev rode in the first car, but unlike American or British leaders – Eisenhower or Eden would sit in the back seat with their bodyguards running behind the car – they still had a few things to learn about photo opportunities. The two Russians were crammed onto tiny jump seats just behind the driver with three huge bodyguards more comfortably installed on the rear seat behind them. True, it was almost impossible for anyone in the crowd to mark them as a target. But at the same time it was just as difficult for anyone in the crowd to see them.

The main part of the conference took place in the cavernous central hall where huge murals stared down from the walls and the ceiling-height windows provided a splendid view of the lake. But the tables, arranged in a rectangle, were too far apart for intimate discussion, seats for spectators were set up around the room and television cameras lit up the place, making it look more like a boxing arena than a 'Big Four' caucus. Those public meetings quickly degenerated into long-winded speeches for the cameras. There was however a small room off to the side for private meetings. The delegates also saw each other informally every evening. The Americans brought their own food with them – frozen steaks for dinner, pancakes, bacon and eggs for breakfast – but the French laid on terrific suppers and every day there was also a buffet lunch. It was in private, away from the glare of the press, that much of the serious talking was done.

Prior to the Russians' arrival, it wasn't evident who'd be in charge. Eisenhower saw Bulganin as the genial, slightly buoyant, public-relations type; Molotov as a man intent on studiously maintaining his reputation as 'the Hammer;' Gromyko as stern, unapproachable, unhappy and with little taste for the whole idea of a summit; Zhukov as a friendly catalyst but frightened; and Khrushchev as rotund and amiable but with an only slightly concealed iron will.

Macmillan likened Bulganin to a radical socialist mayor of some French industrial town, a 'bon papa;' while Khrushchev was a mystery. 'How can this fat, vulgar man, with his pig eyes and ceaseless flow of talk, really be the head, the aspirant Czar, of all these millions of people and this vast country?'

Until the Russian plane touched down at Geneva, no one knew if Khrushchev would come at all. Bulganin stepped off the plane first, a sign of senior rank. When Khrushchev showed up, he was listed not as the First Secretary of the Communist Party but as a member of the Presidium of the Supreme Soviet. Later, when it came time for the official photograph of the 'four leaders,' it was Eisenhower, Eden, Faure and Bulganin who posed in the gardens of the Palais des Nations.

Yet it was Khrushchev who was definitely in charge.

Every day, when the Soviet delegation pulled up to the Council Chamber, it was Khrushchev who always got out of the car ahead of Bulganin. Just as significantly, throughout the five days, whenever the Russian contingent walked down the hallway to the conference table, it was Khrushchev who led the way. During the meetings, it was Khrushchev who did most of the talking. And that suited Eisenhower fine because it was Khrushchev he'd come to Geneva to meet.

Khrushchev himself claimed they'd already met. Eisenhower didn't recall but Khrushchev told him they'd stood side by side on the top of Lenin's tomb for the Victory Parade on 24 June, 1945. News photos don't support that, although it is possible that as Ukrainian Party Chief Khrushchev might well have been invited along for the ceremony. That said, Geneva was the first occasion Eisenhower had to take full measure of Khrushchev. And right from the start, it appears the two got along fairly well. On the flight from Washington, Eisenhower had called everyone into his private cabin on the *Columbine*, the presidential plane, to stress the importance of being firm with the Russians while always treating them with respect. 'Strength and civility' became the key words, made all the more important by the fact that the Soviets, especially Khrushchev, seemed to respond favorably to them.

Khrushchev arrived in Geneva prepared to like Eisenhower, not just because he appreciated what Ike had accomplished during the war, but because Stalin had liked Eisenhower.

74

He too had civility in mind.

Khrushchev dragged Zhukov along specifically to appease Ike. Unfortunately, Zhukov's presence was less comforting to the President than Khrushchev had counted on. In a private chat, Zhukov confessed to Eisenhower, 'There are things in Russia which are not as they seem.' The remark went unexplained. Zhukov also mentioned that his daughter had been married the day before and that he'd missed the wedding to make the trip to Geneva. As soon as he could, Eisenhower discreetly ordered an aide to find a wedding present for Zhukov's daughter – a pen set and portable radio.

Seeing Zhukov for the first time since August 1945, Eisenhower got the distinct impression that life had not treated him well. Once independent and self-confident, Eisenhower now found a subdued and worried man who no longer smiled and joked. Whenever a serious subject came up, Zhukov toed the party line in monotone, as if he'd been rehearsed, as if he'd memorized what the others wanted him to say. In the end, Eisenhower decided it was easier to speak with Zhukov about fishing. A week later, once he returned to Washington, Eisenhower sent Zhukov a fancy American rod and spinning reel. He wrote, 'I trust that you will catch a lot of big ones with it, and have a lot of enjoyment during the process. It was fine to see you again – possibly some day I shall have the pleasure of once more meeting with you personally.' But it was never to be. Eisenhower later told his White House staff secretary – a career Army officer named Andrew Jackson Goodpaster – that the Grigory Zhukov he saw in Geneva was a broken man.

Still, that Khrushchev had made a gesture by bringing Zhukov was not lost on Eisenhower.

It was, in fact, the opening gambit in what was to become an important personal relationship.

The two were roughly the same age and both had come from a rural background. Even though Khrushchev tended to use some 'fairly pungent peasant remarks' – the interpreter often stumbled as he tried his best to clean them up for the English version – Eisenhower quickly discovered and liked the fact that Khrushchev could be very amusing. By the time the conference ended, Khrushchev was even complaining to Ike about his kidneys.

In any case, for six days that July, the leaders of the four most powerful nations on earth discussed disarmament, the development of East-West relations, the reunification of Germany and European security. Macmillan came away convinced that the Soviets did not want war. They feared NATO and called for the Allies to disband it. But most of all they hated and feared the Germans and would do everything possible to see that the two Germanies were never reunited.

Eisenhower tried to reassure the Soviets that a united Germany, which he favored, posed no threat to Russia. He promised that any renewal of Hitlerism would be met by a United States determined to prevent it. But the Soviets refused to budge. They wanted Germany disarmed and turned into a neutral state. However, there was no way Eisenhower could give in to them there without undermining Konrad Adenauer's political base and weakening the Western alliance. From that standpoint, the summit produced no tangible results.

The one moment at the conference when it appeared as if something monumental might happen was when Eisenhower proposed 'Open Skies.' It was a three-part proposition made directly to the Soviets. First, Eisenhower wanted to exchange charts and maps which would locate and describe in detail the military installations of each participating nation. Included would be ground, air and sea strengths. Second, each nation would be given the right to station detachments in the other nations' territory, in predetermined numbers of personnel, aircraft, cameras, maintenance units, and so forth. Third, those detachments would have the right, subject to mutually agreed regulations, to overfly, inspect and photograph the military installations of the host nation.

Oddly, the moment Eisenhower finished presenting his plan to the Soviets, a violent thunderstorm broke out over Lake Geneva and the Council Chamber was plunged into total darkness. It startled everyone present and, in the moment of shocked silence that followed that first roar of thunder, Eisenhower quipped, 'I hadn't dreamed I was so eloquent as to put out the lights.'

Everyone laughed, breaking the obvious tension coming from the Russian side of the room.

Eden and Faure both spoke favorably of the idea. Then Bulganin rose. The same man who had, with a perfectly straight face the night before, labeled NATO an obviously aggressive alliance – 'Because when we applied to join we were denied' – now acknowledged that 'Open Skies' had real merit and that the Soviets would consider it carefully. His tone was encouraging and, as the meeting ended, Eisenhower felt this could lead to a significant breakthrough in US-Soviet relations. But as the delegates filed out of the Chamber on their way to an afternoon cocktail, Khrushchev came up to Eisenhower, wagged his finger sideways and said in English, 'No, no, no, no, no.' Reverting to his interpreter, he then told Eisenhower, 'We cannot accept you trying to look into our bedrooms.'

Later that evening, Bulganin pulled the President aside and told him that he and Khrushchev would accept an invitation to visit the United States if one was made. Understanding that this was a tremendous step towards peace, Ike instantly said, 'Good, come on over.' But, when he told Foster Dulles about it, the Secretary of State chided him for being too impulsive. The message quickly went back to the Soviets that the possibility of a visit would be considered. What Dulles almost certainly wanted to add, but dared not, was 'Over my dead body.'

Which is exactly how it turned out.

Bulganin made the same approach to Anthony Eden. The British took a different view and said the Soviets would be most welcome. That suited Khrushchev and Bulganin. A trip to England would be a good dress rehearsal for the US visit if and when it could be arranged.

That the Russians rejected 'Open Skies' didn't come as a surprise to anyone at Geneva. That Eisenhower put it on the table was enough to declare him the winner. In the world's eyes, for the first time, he looked like a statesman. To the American electorate, he returned home looking like a man who couldn't be beaten by anyone in the election of 1956. But that doesn't mean Khrushchev lost. Harold Macmillan believed he was serious about detente, that he would have liked to reduce the expenditure and effort on armaments, but was genuinely frightened by the American bases in Europe. Presidential press secretary James Hagerty went one step further. He believed that, throughout his stay in Geneva, Khrushchev was keenly aware of the fact that, should there be a nuclear war between the US and the USSR, the result would be 50 million Americans left alive and 50 million Russians left alive, but 450 million Chinese left alive. That, Hagerty sensed, was a pretty startling fact to have to live with.

Without knowing that on his return from Geneva, Khrushchev had started telling people he'd formed a friendship with John Foster Dulles – 'He was the most important man there' – when Dulles got back to Washington he'd begun telling people that Khrushchev needed to be watched.

'I'm not worried about calculating people,' he explained. 'Stalin was a calculating man. What I'm worried about is a miscalculation that might bring on war. Khrushchev is not a calculating man. He is excitable, irresponsible, prone to lose his temper.'

That, said Dulles, made Khrushchev more dangerous than Stalin. 'While pursuing the same objective as Stalin – Communist domination in the world – he will do so in more subtle and devious ways.'

It wouldn't happen for another 27 months, but once again, Dulles would be proved correct.

Chapter Five

The General, the Lawyer and the Spy

By joining the light atomic nuclei of hydrogen you can create a reaction of uncontrolled nuclear fusion which releases phenomenal amounts of energy.

It's called a hydrogen bomb.

In the earliest years of the 1950s, exactly how to put one of those together was undoubtedly the most tightly classified secret in the world. These days you can get books on hydrogen bombs from the public library, complete with step-by-step directions and diagrams down to the minutest detail. Needless to say, building one would be an extremely complicated, extremely expensive weekend hobby. But then, the result is something like a thousand times more powerful than a standard atomic bomb, which itself produces nuclear fission one million times more potent than comparable amounts of TNT.

Although the theory behind this 'super-bomb' had been bandied about for many years – it was considered to be the next logical step after the A-bomb – America only began serious development of it once the Russians detonated their first atomic device in 1949. There'd been initial resistance to the concept of a hydrogen bomb, most particularly from men like Robert Oppenheimer, who'd headed the Manhattan Project which developed America's atomic bomb. A majority of the members of the General Advisory Committee of the Atomic Energy Commission – then chaired by Oppenheimer – agreed that the H-bomb was going too far. Their case was based largely, but not exclusively, on the moral implications of such a horrendous weapon. However, the National Security Council felt otherwise and Truman signed the order to begin work on it in January 1950. This was, the President perceived, a rational next phase in the policy of containment. As the United States no longer possessed an atomic monopoly, the country would have an ultimate weapon of massive retaliation.

Three days after Dwight Eisenhower was elected President, America's first thermonuclear device was tested on Eniwetok Island in the Marshalls. Nicknamed 'Mike,' its yield was 10.4 megatons – or the equivalent of 10.4 million tons of TNT – enough to leave a crater 1 mile long and 175 feet deep on Eniwetok and to obliterate nearby Eleugelab Island. Having upped the stakes, so that possible aggressors risked overwhelming destruction, America was definitely banking on the Russians to think twice before picking a fight.

The theory was fine, at least on paper, and might well have worked had the Soviets not interpreted this as a direct threat to their own security. They agreed that the best way to deter an attack was by offering tit for tat – catastrophic retribution – and with that in mind, they set about developing their own super-bomb. The first successful test of a Russian hydrogen device was announced on 8 August 1953. Although the yield was less than the average A-bomb and only about one-twentieth the size of America's H-bomb, as far as Washington was concerned the Russians were – annoyingly – keeping up with American technology. On 1 March 1954, the United States responded with a series of thermonuclear bomb tests, the first of them having a 15-megaton yield. Twenty months later, in November 1955, the Soviets produced and tested a full-scale hydrogen bomb.

The fate of the world, Churchill prophesied, now rested on a 'delicate balance of terror.'

Eisenhower inherited Truman's containment policy and put his own stamp on it by inexorably linking it to the concept of deterrence. He'd also inherited a Defense Department planning for a variety of different kinds of wars. The separate strategies were all the more confusing because no one had yet taken a firm decision about whether or not nuclear weapons would definitely be used against the Russians. The Navy and the Army shared the view that, if attacked, America wouldn't use them first, so they opted for bigger aircraft carriers and more ground troops. The Air Force, however, contemplated using nuclear weapons specifically to prevent the Russians from firing them first. Muddled in with this were plans for short wars, police actions, peripheral wars and infantry wars. Eisenhower wanted to end the confusion, so he told the Pentagon to assume that a war with the Soviets would be fought with nuclear weapons. One result was that the Army and Navy lost funding while the Air Force gained, which had the sorry effect of heightening an increasingly determined rivalry between the services. But that suited John Foster Dulles because he'd been urging Eisenhower that America's best defense was a strong deterrent force based on atomic and thermonuclear power.

On 12 January 1954, as the guest of honor at a meeting of the Council on Foreign Relations in New York, Dulles warned a distinguished audience of the danger of permitting any aggressor – namely the Soviet Union – to assume that manpower would be the decisive factor in the next war. 'We need allies and collective security. Our purpose is to make these relations more effective, less costly. This can be done by placing more reliance on deterrent power and less dependence on local defensive power.'

He wanted it understood that the only way to deter aggression was for the free world – namely the United States – to be willing and able to respond vigorously wherever and however it chose to do so. 'Local defenses must be reinforced by the further deterrent of massive retaliatory power.'

Reading slowly from his prepared script, he clarified the President's belief that America's security must now depend primarily on 'a great capacity to retaliate, instantly, by means and places of our own choosing.'

The following day, when Eisenhower was asked to comment on the Dulles speech, he displayed full support for the policy by saying that the greatest danger lay in a surprise attack – 'Pearl Harbor multiplied' – and that the only defense for that 'is the knowledge that there is a strong retaliatory power.' A few days later, in his State of the Union address, Eisenhower went even further. 'We take into full account our great and growing number of nuclear weapons and the most effective means of using them against an aggressor if they are needed to preserve our freedom.'

The immediate response to all of this was a spate of criticism levied at Eisenhower and Dulles. Attempting to explain their position, Dulles wrote an article for the March issue of *Foreign Affairs* magazine in which he plainly stated that America's will to use nuclear weapons was a warning to the Russians that they could not expect to start a war without suffering the consequences of evident retaliation. He also conceded that massive atomic and thermonuclear retaliation would not necessarily prove useful under all circumstances and that no one intended to turn every local war into a world war.

A month later, Eisenhower went on television to reassure the American people that no one in Washington was advocating war, that nuclear arms were a threat only if a potential aggressor decided to use them against the US and that, as long as America maintained the power to retaliate massively, the possibility of war remained minimal. Sitting in front of a roaring fire, speaking to the nation like everyone's grandfather, he portrayed the men in the Kremlin as power hungry but sane. 'The very fact that those men, by their own design, are in the Kremlin, means that they love power. They want to be there. Whenever they start a war, they are taking the great risk of losing that power. They study history pretty well. They remember Mussolini. They remember Hitler. They have even studied Napoleon very seriously. When dictators over-reach themselves and challenge the whole world, they are very likely to end up in any place except a dictatorial position. And those men in the Politburo know that.'

While the possibility of all-out war existed, and although men like Dulles were insisting that the Soviets were not particularly keen on establishing a permanent peace, it was becoming apparent that no one in the Kremlin was overly anxious to provoke a final showdown. The thinking behind their policy seemed to be 'to seek to manage the inevitable flow of history, to bring about the attrition of the enemy by gradual increments and not to stake everything on a single throw of the dice.'

At the end of 1955, Dulles formulated an American version of that approach, which came to be known as 'brinkmanship,' and nearly cost him his job. On 4 December, he met privately with three journalists in the library of his mock-Tudor Georgetown home at No. 2740–32nd Street. James Shepley, then head of *Time* magazine's domestic news bureau, was writing an article for *Time*'s sister publication, *Life*. John Beal, who covered the State Department for *Time*, was writing a book about Dulles. And Charles Murphy, Washington editor of *Fortune*, was doing a series of articles on Eisenhower's first term.

The four men spent a couple of casual hours on a wintry Sunday afternoon covering a wide range of subjects. Dulles was fairly relaxed with his guests. They were all pretty senior, he'd known them for a long time and, anyway, it was a 'background only' session. If they wanted to attribute anything to him – he'd stipulated right from the beginning and they'd agreed – he might consider it at a later date, but they'd have to clear it with him first. All the more reassuring to Dulles, Beal had a tape recorder with him, something not commonly done in those days because tape recorders in the 1950s were awkward to carry about, being the size of suitcases.

When they got onto the subject of world tension and Charles Murphy asked about the risks of war, Dulles reportedly said, 'You have to take chances for peace, just as you must take chances in war.' That was a harmless enough throwback to his theme of the 1940s when he'd claimed, one wins the peace the way one wins a war. But at this point he purportedly added, 'Some say that we were brought to the verge of war. Of course we were brought to the verge of war. The ability to get to the verge without getting into war is the necessary art. If you try to run away from it, if you are scared to go to the brink, you are lost. We've had to look it squarely in the face – on the question of enlarging the Korean war, on the question of getting into the Indochina war, on the question of Formosa. We walked to the brink and we looked it in the face. We took strong action.'

A draft of Shepley's article was in fact submitted to the State Department within hours of *Life's* deadline. For whatever reason, it never arrived on Dulles' desk. Or if it did, then he was lying when he said he never saw it. Shepley published it on 16 January 1956 under the title, 'How Dulles Averted War.'

The furore that followed was monstrous.

Some people thought Dulles' statement cast doubts on the administration's efforts towards peace. Others felt they were at best unsubstantiated, at worst untrue. The *New York Times* suggested, 'The Secretary of State doesn't stumble into booby traps, he digs them to size, studies them carefully, and then jumps.' The British Foreign Office issued an official statement disassociating themselves from any references about the UK made by Dulles in the article, and *The Times* called him 'an edgy gambler.' The Soviets joined the bandwagon, attacking Dulles as the complete 'rollbackboy' and the epitome of the Cold War approach. There were calls in Congress for his resignation, prompting Eisenhower to acknowledge publicly that Dulles was the finest Secretary of State he'd ever known.

To give the man his due, Dulles was a lawyer who never learned to stop thinking like a lawyer. As Secretary of State he was still an attorney acting for his client. It was both his great strength and his major weakness.

Dulles the Secretary of State took a hardline view of the world and was dogmatic about his opinions, at times too dogmatic for the often conciliatory Eisenhower. Dulles the man was unremitting in his belief that God was on America's side because theology and the American Constitutional system were righteous and would prevail over the atheistic Marxists. As he saw the world divided between good and evil, it was only logical that he also considered neutrality as immoral. His Judeo-Christian bearing eventually led Eisenhower to label him 'a militant Presbyterian.' Dulles the lawyer was committed to conventional forms of diplomacy and Eisenhower the general was comfortable with that. But Dulles the lawyer also had a rather dour outlook on the possibilities for international order whereas Eisenhower the President was more optimistic, putting great stock in the values on which the American political system was founded. As Andrew Goodpaster observes, 'Eisenhower felt that if we could project that around the world, it would be the strongest armament we had, the strongest diplomacy we had. Dulles was always skeptical.'

Even Nikita Khrushchev was willing to concede that Dulles was at his most skillful when it came to understanding the Soviets. 'I'll say this for him,' he wrote, 'Dulles knew how far he could push us and he never pushed us too far.'

Eisenhower appreciated Dulles as a vigorous Republican and 'a man of strong opinions and unimpeachable character.' A few years later he wrote that he sometimes disagreed with Dulles' lawyer's approach to the Soviets because, 'He shows the steps and the actions that are bad on their part; we seek to show that we are doing the decent and just thing.' Yet, in his memoirs, Eisenhower says quite plainly that he and Dulles were in daily touch with each other and that Dulles always cleared public statements and pronouncements with him first. Noting that Dulles had often been accused of being responsible only to his own convictions and inclinations, Eisenhower revealed, 'What his critics did not know was that he was more emphatic than they in his insistence that ultimate and personal responsibility for all major decisions in the field of foreign relations belonged exclusively to the President, an attitude he meticulously maintained throughout our service together. He would not deliver an important speech or statement until after I had read, edited and approved it; he guarded constantly against the possibility that any misunderstanding could arise between us.'

When the 'brinkmanship' article appeared and the scandal broke around it, Dulles turned down the chance to contradict it publicly. He – mistakenly – felt it was best to let it fade away on its own. However, he told friends that what he'd actually said was that the United States had been 'dragged to the brink of war.' The art of crisis diplomacy, as he saw it, was in recognizing danger and facing it. That was what 'brinkmanship' meant to him.

The term is still today associated with Dulles and his foreign policy approach towards the Soviets. And it is hard to believe that he unknowingly let it happen. James Reston, writing about it in the *New York Times*, hinted that Dulles had made 'a planned mistake.' Therein lies an intriguing supposition – that Dulles said exactly what Shepley alleged and said it in the way Shepley reported it, all the time knowing full well how the world would react. With a presidential election due later that year, Eisenhower would be hard pressed to do anything but defend his Secretary of State and in doing that, he would be sending a message to Khrushchev that he too embraced Dulles' harder-line foreign policy position.

If it was a ploy, it was political brinkmanship of the most sophisticated kind.

Where John Foster Dulles was a rigidly serious man in ambitious pursuit of a serious career, his brother Allen Welsh Dulles was a man who followed his own sense of adventure. Five years the junior, Allen finished Princeton in 1914, didn't know what to do with himself, so he blew what little money he had on a ticket to Europe. He traveled through Spain and into the Middle East. After a time he moved on to India and then made his way to China. Whenever he ran out of money, he stopped somewhere long enough to get himself a job teaching English. He returned home more than a year later, a 22-year-old filled with the confidence of a young man who'd already conquered the world, only to face the same dilemma he'd left behind – what to do with his life. His uncle, Robert Lansing, invited him to join the State Department, which he did, and before long he found himself posted in Vienna. From there he went to Bern, to work as an intelligence officer gathering information about the Germans from behind the diplomatic shield. In 1919 he was assigned to the Paris Peace Conference, where he spent time on the Czechoslovak Boundary Commission. Years later, he jokingly denied any responsibility for shaping Czechoslovakia like a banana lying on its side. He helped open the US mission in Berlin in 1920, did a tour of duty in Constantinople, then returned to Washington for a four-year stint as chief of the State Department's Near East Division.

By that time, he was just about broke.

Foster had convinced Allen to get a law degree, which he did at night at George Washington University, and left the State Department to go to work for his brother at Sullivan and Cromwell. He steadfastly maintained his Washington contacts however, was elected President of the New York Council on Foreign Relations and was also appointed legal adviser to the American delegation at the League of Nations conferences on arms limitation in Geneva.

In late 1940, he received a call from his childhood friend 'Wild' Bill Donovan. Winner of a Congressional Medal of Honor in World War I, and a fellow Wall Street lawyer, Donovan had been asked by his friend Franklin Roosevelt to set up an American intelligence service. Donovan wanted Allen to join him, which he did, and together they built the OSS – played at cloak and dagger throughout the war – then designed the CIA. Truman appointed Allen to be the Agency's number two man and, in 1953, Eisenhower promoted him to Director of Central Intelligence (DCI).

Allen was tall, like Foster, but not nearly as ungainly. He wore clothes better and had a dapper moustache. Nor was he as ponderous. Foster spoke with solemn authority. Allen was more gregarious, more relaxed. Allen also displayed a streak of courage that his brother never showed when confronted with Joe McCarthy. Foster was decidedly mealy-mouthed in the face of McCarthy's accusations that the State Department was riddled with Communists, and a lot of the old hands at the State Department resented him for it. Allen refused to be bullied by McCarthy and his personal stock shot up in many people's eyes.

The Dulles brothers shared a resolute antipathy for Communism, and never saw friendship with the Russians as a viable option. Eisenhower shared their distrust of the Soviets and would immediately remind anyone who lauded their sincerity, 'Every agreement with the Soviets entered into at Teheran in 1943 and Yalta in 1945 was ruthlessly broken, save for those palpably to their advantage. The same holds true for the Potsdam Conference of 1945.'

Still, however much he hated the Communists, Ike's fear of World War III was even more intense. And the Joint Chiefs of Staff's 'Dooms-day' date was now less than two years away. So with Foster Dulles slowly shifting national policy from containment to one of 'massive retaliation' – the idea being that the best way to prevent a surprise attack by the Russians was by having a military force poised to offer such a devastating reprisal that total destruction of the aggressor would be guaranteed – Eisenhower asked Dr James Killian, President of MIT, to head something that would be called the Technical Capabilities Panel (TCP).

The Killian group met for the first time in March 1954, having been asked by the President to study the risk of a surprise attack by the Russians and come up with suggestions to protect against it. One obvious way, they soon concluded, was to catch the enemy preparing for an attack. Exactly how to do that was left to a TCP sub-committee, the Intelligence Panel, chaired by Dr Edwin Land, inventor of the Polaroid camera. He suggested putting a camera on a plane and flying it at high altitudes over the Soviet Union. Some members of the panel, among them the exalted Air Force General Jimmy Doolittle, argued that couldn't be done without specially designed aircraft equipped with specially designed cameras. Coming up with that, Doolittle said, would take 10 years and, by that time, it might be too late.

Except the United States had been doing it for years.

From the end of World War II until the Soviets exploded their atomic bomb in 1949, American and British reconnaissance pilots had been flying missions along the borders of all the Eastern bloc countries, systematically violating their airspace with a fast-dash foray whenever they thought they could get away with it. Shortly after the Russian bomb test, an unmarked American plane flew over the Ukraine, parachuting a pair of spies into the area. Both the Navy and the Air Force also had camera-equipped balloons which they floated in the currents moving west to east across the USSR. The idea was that when they reached the Pacific the balloons could be reclaimed. Needless to say, it was not one of America's more successful intelligence-gathering attempts. By 1950, the Joint Chiefs decided they wanted to penetrate deep into Soviet airspace. The Air Force took on the project and at one point Vice-Chief of Staff General Nathan Twining is reported to have said that he had no fewer than 47 aircraft flying all over Russia. What's more, he added, no one had yet heard a peep from Stalin. That changed pretty quickly when the Russians started shooting at American planes. They bagged a US Navy bomber over Siberia in November 1951 and a USAF B-29 near the Sea of Japan in June 1952. Two more American planes were shot down in the same area during the next 12 months.

The British took their turn spy-flying over Russia, and in 1953 nearly lost a B-57. They'd stripped it down, added extra fuel tanks and loaded it with cameras. It left West Germany one night, flying southwest over Soviet airspace, trying to get pictures of a specific missile site. The Russian air force filled it full of holes, although the pilot managed to bring it back to the recovery base in Iran. Conjecture has always been that the Russians knew the plane was coming, tipped off perhaps by Kim Philby or one of his group from inside M.I.6. The immediate result was that the British now told the Americans to go it alone.

So they did.

Land's committee reported that overflights of the USSR would be a superb source of intelligence. Killian took a recommendation to Eisenhower, who agreed that a special plane should be built. With the authority of the White House behind him, Killian approached the Air Force and Lockheed's Clarence 'Kelly' Johnson, arguably the best aircraft designer in the world at the time. He was asked to create a spy plane that could fly at more than 70,000 feet, over a range of 5000 miles. Because such missions might last for as much as 12 hours, the sheer weight of the fuel required meant Johnson had to reject standard aircraft designs. He broke new ground, opting for the glider look.

Killian and Land brought Johnson's initial sketches to Allen Dulles in his office at 24th and E Streets, a plush suite of rooms in a thoroughly innocuous building behind the Navy's Bureau of Medicine and Surgery, a block from the State Department. They sold him on the idea and he in turn called for a top secret, need-to-know, executive session of the Agency's Intelligence Advisory Committee.

Meeting behind locked doors on Tuesday, 30 November 1954, the service intelligence chiefs, together with the State Department's intelligence chief – no deputies allowed – unanimously endorsed the program.

Twenty-four hours later, Killian and Land were in the Oval Office, this time with the Dulles brothers, briefing the President. Eisenhower liked what he saw, but wondered who was going to pay for the development of the airframe and the first batch of planes. Allen Dulles said right away he could authorize it out of the Agency's 'reserve funds,' a pile of 'invisible' money which Congress knew nothing about. As the DCI was accountable only to the President for the use of those funds, the plane's existence would be the best-kept secret in the country.

Just like that, Allen Dulles transformed the CIA from bureaucrats in trenchcoats to a secret air force beyond the reach of Congress.

Under the code name 'Aquatone,' Johnson and a tiny specialist team at Lockheed's high-security plant in Burbank California – known as the Skunk Works – agreed to deliver a plane in under eight months. Working 100-hour weeks, they finished the prototype in 88 days.

It was a beautiful single-seat plane, constructed in advanced light-weight materials, such as titanium. Its wingspan of 80 feet was almost twice the length of its fuselage. Initially capable of a range of 4200 miles and a maximum altitude of 75,000 feet, it was equipped with specially designed cameras, specially designed lenses and 12,000 feet of specially designed film – nearly enough, it was said, to photograph the entire flight path from southern California to Washington. Johnson christened the plane 'Angel.' But Dulles and the CIA wanted a better name. Instead of using the letter 'R,' which was the standard designation of a reconnaissance plane, they decided that for security reasons they'd choose the less specific 'U,' which usually designates a 'Utility' plane, and called it the U-2.

Eisenhower loved it and the first one entered service in 1956.

Killian and Land's pet project had become Allen Dulles' triumph.

After the first few overflights – once the novelty wore off, and the President got used to seeing high-detail, ultra-precise intelligence photographs taken at 75,000 feet – Eisenhower assumed overall control of the program. Every time Dulles wanted to make an overflight, he needed to have Eisenhower's personal approval. He and Richard Bissell, the CIA deputy in charge of 'Aquatone,' would meet in the Oval Office with the President. The other men who were usually present included John Foster Dulles, General Goodpaster, the President's son John, Air Force General William Campbell, who was Deputy Director of the CIA, and Don Quarles, the Assistant Secretary of Defense for Research and Development. Allen Dulles and Bissell would make their presentation, spreading a map of the Soviet Union across the President's desk and saying, here are the targets we want to cover. Eisenhower would put on his glasses, study the map and start asking questions. He'd say, if I approve this, I don't want you to go from there to there, instead I want you to go this way and over to here. He outlined the criteria for each mission himself. Detail by detail, he personally plotted everything. Then, once the flight plan was set, he'd invariably say, I'll let you know. He never made decisions to go ahead there and then. A day or two later Bissell would get a call from Goodpaster, who'd inform him, the boss says no, or, the boss says do this if you can accomplish it within a specific period of so many days.

Eisenhower was hands on with the U-2 because, as Goodpaster used to tell Bissell, it was one of his favorite projects. He gave the Agency high marks for it and loved being a part of it. Because the U-2 was handled out of all normal channels, Eisenhower felt in total control, which made him look upon the CIA as responsibly accountable. If he wanted them to skip a city or a target, they did. His orders were obeyed. Once a military man, always a military man. It was a rare treat, Eisenhower knew, when a President's instructions weren't cushioned by layers of bureaucrats.

Somehow, responsibility for America's participation in the International Geophysical Year (IGY) landed on the Secretary of State's desk. It probably happened because no one in the White House could figure out where it actually belonged. As it was definitely not the sort of project that would have interested him, Foster Dulles passed the buck to a committee which was formed for the specific purpose of supervising American participation in the event.

The IGY came about because in the first half of the century, the International Council of Scientific Unions (ICSU) had sponsored something known as the Second Polar Year. The First Polar Year, 50 years before, had been a massive coordinated study of the earth's polar regions. In 1950, the ICSU's Mixed Commission on the Ionosphere suggested that they sponsor a Third Polar Year. So a committee of prominent scientists was put together and their recommendation was that the concept should in fact be extended to cover all areas of earth science. Set to span 18 months from 1 July 1957 to 31 December 1958, the idea was that any nation wishing to undertake a project would do so under the auspices of the IGY, entitling them to assistance and encouragement from the world scientific community, in exchange for sharing project results with all other members.

On Friday 29 July 1955, during the course of a briefing for the White House press corps, James Hagerty announced that, in connection with the forthcoming IGY, the United States intended to launch an artificial earth satellite. That would be America's contribution. He said the satellite, which would probably be about the size of a basketball, might carry scientific instruments but would have no military role. A few journalists bothered to ask questions. Most wondered if they'd be able to get away early for the weekend. The text of Hagerty's statement was reported in Soviet newspapers, where the official reaction was said to be 'non-tendentious.' A week later, at a meeting of the International Congress of Astronautics in Copenhagen, Soviet Academician Leonid Sedov claimed – in response to the American announcement – that the USSR was already at work developing a satellite.

It was a lie.

A few days after that, an article appeared in *Red Star*, supposedly in response to questions asked of the magazine by three Soviet Army officers. Called 'Artificial Satellite of the Earth,' the author was Academician K. P. Stanyukovich, apparently a scientist assigned to the Department of Physico-Mathematic Science at the Institute for Physical Problems. He repeated Sedov's fib by promising, 'Preparation is also taking place in the Soviet Union for launching a satellite in the comparatively near future.'

That was followed two days later by an article in *Pravda* under the heading 'Cosmic Laboratory – Projects for an Artificial Satellite of Earth are now being Organized.' In that one, A. G. Karpenko, Secretary of the Permanent Inter-Departmental Commission on Inter-Planetary Communication noted, 'At the present time there exist many designs for the construction of artificial satellites of varying dimensions and weight, from several kilograms to several tons. The engineers, designers and scientific workers who are concerned and interested in rocket technique well know the realism of such projects.'

This was also untrue.

'Chip' Bohlen, the US Ambassador in Moscow, having no way to differentiate between truth and falsehood, ordered full translations of the articles and dispatched them to the State Department. Copies were also forwarded to, among other addresses, the CIA, the Army, the Navy, the Air Force, the Office of Strategic Development and the US Information Agency.

But Foster Dulles couldn't have been less interested. He was the last American to be so naive as to overlook the Russians' reputation for such bravado. The President was also acutely indifferent and if anyone else in Washington who read Bohlen's messages bothered to take them seriously – including Allen Dulles – there doesn't appear to be any record of it today.

As it happened, there was good reason to doubt what the Russians were saying. Sedov and the others who were making public statements about a Russian satellite program didn't know anything about the Russian satellite program, which was precisely why they were being permitted to talk. Khrushchev had been told that several papers on satellites were being presented at the International Congress of Astronautics in Copenhagen, understood that the scientific community considered it an idea whose time had come and decided there was some propaganda mileage to be gained by boasting of Soviet scientific achievements. Not daring to risk any of his truly important scientists, he sent shills. Sedov, for instance, who would soon become known in the West as 'the father of Sputnik,' not only didn't have anything to do with Sputnik, he was purposely kept away from anyone who did in order to avoid the danger of his leaking secrets.

In September 1955, Khrushchev openly boasted that the USSR was ahead of the United States in preparations for space satellites. But, in reporting this, the CIA was quick to add that in a private conversation with someone, Leonid Sedov had expressed his personal opinion that the United States might still be ahead of the Russians in this field.

It's true that the Soviet Academy of Sciences had at one point debated the idea of an artificial earth satellite. But they'd voted against it. It wasn't until January 1956 that Khrushchev agreed to allow a special commission headed by Academician Mstislav Keldish to look into the possibility of the creation of a satellite in connection with the IGY and report back to the Presidium. Then too, the Russians were convinced, just like everyone else in the world, that only the Americans could actually pull off such a feat. When the White House made the announcement, no one in the USSR doubted for a moment that America would be the first to put a satellite in space.

If Eisenhower and the Dulles brothers couldn't get excited about international geophysics, it was because they had more important things to worry about, like the creation of the 5412 Committee, the most secret organization in the United States of America.

A sub-cabinet-level group charged with reviewing and approving all of the nation's clandestine operations – other than intelligence collection and pure espionage activities – it was conceived in 1955 by the National Security Council and originally named for NSC Paper No. 5412 which first put forth the idea.

Established specifically to protect the President from clandestine operations gone wrong, the committee was considered so sensitive that the NSC was not kept informed of its activities and those few men who knew about it referred to it simply as 'The Special Group.'

It still exists today, functioning pretty much the way it did in the 1950s, although various administrations have changed the name from 5412 to such obscurely derived numbers as 303 and 40. The idea has always been that it would be the Special Group, not the President, that officially approves certain plans – for example, activities which entail illegal interventions into the internal affairs of another sovereign state.

The committee traditionally consists of a chairman – often the President's National Security Advisor – the Secretaries of State and Defense and the Director of Central Intelligence.

For obvious reasons, the President is not a member.

There's no denying that the buck stops at the Oval Office and it is ultimately the President who must authorize such projects, but his approval of a Special Group proposal is only ever given verbally. The members of the group work it out among themselves, then brief the President. Nothing is written down with his name on it. Nothing is ever signed by him. That way, should something go wrong, the CIA can rightfully claim it acted on the authority of the Special Group, which means the President can ostensibly deny that he has ever approved of such an activity.

If there ever was a White House sanctioned plot to assassinate Fidel Castro, it would have been John Kennedy's 'Special Group' that discussed it. If, as it has been alleged, the CIA murdered Salvador Allende in Chile in 1973, Richard Nixon's 'Special Group' would have been the ones to discuss that. And if, as has been suggested, Ronald Reagan approved what has become known as the Iran-Contra Affair, that again would have been down to his administration's equivalent of the 5412 Committee. It is, in fact, a perfect example of what the committee is supposed to do. If you accept the premise that William Casey, as Director of Central Intelligence, committed the CIA to engage in the illegal activities for which Marine Colonel Oliver North was tried, then the plan would have almost certainly had to have been brought up in a Special Group meeting. The Secretaries of State and Defense would have known about it, agreed to it and presented it for final approval to the President. But because nothing is written down and therefore nothing can ever be traced back to the President, Reagan's denial of any knowledge of the affair was an impenetrable defense.

In setting up this group, Eisenhower appointed Gordon Gray, his Special Assistant for National Security Affairs, to chair the committee, which consisted only of the Dulles brothers and Secretary of Defense

Charles Wilson. While both Foster Dulles and Wilson were in policy-making positions, the Special Group provided a unique opportunity for Allen Dulles also to get involved with policy, despite his supposed 'bad conscience' about such things. He, like many other intelligence chiefs, had always laid down the long-standing rule that intelligence officers don't make policy, that their mission is to report and to analyze. But Allen was not one to miss an opportunity to say what he thought ought to be done and, in fact, welcomed discussions that had policy implications. At the same time, he was extremely careful where and when he voiced his opinions and did not necessarily volunteer policy counsel directly to the President.

However, the Special Group gave Allen the perfect forum to sell his views to the President. At the same time, he was shrewd enough that those views were never put to the 5412 Committee without first conferring privately with his brother.

Foster and Allen met almost every evening after work and discussed just about everything between themselves. Neither ever admitted that they'd discreetly agreed on a certain stance. They never wanted it to appear as if the relationship between the State Department and the CIA was based on private conversations between brothers. But it clearly was.

Especially when it came to the 5412.

Allen would present his plans to his own staff, saying, we can do this because I'm reasonably sure that when we take it up with the committee it will be approved. That meant, his brother had already approved.

It's not clear whether Eisenhower ever realized that the Dulles brothers had loaded the dice by working out their strategy ahead of time. However, to give the man his due, if he never actually came right out and asked them, it's likely he suspected as much. In any case, the end result was what the Dulles brothers had clearly intended – increased influence over Eisenhower.

In Allen's case, this manifested itself in the CIA becoming more 'action-oriented.' Covert operations had already proven successful on behalf of Western oil interests in Iran by unseating the Mossadeq regime in 1953 and on behalf of American fruit interests against Guatemala's leftist President Jacobo Arbenz Guzman the following year. Allen began turning his bureaucrats into supermen who thought they could over-throw governments at will. And it is from this that the great mystique about the Agency's prowess grew.

Eisenhower, watching Allen Dulles and the CIA rush off to play covert games, worried about two things. Firstly, he sensed the inherent danger of covert activities and their ramifications on his own foreign policy responsibilities. Secondly, he felt such activities might be undertaken at the expense of the CIA's intelligence-gathering function, which he greatly admired. After all, it may be well and good to overthrow a banana republic, but not if it means that the Russian bomber counters are no longer counting Russian bombers.

The crux of the problem lay in the different way that the two men read the DCI's job description. During the war, Eisenhower's chief intelligence officer, General Kenneth Strong, maintained a regular flow of intelligence information which allowed Eisenhower to set policy and take decisions. The President liked that system, had seen it work, was comfortable with it and wanted Allen Dulles to serve as his chief intelligence officer exactly the way Strong had. Allen Dulles, on the other hand, preferred 'Wild' Bill Donovan and his wartime OSS as a role model.

Based on his first-hand field experience with both overt and covert intelligence matters, the President rightfully doubted the merits of Allen's new-look agency. He viewed Allen Dulles as an experienced operator whose role as DCI was to provide integrated intelligence. And, while he was not strong in management, Eisenhower found him to be effective in terms of generating intelligence. He was 'G-2' – the old Army term the President used when he referred to Allen Dulles – but then, after 40 years in the Army, Ike was well aware of the limited services G-2 could provide.

Eisenhower also took a fairly jaundiced view when it came to covert and clandestine operations. Before long, the CIA would fail to stop the Soviets from putting down the 1956 Hungarian revolt, would fail to provide the President with sufficient information about Suez, would fail him again in Indonesia and would fail his successor in Cuba at the Bay of Pigs.

But Ike wasn't dealing here with just any DCI. This was Foster's brother.

So, in January 1956, Eisenhower set up the President's Board of Consultants on Foreign Intelligence Activities. He appointed men whom he trusted explicitly – among them Omar Bradley and Jimmy Doolittle – and asked them to advise him on intelligence matters. Specifically, he wanted them to reevaluate the mission of the CIA.

When they finally came back to him, one of their suggestions was that Allen Dulles should be moved from his post at the CIA and brought to the White House where he would coordinate intelligence gathered by various agencies. It was what Eisenhower had hoped to hear. But Allen Dulles wouldn't have it.

The President now found himself in a dilemma of his own making. The respect he held for Foster spilled over, at least to some extent, onto Allen. He therefore didn't want to do anything which might, in any way, put pressure on his own relationship with Foster. Then again, he knew he couldn't change Allen, shouldn't fire him and wouldn't be able to appoint someone over his head who might assert more authority and keep him in line.

In the end, Eisenhower did nothing. He rationalized his indecision by saying, 'I'd rather have Allen as my chief intelligence officer with his limitations than anyone else I know.'

In less than three years, the Dulles brothers had become the most powerful double act in the country.

Chapter Six

Paranoia and Confrontation

On a warm evening in June 1955, just as Dwight Eisenhower was leaving the Oval Office for supper, a military aide walked smartly up to him to announce that the Soviet Union had attacked the United States.

He informed the President that 53 major North American cities had been decimated, nuclear fallout was spreading throughout the continent and initial casualty estimates could be running as high as 100 million.

Needless to say, Eisenhower's dinner was ruined.

Operation Alert continued throughout the night, driving home in real terms to everyone who participated in the surprise mock exercise, the calamitous potential dangers facing the nation.

Seven months later, in January 1956, a small group of men, all dressed in civilian clothes, filed into the Oval Office and greeted the President. He shook their hands and introduced them to the Dulles brothers and the few selected members of his staff who were also present. When everyone was settled, he asked them to make their report. The leader of the group, a retired Air Force General, announced, 'An Evaluation of the Anticipated Damage in the Initial Stages of a Nuclear War with the Russians.'

For the sake of the study, he said, the outbreak of war was determined to be 1 July 1956. His group looked at two variations of the same scenario. The first assumed that on that date the Russians launched a surprise attack which American defenses detected only at the very last minute as hordes of Soviet bombers reached the DEW Line. The second noted a one-month strategic build-up but assumed that US intelligence could not confirm a specific launch date.

In the first case, he indicated to the President, the United States experienced such devastating economic collapse that the country could not be restored to any kind of operative condition for six to twelve months. The Federal government was completely wiped out and the population suffered enormous casualties. He said his study group estimated that as much as 65% of the population would require medical attention and, in most instances, none would be available. The only good news, if he could call it that, was that retaliatory damage inflicted on the Soviets would be three times greater.

A grim Eisenhower asked, 'And with a month's warning of a build-up?'

The retired Air Force General responded, 'There would be no significant difference.'

The official Congress of the Communist Party of the Soviet Union had convened its 20th meeting on Valentine's Day, 14 February 1956. For ten days, delegates had laboriously worked their way through the formal business of the Party. Speaker after speaker had droned on to the Presidium's pre-orchestrated tune. Although this was the first sitting since Stalin's death, his name had been mentioned just once, and that was only during the opening session in connection with a brief tribute to three recently departed members of the movement. By Friday evening, 24 February, the Congress was ready to wind down. The final items on the agenda were the resignations of the old Central Committee and elections for the new one. In accordance with the established rules of order, members voted, then adjourned for the night, intending to reconvene early Saturday morning, at which time Nikita Khrushchev would resign as First Secretary, be automatically reappointed, announce the names of the newly elected members and close the Congress. But through an odd quirk in the system, the time between the resignation of the old Central Committee and the appointment of the new one – which was never meant to be longer than overnight – left the Central Committee of the Communist Party vacant except for one man, the First Secretary. It meant that, for this one night, Nikita Khrushchev wasn't answerable to anybody in the country. So just after 11 p.m. he summoned a special closed-door session. He wanted all Soviet delegates recalled. Foreign Communists who'd been invited as special observers, he said, would be excluded.

No one knew what was happening.

Amid confusion and excitement, men and women wrapped in heavy coats and fur hats hurried through bitter cold dark streets covered in fresh snow to the crest of Kremlin Hill and the 700-room Great Kremlin Palace. Filing in through the spot-lit State Entrance to the right of the center of the south facade, they came into the huge white foyer with its four granite columns, stomped snow from their boots, checked their coats, and, after asking each other what this was all about, climbed the State Staircase, with its walls lined in Italian marble, to the massive golden doors of the splendid white Hall of St George. It had always been intended by the court architects that this room would be the largest in the palace – nearly 200 feet long and 67 feet wide with a decorated coffered ceiling 56 feet high supported by 18 pilasters and from which, even today, hang six extraordinarily beautiful gilded chandeliers. In the days when the Czars lived here, two lavishly decorated rooms were laid at right angles to the Hall of St George. One was dedicated to the Order of St Alexander Nevsky. The other was the Imperial throne room, consecrated to the Order of St Andrew. But those two rooms were destroyed in 1932 to make way for the 263-foot Meeting Hall, an austere place with no decorations except for a life-sized statue of Lenin – posing with his head held high, stuck into an alcove on the wall behind the podium – and enough uncomfortable seats to hold 3000 people.

The speaker's rostrum – a heavy, dark wooden lectern with three black microphones at the front and a wide top for papers, a small lamp and a pitcher of water – was halfway up carpeted steps, elevating it from the main floor. Behind it and up a few more steps, with a clear view of the speaker's back, were two rows of dark wooden tables. On each side of the rostrum were more tables, facing the room, closed in by wood paneling, like a jury box.

It was well after midnight when Khrushchev took his place at the rostrum. Some people applauded. Others simply stared. Everyone seemed slightly confused. He gripped the sides of the podium as if they were rails on a ship and he was caught in a storm, then launched into a four-hour denunciation of Stalin and his reign. He called his tirade, 'The Cult of Personality and Its Consequences.'

Even though he had a pile of notes in front of him, much of what he said that night was off the cuff. But then, he hardly ever scripted speeches because he found writing difficult. Spelling mistakes abound in the few papers and letters written in his hand. His lack of a formal education and his inability to write well plainly bothered him because he dictated almost everything. When speeches were required, he'd ramble through a rough draft with his secretary. Once she'd typed it, he'd add his own notes to it, creating a working outline for what he'd say. But once he got up to speak he'd deviate from his notes, especially whenever he got carried away with his emotions. A talented agitator and experienced propagandist, his ad-libbed outbursts were usually the most stimulating parts of his speeches.

Tonight was no different.

Risking cries of heresy for such audacity, he presented a letter to the delegates that he claimed Lenin had sent him in December 1922 which cast doubts on Stalin's ability to lead the Party. 'Comrade Stalin,' Lenin wrote, not to Krushchev but to the Party leadership at the time, 'having become Secretary General, has concentrated in his hands an immense power. I'm not sure if he will always use it wisely enough – Stalin is too harsh, and this fault, acceptable in our circle in relations between us Communists, is unacceptable on the part of the Secretary General. This is why I am proposing to my comrades to think about transferring Stalin to another job and naming, in his place, someone with similar qualities to Stalin but someone who will be more tolerant, more loyal, less capricious, etc.'

It wouldn't happen. Once Lenin was gone and the road to total dictatorship was his for the taking, Stalin became more than just *vozhd* – the leader – he was also the Great Teacher, the Helmsman, the Father of the People and Our Sun. By 1943, he'd replaced the 'Communist International' with the Soviet National Anthem which contained a verse about his own glories. Not only did every meeting and every announcement in the country open with the phrase, 'On the initiative of Comrade Stalin,' but the official Soviet battlecry during World War II was 'For the homeland and Stalin.' To celebrate Stalin's 70th birthday in 1949, *Pravda* devoted nearly three-quarters of the entire paper every day for nine months to birthday greetings. The following year, no fewer than 62 Soviet postage stamps were issued with Stalin's picture on them. Three others bore likenesses of Stalin and Lenin together. Only three were printed with Lenin alone. So if Lenin was the Christ, then Stalin was all of the disciples, all of the saints and all of the popes rolled into one. He was also the person who now officially translated the scriptures. It therefore bordered on both high treason and sacrilege when Khrushchev embarked on a detailed list of Stalin's crimes – his imprisonment of tens of thousands of innocent people, his use of torture and executions and deportations, his gross mishandling of the war and his overwhelming abuse of power.

'Stalin was a very distrustful man,' Khrushchev said. 'Sickly suspicious. We knew this from our work with him. He could look at a man and say, "Why are your eyes so shifty today?" Or, "Why are you turning so much today and avoiding to look me directly in the eyes?" The sickly suspicion created in him a general distrust even toward eminent Party workers whom he had known for years. Everywhere and in everything he saw enemies or spies. Possessing unlimited power, he indulged in great wilfulness and choked a person morally and physically. A situation was created where one could not express one's own will.'

Khrushchev reproached Stalin for completely losing touch with reality, for being suspicious of everyone and everything, and for his haughtiness. 'Comrades, the cult of the individual acquired such monstrous size chiefly because Stalin himself, using all conceivable methods, supported the glorification of his own person.'

The men and women in the hall hung on his every word. In the old days, this would be nothing less than high treason, summarily punishable by death. Now, no one knew what to expect. Occasionally someone interrupted with a shriek of approval or a cry of indignation. But for the most part the delegates sat facing Khrushchev in stunned silence, listening to a virtuoso performance by a man whose talent for world-class histrionics would soon become legendary.

The fact that this was billed as a 'secret' speech was a pretense. Realizing that he and the others who'd been with Stalin would, sooner or later, have to face up to their crimes, Khrushchev had spoken to Molotov, Malenkov and Voroshilov about what he intended to do. They'd tried to talk him out of it. He'd invited Molotov to join him in publicly denouncing Stalin – an obvious candidate as Stalin had imprisoned his wife – but Molotov had refused. Then again, even three years after Stalin's death, Molotov wasn't the only one in the Soviet Union who was still afraid of Stalin. It wasn't until March 1989, a full 33 years after the event, that the newspaper *Izvestia* printed the full text of the speech for the very first time in the Soviet Union. Yet word of it spread through the intelligentsia within hours and copies of it were in circulation across the Soviet Union within a few days, supposedly with instructions that it be read at closed-door meetings in factories, offices and collectives.

Although 1 million copies of the speech were reportedly printed, then destroyed, the main points of it were reported in the foreign press. Allen Dulles ordered a 'document hunt' to get a transcript of the speech. Coded directives were flashed from Washington to all foreign stations, sending agents out to check their sources and follow every lead until the text was acquired. Once his men managed it – they supposedly got it from a Polish source – Allen and his brother had little trouble convincing Eisenhower to allow the CIA to leak it to the press. The *New York Times* printed the full text on 4 June 1956.

Over the next several weeks, the echo of Khrushchev's words shook the Communist establishment. By exposing Stalin, Khrushchev had taken on the air of a liberator. Editorials in Soviet bloc papers praised him. Party leaders in Albania and Bulgaria joined in, criticizing Stalin for putting himself above the Party and the people, and honoring Khrushchev for his 'merciless struggle against the remnants of the cult of the individual.' Riots in Poland led to radical changes in the Party's Central Committee there and brought Wladyslaw Gomulka back to power. There were rumblings of unrest in Czechoslovakia. Students at one Romanian university destroyed a Stalin statue without police recrimination. And in Hungary, where Matyas Rakosi had modeled himself after Josef Stalin and ravaged the nation with his own reign of terror, the Party's hold on the people began to disintegrate.

But Khrushchev also exposed himself to criticism from sectors still loyal to Stalin's memory or apprehensive that some sort of mass recrimination for the Stalin years was in the works. He was berated for the shallowness of his report, for not putting the cult of personality into a proper historical perspective and for confining himself to the period 1934–1953. He'd purposely neglected the 1920s, which were characterized by Stalin's terrorization of the opposition movements. Just as significantly, he'd overlooked the appalling criminal behavior of those men who'd made up Stalin's entourage – Molotov, Malenkov, Voroshilov, Kaganovich, Bulganin and, of course, himself.

They were hardly blameless.

Still, by being first to castigate Stalin, he put his rivals into the ungainly position of either justifying their actions under Stalin or supporting Khrushchev's initiative. With hindsight, there are some who would claim that those four hours in the middle of the night in front of the 20th Party Congress were the single most significant event of his life.

At the 28 June meeting of the National Security Council, Foster Dulles updated his opinions of Khrushchev. Now, instead of being 'more dangerous than Stalin,' Dulles claimed, 'He is the most dangerous person to lead the Soviet Union since the October Revolution.'

Briefing the NSC as if he were making closing arguments to a jury, he said Khrushchev was drunk much of the time and could be expected to commit irrational acts. 'The previous Soviet leaders had been, for the most part, the chess-playing type. Khrushchev was the first top authority in the USSR who was essentially emotional and perfectly capable of acting without a calculation of the consequences of his action. Stalin always calculated the results of a proposed action. Bad as he was, you at least knew what you were up against in dealing with him.' He said he would be glad to see Khrushchev go, except there didn't appear to be any easy means to get rid of him.

Unable to assure his demise, Foster Dulles undertook a top secret offensive to exploit Khrushchev's criticism of Stalin, especially his admission that one-man rule was undesirable and carried with it the seeds of dictatorship. He not only called on Allen and the CIA to help, but invited all US government agencies to participate surreptitiously. Through non-attributable press briefings – these days known as 'deep background' – Dulles aimed to sow confusion and doubt in the Communist world by underlining Khrushchev's attempt to disassociate himself from unpopular doctrine. Stories were judiciously placed with friendly journalists to remind people that Stalin's men were still running the country and that Stalin's policies – collectivism, the police state, domination of the Eastern bloc, domination of the Baltics, and firm control of foreign Communist parties – were still the order of the day.

Dulles took it upon himself to solicit cooperation from the British and the French, and stories began appearing throughout Europe echoing American objectives. Groups like the Paris-based Peace and Liberty were 'encouraged' to issue a whole series of satirical posters which ridiculed Stalin.

The Secretary of State's efforts were not, however, without a certain backlash. Faced with the anger of hardline Stalin loyalists, Khrushchev quickly began hedging his bet. In June he ordered the Central Committee to issue a special resolution – 'On Overcoming the Cult of Personality and Its Consequences' – which soft-pedaled his original report. By autumn, his public addresses were being peppered with references to Stalin as a great Marxist-Leninist revolutionary. Khrushchev reverted to crediting his service to the Communist Party and his role as a leading player in the movement towards international revolution. He continued to condemn Stalinism, continued to acknowledge excesses, corruption and the man's abuse of power, but at the same time promised he would not permit Stalin's name to be 'surrendered to the enemies of Communism.'

It was not an easy tightrope to walk. At one public meeting when a heckler in the audience dared, 'You were one of Stalin's colleagues. Why didn't you stop him?' Khrushchev demanded, 'Who said that?' No one answered. Khrushchev glared at the faces staring back at him. 'Who said that?' No one was brave enough to come forward. 'All right,' Khrushchev told him, 'now you know why.'

Trapped to some extent in a largely contradictory world – he needed the hardliners to maintain his power base but also recognized that without reform the country could no longer function – he established dozens of special commissions to oversee the release of political prisoners encamped by Stalin. He offered compensation to the families of Stalin's political victims. He brought ex-prisoners – many of whom now owed their liberty to him – into the Party and gave them significant posts. He permitted previously banned works to be published and created what came to be known as 'the cultural thaw.' He also eliminated Stalin's notorious 'envelope' system, whereby certain Party officials were handed packets of cash every week as one of the many perks for supporting the regime. Burdened with a sluggish and corrupt bureaucracy, he needed to change a lot of things. But change in the Soviet Union has never come easily.

Khrushchev was hardly a typical Soviet apparatchik. He was, in fact, the first 'worker' – in the sense that Lenin used the word – to ever achieve real power in the USSR. Yet for a man of the people he often fell short in his understanding of people. He was frequently influenced by unscrupulous men and on more than one occasion replaced corrupt officials with others who were worse. He put little faith in documents, being an instinctive leader who, when he felt something was right, ordered it done, even if he didn't necessarily know how it would get done.

Although he remained for some time under the restraining influence of the Stalinist conservative wing of the Party, Khrushchev was not the sort of man who easily tolerated opposition to his own authority. At Presidium meetings, he made a point of always stating his view first, specifically so that everyone in the room knew what he wanted and no one contradicted him. He demanded the Party execute his orders and, like Stalin, monopolized control of the media, saturating them with Party propaganda and otherwise monopolizing outlets for any political programs which might arise to challenge his own.

Years later, John Kennedy would ask Nikita Khrushchev if he ever admitted any mistakes. An unruffled Khrushchev said, of course he did. 'I once admitted all of Stalin's mistakes.'

Eisenhower suffered a coronary in September 1955. In June 1956 he was rushed from the White House to Walter Reed Hospital in Bethesda, Maryland, for an emergency operation after an attack of ileitis. In both instances, Richard Nixon thought to himself he was about to become President of the United States.

But that was not part of Eisenhower's game plan.

He'd purposely never permitted Nixon to play a significant role in the administration. Ike even tried to get him off the ticket in 1956 by offering him a cabinet post, under the ploy that such experience would make him a better presidential candidate in 1960. Nixon refused to fall for it and Eisenhower, later criticized for being too soft, refused to fire him.

The two were an odd mix. Eisenhower was a team player, Nixon was a loner. Eisenhower was interested in substance, Nixon was more concerned with appearances and public perception. When it came to getting something into *Time* or *Newsweek*, Nixon was the best. He displayed great media skills. But he never showed as much interest in what needed to be done as in what could or could not be done to manage his image. Nor did Richard Nixon ever display much warmth towards anybody in the administration. He was not as personally close to Eisenhower as he often pretended to be. But then, part of the distance between the two men was built in to the President's job. Eisenhower could delegate certain responsibilities but he had to keep the bulk of them for himself. Nixon was given chores to do – it's the usual method of keeping the Vice-President out of everyone's way – while the major policy decisions were made by the President, who could not and would not divide his responsibilities.

Eisenhower understood Nixon very well. So did the men around Eisenhower. Which is why, when Ike fell ill, one of their concerns was to protect the President from his Vice-President. Andrew Goodpaster stayed with the President and kept him informed on an hourly basis of developments around the world, especially where defense was concerned. He also kept communications open with the State Department. The White House Chief of Staff, Sherman Adams, made a point of staying with the President, as did Ike's old friend and aide, General Jerry Persons. At no time could Eisenhower be out of commission long enough to warrant a reassignment of presidential duties.

★   ★   ★

By the middle of 1956, Eisenhower had pretty much given up on the idea that America held any great nuclear superiority over the Russians. The operative expression around the White House became 'sufficient deterrence,' the idea being that America didn't have to be stronger than the Soviets, just strong enough to inflict incalculable damage on them if they attacked.

For a while, he also discounted any supposed ballistic missile advantage the Soviets might have. As he wrote in his diary, until someone found a way to make a bomb of megaton size and put it in a small package, capable of being transported by ballistic methods, the ballistic missile would not be a serious threat. Yet he felt that because the world would see ballistic missiles as the 'ultimate' weapon, and fear guided missiles raining out of the skies in almost uncounted numbers, it was extremely important that the Soviets did not get ahead of America in the deployment of such weapons. But then he didn't see any problems there. All the services had missile development programs and the Navy had just put into commission their Polaris submarine-based missiles. What's more, the United States had an ace in the hole.

The same evening that Khrushchev rejected his 'Open Skies' proposal, Eisenhower said that it was time for the U-2 to fly. Allen Dulles and Richard Bissell, the man he'd placed in charge of the spy plane program, began supervising test flights. Their trick was to have the plane overfly some of Ike's favorite golf courses and present him with photographs taken at 70,000 feet which were clear enough to show the pin positions on each green. In early 1956, Allen Dulles got Anthony Eden to allow the first detachment of planes to be sent to the Royal Air Force base at Lakenheath, Cambridgeshire, near Newmarket. An American Strategic Air Command wing was stationed there. The U-2s arrived in May, were hidden in a desolate corner of the base and began a series of test flights into Eastern Europe.

Unknowingly, Nikita Khrushchev put a stop to that.

On Tuesday afternoon, 16 April 1956, a Soviet air force TU-104 jetliner arrived at Heathrow Airport with a contingent of KGB guards, secretaries and assistants, plus a cargo of a dozen huge crates, each marked with diplomatic seals which meant they were not subject to British Customs control.

The crates were taken in specially hired vans, with Russian drivers, to the Soviet Embassy at Kensington Palace Gardens. After they were inventoried, they were delivered, along with the guards, secretaries and assistants, to the Brooks Mews service entrance of Claridges Hotel in the heart of London's Mayfair district. Hotel staff joined with the Russians in unloading the crates. Some, containing clothes, security equipment and specialized office equipment – such as Cyrillic typewriters – were delivered to rooms on the first and second floors. But the bulk of them were signed over to the hotel's security staff for safe keeping. These were the important ones.

Nikita Khrushchev, with Nikolai Bulganin in tow, sailed into Portsmouth Harbour early the next morning on board the Soviet cruiser *Ordzhonikidze*. A private seven-car Pullman train brought his entourage up to London.

His first trip outside the USSR had been to see Mao in Peking. Next he'd gone to see Tito in Yugoslavia. Then there was Geneva to meet the big three Western powers. On the way home from Geneva he stopped in West Berlin. Later that same year he visited India and Burma, where he vigorously berated British colonialism and Western imperialism. Now he was in England, reaching out to the West in what became a deliberate policy of suitcase diplomacy. Khrushchev intended to show the world that Russians look like everyone else.

Khrushchev had realized in Geneva, much to his own embarrassment, that he and Bulganin were the odd ones out. To begin with, the three Western delegates arrived in the latest four-engine planes. The Russians showed up in an old twin-engine Ilyushin. Khrushchev vowed that sort of thing would never happen again. Then, Eisenhower, Eden, Faure and the other Western diplomats wore smart business suits. Khrushchev and Bulganin were dressed in baggy pale-mauve outfits. Bulganin also had a light-beige summer overcoat that fell to his ankles, making him look like something out of a silent movie. Although Khrushchev never became much of a clothes horse, insisting on wearing suits made in Moscow, by the time he came to London his tailoring had notably improved.

At Victoria Station, a crowd of nearly 4000 people waited for the Russians, some of them distributing leaflets and holding placards denouncing the visit. One banner, in reference to a certain wedding taking place in Monaco that week, read 'Welcome Grace and Rainier.'

Bulganin was once again officially the head of the delegation, but it was Khrushchev who was shown into Room 112, Claridge's Royal Suite, complete with a dining room. Bulganin was given a smaller suite, and no dining room, one floor above. To further accommodate the Russians, the brass ashtrays that now stand in front of the lifts on each floor of the hotel were emptied and put into those two suites to be used as spittoons.

Over the next ten days, there were the usual rounds of luncheons and dinners. Khrushchev decided that he liked Eden – the storybook English gentleman – but couldn't say the same for Macmillan, whom he found too distant. Khrushchev also met up again with Churchill. Eden hosted a dinner one night at No. 10 and Khrushchev was seated next to him. Khrushchev continued to think of Churchill as 'a smart man but exceedingly rude,' although on this occasion he saw the 82-year-old as 'fat and doddering.' Talk at the table was kept to neutral subjects, such as the food. At one point Khrushchev's secret speech was mentioned. The ever-wily Khrushchev refused to admit that he'd actually made the speech, but willingly spoke of Stalin's crimes. At the end he cautiously added that Stalin had accomplishments worth mentioning too. When Khrushchev reminded his hosts that change was a complicated, painful and gradual process, Churchill lectured him, 'It is just because the problem is so painful that you must resolve it once and for all. Any delay could result in the most serious consequences. It is like crossing a precipice. One may leap over it, if one has sufficient strength, but never in two jumps.'

That remark was one of the things Khrushchev took home with him. He liked it enough to repeat it often, especially when someone tried to slow down his de-Stalinization reforms.

While his meals with the Conservative government were cordial, he fared less well with the Labour Party. On Monday night, 23 April, Khrushchev and Bulganin were invited to join the opposition for dinner in the House of Commons. No sooner had they finished than a boring, drunk front-bencher named George Brown began insulting the Russians. The leader of the opposition, Hugh Gaitskell, compounded the insult by handing Khrushchev a list of names of prominent Eastern European socialists who had vanished from the political scene since the war. Gaitskell wanted Khrushchev to confirm they'd all been shot. It didn't take long for the Soviets to cancel the rest of the evening by walking out. The next night, over dinner with the Tories, Khrushchev told the Minister for Pensions, John Boyd-Carpenter, 'If I lived in England I'd vote Conservative.' He repeated the remark when he returned to Moscow and met with the British Ambassador there, Sir William Hayter. 'Bulganin can vote Labour if he likes, but I'm going to vote Conservative.'

Their visit to the House of Lords was considerably more amusing. Greeted by the Lord Chancellor, Viscount Kilmuir, Khrushchev was shocked to meet someone 'wearing an absolutely comic outfit. He had on a red gown and a red robe and a huge wig. He showed us the seat from which he chaired sessions of the House of Lords. It was nothing but a sack of wool! I was astonished that serious men could conduct such serious meetings in such silly clothes surrounded by so much humbug. I couldn't help smiling.'

Because this visit was considered so momentous an occasion, there was a night at the Prime Minister's 'dacha' – Chequers – and afternoon tea with Queen Elizabeth and Prince Philip. For the sake of international good relations, no mention was made over tea that the men who'd founded the Communist Party of the USSR had come to power only after murdering the Queen's cousins. Another embarrassing incident was averted when Khrushchev, who'd announced the day before that he would not do any bowing or wear any special clothes to meet the Queen, was assured that would not be necessary.

In their discussions with the government, peace was foremost on the agenda but nothing concrete in that regard came out of the visit. At the end of their stay, Khrushchev and Bulganin both stressed the need for closer ties with Britain, said thank you and sailed away. But not before they managed one last propaganda coup.

Having watched the French at Geneva and the way the delegates took to their food, Khrushchev decided that some Russian hospitality might help charm the British. So he hosted a gargantuan cocktail party at Claridges. And that's what the bulk of those KGB-guarded crates were all about. The hotel security staff released their contents to the kitchen staff, who proceeded to serve the Soviet bounty . . . enough vodka and caviar for 4000 people.

In retrospect, one incident was to mar the visit.

A few days after the Russians left England, the Admiralty issued an official statement to the effect that a Royal Navy frogman, Commander Lionel Crabbe, had 'not returned from a test dive in connection with trials of certain underwater apparatus in Stoke Bay, in the Portsmouth area, about a week ago.' Five days later the Soviets officially protested that a frogman had been spotted by Soviet sailors floating near the Russian warships during the Khrushchev-Bulganin visit. Eden's government apologized for the episode, denied all knowledge of it and claimed that, if indeed Commander Crabbe was in the vicinity of the Russian ships, he was acting without authority.

That the Russians knew Eden was lying was obvious. Crabbe was found dead, presumably murdered by Russian frogmen. But this was typical of the games nations played in those days. Six months before, Soviet frogmen had taken a keen interest in the hulls of British ships on a visit to Leningrad. The Royal Navy was just as anxious to inspect the Russian Navy from below the waterline and the Russians were plainly expecting it. Eden had been made aware of the Navy's interest and issued firm orders that it was not to happen. But if he then verbally gave the Navy permission to go ahead – and it's fair to assume that such an undertaking, with all its inherent risks, would not happen without his approval – then it wouldn't have been the first time a Prime Minister or President made certain he had something down on paper to prove he wasn't party to an action before getting involved.

Not being one to push his luck, Eden now decided that perhaps allowing the U-2 to fly out of Britain was not such a good idea. If the Soviets ever found out that Eden had been connected with the planned violation of their airspace, it might expose him as a liar where the Crabbe incident was concerned. So he let the CIA know that it might be best if they found somewhere else to keep their planes. Dulles and Bissell moved the U-2s to the huge American base at Wiesbaden, Germany and on 4 July – the 180th birthday of the United States – the plane's first mission over Russian territory photographed Moscow and Leningrad.

If Eden took a cautious approach with the Russians it was because, in many ways, Khrushchev struck him as a sensible man and much easier to deal with than his predecessors. In a cable to Eisenhower, he labeled 'the Bears' considerate guests and was pleased they hadn't tried to turn the trip into a propaganda exercise. 'There was no effort at wedge-driving between us and you may think that this was clever on their part. I am inclined to think that it was an acceptance of the facts. They made few references to the United States and always spoke with respect of you.'

Another thing that impressed Eden was the grasp displayed by Khrushchev and Bulganin of the topics they discussed. 'I hardly saw them with anything that amounted to a brief. They were confident about their own country but I did not think that they were arrogant about their economic situation.'

When the Middle East was raised, Eden said he made it plain to them that Britain was prepared to fight for oil. He believed the Russians accepted this and that going to war in that part of the world had no place in their plans. He ended by saying that he found these men 'more ready to admit other points of view than any Russians I have known, which does not of course mean that they accept them. It seems strange that they should exercise so much power. At times one wonders how long it can last.'

The answer had to be, not long.

Khrushchev spent those ten spring days in England talking peace. By autumn, he was sending Russian tanks through the streets of Budapest.

'The help given to Hungary by the Soviet Union,' wrote Andrei Gromyko, 'was absolutely justified. The forces that were bent on overthrowing the Hungarian leadership intended to liquidate the social order and restore the previous system that had been responsible for making Hungary a bridgehead for Hitler's aggression against the Soviet Union.'

Khrushchev saw it the same way. 'The help we gave the Hungarian people in crushing the counterrevolution was approved unanimously by the working people in the Socialist countries, by all progressives throughout the world.'

In the West some people thought otherwise. Especially John Foster Dulles. The rape of freedom in Hungary merely reinforced his innate suspicion of Russian motives.

But then, before long, Khrushchev began saying the same thing about the British and their foray into Egypt.

Anthony Eden was a chronically restless man, often erratic, a stickler for detail who was forever dotting i's and crossing t's. A meddler who'd ring his ministers in the middle of the night, he was constantly interfering – infuriating Chancellor Harold Macmillan and Foreign Minister Selwyn Lloyd – and unknowingly laying the groundwork for his own demise.

Emerging from under Churchill's shadow, he designed the July 1954 agreement with Egypt wherein British troops, who'd been pledged to defend the Suez Canal, would withdraw from the zone by mid-1956. The British would, however, return to defend the Canal should Egypt be attacked by any outside power, with the exception of Israel. At the time, Eden felt such an agreement would help bring the new Egyptian leader, Gamal Abdel Nasser – who'd overthrown King Farouk only two years before – closer to cooperating with a regional security pact he was sponsoring. He was wrong.

It had been part of an Eisenhower-Dulles masterplan to surround the southern reaches of the Soviet Union and contain Russian expansion into the Middle East. Turkey and Greece were already part of NATO, so Iraq was brought into the fold through a ten-year-old treaty with Turkey. That became the shell for a Middle Eastern structure known as the Baghdad Pact. England joined in the spring of 1955, followed shortly by Pakistan and Iran. But Nasser wouldn't have any part of it. He had his own ideas.

Pressure mounted along the Egyptian – Israeli border. The Israelis, fearing an attack, asked the US to guarantee their safety. Basically, Dulles said no. Nasser turned to the Soviets and convinced Khrushchev to supply him with arms. This put the US and Great Britain in a particularly delicate situation. If they responded by rearming Israel, they'd lose what influence they had with the Arabs. If they didn't, the Israelis might try to even the odds with a preemptive strike against Egypt.

Eisenhower, Dulles, Eden and Lloyd decided they might be able to buy off Nasser by financing the construction of a dam across the Nile to the south of Aswan. But when Dulles told Nasser that Congress was lukewarm on the project, Nasser alleged that Khrushchev was willing to build it if the US pulled out. Incensed by such a naked threat, Dulles withdrew the offer. In part, Nasser retaliated by nationalizing the Suez Canal. Eden wouldn't hear of it and together with France – which resented Nasser's hand in stirring up unrest in French colonial Algeria – plotted to take back the Canal. As Nasser was intent on seeing the destruction of Israel, Britain and France had no trouble bringing the Israelis into the plot.

It was childishly simple. Israel would invade Egypt, at which time Britain and France would demand a cease-fire. When it didn't happen, they'd move into the Canal zone, pretending to act as a buffer between Israeli and Egyptian forces. Although this would contravene the July 1954 agreement – which allowed Britain to protect the Canal against any forces with the exception of Israel – Eden felt that Britain and France, in their self-appointed role as international policemen, would be welcomed. Not only would they be keeping the peace, they'd be guaranteeing that the Canal remained open.

Eisenhower felt this plan was shortsighted and warned Eden it would fail.

The Prime Minister resented the lack of American support and wired the President, 'If we take a firm stand over this now, we shall have the support of all the maritime powers. If we do not, our influence and yours throughout the Middle East will, we are convinced, be finally destroyed.'

The response from Eisenhower was not encouraging. He said, even if the invasion and subsequent occupation of the Canal zone succeeded, 'The eventual price might become far too heavy.' He wasn't anxious to send American forces into Egypt and anyway couldn't do so without the approval of Congress. That, he emphasized, wouldn't be forthcoming until every peaceful means of resolving the difficulty had previously been exhausted. 'Without such a showing, there would be a reaction that could very seriously affect our peoples' feeling toward our Western allies.'

Now Eden tried to play on Ike's sense of history. 'I have never thought Nasser a Hitler, he has no warlike people behind him. But the parallel with Mussolini is close. Neither of us can forget the lives and treasure he cost us before he was finally dealt with. The removal of Nasser and the installation in Egypt of a regime less hostile to the West must therefore also rank high among our objectives.'

In Eisenhower's opinion, Eden was confusing two distinct and separate problems. Control of the Canal was one thing, Nasser's influence in the Middle East and his emergence as leader of the Arab cause was very much another. The two problems should not – and possibly could not – be solved simultaneously and by the same methods. The future of the Canal was the more immediate of the two. He believed the most dangerous thing Eden could do was to give anyone grounds to say that the British and French were using the Canal problem as an excuse for proceeding forcibly against Nasser.

Ike berated Eden, 'We have friends in the Middle East who tell us they would like to see Nasser's deflation brought about. But they seem unanimous in feeling that the Suez is not the issue on which to attempt to do this by force.'

By invading Egypt, Ike continued, Eden was vastly increasing the consequential risks. 'I do not see how the economy of Western Europe can long survive the burden of prolonged military operations, as well as the denial of Near East oil.'

Eden answered by recalling how the Allies had allowed Hitler to establish his position firmly before any action was taken. He promised that Nasser's seizure of the Canal was just the first move in a campaign designed to expel all Western influence and interests from the Arab countries. 'If he can get away with this, and if he can successfully defy eighteen nations, his prestige in Arabia will be so great that he will be able to mount revolutions of young officers in Saudi Arabia, Jordan, Syria and Iraq. These new governments will in effect be Egyptian satellites if not Russian ones. They will have to place their united oil resources under the control of a united Arabia led by Egypt and under Russian influence. When that moment comes, Nasser can deny oil to Western Europe and we here shall be at his mercy.'

He concluded with a call to arms. 'I can assure you that we are conscious of the burdens and perils attending military intervention. But if our assessment is correct, and if the only alternative is to allow Nasser's plans quietly to develop until this country and all Western Europe are held ransom by Egypt acting at Russia's behest it seems to us that our duty is plain. We have many times led Europe in the fight for freedom. It would be an ignoble end to our long history if we tamely accepted to perish by degrees.'

But Eisenhower wouldn't have it. 'When you use phrases in connection with the Suez affair like "ignoble end to our long history," in describing the possible future of your great country, you are making of Nasser a much more important figure than he is.'

He agreed with Eden's assessment of Nasser's ambitions, but couldn't understand why Eden was so blind to the inherent dangers of military action. Not only was he risking the wrath of an Arab world united behind Nasser against the Western aggressors, all of this was leading to a serious misunderstanding between the United Kingdom and the United States. Eisenhower, who was running for reelection, knew very well that public opinion in the country would not support the use of US troops in Egypt. While he and Foster Dulles were not ruling out the possibility that force might eventually have to be used, he needed to make Eden understand, 'To resort to military action when the world believes there are other means available for resolving the dispute would set in motion forces that could lead, in the years to come, to the most distressing results.'

Dulles added to the pressure on Eden when he made his infamous 'Freudian slip' in a press conference on 2 October. 'The US cannot be expected to identify itself 100 percent either with the colonial powers or the powers uniquely concerned with the problem of getting independence as rapidly and as fully as possible.'

Having made it appear as if he was, at worst, advocating support for the Egyptians and, at best, denying support for Britain and France, he compounded the sin by saying, 'Any areas encroaching in some form or manner on the problem of so-called colonialism find the US playing a somewhat independent role.'

The British Ambassador in Washington, Roger Makins, wired the article to Eden with the remark, 'I have noted before this deep-seated feeling about colonialism, which is common to so many Americans, occasionally welling up inside Foster like lava in a dormant volcano.'

Furious, Eden penned the word 'Futile' on the top of it, then added along the bottom, 'The article describes the most dishonest policy I ever read.'

The growing split between Eisenhower and Eden included a distressing telephone call from the White House to the Prime Minister at the House of Commons. Eden had been on the front bench when a message was handed to him that the President of the United States was on the phone. He left the floor – an extremely rare occurrence – to take the call.

The Prime Minister's suite at the House of Commons, four relatively small rooms, is down a short hallway from the back of the chamber. Under the shadow of Big Ben on the ground floor, looking onto the parking lot called New Palace Yard, there's an ante-room for the secretaries, a small meeting room, a larger meeting room and the Prime Minister's study – a room with wood paneling halfway up the walls, a desk, a couch and several straight-backed green leather chairs bearing the seal of the House of Commons. Eden's Parliamentary Private Secretary handed him the phone as he rushed into his study.

Andrew Goodpaster was in the Oval Office that afternoon when Ike made the call and remembers how the President and the Prime Minister never quite managed to get on the same wave length. 'They were passing each other, not really addressing the same issue. Eden kept saying that if this was not corrected, Britain would go down. Eisenhower tried to make him see that we had to respect the sovereignty of Egypt. He kept asking Eden, to what end would this be brought? The two never satisfied each other. There were some reports that Eisenhower was abusive or profane on the phone with Eden. It's not so. All I sensed was real concern on Eisenhower's part. It was incorrect to say the President lost his temper, entirely wrong.'

At one point Eisenhower even suggested that Eden should come to the United States so that they could find a solution. But Dulles heard about it and complained that such a trip would be misconstrued by the Egyptians. Dulles convinced the President that it would appear as if the United States and Britain were ganging up against Egypt. So at Foster Dulles' urging, Eisenhower withdrew the invitation, leaving Eden isolated.

The British, French and Israelis moved closer to war.

Khrushchev kept a keen eye on developments in the Middle East, using Western preoccupation with Nasser as the perfect cover for his foray into Hungary. And he basked in Britain's discomfort. At a Moscow reception during the crisis, he called out to a French dignitary, 'Did you know that Eden is sick? He's suffering from an inflammation of the Canal.'

When Eden deliberately cut off the flow of intelligence information to the United States, Eisenhower sent a U-2 over the Mediterranean to see what was happening. As soon as he saw the first few photos he knew that an attack on Egypt would fail and duly advised Eden. But the Prime Minister was determined to make his own mistakes. He and the French agreed to keep the Americans out of the equation. Eisenhower would not be briefed on their plans.

The 'special relationship' was deliberately ruptured.

Israel launched a strike against the Sinai Peninsula on 29 October. The next day – following the script – Britain and France demanded there be a withdrawal of all troops from within 10 miles of the Canal Zone. But, in a sudden ad lib, Eden gave Nasser an ultimatum, insisting that the Egyptians allow a temporary Anglo-French occupation of key points along the Canal. Eisenhower couldn't believe it. Eden didn't have a single ship in the area.

It was the height of folly.

The British had no way of backing up Eden's ultimatum if Nasser refused, which, of course, he did. This forced Britain and France into an ill-suited air offensive. The Russians now threatened to intervene with rockets. Eisenhower let it be known that, if the Soviets brought their missiles into the area, America would escalate the conflict. By 2 November, Gaza had fallen and Israeli forces had taken up key positions inside the Sinai Peninsula. Three days later, the British and French attacked the northern end of the Canal. Khrushchev, sensing a propaganda coup, said the USSR would be willing to join with the United States to stop the war. Even without Dulles' prompting, Eisenhower labeled the plan 'unthinkable.' The UN called for a cease-fire, which was put into effect on 7 November. But by that time, Eisenhower and Dulles had already pulled the plug on Eden.

On 6 November, they'd secretly threatened to withdraw their much-needed support of sterling. The Chancellor of the Exchequer knew that if the pound collapsed the country would plunge into economic chaos, so he orchestrated a cabinet mutiny. Eden and a few others wanted to carry on, but Macmillan had rallied enough of the cabinet to stop it. Britain and France eventually withdrew, leaving the Canal clogged with sunken shipping and the Israelis occupying Egyptian territory.

A sad and broken Anthony Eden now wrote to Eisenhower, 'I believe as firmly as ever that the future of all of us depends on the closest Anglo-American cooperation. It has of course been a grief to me to have had to make a temporary breach into it which I cannot disguise, but I know that you are a man of big enough heart and vision to take up things again on the basis of fact. If you cannot approve, I would like you at least to understand the terrible decisions that we have had to make. I remember nothing like them since the days when we were comrades together in the war. History alone can judge whether we have made the right decision, but I do want to assure you that we have made it from a genuine sense of responsibility, not only to your country, but to all the world.'

Thirteen years after his retirement from No. 10 Downing Street, Eden published his memoirs. Eisenhower was still alive but John Foster Dulles was dead, which meant Eden had a scapegoat. He minced no words in blaming Dulles for the Suez fiasco. Describing him as a preacher in the world of politics who had little regard for the consequences of his words, Eden explained, 'My difficulty in working with Mr Dulles was to determine what he really meant and in consequence the significance to be attached to his words and actions. I know that I was not alone in this, but the consequences were unfortunate for Britain, the weaker partner.'

If Eden had been an honest man, he would have looked closer to home. Whether it was his ego trying to live up to the image of his predecessor or the stupidity of allowing himself to get caught up in what always promised to be political suicide, Eden had, almost single-handedly, sacrificed Britain's traditional role as a power in the Middle East. Eden left a legacy of failure, as the *Economist* summarized, in refusing to accept a basic fact of life, 'That empire mattered less than

Britain's special relationship with the United States. That Britain was now a second-class power.'

A wave of anti-American feeling swept through Britain. 'We are rapidly reaching the point,' US Ambassador Winthrop Aldrich cabled Foster Dulles, 'where we are thought of by the British public as enemies of Britain working against them with the Russians and the Arabs.'

At one point things got so bad between the two governments that the British threatened to withdraw from the UN and ask the US to give up all her bases in the UK. Eden had not only come within inches of irreparably damaging the special relationship, he'd opened the door to the Soviets, allowing them greatly to increase their influence in the Middle East.

Nikita Khrushchev couldn't believe his luck.

East School is a two-story red-brick building that takes up a couple of blocks, running north along Neptune Boulevard in Long Beach, a pleasantly developed 2-mile stretch of sand a few hundred yards off the south shore of Long Island, just below the final-approach flight path for planes landing at New York's Kennedy Airport.

Built in 1926, it's shaped like a capital letter I lying on its side. At one end is the auditorium where a nice man named Chuck used to hold gym classes, which consisted largely of jumping jacks and dodge-ball. At the other end is the cafeteria, which in those days was next to the music room, making the sound of off-key clarinets forever reminiscent of overcooked cheese ravioli.

The hallways were lined with daily polished linoleum. Each classroom had ceiling-height windows and big, noisy radiators. Some still had those one-piece desks, where a large oval writing tablet was bolted onto the chair, sloping around from the right side so that it was impossible for anyone who was lefthanded to write on them. Above every blackboard was a printed chart demonstrating the correct way to form each letter of the alphabet. Below every blackboard was a wooden tray to hold large chunks of dusty white chalk that screeched whenever someone wrote too hard with them. If you got the angle just right, the screech could make the hairs stand up on the back of your neck.

East School was 30 that year.

Thanksgiving was only a few weeks away, which meant the Halloween pumpkins and hobgoblins on broomsticks had been removed from the bulletin boards, replaced by drawings of turkeys and pilgrims in three-corner hats. Not long before, the school had been thrown into a panic because, somewhere in America, Strontium 90 had been munched by cows at pasture and passed on to humans through milk. A chemical similar to calcium, it was produced by nuclear fallout and poisonously came to rest in children's bones and teeth. When none of us at East School wanted anything to do with those yellow cartons of Borden's milk that you automatically put on your tray at the start of the lunch line, the principal – a stout, short-haired woman named Velma Hendrickson, who waddled when she walked and seemed very old but was probably only 50 – promised everyone at Assembly one morning that there was nothing wrong with our milk, and that, even if the Russians wanted it to be dangerous, we didn't have to worry because we were safe.

Everyone liked her a lot.

But no one believed her.

Poisoning our milk was all part of the conspiracy. The Russians were going to take over the world by giving every kid in East School rotten teeth.

Then came the election.

Dwight Eisenhower once again faced Adlai Stevenson. During the campaign, the President's health was an issue. So was his golf. Some newspaper added up the number of days he'd spent playing golf during his first administration and implied it might be better if everyone voted for Ben Hogan for President. 'If we're going to have a golfer in the White House,' went the slogan, 'let's at least have a good one.' Still, Ike was all but unbeatable. Many people thought then, and look back now, at that era as the happiest time in American history. The goodtimes had rolled in and now he was taking the glory. Few Presidents have ever been as enormously popular. With a commanding lead over Stevenson throughout the campaign, Eisenhower could afford to have a sense of humor. When a Democratic Senator suggested that the government establish a fund to protect squirrels from the President's mis-hit golf balls, Eisenhower responded, 'I don't see any reason for creating another pressure group.' Naturally, the television comedians played it up as well. One of them told the story of the day Ike and his party came upon a foursome ahead of them and asked to play through. Someone asked, why, what's your hurry? The President answered, 'New York's just been bombed.'

No sooner was the 1956 presidential election out of the way, when some startling news flashed across NBC's Huntley and Brinkley Report. And on CBS with Walter Cronkite. And in all the newspapers too. On 18

THE BEST OF TIMES – THE WORST OF TIMES

November, Nikita Khrushchev had been to a Sunday evening reception at the Polish Embassy in Moscow, gotten fairly drunk and told some Americans there, 'Whether or not you like it, history is on our side. We will bury you.'

So the truth was out, he indeed planned to kill us.

That must have been what Khrushchev had always intended because, whenever he talked about peaceful coexistence, John Foster Dulles reminded us that peaceful coexistence didn't mean Khrushchev was going to put away his atomic bombs. Dulles kept telling us how the Russians were trying to make us think they wanted peace so that we would put our atomic bombs away. One of the teachers at East School was so impressed with the Secretary of State – we used to say she was in love with him – that she made us copy a quote of his. 'The Communist leaders know that, if pacifism becomes a prevalent mood among the free peoples, the Communists can easily conquer the world. Then they can confront the free peoples with successive choices between peace and surrender; and if peace is the absolute good, then surrenders become inevitable.'

Most of us didn't understand what Dulles was talking about, but we did know we weren't ever going to surrender to the Russians. In just 40 years the Communists – if you added in the Red Chinese – had gained control over one-third of the earth's population and were spreading outward. Before they overran America, they'd have to kill us. Which is what Khrushchev had finally admitted he was planning to do. And it wasn't just those of us at East School who were afraid of the Russians. People all over the country started digging bomb shelters in their back yards – family-sized, reinforced concrete underground bunkers, stocked with rations in radiation-proof cans to keep one set of average American parents with their 2.3 children alive for a month. They had doors which could be locked, so that the family next door couldn't get in to contaminate you, and a place to hide a gun for when Russians soldiers tried to rape your sister.

At East School, that's when we began having air raid drills.

Every week, unannounced, alarm bells would ring and we would be taken out of our classrooms, moved away from windows, and made to sit in the darkened hallways with our knees up, our heads down and our hands clasped above our heads to protect ourselves from falling debris once the bombs hit the roof. No one was allowed to talk.

Teachers monitored the hallways, walking eerily up and down, until Mrs Hendrickson sounded the all-clear.

Those air raid drills seemed to take forever, although in reality they only lasted long enough for most of us to wonder, why do the Russians want to kill us? And, is Khrushchev really going to bury us? And, we're too young to die!

In the mid-1950s, the world was a scary place to be 12 years old.

PART II

The Dreamers

We must master the highest technology or be crushed.

Vladimir Ilyich Lenin

Chapter Seven

The Nazi Connection

In January 1920, as the last of the doughboys were leaving the battlefields of France, on their way home to a dry America where the 18th Amendment made Prohibition the law of the land, the Smithsonian Institute published a 69-page monograph titled, 'A Method of Reaching Extreme Altitudes,' by Robert Hutchings Goddard.

The doughboys and Prohibition made the papers.

Goddard and his monograph didn't.

It was, however, heady stuff, being the first modern mathematical study of rocket motion. Breaking new ground, the 38-year-old physics professor from Clark University in Massachusetts described how various types of gunpowder could be used as solid fuels, and went far out on a limb to predict that someday liquid fuels would send a rocket into space. Six years later, Goddard successfully launched the world's first liquid-propellant rocket. Even though it was nothing more than a simple, pressure-fed missile that burned gasoline and liquid oxygen, and despite the fact that it only reached an altitude of 184 feet, he nevertheless proved beyond any doubt that the principle of rocket flight was a valid one.

Three years after Goddard's monograph appeared, the German scientist Hermann Oberth published a 92-page tome, *The Rocket into Interplanetary Space*, going beyond Goddard's calculations to include designs for rockets and firm proposals for the use of liquid fuels.

Oberth's passion for space travel stemmed from childhood. He was so enthralled by Jules Verne's *From the Earth to the Moon* that in 1905, at the age of 11, he abandoned his goal to study medicine and switched to physics. By 1917, he'd already designed a basic liquid-propelled rocket, although it never flew. In spite of the tepid response to his book from his publishers – they'd frivolously shrugged off astronautics as a side-show to science fiction – Oberth struck a chord with the public and two printings sold out quickly. In 1929 he expanded that book into a massive thesis,

The Road to Space Travel, which cemented his reputation as 'The Father of Astronautics.' It also inspired the birth of an amateur rocket club known as 'The Society for Space Travel,' whose stated mission was to explore every aspect of rocketry, from trips to the moon to delivering mail across the Alps.

For anyone interested in rockets, Germany between the wars turned out to be the right place at the right time.

At the end of World War I, the Allies had written provisos into the Treaty of Versailles aimed at preventing the Germans from rebuilding their military machine. Severely limited in both size and mission, the Army was reduced to little more than a dubiously effective defense force. The Navy was prohibited from having submarines. The Luftwaffe could not fly warplanes. But the treaty made no mention of rockets. Spotting the loophole in 1930, the German Army Weapons Department directed Walter Dornberger, a 35-year-old artillery officer, to create a missile branch at Kummersdorf, south of Berlin.

In the meantime, Oberth's club had begun launching rockets with some success. They'd designed a pencil-shaped liquid-fuelled missile which they were now regularly firing to a height of 1200 feet. But they had only one, which meant they had to recover it after each flight. So they worked out a system where, at the top of its climb, a parachute would pop out of its tail. Club members, who chased the rocket's trajectory in cars, would then have to scramble to catch it before it smashed to the ground. To pay for their experiments, they charged people admission to attend their launches.

It was the spring of 1932, some six months after the group had launched their first rocket, when Dornberger heard about them. He and two senior officers showed up one afternoon, paid their money, watched the launch, realized how advanced they were and asked to meet with certain key members of the club. When the young rocketeers arrived at Dornberger's office a few days later, he disclosed the Army's intention to take over their work. Staring into their shocked faces, he gave them three options: They could hand over their patents and stop work; they could withhold their cooperation and be sent to jail; or they could come to work for the Army. Among the first to accept Dornberger's invitation for employment was a charter member of the society, a 20-year-old engineering student from the Technical Institute in Berlin named Wernher von Braun.

'We needed money and the Army seemed willing to help us,' von

Braun later explained. 'In 1932 the idea of war seemed to us an absurdity. The Nazis weren't yet in power. We felt no moral scruples about the possible future abuse of our brainchild. We were interested solely in exploring outer space. It was simply a question with us of how the golden cow could be milked most successfully.'

Dornberger's crew at Kummersdorf had just designed *Aggregat* 1 – also called the A-1 – a 330-lb, seriously flawed, top-heavy missile which never got off the ground. Von Braun was among those who helped restabilize the rocket, now known as the A-2, and in December 1934 fired it to an altitude of 7000 feet. Based on that result, the Army approved development of the A-3, a larger version which they hoped could eventually be transformed into a military weapon.

At this point, Adolf Hitler – who'd come to power in 1933 and had declared himself Führer the following year – deliberately set out to violate the Treaty of Versailles. One of his first decrees was that all military activities had to be administered clandestinely. Dornberger and von Braun were ordered to find a secret location for their work. Recalling that his grandfather used to hunt on a secluded, pine-forested island off the Baltic coast, von Braun mentioned Usedom, concealed in the northeast corner of Germany, not far from what is today the Polish border. It was the ideal solution. Being an island, it was easily secured. As it was covered with forests, any installation there would be well hidden. Because it was largely uninhabited, there was plenty of room for testing facilities, offices, a landing strip and housing. Best of all, it came complete with its own 300-mile stretch of sea to use as a firing range. The Army claimed the western side for themselves. The Luftwaffe requisitioned the eastern half. And they named the military complex after a tiny, nearby fishing village, Peenemünde.

Construction of the base began in 1936 and, although it was not fully operational until spring 1943, Dornberger and von Braun – who was by this time Dornberger's star designer – moved into Peenemünde-West during the summer of 1937. They tested the A-3 there and started work on the more advanced A-4. But in late 1939, with Hitler preparing to bring his newly remodeled army out from behind the Siegfried Line, orders arrived to shelve the A-4. That it offered little more than a 1-ton warhead – hardly a phenomenon by military standards even in those days – was only part of the problem. Another stumbling block was the Führer's inability to see how a rocket would matter in an offensive against the Low Countries and France. It wasn't until the

Battle of Britain was lost by the Luftwaffe that Hitler resurrected the project.

Tested for the first time in March 1942, the 46-foot, black and white rocket blew up on the pad. In June, on their second attempt, it crashed into the sea. Munitions Minister Albert Speer now reported that Hitler was again 'having grave doubts' about it.

Their next try, in August, did nothing to boost Hitler's confidence. The missile exploded just after launching. But on 3 October, they got one to fly. Von Braun supposedly commented, the only trouble with the missile this time was that it landed on the wrong planet. Hitler was elated, telling Speer that he wanted two models of the A-4 built. The first should have a 100-mile range, the second should have a range of 180 miles. But both of them, he specified, must carry a heavier warhead. He also demanded that 5000 of the shorter-range model should be made available immediately so that he could wreak havoc on England.

His orders became impossible to fill as October's success rapidly turned into a winter of launchpad explosions and misfirings. Years later von Braun would testify that, from start to finish, they made 65,000 alterations to the initial design of the A-4. In the face of consistent failure, Hitler changed his mind yet again.

One version of the story goes that he canceled the A-4 project because he'd dreamt it would never be effective against Britain. The other is that someone at the Ministry, perhaps even Speer himself, concocted the dream story to cover up either a failure to secure funding or his own doubts about the A-4. Making matters worse, the Luftwaffe's 'Flying Bomb' was getting good marks at Peenemünde-East. Begun in March 1942, it was called the FZG 76 – for *Flakzielgerat*, or Anti-Aircraft Target Device – a misnomer to confuse spies. Tested for the first time on Christmas Eve of that year, production was soon underway at several converted Volkswagen factories. Twenty-six feet long and with a 17-foot wingspan, it was little more than a pilotless plane that flew at 350-400 mph for 150 miles. When it ran out of fuel, the engine cut out and 1800 pounds of explosives nose-dived onto its target. The Nazis stockpiled 25,000 of them to retaliate against Britain for bombing German cities. Nicknamed 'the doodlebug,' or 'the buzz bomb' because of the noise it made, Hitler preferred the word for revenge, *Vergeltung*, and dubbed it the V-1.

Worried that the V-1 program would be funded at the expense of the A-4, Dornberger and von Braun went into the junket business. High officials were flown in from Berlin, briefed on the merits of the A-4, given a guided tour of the works, filled with food and drink and, as a grand finale, treated to a live firing. The parade of Nazi brass included Gestapo Chief Heinrich Himmler, Reichsmarschall Hermann Göring, and Grand Admiral Karl Dönitz. As long as the missile flew, everyone was suitably impressed. But not all of these 'celebrity' launches turned out well and, in June 1943, disaster struck. With Himmler in the reviewing stand, an A-4 spun out of control and crashed at Peenemünde-East.

Suddenly facing a precarious future, Dornberger and von Braun decided to put all their chips on one spin of the wheel and requested an audience with Hitler. They met him in July, at his Wolf's Lair in East Prussia, presented him with scale models, drawings and photos of the A-4, and showed him color footage of the successful October launch. The gamble worked. An astonished Führer reportedly exclaimed, 'If only I'd had faith in you earlier. Now that the long-range rocket is developed, Europe is too small for a war.' He ordered that the A-4 be given top priority.

At the height of the Peenemünde effort there were about 4000 men and women stationed there, although nearly half of them were SS Guards. Not surprisingly, so much activity concentrated in so small a place eventually attracted Allied attention and, on the night of 17 August, no fewer than 600 British bombers descended on Peenemünde. The base housing area was badly damaged and two fairly senior scientists were killed. But luck was not on the Allied side and most of the rocket complex was spared. According to Speer's estimate, work on the A-4 was set back only a couple of months. Dornberger and von Braun continued, uninterrupted by further bombing attacks, for nearly a year. It wasn't until the summer of 1944 that the US Eighth Air Force launched three more raids on the site. And, for the second time, the Allies failed to knock out the A-4 facilities.

Towards the end of autumn 1943, with the War Office in Berlin looking for 12,000 A-4s to begin rolling off the assembly lines at the rate of 900 per month, the rockets started exploding in mid-air. Forced back to the drawing boards, it was well into 1944 before von Braun discovered that heat and vibration created by the lift-off were cracking the fuel tanks. He tried to rectify the problem as quickly as he could, but Hitler's A-4 ardor once again waned.

Unbeknownst to the Führer, Himmler was plotting to put all German rocket programs under his command. In late February, he summoned von Braun to meet with him privately, hoping to find a co-conspirator. He made a handsome offer but von Braun's loyalty remained with Dornberger and the Army. Three weeks later, a dossier on von Braun and two other scientists was secretly passed to the Gestapo. It contained transcripts of alleged conversations where the three privately agreed that Germany could not possibly win the war. It suggested that von Braun cared less about the war than he did about designing rockets for space and had a plane standing by to take him to England the moment the war ended. On 15 March, based on those allegations, von Braun and the others were arrested. Dornberger tried to rescue his protégé by lobbying Himmler. When that failed, he went to speak with the commander of the SS in Berlin. In the end it took the direct intervention of Albert Speer to secure von Braun's provisional release a fortnight later.

Over the 24 months that stretched from March 1942 until von Braun's arrest, some 3000 A-4 rockets were used for testing and training at Peenemünde. But almost a quarter of the launches failed. When a report on those failures reached Hitler, he came to the conclusion that the V-1 was a reality while the A-4 was anything but. He ordered cutbacks on the A-4 and increased production of the V-1. Then on 13 June, one week to the day after the landings at Normandy, he unleashed his wrath on England in an onslaught that saw more than 8000 'buzz bombs' targeted against London alone, and lasted almost non-stop until 1 September. Exactly seven days later, the promise of von Braun's A-4 was realized. On 8 September, Germany launched an assault on England with this second 'retribution' weapon – forever known as the V-2 – which continued incessantly until 28 March, 1945.

In many ways, the V-2 offensive against England resembled the Iraqi SCUD-B attacks against Saudi Arabia and Israel during the 1991 Gulf War. Although von Braun's rocket was larger than the SCUD, the two were very basic in design, had a fairly limited range, carried a small warhead, and neither was particularly accurate. What both of them did remarkably well, however, was bring terror to the home front. Germany launched no fewer than 1115 V-2s against England, with 517 of them aimed at London, to average nearly 60 attacks per week.

The impact of the V-weapons on the outcome of the war is still debated. Dornberger believed they came too late to be truly effective. Speer concluded that Germany foolishly spent too much money on them, one of Hitler's many 'investment' mistakes. Nor was Churchill overly impressed. He felt the V-1 and the V-2 were both too inaccurate and their payload too light to have created the damage Hitler had been banking on. However, Eisenhower saw it differently. He came to the conclusion that, had the Germans succeeded in perfecting and using these new weapons six months earlier, the invasion of Europe might have been impossible. He wrote, 'If they had made the Portsmouth – Southampton area one of their principal targets, "Overlord" might have been written off.'

In early April 1945, with the Red Army advancing towards Peenemünde, the decision was made to evacuate the base. Wernher von Braun and a large contingent of the German rocket team fled south, to the small Bavarian town of Oberammergau, not far from Garmisch-Partenkirchen. They installed themselves in a hotel there and waited for the right moment to surrender. As von Braun later explained, 'Hitler was dead, the war was over, an armistice was signed, and the hotel service was excellent.' On 10 May, five days after the Russians took Peenemünde, von Braun and the others gave themselves up to the Americans.

With the foresight to see that he would have to barter for his future, von Braun spent his time at Oberammergau writing 'A Survey of Previous Liquid Rocket Development in Germany and Future Prospects.' It was a sort of audition, a way of showing the Americans what he had to offer. After all, he and the others wanted to continue their work and he felt the Americans presented the best opportunity. Some of the others believed they in fact had no choice. As one put it, 'We despise the French. We are mortally afraid of the Soviets. We do not believe the British can afford us. So that only leaves the Americans.' But von Braun argued that they could not side with the Americans 'at any price.' And definitely not if they were simply going to be 'squeezed like a lemon and then discarded.'

The bulk of von Braun's designs and papers, some 14 tons worth, had been hidden in a disused mine shaft in the Harz Mountains. Included in the cache were plans for the A-9, a rocket featuring a pressurized cabin for a pilot, and the A-10, basically a two-stage version of the A-9. The Americans located the papers on 26 May and managed to get everything, less than 18 hours before the British were to assume control over that part of Germany. At one point, some British soldiers appeared at the mine shaft and asked what was going on. They were told that German geologists were assessing iron-ore samples. The British did not question the story and unknowingly allowed the Americans to confiscate the Peenemünde files.

While the Germans were being interrogated, American troops raided the V-2 factory at Nordhausen and found hundreds of rockets in various stages of assembly. However, that part of the country was about to fall into the Russian zone. Officially, the troops were ordered to leave everything for the Soviets. Unofficially, they were told to steal whatever they could before the Russians arrived. Given less than three weeks to pillage the place, the Americans hurled themselves into a frenzied, round-the-clock effort and the first shipments left Nordhausen on 22 May. Over the next nine days, 40 railway cars were packed each day and sent to US Navy cargo ships waiting in Antwerp. The looting of Nordhausen was in full swing when the British realized what was happening and sent word directly to Eisenhower, proposing it might be reasonable for the British to expect that their closest ally would invite them to share the booty. To Churchill's indignation, Eisenhower held off taking any action until the convoy sailed. Then came the excuse, sorry but it's too late.

Back in Washington, on 19 July, 1945, the Joint Chiefs of Staff established 'Project Overcast,' a plan to 'temporarily' exploit German scientists. When the code name was somehow compromised, they changed it to 'Operation Paperclip.' The original idea was to use the Germans in the war against Japan. After VJ day, the project was reexamined and the Pentagon decided they could afford to be more selective. A list of criteria was drawn up, stipulating that only outstanding scientists in fields where the Germans were notably superior would be chosen and then only those scientists whose work could not be exploited in Europe would be brought to the US. The program was on a strictly volunteer basis, with the understanding that while in the States the Germans would remain in military custody. They would not have access to classified material and, once their job was done, they'd be returned to Germany.

In other words, the Americans were going to do exactly what von Braun feared they would – squeeze the Germans like lemons.

The Americans were still working out what sort of contract the Germans should have when the British put into motion their own plan to exploit German technology, 'Operation Backfire.'

Walter Dornberger and Wernher von Braun were both brought to the UK. Held at a school in Wimbledon which had been turned into an internment camp for Nazi scientists, von Braun flatly refused to cooperate and was handed back to the Americans. But Dornberger was treated differently. Because he'd been an army officer, the British considered him a prisoner of war and did not accord him the same respect as the civilian rocket team. From Wimbledon he was moved to Cuxhaven, due north of Bremerhaven on the mouth of the Elbe River, where the British hoped he would help them build their own V-2 plant and launch site. Protesting his POW status, he was not particularly forthcoming and was soon returned to the UK.

Operation Backfire ended with a whimper. More interested in learning how to fire a rocket than in mastering the techniques of building them, the British wound up watching complaisantly as the German scientists left en masse for America. The one man who might have made a difference was Dornberger. But the British were unwavering about his POW status and, although he was never charged with any war crimes, he was incarcerated along with other Nazi officers at a camp in Wales. Just as puzzling, there is no record anywhere in British War Office files to suggest that, once he was interned, anyone ever bothered to question him about German rocket technology.

Under pressure from Washington, Dornberger was released in 1947 and permitted to join the others in the States.

The United States Army had originally taken an interest in rockets because rockets extended the range of their artillery. In 1944 they'd established the White Sands Proving Ground, 2 million acres of New Mexico desert. So desolate was that part of the country in those days that personnel and logistical support for White Sands came from the ironically named Fort Bliss, 40 miles across the state line at El Paso, Texas. When the Germans began arriving in the US, that seemed like the most obvious place to send them. The shipments of materiel that followed – nearly 100 complete V-2s, together with 40 tons of reports, plans, manuals, charts and drawings – went first to the Aberdeen Proving Ground in Maryland where seven German scientists, including von Braun, catalogued everything before it was shipped to White Sands. A few months later, the seven working at Aberdeen joined 120 of their comrades at Fort Bliss, where the Army had been testing their WAC Corporal missile. Now that they had V-2s to play with, the WAC Corporal took a back seat.

Yet, despite the great enthusiasm that greeted the Germans at White Sands, rocket technology didn't muster a lot of passion in Washington. At least in the first few years after the war, there wasn't any interest whatsoever in funding an important missile program. A Rand Corporation study in 1946 suggested that missiles be developed to launch satellites into space, noting how such a project would 'inflame the imagination of mankind.' In commending it, Rand warned of the apprehension that would be felt were another nation to beat America into space. A scattering of Army generals believed in it, but they couldn't get anyone with heavyweight influence to back them. The Air Force awarded a contract to the Convair Corporation to help develop an Atlas missile, but that lapsed after a year. Even highly respected men like Dr Vannevar Bush, who was then Director of the Office of Scientific Research and Development, couldn't see what all the fuss was about. He'd been instrumental in calling for the creation of the National Science Foundation and for making a national commitment to atomic energy research. Yet, when it came to testifying on rocket research before a 1945 Senate Committee, he maintained, 'A 3,000 mile high angle rocket, shot from one continent to another, carrying an atomic bomb and so directed as to be a precise weapon which would land exactly on a certain target . . . I don't think anybody in the world knows how to do such a thing, and I feel confident it will not be done for a very long period to come.'

But the Germans knew better. They launched the US Army's first V-2 in June 1946. Over the next four years they fired 51 more of them, using White Sands and occasionally the Florida Missile Testing Range, which later became the Kennedy Space Center. The Navy convinced the Germans to try launching one from a ship, which was the first time anybody ever did that. Next, the Germans modified a V-2 so that it could be used as a booster, with a WAC Corporal second stage, to create the Bumper series, one of which reached an altitude of 250 miles. Perhaps the most famous shot in those years was the V-2 aimed to go north along White Sands' 125 mile range but which somehow wound up heading south instead. Radar lost it crossing the border at 5000 mph over El Paso. A few seconds later it crashed into a hill outside Juarez, Mexico, where a fiesta was taking place. The warhead was not armed, so it caused only minimal damage. At least no one was hurt. But it scared the hell out of a lot of Mexicans who, with enterprising ingenuity, roped off the area, charged admission to see the crater and sold souvenir pieces of the rocket.

Even though they were back in the missile business, life in the middle of nowhere was not easy for the Germans. Everything seemed ramshackle and greatly inferior to the big-time research facilities they'd known at Peenemünde. They were frustrated with their working conditions – especially having to commute 40 miles between Fort Bliss and White Sands – uncomfortable in their accommodation and missing their families left behind in Europe. They resented being under constant surveillance by military guards and restricted in their movements. What's more, they couldn't stand the food. Some years later von Braun recalled, 'We were disappointed with what we found in this country during our first year or so. At Peenemünde we'd been coddled. Here you were counting pennies. Your armed forces were being demobilized and everybody wanted military expenditures curtailed.'

They were, he claimed, 'prisoners of peace.'

It was around 1949–1950 when things began to change. General Omar Bradley, then Chairman of the Joint Chiefs of Staff, deemed that each service would develop missiles in keeping with its own particular operational requirements. In other words, the Army would develop ground-based rockets, the Navy sea-based, the Air Force air-launched. On paper this seemed absolutely appropriate. In reality it created extensive confusion and opened old wounds which steadily led to inter-service jealousies and funding battles. The primary benefit to the Germans was that it got them out of the desert. The Army designated Redstone Arsenal in Huntsville, Alabama, as the home of their rocket and missile activities and so the Germans – now with their families in America – were moved to the deep South. Shortly after they settled in, work started on the Army's first heavy ballistic missile – a kissing cousin of the V-2 – appropriately named 'Redstone.'

In 1952, the Atomic Energy Commission detonated the first thermonuclear device. Eighteen months later, a group of respected American scientists, calling themselves the Strategic Missiles Evaluation Committee, met under the auspices of the Defense Department and the Rand Corporation. They prophesied that over the next few years, as physicists learned how to multiply the yield of the explosion, nuclear warheads would not need to be as heavy as they were at the time. That's when the Soviets conducted their first thermonuclear test. The CIA deduced they were developing intercontinental ballistic missiles specifically to carry nuclear warheads and the Air Force/Convair Atlas program was revamped, this time funded as a high-priority project. A first-rate coup for the Air Force, it was an ominous sign for the Germans employed by the Army. If they couldn't compete, they'd be out of work.

Early on Saturday morning, 25 June, 1954 Wernher von Braun walked into a US Navy office building in downtown Washington to meet privately with a group of like-minded men who were interested in seeing the United States begin work on an artificial earth satellite. He'd flown up from Redstone the night before at the request of Frederick Durant III, President of the International Astronautical Federation. Among the men present that morning were Harvard astronomer Dr Fred Whipple, Dr S. F. Singer from the University of Maryland's physics department and Commander George Hoover from the Office of Naval Research (ONR).

Sitting around a large table in a nondescript conference room, the group discussed whether or not it would be possible to put a satellite into orbit at some point over the next couple of years. Von Braun, preaching to the converted, insisted it was merely a question of thrust. He said that by using his Redstone rocket as a booster, with a cluster of solid-fueled Loki missiles as a second stage, he could orbit a small satellite, something in the range of, say, 5 lbs. Everyone approved of von Braun's concept. The problem was getting the government to fund it.

When von Braun returned to Redstone Arsenal and made his pitch to the Army, they agreed to let him work on a satellite project, but only as an extra-curricular activity. It could not interfere with his main responsibilities to them. That done, George Hoover arranged for senior officers from the ONR to meet with their Army counterparts. Interservice rivalries being what they were, the Army and Navy kept this to themselves, seeing no reason whatsoever to invite the Air Force along. At that meeting, in Huntsville on 3 August, Hoover was asked to draw up preliminary studies. The working code name for the scheme became 'Orbiter,' but, to show the importance that the government gave to it, the overall security classification was a lowly 'Confidential.'

In planning those initial studies, Hoover and von Braun concurred that the Navy would design the satellite and deal with such matters as tracking and data collection, while the Army would have the job of getting it into orbit. Preliminary contracts for design and development were awarded.

By the middle of September, von Braun had completed a report aimed at convincing the service chiefs to finance Project Orbiter. He

stressed that a man-made satellite would be a scientific achievement
of tremendous impact and that America could manage it within the
next few years based entirely on rocket and missile know-how already
available. But he also warned, 'It would be a blow to US prestige if we
did not do it first.'

Von Braun's report made its way up the chain of command to
Assistant Secretary of Defense for Research and Development, Donald
Quarles. The idea was he'd ratify it, pass it along to Secretary of Defense
Charles Wilson for final Pentagon approval and from there it would go
to the White House. Once they had DDE initialed on the front page,
America would be on its way into space.

The fly in the ointment was Charles Wilson.

Eisenhower had recruited Wilson into the government from General
Motors, where he'd been chairman of the board. Ike had believed
that, simply by virtue of his being that, Wilson was qualified to be
Secretary of Defense. The way the President saw it, any man with his
kind of corporate experience should have no trouble teaming up with
professional soldiers to deal with the military's enormous personnel,
distribution, storage, transportation and procurement problems.

His mistake was in assuming that every chairman of GM would be
bright, articulate and forward thinking.

Wilson wasn't any of those.

Making matters worse, Wilson had a reputation for saying precisely
the wrong thing at exactly the wrong time. The moment he was
appointed, the story quickly spread around Washington, as James
Reston reported in the *New York Times*, that Wilson had invented
the automatic transmission so he'd have one foot free to put in his
mouth.

Not only did Wilson totally lack imagination, he was the kind of
practical man who spent most of his time 'looking about his vast domain
for candle ends to pare.' Wilson was once described by an Eisenhower
confidant as someone who had no interest in knowing why grass is
green or why potatoes turn brown when they're fried. Yet the President
undoubtedly felt comfortable with Wilson. After all, this was the same
Dwight Eisenhower who'd once defined an intellectual as 'a man who
takes more words than necessary to tell us more than he knows.'

During briefings, Wilson would gaze out the window, chain smoking,
then ask questions that had no relevance whatsoever. As one Chief of
Staff put it, he was 'the most uninformed man and the most determined

to remain so, that has ever been Secretary.' Worse still, he treated the Joint Chiefs like recalcitrant union bosses seeking shorter working hours for the men on the assembly line.

As soon as he took charge of the Pentagon, the new Secretary of Defense cut research and development funds at all of the services, arguing that there was too much overlap and 'boondoggling.' On paper it looked to the White House like good fiscal management. In reality, the appointment of Charles Wilson was about to become a very costly error.

Unbeknownst to anyone at Redstone Arsenal or the ONR, the National Science Foundation (NSF) had also been thinking about artificial earth satellites. They'd been approached by the American Rocket Society which, as part of the proposed International Geophysical Year, offered to sponsor a satellite carrying scientific instruments. The NSF then approached the President. Eisenhower wasn't terribly infatuated with the idea, but as long as it was in the realm of scientific research it seemed harmless enough. He directed the Pentagon, which in turn asked the National Security Council's Planning Board, to look into it.

NSC Report No. 5520 was issued on 20 May, 1955. It not only recognized America's capability to orbit a 5–10-lb satellite in the 'fairly near future,' it acknowledged that, while there were certain scientific gains to be made, considerable prestige would come to the first nation successfully launching a satellite.

As it would be part of the IGY, a distinction was necessarily made between the scientific nature of the satellite – which could be shared with other nations – and the classified means of launching the satellite, which would be handled by the military.

Annexed to NSC 5520 was a letter from Nelson Rockefeller to the Executive Secretary of the NSC. Rockefeller, who was serving as Special Assistant to the President, wanted it understood, in no uncertain terms – echoing Wernher von Braun – that there would be costly consequences if the Russians launched a satellite first. 'The stake of prestige that is involved makes this a race that we cannot afford to lose.'

Immediately, all three services threw their hats into the ring. The Army led with Orbiter. The Air Force had an idea that they could launch a very heavy satellite but to do so they'd have to use their problem-plagued Atlas ICBM. The Navy, disregarding the fact that the ONR was already involved with Orbiter, proposed to put a 40-lb satellite into orbit using a three-stage rocket in development for their inventory called Vanguard.

At 1:30 in the afternoon, on Friday 29 July, 1955, Jim Hagerty brought reporters into the White House press room, introduced several prominent members of the National Science Foundation and the National Academy of Sciences and announced that the President had approved a proposal to launch a satellite in conjunction with the IGY. He didn't give any specifics of the proposal for the simple reason that there wasn't yet one.

Charles Wilson then called on eight of the nation's most respected scientists – as the Ad Hoc Advisory Group on Special Capabilities – to choose one of the three competing proposals. Chairing the group was Dr Homer Stewart of the Jet Propulsion Laboratory at California Institute of Technology. In briefings with all the services, it became evident that the Air Force was way behind schedule with the Atlas and anyway didn't appear too willing to commit themselves to a time schedule. By contrast, the Army and von Braun did everything they could to convince the committee that they had the most suitable plan. The Navy, equally anxious to make the committee think they should win the prize, played down the fact that Vanguard was still in the design stage. It all boiled down to a new version of the Army-Navy game, and Don Quarles indicated several times and to various people that he personally favored the Army's scheme.

Now fate played its hand.

The Secretary of the Air Force, a man named Harold Talbott, had been slightly indiscreet in some of his personal financial dealings. Severely criticized for possible conflicts of interest, he continually denied the accusations, until columnist Drew Pearson uncovered the fact that Talbott had used Air Force stationery to offer a friend some investment advice. Even though the letter was fairly innocuous, it added enough fuel to the fire that Talbott was forced to resign. Eisenhower appointed Quarles to succeed him. The swearing-in ceremony, to be attended by family and friends, was scheduled for 15 August, at precisely 11 a.m., in the office of the Secretary of Defense. But Quarles had arranged a meeting for earlier that morning with the Stewart Committee to decide the fate of the satellite program. He couldn't postpone it and, anyway, felt this was a fitting last official act as Assistant Secretary of Defense.

Only seven of the eight scientists were able to attend. As they presented their views, it became obvious to Quarles there was no clear majority one way or the other. Three appeared to favor the Navy program, two were set on the Army's Orbiter – including Chairman Stewart – and two were undecided. The one missing member, Dr Robert McMath from the University of Michigan, had already informed Quarles that he favored the Orbiter.

The group argued until 10:50 that morning, when Quarles, who by this time was nervously checking his watch every few seconds, had no choice but to call for a vote. He went around the room, asking each person to make a decision. Two men abstained. McMath was absent. Quarles could only vote in case of a tie. The Navy won 3–2.

Now it was 11 o'clock. Quarles had no time left to do anything but declare the decision final.

With the benefit of hindsight, there's no doubt that Orbiter was the best of the programs. Oddly, second choice probably should have been the Air Force with Atlas. In any case, the decision in favor of the Navy and Vanguard not only was difficult for everyone at Huntsville to swallow, it was just about impossible to understand.

Charles Wilson could have overruled the Stewart Committee but chose not to. He couldn't have been less interested. As long as Vanguard was sufficiently disassociated from any particular weapons system it characterized the civilian nature of the program, and he liked that. All he cared about was pleasing the President, who remained steadfast in his belief that putting a satellite into orbit was not a matter of any great military significance. Wilson simply closed the door on the subject and refused to allow anyone to reopen it.

The one thing that worried the President was that certain factions in the Pentagon might turn this into a race against the Russians and use it as a lever to gain funding for their own missile interests. He was prepared to fund an orderly approach but emphatically ruled out any sort of crash program.

Years later Major General John B. Medaris, von Braun's boss at Huntsville, would insist that the decision to go with Vanguard was based on either poor judgement or misinformation. He couldn't see any other valid explanation as to why the proven talents of Wernher von Braun were ignored. Among the culprits, he named the Joint Chiefs of Staff, who should have done something and didn't. He labeled them no better than a debating society, and otherwise totally ineffective.

It's possible that the decision was not so much in favor of the Navy as it was against the Army, whose project was manned by Germans. If the object of this was national prestige, the hypothesis goes, putting a

German-built rocket into space would be one hell of a strange way of going about it. That 40 former Peenemünde team members had by this time been granted American citizenship didn't seem to matter.

But then, the era was plagued with inexplicable stupidity.

For instance, in July 1955, Hermann Oberth accepted a contract to come to Redstone to work with his protégé, von Braun. Assigned to the Research Project Office, he spent four years at Huntsville, mostly doing theoretical studies on space flight. The problem was that he was never given top security clearance, which meant there were times when he wasn't authorized to see his own work. Understandably, when his contract was up, he returned to Germany.

The Army decided to consolidate their efforts in the field of rocket research and formed the Army Ballistic Missile Agency (ABMA) in February 1956. Medaris took command at Redstone Arsenal and tried to motivate everyone there with a great sense of urgency. The Redstone rocket was modified to create the Jupiter-C and the ABMA launched it for the first time in July. Talk around the Pentagon was that the Army had a missile capable of putting America into space. Two months later, Charles Wilson issued a directive under the heading of 'Roles and Mission,' which – totally out of the blue – limited the ABMA to the development of missiles with a range not exceeding 200 miles. Anything greater was to become the property of either the Navy or the Air Force.

In March 1956, General Goodpaster heard that von Braun could launch a satellite before the year was out. He was also told the Army was anxious to do so, if only someone would say go. Goodpaster phoned Deputy Secretary of Defense Reuben Robertson and wondered if that was true. Robertson promised to look into it. Two weeks later, having heard nothing from Robertson, Goodpaster phoned to ask if he'd made any progress with the inquiry. Robertson replied, 'Well, there are all sorts of considerations here.' And that was the last Goodpaster ever heard of it.

Next came the rumor that Wernher von Braun might 'accidentally' launch a satellite as part of his on-going ICBM work. Such was the fierceness of inter-service rivalries that the Department of the Army was ordered to send inspectors to Cape Canaveral to make certain that there were no available Jupiter-C fourth-stages – the satellite deployment stage – just in case.

The NSC continued to discuss the artificial earth satellite program for the next two years. They sat around arguing whether to launch six or twelve – the size of each ranging from 'much larger than a basketball' to 'still larger than a basketball' – while costs shot upwards. Scientists wanted satellites packed with instruments and the Pentagon worried they'd have to scrap an infantry division or some B-52s to pay for it all. When Congress demanded to know how much this was costing, the President ordered 'less gold plating.' From an original $20 million estimated by von Braun for October, the bill for Vanguard was fast approaching $110 million.

The Navy sent a progress report to the NSC in October 1956, promising that six launch vehicles would be ready, together with six satellites, within 13 months. They said they couldn't launch any earlier than 31 October, 1957, but after that they'd be in a position to try one rocket every two months, predicting that at least one of the six would be successful. That would put an American satellite into orbit before the IGY expired at the end of 1958.

Both the American IGY Committee and the National Science Foundation were hoping that a dozen launchings might be possible. But the NSC insisted that only six launch attempts had been authorized and that anything more than that would tie up manpower and resources needed for various military weapons programs. In other words, you get six chances to make it work and that's all. After that, no more fooling around with satellites.

Somehow disregarded in all of this was the fact that the Navy still did not have a rocket that worked.

Charles Wilson was now utterly determined to keep everybody out of the Navy's way. In February 1957, following a speech by General Bernard Schriever, the officer in charge of the Air Force's ICBM program, in which Schriever explained how the Air Force could put a satellite into space, the Secretary of Defense ordered Schriever not to use the word 'space' in any future speeches.

On 9 April, 1957, a report written by von Braun and signed by John Medaris was forwarded to the Army's Chief for Research and Development at the Pentagon. Confident he could orbit a satellite by September, von Braun proposed that the ABMA back up Vanguard with their Jupiter-C rocket. On 7 May, the answer came back that there were no plans for a Vanguard back-up. Six weeks later, Wilson sent an official party down to Alabama to remind the ABMA that their mission had nothing to do with satellites.

'In various languages,' Medaris explained after the fact, 'our fingers were slapped. We were told to mind our own business, that Vanguard was going to take care of the satellite problem.'

On 20 June, 1957, the *New York Times* reported that Soviet Academician Yevgeny Fedorov had announced that the Russians, as part of their IGY contribution, would put a series of artificial earth satellites into orbit before the end of 1958. He remained vague about their plans, saying only that the satellites would contain certain scientific instruments – 'gadgets to record the density of air, to register and count meteoric particles and to determine the energy and composition of cosmic ray particles.' The truth is he couldn't have said much more, not only because he didn't know anything else, but because the Soviets hadn't yet begun to build any satellites.

The press secretary at the National Academy of Sciences prepared a response from his President, Dr Detlev Bronk, welcoming the Russian effort, but pointing out, 'We have known for some time that the Soviet Union intended to undertake such a program.' He cited similar announcements in 1955 and 1956. Except for Bronk's press release and the *New York Times* article, Fedorov's statement generated almost no interest. When the IGY office in Washington checked with their media sources, they found that most of them considered the Russian announcement 'old hat.'

So did the CIA. They reported that the announcement 'revealed nothing new.' They also picked up a 9 June boast by the President of the Soviet Academy of Sciences, A.N. Nesmeyanov, that Russia would launch its first artificial earth satellite within the next few months. The Agency concluded, 'Since the USSR has committed itself publicly to launching an earth satellite within the next few months and is well aware of the psychological and political advantages of a 'first' in this field, a major effort on its part towards this end is expected.'

When Richard Bissell at the CIA heard that, he figured the Agency could – and must – do something about it. So he proposed that the CIA go into the satellite business. He told Allen Dulles he'd been going through intelligence reports on Soviet missile development and everything he'd read pointed to the likelihood that the Russians would try to launch a satellite in the very near future. He underscored, 'This country is heading for a great shock if we allow the Russians to put a satellite into orbit before us.'

Dulles asked him what he was proposing.

Bissell went on, 'We have a responsibility for psychological warfare. I suggest we pick one of the rockets currently being developed and offer to secretly add funding to get it into space.'

Dulles pondered that for a moment. If the Agency was going to get involved, Congress couldn't know about it. But that wouldn't necessarily be a problem as long as there was enough money in the Director's slush fund to finance it. He knew there was. He also knew he could get the 5412 Committee to approve it. This was just the kind of thing his brother would back him on. So he gave Bissell authority to speak about it with Don Quarles.

The next day, meeting with Quarles, Bissell didn't explain that he and Allen Dulles had cooked this up on their own. He said 'the Agency' was concerned about the possibility that the Soviets could launch a satellite before America did, that 'the Agency' did not want to see that happen and that 'the Agency' was determined to deny the Russians any opportunity to score what would inevitably be a major psychological victory. What 'the Agency' was therefore proposing, Bissell said, was the additional funding the Navy needed to get Vanguard off the ground.

Quarles was taken aback. What had originally been designated by the President to be a purely scientific project was about to become a clandestine Department of Defense/CIA offensive against the Soviets.

Bissell continued, 'If the Russians launch first, even if it doesn't put them far enough ahead in weapons development to threaten us, their satellite will be seen throughout the world as a symbol of their advanced technology and our lagging technology.'

Quarles agreed, but had to confess, 'I don't know if I can sell that to anyone upstairs. And even if they'll buy it here, I don't know about the White House. The Cabinet is filled with types who'll say, this is one more goddamned fool idea and we shouldn't be doing this sort of thing.'

Bissell reported back to Allen Dulles, who knew the answer to that problem was obvious. With his brother's help, the cabinet was not informed and by the middle of the summer of 1957 the CIA was the Navy's silent partner in the Vanguard project.

On 20 July, Alan Waterman, President of the National Science Foundation, had an odd telephone conversation with Hugh Odishaw, who was serving on the US National Committee for the IGY. Odishaw alleged that the Department of Defense (DoD) was secretly planning to take short-cuts with the American satellite program in order to put a 4½–6½-lb satellite into orbit as early as November. Odishaw said he was concerned that such an attempt – to be billed by the DoD not as an official launching but as a test – had certain less than favorable international implications. In particular, he felt that the DoD was, despite Eisenhower's deliberate effort to avoid such chaos, turning this into a race against the Russians.

Neither Waterman nor Odishaw knew enough to look for the Dulles brothers' fingerprints.

But they were everywhere.

Towards the middle of Eisenhower's first term, Foster and Allen jointly championed a plan through the 5412 Committee to build the most powerful fixed-beam radar station on earth near the town of Diyarbakir, in the Turkish mountains, some 300 miles to the east and slightly north of Adana. From there, the radar reached nearly 1000 miles, across the Caspian Sea and into Kazakhstan, blanketing the area around the original missile testing site at Kapustin Yar. Backed up by a huge radar station at Samsun Air Force Base, on the northern Turkish coast, the White House was kept informed on a regular basis of Soviet rocket tests. Before long, the U-2 was mapping the area with aerial photographs. The Kapustin Yar complex was thoroughly documented and the extent of the Soviet intermediate-range ballistic missile (IRBM) program was clearly determined. But it wasn't until June 1957 that a U-2 pilot flying out of the CIA's secret base at Peshawar, Pakistan, veered off course and accidentally discovered the Russian's top secret missile base at Baikonour. Within five days, Allen Dulles was showing the President a cardboard model of the site, complete with feeder roads and railway sidings. The radar at Diyarbakir was then refitted and redirected to cover the path east from Baikonour along the missile test range.

Sometime before 26 August, the day Tass officially announced that the Soviets had successfully tested their ICBM, the President was informed that they'd launched. But he took the news with a certain amount of skepticism. The best intelligence from the CIA was not in the form of 'positive information,' but through what is referred to as 'negative information.' The Russians had often announced things, like submarine and rocket capabilities, which the U-2 was now proving false. They didn't have as many long-range bombers as they'd bragged, nor were they building the vast numbers of ships that they'd laid claim to. The U-2 also refuted Khrushchev's figures on exactly how many IRBM facilities the Soviets had. That they were testing an ICBM at Baikonour was one thing. The U-2 spotted it. Whether or not it actually worked was another matter. Just because Tass said so, that didn't mean Eisenhower was going to believe it.

When Charles Wilson informed the President that he wished to step down as Secretary of Defense, Eisenhower reluctantly accepted his resignation and designated Neil McElroy, then President of Procter & Gamble, to be his successor. Firm in his belief that outstanding businessmen could successfully run as complex an industry as the Defense Department, it appeared at first as if Eisenhower was merely trading cars for soap powder. Few people in the military knew anything about McElroy. Then again, no one at the Pentagon bothered to shed any tears when they heard Wilson was leaving.

McElroy – who was not due to be sworn in for another week – arrived at Redstone Arsenal to get acquainted with the Army Ballistic Missile Agency and talk about intermediate-range rockets on the afternoon of 4 October, 1957.

Accompanied by Secretary of the Army Wilbur Brucker, Army Chief of Staff General Lyman Lemnitzer and various Pentagon officials, the party was met with full military honors by Medaris, Lt. General James Gavin – who, as the Army's Chief of Research and Development, was a major proponent of Project Orbiter – von Braun and their key staff members. A tour of the base would be followed by a full briefing and a formal dinner later that evening.

The base tour went off without a hitch.

The briefing didn't.

When it was von Braun's turn to discuss the work he'd been doing at Redstone, and specifically to detail the Army's IRBM program, he launched into a speech about satellites. Having had lots of experience pampering egos at this level of decision making – after all, he'd dealt with Hitler – von Braun played up to McElroy, offering him the chance to take credit for righting a wrong.

He explained how Wilson had ordered the Army to put Project Orbiter in a warehouse and forget about it because 'satellites are not your business.' This was bad judgement, von Braun maintained, because rockets and satellites *were* the Army's business. It was the Army who marched into Peenemünde and it was the Army who brought the German scientists together. With Wilson out of the picture, he went on, the plan could be successfully resurrected. The Navy should never have been given the go ahead. The Army could have launched a satellite a year ago. The Russians would be launching one before too long and, if they did it before the Navy got Vanguard into space, it would be a serious embarrassment. 'We have the hardware ready to put a satellite in orbit,' von Braun pleaded with McElroy, 'let us do it.'

Medaris now urged McElroy, 'Make the launching of a satellite a national priority.'

A bemused McElroy tried to sidestep the issue. 'This is not why we're here.'

Lemnitzer, sitting next to McElroy, couldn't help but notice 'a bit of bad odor' around the place, and suggested that the subject might be discussed at another time. He knew there'd already been enough blood spilled between the services under Wilson on the future of the satellite program and wanted the subject dropped.

So did McElroy.

And so it was.

At 4:30 p.m. on 4 October, 1957 the incoming Secretary of Defense didn't want to know what Wernher von Braun thought about Charles Wilson's regime, or that the Army could have put a satellite into orbit a year ago, or that America might possibly be beaten someday into space by the Russians. He had other things on his mind. Being lectured to by an arrogant refugee rocket scientist simply wasn't high on his list of priorities.

Chapter Eight

The Day the World Changed

As a child, Konstantin Eduardovich Tsiolkovsky suffered from scarlet fever and lost most of his hearing. Because he couldn't attend regular schools – and in the middle of Czarist Russia in the middle of the 19th century there were no special schools for deaf children – he was forced to educate himself. He managed it well enough that sometime around 1878, at the age of 21, he was able to get a job teaching mathematics in a tiny village 90 miles south of Moscow. And he might well have spent the rest of his life teaching in that village had he not discovered Jules Verne's *voyages extraordinaires*.

Like Hermann Oberth, he too was enraptured by Verne's images of airships and rockets, and soon began asking questions about the possibility of space flight. Starting with rudimentary calculations, he devoted the next 20 years of his life to systematically refining his theories. By 1896 he was regularly publishing his ideas in Russian journals, although he was not yet attracting any serious attention. Imitating Verne, he also wrote science fiction adventures, detailing such far-out concepts as space colonies, satellites, spacesuits and the mining of asteroids. 'Our planet is the cradle of reason,' he wrote, 'but one cannot always live in a cradle.'

It wasn't until 1923, with the publication of Oberth's masterwork on astronautics, that Russian scientists realized how far ahead of his time Tsiolkovsky had been. Now heralded as a genius, not just for his calculations on flight but for his wider perspective on space and life in space, all his earlier articles were reprinted. Within a year, amateur astronautical clubs dedicated to Tsiolkovsky's vision of the future were springing up in the USSR. Lenin himself approved the creation of the Central Bureau for the Study of the Problems of Rockets. Out of that came the Society for Studying Interplanetary Communications, founded by Tsiolkovsky, the scientist Friedrich Tsander and the father of the KGB, Lenin's security chief, Felix Dzerzhinsky.

One of Tsiolkovsky's greatest visions was of a 'rocket train,' a multi-stage missile that could carry man-made objects into space. And one of those young Society members who was smitten by that fantasy was a roof tiler from the Ukraine named Sergei Korolev.

Born in December 1906, in the village of Zhitomir, not far from Kiev, Korolev had also been obsessed with aviation and space travel since childhood. After attending trade school in Odessa, he quite happily abandoned his future in slate roofs to study aeronautical engineering at the Kiev Polytechnic Institute. By 1925 he'd built and was flying his own glider. A year later, when his parents moved to Moscow, he transferred to the Bauman Higher Technical Institute where the great aircraft designer Andrei Nikolayevich Tupolev was on the faculty. Tsiolkovsky had once taught Tupolev and Tupolev was now teaching Korolev.

Immediately upon graduation, Korolev was invited to join a private rocket society known as GIRD – the Group for the Study of Rocket Propulsion Systems. Its members had visions of flying to the moon and it was through GIRD that Korolev met men like Mikhail Tikhonravov and Valentin Glushko, who would one day help him do just that. At the same time, there was a group in Leningrad known as the Gas Dynamics Laboratory (GDL) which belonged to the military. Under the auspices of Marshal Mikhail Tukhachevsky, an ambitious member of Stalin's general staff, they'd been working on artillery bombs and shell velocity. Tukhachevsky heard about GIRD's experiments with small liquid-propelled rockets and convinced Stalin to let him combine the two, naming the new organization the Rocket Research Institute. Overall command was assigned to the director of the GDL, an otherwise disagreeable political appointee called Ivan Kleimenov. Sergei Korolev was chosen to be his deputy.

But these were not happy times for Korolev. Incessant womanizing was ruining his marriage and even the birth of his daughter in 1935 couldn't stop his wife from talking divorce. Furthermore, he and Kleimenov bickered all the time. Korolev did not have the right temperament to be anyone's subordinate. He suffered fools badly, saw Kleimenov as a fool and never bothered to hide his loathing for him.

Very much a loner, Korolev was a typical workaholic, a man without any hobbies whose life was almost exclusively focussed on his work. His only other interest was women. He seldom went to the theater or concerts and almost never socialized, except when his wife forced him to.

He was not easily approachable and always walked with his head down to avoid making eye contact or inviting idle conversation. His thick black eyebrows gave him a permanently angry appearance. He made snap judgements about people, was very demanding and totally unforgiving. His clothes were usually rumpled and he hardly if ever wore a tie. His single concession to fashion was a penchant for soft colored shirts, which was officially frowned upon. Food held very little interest for him, but he loved flowers and always had a vase of lilacs on his desk.

Most of all he loved his work. He wasn't necessarily the first one at the office in the morning but he was invariably the last one to leave at night, staying behind after everyone else left, organizing his papers and singing to himself. He'd often still be there after midnight, and frequently told his secretary, 'I want to die at my desk.' What money he earned he spent, mostly on women and vodka, being forced to borrow what he needed to live on. When he died in 1966 – not at his desk but in a hospital bed – he was one of the most highly decorated heroes in the Soviet Union. Yet he left a mere 16 rubles 24 kopeks in his bank account.

Under Kleimenov, he'd been working on the development of rocket engines for airplanes because in those days he saw aviation as the future to space travel and believed he could design a plane that would one day fly into space. As his work progressed, Stalin became convinced that Tukhachevsky was about to use this new-found technology to launch a coup. So he had Tukhachevsky shot. He then demanded the arrest of Tukhachevsky's 'ring,' which included Kleimenov. On 27 June 1938, Sergei Korolev also fell victim to the purge. He was accused of jeopardizing the work of the design bureau and officially charged with sabotage.

It turns out Stalin had been advised that the Nazis were making significant advances in guided missile development, had flown into a rage and had arrested the KGB agents who'd brought the news to him. Under interrogation, they'd mentioned that Kleimenov had once worked in Berlin for Aeroflot. Stalin had immediately assumed Kleimenov must therefore be a German spy. In custody, Kleimenov had seen the opportunity to get even with Korolev and had denounced him. But Stalin discovered that the two men hated each other and argued all the time, so he had Kleimenov shot and spared Korolev's life by allowing him to stand trial.

In September 1938, without any real evidence against him, a military tribunal sentenced Sergei Korolev to ten years in prison. Protesting his innocence, he spent the next two years trying to get an appeal heard. The original judgement was thrown out and Korolev was found not guilty. The higher court overturned the verdict against him, but would not set aside his sentence. Typical of this era – an utterly asinine period when the brain of the nation was cleanly severed from the body – the court illogically ruled that, even if he wasn't guilty, he'd still have to serve the remaining eight years.

After several months in various jails around Moscow, he was transferred to the notorious Kolyma gulag in the Far East. Forced to work in the gold mines, his health rapidly deteriorated and he became convinced that he would vanish without a trace. His deep-set brown eyes had been badly burned in an aircraft accident a few years before and prison aggravated that injury. He also lost 16 teeth. By March 1940, Korolev was nearly dead.

He was brought to Moscow's Boutirsk Prison only after a second reevaluation of his case was announced. Six months later, a military tribunal ruled that, although he must remain in jail, he should be permitted to continue his work. He was transferred to Butyrki Prison where, it happens, Andrei Tupolev was interned as a 'saboteur ringleader.' Korolev spent two years there, working with his old professor, until he was moved yet again. This time he joined his friend Valentin Glushko and, still under NKVD supervision, designed rocket-assisted jet planes.

In all, Korolev spent six years of his life incarcerated.

He was released in late 1944 with the clause 'Full rehabilitation' added to his official file – these days that's considered a tacit recognition of a wrongful sentence. Korolev's marriage was over, but the possibility of working with rockets looked brighter than ever. Technology was back in favor. Stalin asked Marshal Dimitri Ustinov, then Commissioner for Armaments, to chair a committee to advise the military on the use of rockets. A few months later, the Academy of Artillery Sciences created their committee on rocketry, chaired by Academician Anatoly Blagonravov.

Korolev was sent to Germany on 8 September 1945 by the military to study the V-2. He traveled between Berlin and Peenemünde, as deputy to the man responsible for transferring V-2 production and testing facilities to the USSR. His state records show this was his first and only time outside the USSR, although they never detail his whereabouts. They note he was assigned to 'Special Tasks on

New Techniques,' and that he didn't come back to Moscow until January 1947.

One story that has now become a solid part of the Korolev myth revolves around the British and Operation Backfire. They'd put eight V-2s together at the Cuxhaven camp and, in the autumn of 1945, test-fired three of them. The first two, on 3 and 4 October, were for their own benefit. To celebrate the third, on 14 October, they invited 25 Americans, a dozen French and three Russians to be their guests, including a Red Army General named Guydukov and Valentin Glushko. When the Russians pulled up to the gate, the British were surprised not only to see six of them, but to be told that the man in the Red Army uniform sitting in the back seat with General Guydukov was his driver.

It was, of course, Korolev.

For whatever reason – possibly because one of the uninvited three Russians was an obvious KGB officer – the British refused to allow them inside the gates. So Sergei Korolev had to watch his first V-2 launch from the parking lot.

Nevertheless, when he left Russia he believed rocket engines were nothing more than a means of getting a plane into space. The moment he saw the V-2, Korolev realized the Germans had already found the answer.

He was still in Germany in August 1946 when he was named Chief Designer of the newly created rocket design bureau OKB-1. Five months later he moved into offices at the Scientific Research Institute and Experimental Factory for Guided Missiles, code named NII-88, in Kaliningrad, 13 miles northeast of Moscow.

Today that plant stretches for over a mile along the Moscow-Yaroslava Highway, a heavily congested four-lane road cutting straight through what is now a dark and dingy suburb. There are 9-foot walls topped with barbed wire around most of the area, and plenty of signs warning that this is a military restricted zone. Somewhere behind the walls are guard posts, remnants of those early days at NII-88. Employees still come through the same main entrance – a long, narrow, one-story red shack filled with large wooden turnstiles that don't budge until a KGB guard checks each pass.

Korolev's OKB-1 consisted of a series of dark brick buildings, warehouses and assembly plants, not far from the small military airfield at the rear of the compound, along a street that criss-crosses railroad tracks, overlooking a huge open field used as a siding for flatbeds and freight cars.

Within a few months of coming to Kaliningrad, he met a woman who lived in his apartment building, took her out to supper and moved her in with him that same night, marrying her once his divorce was finalized.

It was at Kaliningrad where, one summer afternoon in 1947, Korolev and his old friend Mikhail Tikhonravov began talking about the possibility of putting an artificial satellite into orbit around the earth.

A competent Sunday painter and a dedicated collector of bugs, Tikhonravov had, like Korolev, always dreamt about exploring outer space. Six years Korolev's senior, he supervised a top secret research group, HVV-4, under the Academy of Artillery Sciences, specializing mainly in theoretical work on ballistics.

Tikhonravov reasoned, if the major obstacle to launching a satellite was getting beyond the earth's atmosphere, and if getting beyond the earth's atmosphere was nothing more than a question of thrust, the goal might be achieved by putting several rockets together into a sort of bouquet.

Seeing great possibilities in the idea, Korolev urged Tikhonravov to publish his calculations and to present them at the June 1948 meeting on rocket technology at the Academy of Ordnance Sciences. Convinced of an enthusiastic reception, the two approached the Academy, and promptly ran into a wall of apathy. Because no one in those days cared about artificial earth satellites, the Vice-President, Anatoly Blagonravov, turned them down.

While Tikhonravov was willing to accept the rejection, Korolev wasn't. He appealed to Blagonravov to reconsider. Warning that Tikhonravov would be facing an audience who thought of such things as pure science fiction, he begrudgingly agreed to allow it. And true to Blagonravov's warning, most of the Academy condemned the paper as an outright waste of their time.

Yet Korolev was convinced that Tikhonravov's calculations could one day point to a major scientific breakthrough. So with permission from a slightly bemused Marshal Ustinov, now Minister for Heavy Industries, Korolev hired Tikhonravov as Head of the Department of Space Research at OKB-1, even though there was no Department of Space Research.

Tikhonravov's bouquet consisted of five rockets in the first stage, three in the second, one in the third. On paper it was perfect. But Korolev couldn't find anyone to take it seriously. He argued that this might provide enough thrust to put a satellite into orbit, only to be reminded that he was employed by the military and the military wanted missiles. The idea of diverting work from missiles to something like satellites, which served no military purpose, was out of the question.

Forced to put that aside, Korolev turned the V-2 into his R-1, and that gave birth to the R-2. Both of those rockets flew. His next two designs, the R-3 and the R-4, never got off the ground, but they brought him to the R-5 which did. By the end of 1952, Korolev was using R-5 rockets to launch dogs into the upper reaches of the atmosphere. The animals were dressed in space suits, sent aloft and brought back to earth with parachutes.

That's when Stalin ordered the military to build an ICBM. The USSR was being surrounded by American bases where, the Russians believed, nuclear weapons had been deployed. This made Moscow an easy target. Because the Soviets knew their bombers didn't have the capacity to fly to the United States to answer an attack, rockets became their main priority. Korolev scrapped plans for the R-6, still in the very early design stage, and began work on a full-scale ICBM.

With Tikhonravov's help, the bouquet concept was modified and became a two-stage rocket. Called *semyorka* – number seven – the design was accepted by the academies concerned with ICBM development. In May 1953, Malenkov unified the various laboratories working in missile research and nuclear weapons technology because, in his eyes, they were both directed at the same purpose.

Towards the end of that year, Alexander Nesmeyanov, President of the Soviet Academy of Sciences, claimed that science had reached the point where it was realistic to speak of sending a 'stratoplane' to the moon and of creating an artificial satellite of the earth.

Theorizing that the R-7's advanced thrust might indeed be enough to put an object into space, Korolev wrote to Marshal Ustinov seeking approval to begin work on a satellite. In a letter dated 26 May 1954, he urged Ustinov to fund such a program and enclosed comments on the future of space travel from several leading scientists, plus what KGB intelligence reports he could get on satellite activities in the US.

Ustinov wasn't convinced.

So Korolev hedged his bet. He forwarded a copy of the dossier directly to Nikita Khrushchev. But when a letter came back from the Kremlin, it didn't sound as if Khrushchev was any more confident about the future of satellites than Ustinov.

However, Khrushchev was willing to give Korolev some benefit of the doubt. He ordered the KGB in Washington to start compiling intelligence information on any US plans for an artificial earth satellite. He also assigned his personal assistant, Vladimir Lebedev, the task of sifting through those reports to keep him abreast of any important advancements. Then, just in case there was something in all of this, Khrushchev permitted the Astronomical Council of the Academy of Sciences to form a Joint Commission on Space Travel.

A year later, when nothing seemed to be happening, Korolev wrote to the Council of Ministers, reminding them that the technology existed to put an artificial earth satellite into orbit in the near future. The Council answered that, while the plan sounded interesting, the nation's primary goal remained the development of an ICBM. They felt it was doubtful that work on artificial earth satellites could, at this time, further enhance that objective. In other words, thanks but no thanks.

In June, Khrushchev was told that rocket research was moving closer towards the stage when an ICBM prototype would be built, and that the Kapustin Yar rocket facility was not adequate for testing this new breed of missile. He signed the orders to begin construction of mammoth launch facilities near Baikonour, in the Kazakhstan Steppes.

Hoping to take advantage of the excitement surrounding the establishment of Baikonour, on 16 July Korolev forwarded to Khrushchev an explanation of Tikhonravov's calculations which showed how, by making minor modifications to the R-7, the Soviet Union could orbit a satellite weighing somewhere between 1000 and 1400 kg.

Korolev was enormously exhilarated by this. Unfortunately, Khrushchev was not.

Enter here the Americans.

When the White House announced in July 1955 that the United States, in connection with the International Geophysical Year, would launch a small artificial earth satellite, Russian newspapers reported it. Academician Leonid Sedov, attending the 6th Congress of the International Astronautical Federation in Copenhagen, was quoted as saying, 'In my opinion, it will be possible to launch an artificial earth satellite within the next two years.' Immediately Korolev wrote to the Central Committee to emphasize that the USSR could also launch a satellite during the IGY. They answered that, while the idea was attractive, it needed more thought. Next, Korolev copied all those newspaper reports and sent them with a specially prepared dossier to the specific military committee concerned with ICBM development. He asked for an appointment to meet with them. They agreed. In the notes he prepared for that meeting, he listed the benefits of putting a satellite into space. First was 'Technical.' Second was 'National Economy.' Third was 'Political.' And he underlined the third benefit three times.

Addressing them at the Defense Ministry, Korolev stressed the political benefit. The main objection of the military was that development of something as obscure as an artificial earth satellite would merely distract from work on the ICBM. Korolev stressed that work on an artificial earth satellite actually furthered the cause of rocket research because, in order to launch a satellite, he'd need an advanced military rocket. Ustinov, who was present at that meeting, remained skeptical while the majority of the military commanders were loudly against the idea. Yet Korolev somehow convinced them to form a working party on satellite research. And Khrushchev, now well aware that a plan to launch a satellite was underway in the US, gave it his blessing.

If nothing else, Korolev was finally out of the starting gate.

Turning his attention to the Academy of Sciences, he had no trouble selling the concept to the Vice-President, Mstislav Keldish. But a large and vocal block of members were firmly against anything to do with space. They likened satellites to toys and resented Korolev wasting their time with such foolishness. Hoping to change their minds, Keldish called a special meeting of leading scientists.

It took a Cambridge don to come to Korolev's rescue.

Pyotr Leonidovich Kapitza is these days remembered as the nuclear physicist who first liquefied helium and won the 1978 Nobel Prize for his life's work in low-temperature physics.

Born in Kronstadt, the island naval fortress near St Petersburg, in June 1894, he studied at the Petrograd Polytechnic Institute, graduated in 1919 and remained on the faculty for the next two years. In 1921, largely thanks to the efforts of his friend Maxim Gorky, Kapitza was granted permission to go to England to join Ernest Rutherford and the Cavendish Laboratory at Cambridge University. Awarded his PhD there in 1923, he stayed for 11 years, building a solid international reputation, first as a fellow at Trinity College, then as director of the British Royal Society's Mond Laboratory, which was specifically for him.

Throughout his years at Cambridge – having changed his name from Pyotr to Peter and taken to wearing tweeds and smoking a pipe – Kapitza regularly lectured in the Soviet Union and always spent his summer holidays there. In 1928 the Academy of Sciences of the USSR awarded him a PhD and the following year named him a corresponding member. But his relations with Stalin's government were, at best, problematical. Stalin saw no reason for a man of Kapitza's standing to be working for the British. And in the summer of 1934, almost as soon as Kapitza arrived in Moscow, Stalin canceled his exit visa.

Kapitza protested but the government turned a deaf ear. He took his case to the British Ambassador, asking that a formal appeal be lodged directly with Stalin. The British government did relay their objections to the exit ban, but to little avail. Once word of his captivity found its way into the British press, the scientific community lodged a series of protests. But Stalin would not be swayed. He was determined that Kapitza was going to work for the motherland. To soften the blow, Stalin ordered the Academy of Sciences to offer him the directorship of their Institute for Physical Problems. Kapitza refused to cooperate, resolute in his fight for freedom.

Rutherford tried to help, exerting what pressure he could on the Foreign Office to take a firmer stand. Objections from noted scientists around the world were addressed to Stalin. But it was a futile battle. In 1935, there was little left for Kapitza to do. He admitted defeat and accepted directorship of the Institute. Ernest Rutherford also resigned himself to the fact that Kapitza would not be returning to Cambridge and, as a gesture of the enormous respect in which he held his protégé, personally negotiated the sale of the Mond Laboratory to the Russians so that Kapitza could continue his work.

At the end of World War II, a rumor spread that Kapitza had worked with Igor Kurchatov on the Soviet atomic bomb. He always denied it. Apparently he consistently defied Beria, who was in charge of the project, by refusing to work on any military programs. When the Americans dropped their bomb on Hiroshima, Kapitza was accused of premeditated sabotage of the national defense, removed from his post at the Institute and placed under house arrest for the next eight years.

On 20 August 1953, the *New York Times* reported he'd been one of the key men, along with Andrei Sakharov, behind the Soviets' hydrogen bomb. He denied his participation in that as well.

It wasn't until 1955 that Khrushchev allowed him to return to his duties. Recognizing his rehabilitation, the *Moscow News* announced on 15 April that Kapitza was to be a member of a committee formed to discuss the launching of an artificial earth satellite. A similar story ran in the *New York Times* on 30 July 1955.

Invited by Mstislav Keldish to address the Academy of Sciences, Kapitza based his entire argument on one very basic premise. 'If it means that we will be developing a new technology, then it's right for the development of science.'

Kapitza's plain rhetoric, in tandem with Keldish's quiet lobbying, was enough to get a majority vote. The Academy of Sciences endorsed Korolev's plan.

A battle was won but the war was still to be fought. Korolev didn't have a rocket. Nor did he have any funding. What's more, deep down he was convinced that, even if he somehow managed to get both, the army still would not let him do it.

In May 1957, Nikita Khrushchev proclaimed that the Soviet Union must overtake the United States in meat and dairy production within four years. On the surface it sounded like an innocent, off-the-cuff remark. But it was an unrealistic goal which he'd taken upon himself to set without the approval of the Presidium. Georgi Malenkov labeled Khrushchev an 'irresponsible adventurist' and tried to remove him from power. It was an especially gutsy thing to do, for among other things, he was married to Khrushchev's sister. Molotov and Kaganovich sided with Malenkov. So did Voroshilov. Eventually so did Bulganin.

The group decided to accuse Khrushchev of 'economic voluntarism.' Left unsaid, but very much on the agenda, was their continued uneasiness about his denunciation of Stalin and their feeling that in so doing he'd undermined the Party's authority. They agreed to offer him the chance to admit his crimes. If he did, he'd be demoted to a junior ministry. If he didn't, he'd be arrested. However, the thought of taking him into custody made some of the group very nervous. Khrushchev's condemnation of Stalin had turned him into the most popular man in the country. Furthermore, it was clear that he had the support of the army, now under Marshal Zhukov, and of the KGB, under Ivan Serov.

Both men had suffered under Stalin and both had been rehabilitated by Khrushchev.

The group nevertheless felt it was a gamble worth taking and informed Khrushchev that a special session of the Presidium had been called to lodge charges against him. Ignoring his protests, the meeting was convened on Tuesday, 18 June. It lasted three days. When the members finally voted, the tally was eight to four against Khrushchev. The Presidium formally dismissed him and Malenkov named himself First Secretary.

But Nikita Khrushchev refused to accept their verdict, indicating that as First Secretary of the Communist Party he was elected by the Central Committee and therefore not subject to the whims of the Presidium's members. He demanded the right to face the entire Party. Stunned by such defiance, Malenkov resolved to have his brother-in-law arrested. No one knows how he intended to explain this to his wife, but like the plotters who would try to unseat Mikhail Gorbachev 35 years later, he failed to move either quickly or decisively enough. Arresting Khrushchev should have been his first thought, not his last, because by the middle of the second day, word of the coup began leaking out of the secret meeting. Some 20 Central Committee members arrived at the Kremlin and tried to force their way in. Among them were Serov and Zhukov. When the Presidium members refused to admit them, Serov ordered his security forces to secure the area. If he and the others couldn't get in, none of the Presidium members were going to get out. Zhukov then ordered military transport to fetch Committee members from the outlying regions and by Friday evening, 21 June, he'd airlifted more than 100 of them to Moscow.

According to the rules governing the Central Committee, a special session could be called by one-third of the delegates. Seeing that the men supporting Khrushchev had enough votes, Malenkov dispatched Bulganin and Voroshilov to negotiate a settlement. When Serov and Zhukov stipulated that nothing short of a full Central Committee meeting would do, Voroshilov accused them of being traitors. Serov grabbed Voroshilov by the throat and threatened his life.

The tone of the confrontation deteriorated from there.

An extraordinary session of the Central Committee assembled the next morning and listened to a debate on Khrushchev's future for seven days. By Saturday, 29 June, the mutiny had crumbled. Malenkov admitted defeat. Only Molotov refused to give in.

Khrushchev promptly neutered Malenkov, Molotov and Kaganovich. Instead of sending them to prison camps, which would have dredged up memories of the Stalin years, he demoted them to junior ministries, then kicked them off the Presidium. Three of the remaining five also lost their seats. Only Voroshilov and Bulganin were permitted to stay. But Khrushchev sufficiently diluted their power by expanding the Presidium to 15 members and padding it out with his own people, including Zhukov, Frol Kozlov – who was First Secretary of the Leningrad Communist Party – plus various 'rising stars' such as Leonid Brezhnev, Alexei Kosygin and Dimitry Ustinov. By controlling the Presidium, Khrushchev now controlled the country.

Yet two things remained just beyond his grasp.

First was his ranking as a major player on the world stage. The men who governed the Western nations had all dealt with Stalin. From their point of view, this 'palace coup' gave off confusing signals. Harold Macmillan felt, 'It may mean a more flexible policy towards the West. But it may be a more personal struggle for power than a conflict of policies.' Selwyn Lloyd told the British cabinet, 'Mr Khrushchev appeared to have emerged as the dominant personality for the time being, but he was of an unpredictable temperament and might no longer be restrained as effectively as hitherto by the need to compromise with points of view which differed from his own.' Eisenhower looked on the Kremlin leaders as politicians and found a certain comfort in the insecurity that forever surrounded their careers. He told Allen Dulles, 'The more trouble the Soviet leaders got into, the better for us all.'

Khrushchev's second concern was the unquestioned confidence of the people supporting him. He had no way of knowing how long he could count on their endorsement. What he needed was some sort of world-class triumph to firmly cement his power base.

It was Sergei Korolev who was about to provide that for Nikita Khrushchev, in spite of himself.

There were times when the Chief Designer would argue with someone and get so angry he wouldn't talk to that person for weeks on end unless he absolutely had to. Then, even if they were only in the next room, he'd ring on the phone, keeping the contact as stiff and formal as possible.

Such tenacity was apparent in everything Korolev did.

Although he never met Wernher von Braun, he thought of him as both a colleague and an adversary. When he heard how Khrushchev was getting KGB reports on the artificial earth satellite program in the US, he bombarded the KGB with requests for information on von Braun and the various American rocket programs. At first, the KGB failed to see the necessity for keying him into any foreign intelligence. But Korolev persisted and from the mid-1950s he was supplied with everything published in the United States about von Braun, rockets and artificial earth satellites. He converted an office down the hall from his own into an intelligence section, recruited a bilingual staff to sort through what soon became daily consignments from the KGB, and received a full briefing from them every morning. He then studied everything in the minutest detail before determining what should be copied and sent to the Kremlin, marked for Khrushchev's attention.

Some of what he received from the KGB was genuine intelligence gleaned from classified information. Through their own sources in the US, Korolev knew, for instance, of the existence of Project Orbiter, how inter-service rivalries were hampering von Braun's satellite work, and about von Braun's problems with Charles Wilson. He received some very precise details about the Redstone and Jupiter-C rockets and about the Navy's Vanguard. From 1956 onwards, von Braun was followed whenever he was in Washington. The KGB knew whom he worked for, where he went and with whom he met. But most of the information Korolev received – such as the contents of the KGB's file on the Army Ballistic Missile Agency – came straight out of newspapers, magazines, technical journals and speech transcripts, plus television and radio interviews. At one point, Korolev bragged to his staff that he probably knew as much about what was going on in the US as anyone in the world.

Something that struck him right away was how the Americans didn't appear equally interested in what the Soviets were doing. Every now and then he'd see a document where someone would warn that the Russians were ahead of the Americans and that a 'missile gap' was beginning to develop, much like the bomber gap of a few years before. But that was about all. What he never knew was that the CIA had been watching him and studying his design bureau at Kaliningrad since the late 1940s. They'd correctly identified 79 senior members of the NII-88 staff, and had even named him Chief Designer. Had he known, Korolev would have been impressed because, under Khrushchev's personal orders, his name was top secret in the USSR. As long as he was alive it was never publicly acknowledged in conjunction with his title.

Korolev came to see the Americans as chauvinists who believed they were technically superior to the Soviets. It might have indeed been true, but he imagined them saying, 'We don't have anything to learn from the Russians.' And that infuriated him. As 1956 turned into 1957, he became more and more obsessed with the idea of launching a satellite before the United States did. He wanted to 'punish the Americans.'

A severe taskmaster who became all the more demanding when he was angry, he never stopped reminding his staff how important it was to 'always be first.' He expected dedication and blind loyalty from those who worked for him. By the same token, he was easily suspicious and constantly had to know what everyone was doing, where they were and how they were working. He'd prowl through the offices and factories, hunting people down, then standing over them while they worked. Uncompromising whenever he spotted inefficiency, he was one of those men who always seemed to be under pressure, stressed out, as if he couldn't manage his time well. As a consequence, he permitted little quirks to get in the way. When he heard how some people at the design bureau spent their mornings on the telephone, he ordered all the telephones removed from the project offices. It was only after the staff complained in unison that they couldn't reach him to ask questions, that he permitted the phones to be reinstalled. But then, he forbade anyone from using them before 11:30 a.m.

To help his own cause, in late 1956 Korolev invited Khrushchev to see the work being done at OKB-1. Satellites were not mentioned. A few months later, he accompanied Khrushchev to Baikonour. Khrushchev later wrote, 'We gawked at what he showed us as if we were a bunch of sheep seeing a new gate for the first time. When he showed us one of his rockets, we thought it looked like nothing but a huge cigar-shaped tube, and we didn't believe it would fly. Korolev took us on a tour of the launching pad and tried to explain to us how a rocket worked. We were like peasants in a marketplace. We walked around the rocket, touching it, tapping it to see if it was sturdy enough, we did everything but lick it to see how it tasted.'

Winning over the politicians and keeping the military happy were not Korolev's only hurdles. He was hampered at every turn by the backwardness of Soviet technology. Without private enterprise to aid him in the design and development stages – the way business in the US was lured into a project with patents and profit for their efforts – Korolev had to devote vast sums of money, time and energy to each problem as it came along. To motivate his people, to get the rocket ready on time, he resorted to 'golden rain,' the Soviet term for cash bonuses. Valentin Glushko, for example, who was being paid 350 roubles a week for designing rocket engines, was offered the enormous sum of three months' bonus for meeting the deadline Korolev set for the R-7 engine.

That engine was tested at Kaliningrad throughout January and February 1957. When Korolev decided it was ready, the first R-7 was assembled and, in late March 1957, shipped to Baikonour. Freight cars were camouflaged to look like a passenger train, with the rocket stretched across the inside of two carriages. The trip took four days. Korolev and his team followed on the fourth day, making the trip by air in just under 8 hours, with one fuel stop in Uralsk.

Preparing the rocket once they got it to Baikonour took another month.

These days the Baikonour rocket testing site stretches over a huge, still largely desolate Kazakhstan. For security reasons – mainly to deceive the Americans – the Baikonour site, which does not appear on any maps, is actually 225 miles away from the city of Baikonour. It's closer to Leninsk, a run-down, unattractive one-factory town of 75,000 people who are crammed into slumlike high-rise apartment houses. Leninsk doesn't appear on any maps either. A tightly controlled security zone, you need a special pass to get anywhere near it. And the only reason anyone would bother is because Leninsk is the purpose-built airport city that serves what is today referred to as The Cosmodrome.

An extremely bleak corner of the world, the temperature can reach 115 degrees Fahrenheit in the summer and dip to −40 degrees Fahrenheit in the winter. There are a few hotels and a few restaurants, but even by Russian standards they're pretty awful. Then too, no one ever comes here except for the rocket base. If there is nowhere else to stay, that's in keeping with the barren and dismal mood of the place, because besides work at the rocket base, there is nothing else to do.

Up the road is the village of Tyuratam. It is equally grim. The buildings are older and smaller, having been built in the late 1950s expressly for the men from Kaliningrad. There are railroad tracks everywhere, and power lines too, bringing electricity to the area. This is also where you find the guarded entrance to the rocket base.

Once inside, you drive for 20 miles with nothing to see but the occasional unmarked prefabricated concrete blockhouse, a few scattered radio antenna farms and, if you're particularly lucky, a herd of wild horses roaming the steppes.

It seems like forever before the rocket base rises above the horizon – a cramped collection of drab multi-story buildings, offices, bunkers, warehouses, assembly plants and factories. You pass yet another checkpoint to get inside. There are now a couple of launch pads and off in the distance is a landing runway for the Russian shuttle. But in the heart of 'old Baikonour,' to the northeast of that last checkpoint, along a road that parallels more railroad tracks, you find the original launch pad – a massive concrete pit with a single gantry.

Still an incredibly lonely place, it must have been excruciating in the spring of 1957 when there were just four buildings here – one huge hangar, a barely adequate assembly plant, a basic testing complex and a very spartan, very uncomfortable inn. Eventually they built a tiny cottage nearby for Korolev. Everyone else had to live in railway carriages on a siding. In those days, even worse than now, for nearly 500 miles in any direction there was nothing else.

When the rocket wasn't ready at the end of April, Korolev's mood darkened. As the days went by, he became more and more menacing. The R-7 was finally wheeled out of the hangar on 11 May and brought to the launch pad where it was painstakingly winched upright. Four days later the order was given to launch.

The rocket lifted off perfectly and flew for 80 seconds before it exploded in a stupendous fireball.

Korolev was elated.

He hugged the men in the underground command post and told Vasily Rabikov, from the State Commission supervising the launch, that even 80 seconds of flight meant they'd achieved something.

Six weeks later, the second launch attempt failed. Korolev explained to Rabikov there'd been a malfunction in the guidance system. But privately he confessed it was down to 'typical Russian bad work.'

They tried again in July. Within seconds of lift-off, the rocket began to whirl. Korolev ordered it destroyed.

The fourth attempt to launch the R-7 took place on 21 August at 3:15 in the afternoon. The rocket lifted off perfectly, headed straight up, the way it was supposed to, then turned downrange. Exactly 22 minutes later, the last tracking station reported that it had reached the target zone, crashing into the sea near the Kamchatka Peninsula, 4000 miles east of Baikonour.

On 26 August, Tass announced that the Soviet Union had successfully tested its ICBM.

In the third week of May 1957, returning to Kaliningard a few days after the initial R-7 launch, Sergei Korolev decided it was time to design a satellite. He didn't have a budget for it, although it would cost nearly nothing. Nor did he have anyone's authorization to do it. He simply took it upon himself to choose 20 close associates from his ICBM team, which by this time numbered nearly 1000 people, and put them to work on it. He was hoping that he'd eventually – somehow – be able to convince the military to let him launch it.

The original design was for a very large satellite filled with scientific instruments aimed at conducting experiments on cosmic rays, solar winds, magnetic storms, micro-meteors and ultraviolet rays. It would weigh more than a ton and Korolev knew from the start it was a folly because there was no way his R-7 could put anything that heavy into orbit. But it got the Academy of Sciences on his side. Enticed by those experiments, they agreed the plan was worthy of their support.

In late June 1957, without informing the Academy of Sciences, he shelved those plans and started thinking more modestly. He called for his chief radio specialist, Vyacheslav Luppo, a young engineer he'd worked with since 1948, and told him to design a transmitter. He explained that it had to be small and light and last as long as possible. Furthermore, he said, it had to use frequencies that could be received easily by ham radio operators throughout the world so they could plot the satellite's exact location. When Luppo asked precisely what he wanted the transmitter to do, Korolev answered, 'I want it to go beep.'

While Luppo was working on that, Korolev tried to get the military's permission to use their rocket. But they insisted his job was to design and deliver a missile that could carry an atomic warhead to the United States. They were not in the least interested in satellites.

Frustrated, he went to Marshal Ustinov and told him that he was going to take his case directly to Nikita Khrushchev. Ustinov warned that, by going over the heads of the generals, Korolev was risking his career. If he failed to get Khrushchev's permission, any future access to the First Secretary would be cut off. If he succeeded, there'd be a great deal of resentment towards him by the military. Either way, Ustinov cautioned, Korolev would lose.

Determined to take his chances with Khrushchev, he put together a folder of press cuttings from the United States on the American satellite program and on Wernher von Braun, added a report on the progress he was making with the R-7 and drew a few sketches of the 1-ton satellite. There was no need to complicate matters by admitting it was too heavy to launch. He'd worry about that after he got permission to launch. He phoned for an appointment and a few days later a call came back saying that Khrushchev would see him.

The First Secretary's office was on the fifth floor of the Presidium building, headquarters for the Communist Party of the USSR, on the Staraya Ploshchad – the Old Square – just inside the Kremlin's walls, past the Savior Tower gate. It is the same office that Mikhail Gorbachev used, the same one Boris Yeltsin uses.

Throughout most of the building, the long, well-lit hallways had highly polished floors, where heels clicked noisily and rubber-soled shoes squeaked. Except for that, in those days the building was a very quiet place. Every door along every corridor was shut. A guard stood silently every few dozen yards. There was no clank of typewriters. There were no ringing telephones. No one rushed around waving papers that had to be seen or signed right away. There was nothing to suggest that any of these hallways led to the office which was the seat of power in the USSR, except, now on the fifth floor, the hallway was covered with a thick red carpet.

A security guard escorted him into a smallish ante-room of the First Secretary's office. A guard there took him through double doors and into a long narrow light-wood-paneled room, with four immense windows opening onto an inner courtyard. The office was arranged in typical Russian fashion. There was a green baize conference table with enough chairs around it to seat 40, and at the head of that, pushed right up against the end – forming a 'T' – was Khrushchev's desk. Covered in papers, there was also a bust of Lenin, a bust of Gandhi, a model jet plane and several large telephones.

Coming from behind his desk, Khrushchev welcomed Sergei Pavlovich, offering him a chair at the conference table and some tea. Once those formalities were out of the way and Khrushchev was sitting down again at his desk, Korolev handed him the dossier and made his pitch. He said he wanted to use the R-7 to put an artificial earth satellite into orbit, emphasized the political aspects of successfully orbiting an artificial earth satellite and suggested that, with the First Secretary's permission, he might be able to manage it before the Americans launched one of their own.

That Khrushchev didn't appear to believe in Korolev's satellite, wasn't unusual. At that point, no one outside his own design team believed in it. But Khrushchev appreciated Korolev's unlimited energy and respected him as a brilliant organizer. He found Korolev's explanations clear and easy to understand. And he could see the passion burning in his eyes. He liked that.

He also liked Korolev's plan to beat the Americans.

Most of all, Khrushchev liked the idea that the scheme offered him certain rewards without posing any risks. If Korolev could launch a satellite before the Americans, he could say to the country, see what a good leader I am. Coming on the heels of the 'palace coup' like that, it would reassure the others that he was in control. If Korolev failed, he could always claim that Korolev had acted without official permission. He'd fire Korolev and still be seen to be in complete control.

Obviously, Khrushchev understood that, by coming directly to him, Korolev was going over the heads of his military patrons. If he had to come this far, it was because everyone else had already said no. Yet by daring to come this far, Korolev was displaying his strong belief in the project. So Khrushchev said, all right, but only in principle. Without consulting anyone else, without going to the Presidium or even discussing it with the military, Khrushchev said Korolev could do it, on the condition that launching this artificial earth satellite did not interfere in any way with the testing of the rocket. Once he got that to fly, he could launch a satellite. But the rocket must come first. An artificial earth satellite, Khrushchev reminded him sternly, could never be anything more than an after-thought.

In Korolev's mind, he was now in a race against the Americans. But to win it, there was more to do than just design a satellite. In its present configuration, the R-7 had a theoretical range of about 5000 miles, that being the distance between Moscow and New York. Traveling at around 4 miles a second, the Soviet ICBM was designed to carry a nuclear device to America in something like 21 minutes. To put a satellite into orbit, he needed a speed of 4.7 miles per second, which was an increase of nearly 20%. He would also have to come up with some sort of deployment system. The nose come, originally created to house an atomic warhead, would have to be completely reworked. But then, as Khrushchev said, before anything happened, the R-7 would have to fly.

For Vyacheslav Luppo, building any old radio transmitter was easy.

Building one that would be able to send signals back to earth was another matter. No one in the USSR had ever done that before. Starting from scratch, he chose to use a pair of silver zinc batteries which would, he hoped, last as much as 14 days. But it was difficult to calculate how long the satellite might keep sending signals because what little data were available were totally unreliable. They didn't know anything about cosmic rays or the higher layers of the ionosphere because no one had ever done this before.

He designed special low-energy radio tubes as the heart of the 1-watt transmitter, which he sandwiched between the two battery packs, hoping they'd protect it if in fact it needed protection from cosmic rays. Again, no one knew.

The transmitter weighed about $4\frac{1}{2}$ lbs. The two batteries weighed nearly 35 lbs. Springs would automatically open the antennae once the satellite was free of the rocket.

Code-named 'Device 200,' he programmed the transmitter for alternating signals on the 20.005 MHz and 40.005 MHz bands. That would, he believed, best fulfill Korolev's requirement that the signals be receivable on any ordinary short-wave radio.

In all, six transmitters were built. The first two were set aside for the actual flight – it was Device 200-No. 2 which went into space – and the other four were used for experiments. They were flown in planes to help establish a string of listening outposts throughout the USSR.

Once they determined the radio frequencies, Luppo and Korolev wrote an article that was published under a fictional byline for a Russian ham radio magazine. They said that a forthcoming experiment with an artificial earth satellite would include a signal that amateur radio operators around the world could hear. Officially naming the transmitter 'The Border Radio Station of the First Soviet Artificial Earth Satellite,' the article asked any ham operators who heard the satellite to send a letter noting the time and location of their contacts to the simple postal address, 'Moscow Satellite.'

The only mail they got was from a few Japanese ham operators.

No one else bothered to write in.

No one yet took this seriously.

On 23 August, exactly two days after the R-7's first successful flight, Korolev rang Nikita Khrushchev and asked if he could try to launch his artificial earth satellite during the next R-7 test. Khrushchev said yes, but insisted once more that satellites would always remain an after-thought.

When the military were informed, they were very dubious and Korolev was constantly reminded that the rocket came first. In the end, the changes Korolev made to the R-7 were minimal. The guidance system needed to be modified, as did the launch program. He also had to change the rocket's velocity. But except for that, the R-7 remained the same ICBM whose primary mission was to blow up American cities.

In June 1957, Academician Nesmeyanov had promised in a public statement that the Russians would launch a satellite, 'literally within the next months.' The betting line among those people in the West who believed him was that the date would be 17 September, the centenary of Tsiolkovsky's birth. When that day came and went, some scientists, like Professor Albert Parry who wrote the 'Behind the Curtain' column in *Missiles and Rockets Magazine*, guessed that the Russians tried to launch, failed and simply never disclosed it. 'The Soviets advertise our failures only,' he wrote, 'never their own.'

In fact, Korolev had, at one point, thought of commemorating the Tsiolkovsky anniversary, but it was technically out of the question. He aimed instead for sometime in the middle of October. That meant, during the final week of August, he had only a few weeks to actually build a satellite. When one of his designers suggested an oval, Korolev said no and opted for something round. It wasn't for aerodynamic reasons, he explained, but because he believed that a round object would be easier to understand. He also said he wanted it highly polished, claiming that a highly polished sphere would better deflect solar rays.

While that might have fooled the politicians and the military, the men working with him knew otherwise. He'd favoured a highly polished round ball, not just because it was the most practical idea, but because it was aesthetically the most pleasing.

Once that was decided, he designed a deployment system. The satellite would sit on a cocked metal arm, its four antennae sticking out of the nose cone along the side of the rocket. As soon as the rocket reached a certain velocity its main engines would switch off. Two seconds later, a blasting cap would blow off the nose cone. The rocket and the nose cone would fly along together for another minute before a second timing device fired the cocked arm, which literally shoved the satellite away from both the rocket and nose cone.

At least that was the theory behind it all. Korolev had no guarantee it would work. He couldn't promise anyone that the satellite would get into orbit or, if it did, how long it would stay there. All he knew for sure was that he was finally going to try.

The original code name for the satellite project was 'Objective D.' By the middle of September, everyone at OKB-1 was referring to the satellite as 'Objective PS.' The initials derived from the Russian words for 'simplest satellite,' although some of the people around the design bureau led others to believe that PS really stood for Sergei Pavlovich, backwards.

Blueprints were drawn up and actual construction of the satellites began. Six were built simultaneously. Korolev ordered everyone working on them to wear white gloves, demanding that each one be treated as gently as if it were a child. And as each one came together, piece by piece, it was placed on a black velvet cushion. But all this was taking time and Korolev, ever nervous that the Americans might launch first, soon abandoned the blueprints to supervise the construction personally, on the spot. He stood at the table and said, do this, and pointed, do that.

One of the six would be launched. Another would be the back-up. The remaining four would be used in tests. When the satellites were ready, they were flown to Baikonour, with each of the components packed separately. PS No. 1, and the back-up PS No. 2, were reassembled in the main rocket hangar there.

At the same time, the R-7 was prepared for flight.

On 23 September, Soviet agents working in the United States reported rumors to Moscow that the US was ready to launch a satellite. Korolev was immediately informed. He grew so incensed with the thought that America might beat him into space, he moved his own launch forward by two weeks. He threw his team at Baikonour into a total panic by telling them that he wanted to go on Friday, 4 October. The next day, he phoned some journalists in Moscow and told them what he planned to do. He announced to the press that on 4 October he was going to put a satellite into orbit. But no one paid any attention to him. Not one single newspaper carried his news.

On 3 October, Korolev and Luppo tested the transmitter for the final time. Alone in the big neon-lit assembly hall, the two of them – always wearing white gloves – placed the transmitter into the satellite and tested it, listening one last time to the sound. Early the next morning, the satellite was positioned on the cocked arm deployment device, the nose cone was locked into place and the final countdown began.

The military filmed the launch, not because they had any interest in the satellite, but because they were concerned about the rocket. Later, those films would be doctored to show a fellow with a bugle announcing the launch. But it never happened. In fact, it was Korolev's biographer, Yaroslav Golovanov, who invented the bugler. He wrote a fictionalized account of the launch which had the bugler sending the world's first satellite into space. When the films were doctored, the story of the bugler entered Russian folklore. Later, with Yuri Gagarin's first manned space flight, films would show Korolev sitting at the command post talking on the radio with Gagarin, but that didn't happen either. It, too, was filmed after the fact.

Such is the stuff of Soviet history.

PART III

The Cold War and Other Games

We are like two scorpions in a bottle, each capable of killing the other, but only at the risk of his own life.

J. Robert Oppenheimer

Chapter Nine

The First Shock

The formal dinner to honor in-coming Secretary of Defense Neil McElroy, hosted by John Medaris at the Redstone Arsenal Officers' Club on the night of 4 October 1957, was not a happy event.

Milling around in the bar over cocktails, a brooding Wernher von Braun refused to disguise his frustration or his displeasure. McElroy, who resented the way von Braun had tried to push the Army's satellite program on him, was noticeably annoyed. Lemnitzer shared McElroy's discomfort. Brucker did as well.

Determined to keep the conversation light, John Medaris was diplomatically positioned between von Braun and McElroy, when an announcement came over the PA system that Gordon Harris, the ABMA's press officer, was wanted on the telephone. A few minutes later, a distraught Harris rushed back into the bar with the news, 'The Russians have put up a satellite.'

Von Braun reeled. 'We knew they were going to do it.'

Medaris couldn't believe it. 'Has it been confirmed?'

'It's on the radio,' Harris said. 'All the news services have it.'

Word spread quickly through the club. A visibly shaken Gavin came over to von Braun, put his arm around him and, as if a loved one had passed away, expressed his deepest sympathies. Someone mumbled, 'So Sedov and his team actually managed it,' as a large group of people formed around them.

'Vanguard will never make it,' von Braun confronted McElroy. 'We have the hardware on the shelf. For God's sake, turn us loose and let us do something. We can put a satellite up in sixty days.'

'Ninety,' Medaris corrected him.

'Sixty,' von Braun insisted. 'Give us the green light and sixty days.'

Dinner went right out the window.

The rest of the night was spent avoiding phone calls from the national press and staying out of the reach of those local reporters who showed up at Redstone's front gate looking for comments. Early the next morning, McElroy, Brucker and Lemnitzer met with Medaris, von Braun and Gavin. Information about the Russian satellite was still sketchy, but the announced weight of it worried von Braun. 'If it really is over 180 pounds,' he wanted McElroy to understand, 'it's ten times heavier than ours. That's a huge difference. To get a payload that heavy into space, the Russians would need a gigantic launch vehicle.'

McElroy, who had no experience with such matters, simply conceded, 'Okay, they beat us.'

'Only,' von Braun snapped, 'because we let them.'

McElroy saw no sense in arguing that point. Anyway, he didn't know the full story of how Vanguard was chosen. 'If I give you the authority to go ahead' – he was evidently trying to keep his options open – 'if I say you can get your hardware out of the warehouse, and set up a parallel project to Vanguard —'

Von Braun cut him off, diving head-first into a spiel on the merits of Jupiter-C and Orbiter. Never hesitating to remind the group how Charles Wilson had been so simple-minded, he outlined his plan step by step. The crux of it was that a pair of Jupiter-C spares were currently in storage at Cape Canaveral and could be quickly reconfigured to handle a satellite. 'We can get into orbit in sixty days.'

Medaris tried again to revise the figure upwards, 'Ninety days.'

In the end, McElroy was content to settle for an outside estimate of four months. But, he pointed out, just because von Braun and the Army believed they could put a satellite into orbit, that didn't mean he was going to let them. He said he'd have to think about it. He said he wouldn't be sworn in for another four days, and then it would take him some time to get into the job. He said he couldn't make any promises now, except that he'd be in touch.

'When you get back to Washington and all hell breaks loose,' Medaris prodded, 'tell them we've got hardware down here to put a satellite up at any time.'

With that, McElroy and his party headed home.

As soon as they were gone, John Medaris made the most momentous decision of his life. He told von Braun, 'Go ahead. Get started.'

The President returned to the White House on Tuesday, 1 October, having spent most of September in Rhode Island, installed in a big home at the Navy base on Coasters Harbor Island, a few minutes by golf-cart from the Newport Country Club.

It was supposed to have been his summer vacation.

But trouble was brewing in Little Rock, Arkansas. At the beginning of the month, Governor Orval Faubus had ordered the state's National Guard to prevent any black children – in those days referred to as Negroes – from attending the all-white Central High School. A federal court instructed the school board to admit those children, Faubus remained defiant, and so Attorney General Herbert Brownell got an injunction issued against him. The Governor publicly vowed to comply, and apparently did for a few days, until mob rule took over. Street gangs, sponsored by Faubus, marched on the school. That provided the Mayor of Little Rock with the excuse, purportedly in the interest of public safety, to remove all the black children from Central High.

For Eisenhower, it was the last straw.

On 24 September, he federalized the Arkansas National Guard, taking control away from Faubus, and sent Army paratroopers into Little Rock. It would be a full month before any of those black students were able to leave Central High without a military escort.

Now, in early October, Little Rock continued to monopolize the front pages. The only other contenders for headline space were an Asian flu epidemic spreading along the east coast and the World Series, which pitted the New York Yankees against the Milwaukee Braves.

Back at the White House on that Tuesday, the President received a group of angry southern governors who objected to his heavy-handed approach to integration. When the meeting ended, nearly two hours later, a furious Ike walked onto the lawn behind the Oval Office to hit golf balls. It was the quickest way he knew to let off steam.

Little Rock took up Wednesday morning too. But after lunch he went to Burning Tree Country Club for a round of golf with the Vice-President.

He dealt with Little Rock again on Thursday afternoon, having played 18 holes with some Republican supporters.

On Friday, 4 October, he walked into the office at 7:55 a.m. for a briefing on the upcoming visit of Queen Elizabeth and Prince Philip. He left at 9:02, flying to his farm at Gettysburg for a golfing weekend.

With the President out of town, the White House slowed down. It was a chance for most people to catch up on paperwork and phone calls. Andrew Goodpaster was still in his office that evening, going through message traffic, trying to decide what papers the President needed to see when, at around 7:30, a call came in from the duty officer at the CIA to say that the Soviets had just launched a satellite.

Goodpaster immediately rang Gettysburg.

He gave the President what few facts he had – the satellite was 22 inches in diameter, weighed 184 lbs and was in a north-south orbit at an altitude of 560 miles . . . and in the fraction of a second before the President responded, Goodpaster got the distinct impression that Eisenhower already knew. It was just a hunch. There was something in the way the President took the news. If he did know, it would have been typical of Eisenhower not to show his hand. He was very cagey when it came to his sources of information. What Eisenhower did tell Goodpaster was, 'This won't throw our own earth satellite effort off course.' He insisted, 'We've studied it thoroughly, we've laid out our plans and that's what we'll continue to do.'

That America had been beaten into space didn't appear to have any great impact on him. Ike considered the Russian launching nothing more than a scientific achievement. Goodpaster discussed the pros and cons of it with the President, but Eisenhower maintained that it did not present any danger to the national security. He saw no reason to worry about a radio transmitter circling around the earth and emphasized, 'This isn't about military might, this is about science.'

Ike played golf all weekend and stubbornly held onto that stance for the better part of a month.

Andrei Gromyko was due in Washington the next afternoon to see John Foster Dulles, the rendezvous having been arranged several weeks before. He'd only just replaced Molotov as Foreign Minister, a consequence of the 'palace coup,' but was already very much a celebrity.

Born in the Byelorussian village of Gromyki in 1909, he studied English and economics, taught at the Institute of Economics in Moscow and earned the equivalent of a PhD in agricultural management. In 1939 he joined the Foreign Ministry where, because of his English language abilities, he was put on the American desk. Two years later, he was sent to Washington as a Counsellor at the Soviet Embassy. Two years after that, Stalin named him Ambassador to the United States. At 34, he was the youngest Soviet ever to hold that post.

Cursed with a permanently dour expression, and referred to behind his back as 'the oldest young man in the capital,' Gromyko led the Russian delegation at Dumbarton Oaks for the founding of the United Nations. He also attended the Teheran, Yalta and Potsdam conferences. In 1946 he was appointed permanent representative to the UN, where he spent six years in open defiance of the West, never hesitating to storm out of the Security Council or to use his veto. It was when he posted 26 consecutive vetoes that the tabloids began calling him 'Mr Nyet.' After serving as Ambassador to the United Kingdom for a year in 1952, he returned to Moscow to work under Molotov as First Deputy Minister of Foreign Affairs.

Morose, even at the best of times, 'Grim Grom' was decidedly straightforward by Soviet standards, possessed a remarkable memory and kept his cool under the most extreme circumstances, such as when Winston Churchill threw cigar butts at him at Yalta because he'd been whispering to Stalin that the USSR should demand Germany's immediate surrender. He was also perfectly at home with blatant mendacity, like when he told John Kennedy in 1962 that the Soviet Union had definitely not deployed offensive missiles in Cuba. Privately, he played chess, lifted hand weights every morning and read histories of the Czarist period. He liked movies and once told Marilyn Monroe that he'd seen all her films. But his somber and laconic public persona overshadowed his private life. More often than not, when asked about himself, he'd reply, 'My personality doesn't interest me.' One day, when a Western reporter wanted to know if he'd enjoyed his breakfast, Gromyko answered, 'Perhaps.'

His cynical view of the world colored Soviet relations during the span of nine US Presidents, fourteen Secretaries of State, nine British Prime Ministers, the entire French Fourth Republic and four Presidents of the Fifth Republic, in addition to four West German Chancellors. He served every Communist leader up to and including Mikhail Gorbachev, with the exception of Lenin.

In the United States, he was, nevertheless, the brunt of a popular joke. It was based on the fact that Stalin's men loved to boast how the Russians had invented everything – from bicycles, radio, airplanes, radar and vitamins to electricity, anesthesia, balloons, telephones and machine guns. It got to the point of being so ludicrous that even the Russians couldn't take these claims seriously. 'Congratulate me,' a well-known Soviet comedian would say to his straight man, 'I've just invented the umbrella.' The straight man would remind him that umbrellas had been invented by the Chinese hundreds of years before. 'Yes,' would come the punchline, 'but I am the first man to invent the umbrella a second time.' In America, the story went, Gromyko was inspecting the latest gadgets at an industrial trade fair when he said to his assistant, 'Just look at all the things we're going to invent.'

Suddenly, on the evening of 4 October 1957, that joke didn't seem very funny.

He was at a diplomatic reception around the corner from the United Nations when the press arrived looking for him. It was the night *West Side Story* opened on Broadway and most people were talking about that. He couldn't imagine what it had to do with him.

They were the ones who broke the news to him about the satellite.

With great natural cunning, Gromyko gleaned what he could from the reporters, called an impromptu press conference, and faked it. He responded to their questions by rephrasing what they'd already told him. Even more skillfully, he left them with the impression that he knew a great deal more than he was letting on to. The truth is, he didn't know anything about the satellite at all.

Another reception was taking place 230 miles away in Washington, DC.

Walter Sullivan, the science correspondent for the *New York Times*, had been attending a conference on rockets and satellites sponsored by the IGY at the National Academy of Science. Throughout the week, several Russians – but especially the head of the Soviet delegation, Anatoly Blagonravov – had been hinting that a satellite was about to be launched. For Sullivan, it created a minor dilemma. Responsible newspapers like the *New York Times* do not generally report rumors. And, at least on the surface, much of what Sullivan was hearing fell into the category of typical Soviet bravado. But his gut feeling told him this time might be different and after much soul-searching he decided to go with his hunch. Late on Friday afternoon, Sullivan filed a story from the *Times*' Washington bureau saying that a Russian launch was imminent. Intending it for the Saturday edition, which would hit the streets at around 11 that evening, he had no idea if the editors would let the rumor run.

That done, he walked over to the Soviet Embassy on 16th Street, two blocks north of the White House, where the Russians were hosting a cocktail party in honor of the conference. After the usual hassles involved in gaining entrance to the heavily guarded building, he climbed the staircase to the ornate grand ballroom and helped himself to caviar and vodka. He was standing with some people, exercising his limited command of Russian, when an attendant told him he was wanted on the phone. Sullivan went downstairs to the lobby and took the call. It was the bureau to inform him that Reuters was saying the Soviets had just launched a satellite.

Once his initial shock wore off, it dawned on Sullivan that no one in the Embassy knew about it yet. He rushed back to the party, spotted the head of the Rocket and Satellite Committee of the National Academy of Science, a man named Dick Porter, and pulled him aside. After a few minutes of huddled discussion, they decided Lloyd Berkner, an American representative to the IGY, should break the news. They told him what had happened and he agreed to say a few words. Sullivan suggested he preface his announcement with something like, 'I have been informed by the New York Times,' just in case Reuters had somehow gotten it wrong. At least that way, the US-IGY Committee wouldn't be embarrassed.

That's exactly what he did. Berkner banged a spoon on a glass, called for silence, then said, 'I am informed by the New York Times that a satellite is in orbit at an elevation of 900 kilometers. I wish to congratulate our Soviet colleagues on their achievement.'

The room broke out in applause.

The Russians spent the rest of the evening crowing, as Sullivan describes it, with grins on their faces 'as though they had swallowed a dozen canaries.'

Sullivan waited until he could politely excuse himself before going downstairs, only to discover all of the Embassy's telephones frantically occupied. He walked across the street to the United Mine Workers' Union building where he dialled the Times' copy desk in New York to tell them he was on his way back to the bureau to file an update to his story.

The Saturday edition carried a three-line, eight-column banner headline:

> Soviet Fires Earth Satellite Into Space;
> It Is Circling The Globe At 18,000 M.P.H.;
> Sphere Tracked In 4 Crossings Over U.S.

With news services around the world clamoring for satellite stories, the White House switchboard lit up. But no one could reach Jim Hagerty and Jim Hagerty didn't reach the President until 9:25 Saturday morning. When he did, the President restated what he'd told Goodpaster, that this was nothing but a scientific achievement and there was no need to issue any sort of statement until he returned to Washington. If pressed, Ike said, tell them we've never seen ourselves in a race with the Russians to put a satellite into orbit. That's all. Period.

Hagerty then phoned John Foster Dulles. He was at the State Department, already in a meeting about the Russian satellite with his brother, Deputy Secretary of State Christian Herter and their closest aides. Hagerty quoted the President, saying there would be no White House statement on the satellite until Wednesday at the very earliest. Dulles stressed his concern that the administration must not appear to be afraid of the satellite and offered to supply a draft text for the President. Hagerty thought that was a good idea. When he hung up, Foster Dulles turned to Allen Dulles and said, you write one too.

Andrei Gromyko arrived at Foster Dulles' Georgetown home shortly after 4 that afternoon. As the two men went into the library, Dulles casually mentioned the satellite. Gromyko said blandly he hoped the achievement would be for the common good of mankind and of universal science.

These two originally met at the first United Nations session in San Francisco in 1945. Although they didn't necessarily like each other, that was not a prerequisite for respect. Gromyko always felt uneasy in Dulles' presence, uncomfortable with the way he fidgeted, the way he constantly shifted from one foot to the other, the way he never looked anyone straight in the eyes. Nor did he appreciate Dulles' stewardship of US foreign policy, especially where he advocated hostility towards Russia. But there was a lot more to this relationship than personal habits and ideology. One day, Dulles invited Gromyko and the Soviet Ambassador to his home for a private lunch. Bringing them into the library, he proudly displayed the selected works of Lenin and Stalin. 'I'm working on the dictatorship of the proletariat right now.' He even passed the books around, pointing out ear-marked pages and notes he'd written in the margins. As the Russians were leaving, Gromyko wished him luck in his study of Marxism and Leninism. Dulles burst out laughing. So did Gromyko, who later noted, 'We understood one another very well.'

In that same room, less than 24 hours after the launch of the satellite, Dulles told Gromyko that relations between the US and the USSR were worsening. He said the United States was not happy with, among other things, the way the Soviets had allowed developments in the Middle East and Central Europe to strain relations between the two super-powers. He was particularly concerned with Soviet designs on Syria. 'We didn't move to get our friends the British and French out [of Suez] merely to see them replaced by the Soviet Union.'

Old hand that he was, Gromyko toyed with Dulles. Despite his total command of English and French, he asked for a translation. It was all part of his act. Whenever he was put in a corner, he'd want to hear the remark in Russian, and would then respond in Russian, paying close attention to the English version of his answer, sometimes even going so far as to correct the translator if he missed any subtleties. This not only gave him time to consider each sentence twice, it slowed things down and disrupted Dulles' ability to control the meeting.

'The Soviet Union,' he eventually replied, 'cannot remain a passive observer where a situation arises involving the peace and security of the USSR.'

Over the next three hours, they talked about Russian intentions in the Middle East and American intentions in Germany. They spoke about the political situation in Central Europe and US influence over Britain and France. Then they got on to the topic of disarmament. Dulles felt he needed to pull in the administration's reins. Without admitting that the satellite proved the success of the Russian ICBM, Dulles said if disarmament was ever going to work there would have to be a way to monitor it and the best way was with aerial inspections. Echoing Eisenhower's 'Open Skies' proposal to Khrushchev in Geneva in 1955, Dulles justified the concept by saying that, if the Russians had nothing to hide, they'd permit it. Specifically, Dulles wanted to inspect large areas of the Soviet Arctic.

Gromyko was in rare form. 'Why does one want to photograph the Arctic? All he would get would be pictures of ice, snow and polar bears.'

Dulles answered, 'Because there have been Soviet explosions of nuclear devices in the area. On our part, there is an important base at Thule [Greenland].'

Gromyko shrugged. 'What does this have to do with surprise attack?'

'Because,' Dulles reminded him, 'everybody knows that surprise attacks are likely to come from the Arctic area.'

But Gromyko wasn't impressed. 'The time is not yet ripe for an agreement. There is a lack of confidence between our two countries. We cannot consider it in earnest. Can anyone imagine British and American planes flying over the Soviet Union and Soviet planes flying over the US at the present time?'

Knowing what he did about the U-2 program, Dulles replied with a very forthright 'Yes.'

The satellite was called 'Sputnik,' derived from the root *put* which is road, the suffix *nik* which is someone or something that uses a road, such as a traveler, and the prefix *s* – in Cyrillic the letter 'C' – to signify 'with.' So the word translates into English as 'Fellow traveler.'

But not everyone welcomed the arrival of this fellow traveler quite as calmly as Dwight Eisenhower.

Senate Majority Leader Lyndon Johnson claimed, 'We have got to admit frankly that the Soviets have beaten us at our own game.' Political columnist Joseph Alsop wrote that one of America's greatest assets, its military and technological supremacy, had suddenly been depreciated to the vanishing point. Calling Sputnik 'a tremendous defeat for US,' the *Chicago Daily News* worried that, if the Russians could place a 184-lb moon into a predetermined orbit around the earth, then they could deliver 'a death-dealing warhead onto a predetermined target almost anywhere on the earth's surface.' The *New York Times* concluded that a serious reappraisal of the Eisenhower administration was required, the launch having raised 'questions of the gravest character regarding the correctness of our present and past national policies.'

Dr Edward Teller, father of the atomic bomb, said, because of Sputnik, the future belonged to the Russians. 'America has lost a battle more important and greater than Pearl Harbor.' John Rinehart, of the Smithsonian Astrophysical Observatory, announced, 'I would not be surprised if the Russians reached the moon within a week.' Eisenhower's friend, financier Bernard Baruch, wrote, 'America is worried. It should be. We have been set back severely, not only in matters of defense and security, but in the contest for the support and confidence of the peoples throughout the world.' The chairman of the Senate Armed Services Committee, Richard Russell, said Sputnik proved that the Soviets could deliver nuclear bombs to any target in the US. Senator Mike Mansfield specified, 'What is at stake is nothing less than our survival.' Jim Gavin agreed that Sputnik put America in a position of 'mortal danger.'

Eric Sevareid, on the CBS Evening News, also saw the sinister side of this. 'If the intercontinental missile is, indeed, the ultimate, final weapon of warfare, then at the present rate Russia will soon come to a period during which she can stand astride the world, its military master. If she refrains from acting the role, the period should be short and we will equal and neutralize her mastery. If she does not refrain, then the freer, the more tolerant parts of the world will be confronted with the ultimate choice that Patrick Henry once expressed . . .' Those words, as every American school child learns, were 'Give me liberty or give me death.'

At the Redstone Arsenal, the local press reflected von Braun's bitterness. The *Huntsville Times* disclosed that America could have put a satellite into orbit three to six months before the Russians, had von Braun and his team not been prohibited by 'the pig-headedness of persons in high levels in the Defense Department.' They revealed that von Braun, who had not yet spoken publicly on the affair, was telling friends, 'This fiasco to American prestige could have been avoided,' and that he was laying blame for the nation's failure directly on 'the bitter fruits of inter-service rivalries.'

Hermann Oberth, who was then living in the United States, mirrored von Braun's anguish by corroborating that the Redstone team 'could already have launched a satellite if assigned the mission at the same time it was given to the Navy.'

Much the same reaction was shared by James van Allen, the American scientist whose name would be forever linked to the radiation belt surrounding the earth's atmosphere. He was sailing in the South Pacific aboard the Navy's USS *Glacier* studying cosmic rays in conjunction with the IGY when he heard the news on Armed Forces Radio. The entry in his field notebook for that day reads, 'Confirms my disgust with decision to favor NRL [the Naval Research Laboratory's Vanguard] over the Redstone proposal . . .'

In England, the *Daily Express* announced, 'The Space Age Is Here,' while the *News Chronicle* trumpeted, 'Russia Wins Space Race.' Science fiction writer Arthur C. Clarke believed Sputnik would have 'colossal repercussions.' Sir Bernard Lovell, director of the Jodrell Bank Observatory, labeled it 'absolutely stupendous, about the biggest thing that has happened in scientific history,' although he then suggested the Soviets had somehow misplaced the decimal point when giving Sputnik's weight, and insisted it should read 18.4 lb. 'That sounds like a much more reasonable figure.' Science writer Ritchie Calder said in the *New Statesman*, 'No one can have any doubts about the reality and range of a Russian ICBM.' Nor did *The Times* of London find much comfort in the fact that a Russian satellite was soaring over US territory. 'What strikes a note of fear is the American scientists' estimate that it must have taken something like an intercontinental ballistic rocket to launch a satellite of nearly double the expected weight – and hitherto the official tendency has been to belittle Russian advances towards the "ultimate weapon".'

In Paris, where French Premier Guy Mollet was trying to form a new government under the seemingly inadequate structure of the Fourth Republic, one radio announcer opened his morning newscast by assuring his listeners they would be quite surprised to learn that the first story of the day was not about the government crisis.

As Jim Hagerty tried to calm the waters by reciting Eisenhower's sentiments over and over again – 'We never thought of our program as one which was a race with the Soviets' – Senator Stewart Symington, the Democrat from Missouri who'd once screamed 'bomber gap,' was now starting to shout 'missile gap.' He asked Richard Russell, chairman of the Senate Armed Services Committee, to convene hearings immediately. 'Recently announced launching of an earth satellite by the Soviets is more proof of growing Communist superiority in the all-important missile field. If this now known superiority over the United States develops into supremacy, the position of the free world will be critical.' He reminded Russell that he'd been warning about this growing danger for a long time, 'because the future of the United States may well be at stake.' Now he wanted a full-blown inquiry into how the US fell behind the Russians. 'Only in this way can the American people learn the truth. Putting it mildly, they have not been getting the truth. Under our form of government, however, they have a right to know.'

Senator Henry 'Scoop' Jackson, a Democrat from Washington state, jumped on Symington's bandwagon, laying the blame for America's defeat squarely on the shoulders of the Eisenhower administration. He called on the Defense Department to restore recent cutbacks in missile programs and to increase production of the B-52 bomber. Another Democrat, Senator Mike Mansfield from Montana, saw Sputnik as proof that America could not afford to underestimate the USSR, while New Hampshire's Senator Styles Bridges, this time a Republican, said Sputnik necessitated an immediate revision of national psychology. 'The time has clearly come to be less concerned with the depth of the pile on the new broadloom rug or the height of the tail fin on the new car and to be more prepared to shed blood, sweat and tears if this country and the free world are to survive.'

To counter the political assault brought on by Sputnik, and in the absence of any noticeable concern from the President, some members of the administration assumed an almost childishly flippant stance. Admiral Rawson Bennett, the Chief of Naval Operations, called Sputnik 'a hunk of iron anybody could launch.' White House Chief of Staff Sherman Adams said, 'The Administration is not interested in serving a high score in an outer space basketball game.' Presidential adviser Clarence Randall shrugged it all off as 'a silly bauble.' Charles Wilson, who spent his final weekend as Secretary of Defense holed up at the Pentagon meeting about Sputnik with members of the National Security Council and the Joint Chiefs, labeled it 'a neat scientific trick.' The same man who, only a few years before had been asked, 'What happens if the Russians get to space first?' and had answered, 'I wouldn't care if they did,' proved that he was, if nothing else, consistent by shrugging, 'I don't need to know if the moon is made out of cheese.' He also promised the nation, 'Nobody is going to drop anything on you from a satellite while you are asleep, so don't worry about it.' And Treasury Secretary George Humphrey prophesied, 'The real danger of the Sputnik is that some too eager people may demand hasty and sensational action regardless of cost and relative merit in an attempt to surpass what they have done. Americans must never lose their sense of balance and proportion.'

When James Reston looked back on those comments a month later in the *New York Times*, he denounced the administration's arrogance. He alleged America had been suffering from a great national superiority complex and that, until 4 October, 1957, the nation had never been defeated in a war or, for that matter, anything else. He said, until Sputnik came along it was easy to believe in the American Century and to reject any idea that a rival power could share in it, especially since the one power which showed an inclination to do so could be stopped just by encircling and containing it.

But for many Americans, the problem was even simpler. The sky suddenly felt different. For many Americans, overnight, the world had become a different place.

Sputnik had made it very small.

The Secretary of State spent the weekend working on a statement for Eisenhower and sorting through the voluminous message traffic that poured into Foggy Bottom from American embassies and consulates around the world. Such was the impact of Sputnik that those reports, depicting local political, social, military and press reactions to the Russian satellite, would continue to come in, almost non-stop, for the next two months.

Ottawa: 'USSR had scored double-barreled triumph. One is satellite itself and other is confirmation it gives to earlier Soviet claim to have successfully tested ICBM.'

Cairo: 'America in panic for fear moon will be used as site launch rockets at US. This positive proof Russian superiority in missile field.' And later, 'Nasser excited over news. Takes pleasure in seeing America's discomfort. "Serves them right" . . . "Puts Dulles on notice he can't rule the world".'

The Hague: 'American pride has not received such severe blow since Pearl Harbor.'

Bucharest: 'Achievement was certain proof their ability to send ICBM to any part of world.'

Damascus: 'Russia can bomb America after fifteen minutes' warning. Military pacts and bases encircling the Soviet Union have been rendered almost useless.'

Tunis: 'Embassy officers have been asked how US could permit Soviets be first launch satellite.'

Quito: 'Sputnik "beeps" are special code that only Russian scientists are able to interpret.'

Buenos Aires: 'The first question to come into people's minds was, "Why was not the United States the first to launch a satellite?"'

Pretoria: 'The USSR could launch an ICBM with an atomic warhead. The whole world must change its defense plans.'

Bern: 'A great political and psychological victory for the USSR and, correspondingly, a grave, though not decisive, defeat for the United States and for the West as a whole.'

Dublin: 'An undertone of fear that this new device might be used for destructive purposes.'

Montevideo: 'A breakthrough over the United States in the Cold War.'

Taipei: 'Constitutes a threat to the free world.'

Lagos: 'The US has had the ground cut from under her feet.'

Manila: 'Soviet launching of earth satellite was scaring the pants off Philippine leaders.'

Tokyo: 'One adverse effect of this has been to destroy the widely-held assumption that the US is always superior to the Soviets.'

West Berlin: 'May eventually render NATO a ghost of the past.'

Paris: 'The average Frenchman's reaction appeared to be tinged with a certain malicious pleasure, as if they derived a vicarious thrill from seeing someone for once score a point against the United States.'

On Monday morning, 7 October, with Sputnik crossing over the United States seven times every 24 hours, Wall Street suffered its biggest one-day fall in more than two years, reaching a 1957 low, on a record volume of 2.49 million shares. The only advances of any substance were seen in companies dealing in guided missiles, solid rocket fuels and aeronautical instruments.

Also badly hit were Czarist bonds, paper certificates these days collected as scripopholy. Issued before the Revolution and repudiated by the Soviets in the early 1920s, at one point during World War II they were trading as high as 23 cents on the dollar, in the hopes that the Soviets might one day need the West badly enough to honor them. Sputnik brought them crashing to under 3 cents. As one dealer explained, 'Now that the Russians have an earth satellite, they aren't going to need any friends.'

As newspaper clippings about Sputnik piled up on his desk, Jim Hagerty must have felt like the young Dutch boy with his finger in the dike, trying to hold back the sea. No one seemed terribly interested in the President's comment that this wasn't a race. The weekend press, especially the important Sunday papers, were crammed with Sputnik stories. Some were fear-mongering. Dr Fred Whipple of the Smithsonian's Astrophysical Observatory proclaimed that the satellite's signals were coded messages, and two prominent scientists with the Naval Research Laboratory concurred. William Randolph Hearst, Jr, editor-in-chief of Hearst Newspapers, chastised the administration for allowing inter-service rivalries to relegate America to second place. He ran his own column on the front page of the chain's papers that Sunday, with the headline 'Red Moon Warns US.' He was putting his readers on notice. 'The beep beep so far is a challenge. Now is the time to act before it becomes a boom boom.'

Some stories expressed theories about who the master mind might have been behind the Soviet triumph. In the US, 'informed speculation' named Blagonravov, and when he was interviewed he did nothing to deny it. Sources in the UK suggested it was Peter Kapitza.

However, the stories that got the most play came out of the big news agencies, like United Press International, which credited the Russians with a smashing victory over the United States. 'The new achievement should go far toward convincing people all over the world that Russia has emerged as a first-class military in the age of missiles and atomic weapons and that it is seriously challenging the leadership of the United States.'

The magnitude of the achievement was given fair play, but most of the ink was spent on the soundness of the American defeat. After all, the Soviets had shattered the myth that 20th-century science belonged to the United States.

Monday's papers were much the same. The *New York Times* lead story was that the Russians were planning to launch a second satellite and this one would be brought back to earth. The *Washington Post* said one effect of Sputnik would be to 'greatly enhance Soviet prestige and to buttress the Moscow claim that Communism is the wave of the future. Americans would only deceive themselves by drawing any conclusion other than that the Soviet Union has scored a brilliant victory.' 'The Russians have the weapon,' said the *Atlanta Constitution*. 'For the first time in history our country is vulnerable to attack.'

One difference between the Monday papers and the weekend papers was that now they were publishing maps to trace Sputnik's flight path over the United States, and side bars telling their readers how to spot it. Throughout America, at dawn and dusk and throughout the night, people stood on their front stoops or climbed on their roof, binoculars and spy-glasses in hand, trying to locate a small blip of light flying overhead. All these years later it turns out that no one saw Sputnik. The 22-inch ball was too insignificant at 560 miles. But when the satellite was deployed from the rocket, the nose cone flew along with it, and that was big enough to reflect the sun's light. That was big enough to see. Still, if you were searching for the satellite, all you had to do was look where the newspapers said to look and, sure enough, there it was, right on time. They said it was Sputnik and you believed it was Sputnik and it left an indelible impression. Walter Sullivan called it 'an awesome reality,' and said anyone who went out to see Sputnik would probably never forget the experience. He's got to be right because even now, even knowing it was only the nose cone, the memory of a little dot streaking across the mid-October Indian-summer night sky doesn't seem any less breathtaking.

One of Charles Wilson's last official duties on that Monday was to draft a memo to the President, providing a brief history of the US satellite program – he conveniently ignored the animosity shown to the Army and in particular to von Braun's proposals – and defending the choice of the Navy's Vanguard program for 'technical reasons.' He flatly rejected the notion that the Army should now be permitted to set up a program parallel to the Navy's. 'Since, in any event, the US satellite would be second rather than first, it appears sound to adhere to our program as presently planned.' And he credited the Soviets with being cunning enough to see their achievement coincide with the visit to Washington of their top scientists. 'The fact that what they claim was their first attempt was successful, and that it was timed perfectly in relation to the IGY conference in Washington, supports the thesis that this was all a very carefully laid plan to make maximum Cold War capital out of their satellite program.'

There were, he wrote, two main Cold War points to consider: the impact on the public of the first successful invasion and conquest of outer space; and the inference that could be drawn, if any, on the status of the Russian ICBM program. To counter these, America might take the position that it's not important who launched first. The important thing is the success of the program and how many scientific goals are achieved. As for the second point, Wilson was not convinced that the satellite corroborated Soviet claims to have successfully tested an ICBM. 'Our public position might well be that our own Vanguard program was divorced from military rocketry as much as possible, and the fact that our schedules have not produced a satellite at as early a date as the Russians have succeeded in doing is without military significance.'

Later that morning, across town at the White House, Jim Hagerty and Don Quarles, who'd been promoted from Secretary of the Air Force to Deputy Secretary of Defense, met with some of the President's military advisers to iron out an agenda which would serve as the basis for a full-scale meeting about Sputnik with the President the next day.

At 2 o'clock, next door on the third floor of the Executive Office Building, the Working Group on Earth Satellites, part of the Operations Coordinating Board (OCB) of the National Security Council, met in emergency session for the second time in 48 hours. Representatives from Defense, State, the CIA, the USIA, the National Science Foundation and the OCB's permanent staff attended, as did ad hoc members from Budget, the US-IGY Committee, the Office of Defense Mobilization and the President's Disarmament Staff. When news of Sputnik had initially reached Washington, an OCB coordinator had asked the Pentagon to offer the press background information, news photos and motion picture footage on Vanguard, and to open three satellite tracking stations to the press. They'd hoped to counter Soviet propaganda with American propaganda. No one cared. So the group had gathered on Saturday to discuss the problem. They'd concluded that the government must not over-respond with official high-level statements and needed to avoid any reference to the military implications of the Russian satellite. When that didn't appear to be working either, they met again on Monday afternoon. Now they hoped they could use the interest aroused by Sputnik to draw attention to the broader programs being conducted under the auspices of the IGY.

It was, needless to say, a lesson in futility.

At about the same time, back at the Pentagon, Wilbur Brucker received a phone call from John Medaris in Huntsville. Medaris, who was taking a substantial risk by going outside the chain of command to phone the Secretary of the Army directly, wanted him to put in writing a request to the Secretary of Defense, formally asking permission to launch a satellite. Brucker agreed with Medaris that there was no harm in trying and dictated a memo to Charles Wilson stressing the importance of Sputnik and recommending that the Army's Jupiter-C rocket be used to launch a US satellite at the earliest possible moment.

Wilson, who might not have even bothered to read it, put it in a pile of papers for Neil McElroy's attention where it sat for the better part of a week.

When Foster Dulles rang Jim Hagerty a few hours later to find out if Eisenhower was back, Hagerty said he was and that they were talking about scheduling a press conference on Sputnik for Thursday or Friday. Dulles reminded him, 'We will have to agree on what to say about the satellite.'

As soon as they hung up, Dulles phoned his brother to tell him about the press conference. 'It's important what we say.'

Allen cautioned, 'Don't give it out that we were caught by surprise.'

Half an hour later Hagerty rang Foster Dulles again to say he'd just heard from the *New York Times* that James Reston spent three hours with Nikita Khrushchev in Moscow today and that the first part of his interview would be running in tomorrow's paper. He said, Khrushchev is claiming the Soviet Union has all the missiles they need for any purpose. Dulles wondered if they should respond to that. Right away Hagerty said no.

The President and his wife returned to the White House from Gettysburg by car, arriving at 3:55. With afternoon temperatures in the low 60s, all he intended to do was see a few people, look at the mail and then go outside to hit some golf balls.

But by now some people in the White House were coming around to the view that the Soviet satellite was a bigger problem than Ike believed it was. Hagerty was the first one to try to get that point across. Later in the week, Murray Snyder – Hagerty's former assistant in the Press Office and since the beginning of 1957 an Assistant Secretary of Defense – would also try to speak about Sputnik to the President.

Hagerty reported that the country was fast approaching a state of panic and the President shrugged that he couldn't understand why. He said he was going to 'play down the whole thing,' because he refused to believe that anyone could make such a commotion over a scientific achievement. He said, look, I've agreed to make a statement for the press, I've agreed to include it on the agenda for Wednesday's NSC meeting, and I've also agreed to discuss it with the staff tomorrow morning. Enough, he mumbled, is enough.

He turned to his 'In' box and picked up the daily Staff Notes, a mimeographed series of numbered paragraphs that can only be described as instant secret briefings on the hot items of the day. Three of the five listed for 7 October dealt with unrest in Haiti, a Japanese–Indian iron ore project and an item that the US was continuing to oppose expansion of the Disarmament Commission at the UN. Number four was 'Soviet Earth Satellite,' referencing a report from Dr Alan Waterman, director of the National Science Foundation, saying that the technical details contained in the Soviet's official announcement seemed to be correct. Number five was 'USIA Coverage On Satellite.' The United States Information Agency had issued guidance to American outposts to avoid giving an impression of sour grapes, to avoid politico-military implications, and to guide public interest away from the satellite in favor of the IGY.

Next he picked up a fact sheet from the office of the Secretary of the Army, forwarded to him by the Secretary of Defense.

'The purpose of this fact sheet,' it said under item one, 'is to describe the Army's capability to place a satellite in orbit at an early date.' It was a not-so-subtle way of telling the boss that they could have launched a satellite as far back as a year ago and that, if given the go ahead, 'the Army would require four months from a decision date to the first launching of a missile designed to place a satellite in orbit.'

Like everything that came across his desk, Ike put his initials on it to show he'd seen it. But unlike some papers, he tossed this one towards his 'Out' box because there was no action necessary.

Tuesday morning all hell broke loose.

The front page of the *Washington Post* trumpeted, 'Reds Fire New-Type H-Bomb.' Citing Tass, that a powerful hydrogen device of new design had been exploded at a great height, the paper explained, 'Today's announcement supposedly sought to take advantage of interest whetted by the recent firing of a ballistic missile and Friday's satellite launching.' The front page of the *New York Times* had that story too, but featured Reston's interview with Khrushchev. And sure enough, there was the Soviet leader saying he had all the missiles he needed. Inside both papers was an interview with Anatoly Blagonravov gallantly offering to launch American instruments with the next Sputnik.

Hagerty's telephones rang non-stop with reporters from newspapers and television networks and radio stations and news agencies all looking for comments.

Eisenhower was in the Oval Office by 8.

He'd known about the Soviet atomic bomb test within hours of it happening on Sunday. He didn't know how it was brought to 'a great height,' whether it was put up by a missile or dropped from an aircraft, but the CIA had picked it up, the Japanese Meteorological Board had announced it and the Atomic Energy Commission had not only detected it but they'd already issued a press release on it. Anyway, the Russians had been actively testing these things all autumn.

It was what Khrushchev was telling Reston that bothered him.

Some of those remarks simply could not go unanswered. For example, Khrushchev accused the United States of trying to stir up a war over Syria by coercing Turkey to launch an attack. His warning, 'If the rifles fire, the rockets will start flying,' was too provocative to disregard.

Eisenhower was coming to understand that, when Khrushchev said he was going to do something that he could do, he did it. At the same time, there was always a lot of bombast with Khrushchev. The trick was in knowing what he could or could not pull off. In 1956, during the Suez crisis, Khrushchev threatened 'to let the rockets fly.' Eisenhower stuck that into the bombast category. Later when he said, 'We will bury you,' that was put down to Khrushchev's pompousness as well. There was some deliberation around the White House about what he meant by that, because the phrase could be read two ways. One is, we will outlast you. The other is, we will put you in the ground. But no one in Eisenhower's inner circle thought he could do either. No one believed for a moment that Communism could outlast Capitalism. And, if Khrushchev was crazy enough to attempt to put America into the ground, it would result in the complete destruction of the USSR. Khrushchev knew that. And Eisenhower knew Khrushchev was no fool. Georgi Malenkov had publicly predicted that if it came to war both sides would be destroyed, and that was contrary to Soviet doctrine which preached that only one side, the imperialist side, would not survive. Ironically, Malenkov's candor, saying what he did, was always believed to have been part of the reason that Khrushchev removed him.

Khrushchev's comment about Turkey and Syria, though, was not as easy to categorize. The best thing was to take him at his word. So the President told Hagerty to issue a statement to the effect that Turkey was an independent nation, capable of creating its own foreign policy and that Mr Khrushchev must not be under any illusion that the United States, 'Turkey's friend and ally,' takes its obligations lightly.

As for Dr Blagonravov's invitation to fly American equipment into space on the next Soviet satellite, the response would be an emphatic, no thanks.

Just after 8:30, the President convened what he hoped would be the first of only two meetings he'd have to take on Sputnik. Waterman was there from the National Science Foundation. The Deputy Secretary of Defense for Research and Development, William Holaday, was there. John Hagen, director of the Vanguard program, was there.

As was Don Quarles. The other seven people who attended, including Sherman Adams, Andrew Goodpaster and Jim Hagerty, were Eisenhower staffers.

The first thing Eisenhower said was, there will be no shift in policy. He wanted it understood, we will proceed in an orderly fashion, which means there will be a test launch of a Vanguard vehicle in December and the actual launch of an instrumental satellite in March 1958. That's what we said we were going to do, that's what we will do. He told the Department of Defense to issue a statement to that effect.

Eisenhower then asked if it was true that the Army could have put a satellite into orbit months ago. Quarles said there was no doubt that the Redstone rocket could have done it a year or more ago. But, he said, the Science Advisory Committee felt it was better to have the earth satellite program well separated from military rocket development. He reminded the President of the need to stress the civilian nature of the program and to avoid using any systems to which foreign scientists could never be given access for security purposes. He added, the Army felt that, with some minor modifications to the rocket, they could put a satellite into orbit within four months. That would still be one month before the estimated March 1958 launch of the Navy's Vanguard.

The President remarked that, when Congress learned about this, they would inevitably ask a lot of embarrassing questions. He said he might tell them, timing was not one of our priorities. And, because this was tied into the IGY, we were never under any pressure to fix a date as long as we orbited our satellite during the IGY. And because foreign scientists were involved, we had to keep military secrets out of it.

Sherman Adams agreed that this was never designed to be a crash program but thought the President should make that point understood to the public. He said, let's stress the fact that we've been working simply to develop and transmit scientific knowledge. Eisenhower liked that. He took the decision that a sudden shift in approach would be to belie that attitude, one he'd had all along. Quarles concurred that such a shift would create service tensions in the Pentagon.

John Medaris and Wernher von Braun had, without even knowing it, lost another round.

Just before lunch, Jim Hagerty got a call from Foster Dulles who said he'd been thinking about the satellite, had seen the Reston interview and felt the President should make a major speech on disarmament. He said the time for it was right, not merely because America's position was not adequately understood but because Soviet propaganda was suddenly very intense, thanks to Sputnik, and the best way to counter that would be something from the President himself. Hagerty suggested Dulles mention it when he met Eisenhower that afternoon.

That's exactly what he did. Eisenhower, Dulles and the President's disarmament adviser Harold Stassen discussed their divergent views, with Dulles accusing Stassen of being ready to meet the Russians 'practically, if not entirely on their terms.' Dulles said he felt a major speech on disarmament was called for to tell the Russians exactly where America stood. At the same time, but clearly separated from the disarmament talks, Dulles wanted to discuss with the Soviets the possibility of establishing a special international study of means to control outerspace missiles and satellites. Eisenhower told him to go ahead. Announcing it the following day, Dulles would concede for the first time publicly, 'I think they have gained a certain propaganda advantage because of it [Sputnik], undoubtedly. I don't think they have gained much more than that.'

When Dulles left, Dr Detlev Bronk of the National Academy of Sciences came in to talk to Eisenhower about Sputnik.

Once that meeting was over, Hagerty showed up with the Dulles brothers' draft statements. Not surprisingly, they were similar in tone and equally loose with the truth.

Foster Dulles wanted Eisenhower to play down the satellite's importance, saying that the value of it to mankind would, for a long time, be highly problematical. He noted that, by capturing Peenemünde, the Russians had the benefit of advanced German technology. They were then able to commit resources to the project far beyond the means of free societies where people engage in pursuits of their own choosing and where public monies are limited by representatives of the people. 'Despotic societies,' he wrote, 'which can command the activities and the resources of all their people, can often produce spectacular accomplishments.'

Allen Dulles took the tack, 'We too have had our firsts. We led in atomic and thermonuclear development including building of the first nuclear reactor which has pioneered the peaceful uses of the atom; a more significant development than the hurling of a missile into outer space.' He also played up the spoils of war. 'They acquired a missile system which enabled the Germans as early as September 1944 to hurl a V-2 some 175 miles to London. We have hard intelligence to support

197

our analysis that they have never stopped their intensive work on rocket propulsion and guided missiles since 1945.'

As importantly, Allen Dulles suggested the President stress that America's primary interest was not in pursuing a race into space with the Soviets but in finding a way to end the race towards mutual destruction. 'The present course leads to suicide. What we can do the Soviets can do and vice versa; so in time can other countries. This we have never doubted. One side may get a slight advantage in one field today; the other tomorrow. It is unlikely that either will get such a monopoly in the field of annihilation as this country acquired for a brief period between 1945–1949 and never dreamed of using.'

The President read both drafts, doodled a teacup on the bottom right-hand corner of Allen Dulles' draft, then crossed out those last five words – 'and never dreamed of using.'

He wasn't going to tell a lie like that.

At the last minute he had some questions he wanted answered and they were sent to Don Quarles:

(1) If an object pierced the earth's envelope of air and entered outer [sic] at too great a speed, would it fail to orbit and simply be lost in space?

(2) If the above is true, is it not likewise a fact that at too slow a speed, the object would merely start falling back to earth and probably be consumed by the heat generated by friction?

(3) If the above is true, would not the height of the orbit above the earth be determined by the balance of forces between the momentum of the object and the mutual attraction between earth and the object?

(4) In this question, my memory is going back more than 40 years, but as I recall, the formula for momentum was MV-squared. Since increasing mass, as I remember, increases the force of the attraction between the earth and the object, would it be true that the heavier the object would require, for successful orbiting, either greater speed or greater height?

Finally, (6) [Mis-numbered, this should have read 5.] Can an object be orbited in any direction chosen by the scientists; that is, circle the earth directly along a parallel latitude, or does it have to have a direction that has in it the north and south components?

★   ★   ★

198

There's no record as to how Quarles answered each question, or if in fact he answered any of them. But by the very nature of the questions, all of them scientific, it's easy to see just how deeply entrenched the President's thoughts were in that first week.

He then got up from his desk and went outside to hit golf balls. He stayed there very late, trying to get Sputnik out of his head.

Chapter Ten

The Russian Offensive

It was just after 3 a.m. Moscow time, on Saturday, 5 October, when Tass announced that the Soviet Union had successfully launched the world's first artificial satellite. After giving a few vague details, they promised in typical prose, 'Our contemporaries will witness how the freed and conscious labor of the people in the new, socialist society turns mankind's most audacious dreams into reality.'

Throughout that morning, radio programming was interrupted every half-hour with martial music and the resonant tones of Josef Levitan, followed by the national anthem. The voice of Soviet radio, he'd been Stalin's favorite announcer, and was the man the state put on the air whenever something major happened. It was Levitan who announced the end of the war. It was Levitan who announced Stalin's death. And it was Levitan who introduced Sputnik to the proletariat. 'As a result of very intensive work by scientific research institutes and design bureaus, the first artificial satellite in the world has been created.'

The story about Sputnik in that morning's edition of *Pravda* was equally terse, a few column inches crammed into a small box on the front page. The paper said the satellite was in orbit and noted that its radio transmitter could be heard in every corner of the globe. *Pravda* explained how Tsiolkovsky had theorized on the possibility of interplanetary travel and how the high level of scientific and technical potential of the Soviet Union was making it possible.

That the Soviets announced Sputnik in the briefest of terms wasn't simply because no one knew much about the satellite. It was primarily because no one yet gave it any political significance. As far as the government was concerned, this was a scientific achievement that didn't necessarily warrant anything more than a small box on *Pravda*'s front page.

The first indication the government had that they might have underplayed the event came from Moscow. As the news swept across the city, the Soviet capital was transformed. Saturday morning turned into New Year's Eve. People congratulated each other, patted each other on the back, opened bottles of vodka and toasted the health of the nation. In less than 12 orbits of the earth, Sputnik had been fêted with immense national pride. By then, news of the reaction in the West began coming in. Reflecting that, on Sunday *Pravda* ran six pages about Sputnik. On Monday, they ran eight. Triumphant editorials set the tone for an orgy of boasting and self-congratulation. 'Socialist order is the best form of organization of human labor,' they claimed. 'Even the capitalist press has been forced to admit the superiorities of the Socialist system.'

The Russian press overflowed with American praise for Sputnik. The warning from the *Washington Evening Star* was given prominent coverage. 'We would appear totally blind if we did not see in this Russian achievement particularly convincing confirmation of Moscow's previous reports about the success of the Soviet Union in creating an ICBM.' And in citing the *New York Herald Tribune's* remark that the United States had suffered defeat in the epic competition of the 20th century, *Pravda* gloated, 'Americans will now be forced to abandon the arms race.'

At last, *Pravda* continued, the United States had 'recognized the falseness of bourgeois propaganda lies about USSR scientific technical backwardness.'

Radio Moscow noted that Radio Free Europe had soft-pedaled Soviet scientific superiority in announcing the launch of Sputnik.

The Soviet Academy of Sciences released a statement exclaiming, 'That we are not as rich as the Americans is no secret to us. But such problems require large teams of gifted scientists and engineers and in our country, under Socialism, it is easier to organize, inspire and direct the work of such a team.' It was signed, Peter Kapitza.

Across 11 time zones, but especially in Moscow, the Soviets began thinking they'd finally proven themselves. They were overcome with a tremendous sense of optimism, a conviction that Russia was the greatest power in the world, that it would soon catch up and surpass the United States in material wealth because it had already caught up and surpassed the United States in technical wealth.

As people were saying the future belonged to the USSR, Nikita Khrushchev set out to remind them who made it happen.

Late Saturday night, at about the same time that John Foster Dulles was meeting Andrei Gromyko in Washington, Sergei Korolev and the senior members of his team, all of them badly hung over from their vodka and champagne celebrations, left Baikonour by military plane for the Black Sea. Because it had been such an important success, Vasily Rabikov felt it warranted an important reward. He'd hastily arranged with Marshal Ustinov, who in turn had arranged with Khrushchev, that Korolev and the senior members of his team be granted special travel authorization to install themselves at Bulganin's dacha in Sochi. They could have as much time there as they needed before going back to Moscow to pick up their work on the ICBM.

But a powerful group of senior military men continued to voice their objections. They resented the way Korolev had gone over their heads to get permission to launch his artificial earth satellite. They resented his use of their rocket. They resented the rumors spreading through Baikonour that he wanted to put more satellites into space.

Referring to them, Korolev started joking that Sputnik had gone into orbit without a permit.

They complained to Ustinov that there was a distinct threat to be met and they wanted ballistic missiles to meet it. They didn't want to hear any more talk about outer space. If they didn't get satisfaction from him, they pledged to take their case to the Central Committee because the defense of the nation had to be their most important priority.

Reluctantly, Korolev had to accept the fact that he'd accomplished what he'd set out to do and now it was time to get back to missiles. In the end, he knew it never really mattered what he orbited around the earth, as long as he did it before the Americans. Deep down he knew Sputnik might wind up being the first and last shot in a one-shot war. Anyway, at this point, despite his dreams, there were no plans to launch any other satellites. And, in the face of such ardent resistance from factions of the military, it didn't appear as if there would be any in the immediate future.

On that Sunday in Washington, Anatoly Blagonravov met the press and pretended to know everything about the satellite. When someone asked him why the Russians hadn't announced the launching in advance, he replied, 'This one was purely experimental. The next one will be for the International Geophysical Year.' He said Sputnik was launched to pave the way for the more ambitious satellites and promised that those satellites would be equipped with an array of scientific instruments. He then lied that work was already underway in the USSR for a manned satellite launching. 'We have prepared for the flight of human beings

Harry Truman so feared the Soviets that he ordered Dwight Eisenhower, then Chairman of the Joint Chiefs of Staff, to plan a pre-emptive invasion of the USSR.

President Eisenhower treated the British as equals out of deference to Winston Churchill. But as the Prime Minister's health deteriorated, so did Britain's status as a full partner in the "special relationship."

left
West met East in Geneva in 1955. (l-r) Nikolai Bulganin with Eisenhower, the French Premier Edgar Faure and British PM, Anthony Eden.

right
However, the star of the show was the First Secretary of the Communist Party of the USSR, Nikita Khrushchev (r), here with American Secretary of State, John Foster Dulles. Bulganin, the official head of the Soviet delegation looks on.

left
It was the first foray into the West for Khrushchev and Bulganin, who clearly had a lot to learn about media events. Hoping to be seen, they arrived at the summit each day in an open car. But security guards took the rear seats, cramming the two Soviets into the jump seats where no one could shoot them, or see them either.

top left
Khrushchev quickly understood the lessons of Geneva. A year later when he visited Britain, he made certain that there were plenty of photo opportunities, like this one with Eden.

top right
Eden and Dulles couldn't stand each other and their inability to get along soon became a significant factor in the Cold War.

bottom
Dulles' influence on Eisenhower was powerful enough to turn the President against Eden too, leaving the British exposed at Suez and contributing to the demise of Eden's Premiership.

above
Secretary of the Army Wilber Brucker (l) administers the oath of office to the new Secretary of the Air Force, Don Quarles, while Secretary of Defense Charles Wilson looks on. Had this ceremony taken place even 30 minutes later, America might have beaten Russians into space.

right
As head of the CIA, Allen Dulles conspired with his brother Foster, giving them an inordinate influence over the President.

below
The Dulles brothers' most significant undertaking was perhaps their resolute sponsorship of the fated U-2 spy plane project.

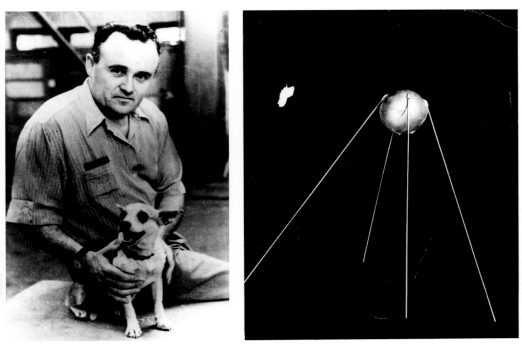

Father of the Soviet intercontinental ballistic missile, Sergei Korolev.

top right
When Sputnik was first launched in October 1957, few people realized how a highly polished steel ball would change the world.

Had they not been ordered to put their satellite project on the shelf, Army General John Medaris (l) and German rocket scientist Wernher von Braun (r) almost certainly could have put America at least a year ahead of the Russians.

left
America's answer to the
Russian Sputniks was the ill-
fated Vanguard project.

above
It was the in-coming Secretary
of Defense, Neil McElroy who
eventually gave von Braun the
green light to launch a
satellite, which he did less than
60 days later.

below
Harold Macmillan used
Sputnik to put the "special
relationship" back together
and bring American atomic
weapons to British shores.

right
It was because of Sputnik that Nikita Khrushchev emerged as a major player on the world's political stage. Now media-savvy, he handily gave Vice-President Richard Nixon a piece of his mind when the two met for the first time in Moscow.

below
Three old warriors: Eisenhower and Churchill visit a dying John Foster Dulles.

Out from under the staunch anti-Communist influence of Foster Dulles, Eisenhower discovers a likeable, human side to Nikita Khrushchev.

Three years later, President John Kennedy had no way of knowing that as he briefed the nation on the American blockade of Cuba, Nikita Khrushchev was arming a Soviet ICBM with a nuclear warhead and targetting the United States.

to space. But it is difficult to say when. We want to be sure it would be safe.'

The next day, while visiting the Naval Research Laboratory, he asked his hosts if he could listen to the satellite's radio signals and, when they tuned into the beep-beep-beep, he nodded convincingly, 'Yes, that's it. I recognize it.' When they showed him some of the instruments intended for the US satellite program, Blagonravov suggested America might want to send those instruments into space on a future Sputnik.

Suddenly he was the hottest Russian in town. The *New York Times* did a major profile on him, and all the news agencies sought his advice. He refused to quash any of the rumors that quickly circulated which named him as the man directly responsible for Sputnik.

By the time he returned to Moscow, Anatoly Blagonravov was beginning to believe his own publicity.

Also over that first weekend, comedian Bob Hope tried to explain away Sputnik with, 'Their Germans were smarter than our Germans.'

But German scientists did not significantly contribute to the ultimate success of the Soviet missile program. After studying V-2 designs and learning how to build them from captured production facilities, Korolev discovered the V-2 was filled with faults. There's no denying that his first rocket, the R-1, was a copy of the V-2, but the Russians found so little to scavenge in Germany that they jokingly referred to their presence there as 'Operation Paper Scraps.' The bulk of what they managed to get comprised little more than unique machine tools which the Americans left behind at the Nordhausen plant, plus a complete set of V-2 production plans. It was hardly enough to put them into space.

Perhaps their single most important find, seldom if ever reported in the West, was a V-2 launching site at Debica, near Warsaw, Poland. They came away from there with enough parts to reconstruct 10 V-2s. Included in the group working at Debica were two men who would become key members of Korolev's team, Vasily Mishin and Boris Chertok.

Those few Germans who were brought back to the USSR were never incorporated into the mainstream of Russian missile development. They were kept away from the important design bureaus, confined to writing reports on their work in Germany. It gave the Soviets a concise picture of the V-2 program up to the moment when the Allies disrupted it, but nothing more. The Soviets used German slave labor to build their testing sites but never used German rocket scientists to move those programs forward. As Wernher von Braun put it some years later, 'The Americans looked for brains, the Russians looked for hands. The Russians have a great many production engineers who can make wonderful copies of V-2s.'

While the V-2 might have been considered good for 1945, it turned out to be pretty bad for 1950. The fuel tanks, for instance, were separate from the main body of the rocket at a time when the Soviets were already incorporating fuel tanks into their rocket design. By then the Soviets reckoned they'd gotten what they could out of the Germans and sent most of them home.

Of course, the moment those Germans arrived in the West, they were interrogated by American intelligence, giving the US a very concise picture of the work the Soviets were then doing. Through those interviews, the CIA was able to identify such major players as Sergei Korolev.

The only German scientist of any note to side with the Soviets was a man named Helmut Grottrup, who'd worked in guidance, control and telemetry at Peenemünde. He was among those originally offered a contract by the Americans in 1945, but when he was told that German wives weren't being invited along, he backed out. The Soviets hired him to help set up a V-2 assembly plant. Once that was completed, in mid-1946, they asked him to suggest technical improvements for the V-2. He completed a study, but Korolev discarded it. In October 1946, Grottrup formed part of a huge German workforce sent to create a V-2 production facility for the Volga rocket range at Kapustin Yar. Once that was established, the Russians gave Grottrup a year to design a more powerful version of the V-2 with a detachable warhead. Arrogantly believing that his rocket was something special, he submitted plans to his Soviet masters and waited for word to come back to start production. Five months later, having heard nothing, Grottrup demanded an answer. He was told, our own designs are better, and that was the end of that.

Grottrup was permitted to go home in 1953. By that time Sergei Korolev was well on his way to solving the problem of how to get a rocket with an atomic warhead from Moscow to New York.

During the 1950s, newspapermen used to refer to the Moscow beat as 'the world's biggest story.' The only problem with it was that the world's biggest story couldn't be told.

To begin with, no matter what happened, nothing had happened and no one could write about it until the happening had been officially acknowledged, which usually came in the form of an announcement from the Soviet news agency, Tass.

Next, even after it was officially acknowledged, there were no sources to verify the facts except official sources, which more often than not also meant Tass.

The origins of the system stem from a Soviet mania for secrecy.

Until *glasnost* and *perestroika* came along, secrecy was not merely official government policy, it was so deeply embedded in the Russian psyche that it took on the aura of a national neurosis. No regime in history, with the possible exceptions of Chairman Mao's China and Chairman Hoxha's Albania, ever stayed tighter-lipped about most things than the Soviets. As long ago as 50 years before Khrushchev's birth, a French writer traveling through Russia observed, 'Secrecy presides over everything, administrative secrecy, political, social secrecy. Here everything is difficult. Everybody wishes to please his master by contributing toward the concealment of some corner of the truth from foreigners.'

The fetish for secrecy reflected itself in all echelons of life. Security Offices, known cryptically as the 'First Department,' were installed in every factory and workplace throughout the country. It was then down to the head of each First Department to determine work procedures and allow access to information. By the time Stalin died, there were 13 scientific institutes designing missiles and 35 factories manufacturing them, but workers at one plant were hardly ever informed about the work going on at any other plant.

Secrecy so permeated Soviet society that Russian comedians used to tell a story about three surgeons meeting to discuss their most demanding operation. The British doctor said it was brain surgery in a bunker during wartime blackout conditions. The American said it was open heart surgery on a warship during a battle. The Russian said it was a tonsillectomy during peace time. When told that surgeons in the West could do a dozen tonsillectomies in a day without thinking twice, the Russian physician answered, 'But here everyone must keep their mouth shut so we have to go in through the ear.'

Exactly like the Czarist bureaucrats who saw railroads as a threat because they allowed people to travel, Khrushchev tried to ban photocopiers because they were an easy way to reproduce *samizdat*, or forbidden literature. Along the same lines, he tried to slow down the proliferation of telephones because they permitted people to have uncontrolled communication. Nor would Khrushchev ever permit a Moscow phone directory to be printed and Moscow remains perhaps the only capital city anywhere in the world without one. For that matter, there's never been a comprehensive street map of Moscow, like London's *A-Z*, Paris' *L'Indispensable*, or any of several detailed guides to American cities. But then, for years, every map made in the Soviet Union was purposely deceptive. Correct geographical co-ordinates were outlawed. Map makers were ordered to move cities and towns to one side or the other so that no one could ever establish their correct position. At the height of the Cold War, such madness became so obsessive that newspaper cuttings more than ten years old were officially classified as state secrets so that no one could check on history.

Yet the crux of the problem, faced by every Western reporter trying to cover the world's biggest story, lay with the Soviets' definition of precisely what the press was supposed to do. The word 'fact,' for instance, was not given the same importance in Moscow that it had in Washington, London or Paris.

'Fact is a Latin word,' a senior Tass official once pointed out, 'and it means that which actually happened. Tass makes no attempt to pass out for facts what are merely reasonable suppositions. Tass reports facts only when they are really facts.' In some cases, that means weeks or months after the event. When, in 1949, the Soviets finally decided to tell the world they'd tested an atomic bomb, Tass broke the news at least four weeks after the event with the words, 'On September 23, President Truman announced that . . .'

In 1956, news of the Hungarian Revolt was kept out of the Soviet press for nearly a week, and the 1957 'palace coup' didn't make it into the papers until four days after Malenkov, Molotov and the others were gone. With disasters, the record of reporting 'facts' was even more dismal. In 1955, when a Russian Navy ship sank with the loss of 1500 lives, nothing appeared. Even under *glasnost*, it was weeks before anything but the barest outline of the accident at Chernobyl was released.

But then, the ruling principle of Soviet journalism, in direct contradiction to Western journalism, dictated that the role of the press was to be the Party's strongest weapon. Lenin saw newspapers not only as a collective propagandist and agitator, but also as a collective organizer. Khrushchev refined the definition. 'The press is our chief ideological weapon,' he said. 'It is called upon to rout the enemies of the working class, the enemies of the toilers. Just as an army cannot fight without weapons, so the Party cannot successfully carry on its ideological work without such a sharp and militant weapon as the press.'

Under the old system – pre-August 1991 – the USSR's two major newspapers were the morning *Pravda*, official voice of the Central Committee, and the evening *Izvestia*, official voice of the Supreme Soviet. The word 'pravda' means truth and the word 'izvestia' means news, and the oldest joke in Moscow was that neither could be found in either.

News came into the papers over wires from government offices. Reporters were not reporters as much as they were technicians charged with putting the Party's version of events into print. Not surprisingly, everything was always seen through rose-colored glasses. Production quotas were always up. Efficiency was always up. Communism was always on the rise. Capitalism was always in the throes of terminal decay. The movement would undoubtedly triumph and the people of the world would soon be liberated.

That everyone on both sides – Russian sources and foreign reporters – knew this was all a load of crap didn't change anything. It was how the system worked. As journalist Max Frankel reported in the *New York Times*, 'Hypocrisy in Russia is bearable as long as all the participants know they are playing the game. It is when you are innocently taken in, or when you fight back, stupidly demanding "the truth" that you are contemptible and loathsome in Russian eyes. But once you've learned this game and it is still the truth you want, it is time to leave.'

It must be said that foreign correspondents were free to write anything they wanted to. But that didn't mean it reached their editors. Every dispatch was heavily censored and it was a crime bordering on espionage to attempt to get any story out of the country without first going through the censor. Obviously, this was before faxes and satellites. In those days, with the KGB monitoring every international phone call, you filed a story by telex and the only telex machines in Moscow were the official ones.

Knowing that Pushkin, Tolstoy and Dostoevsky had been tormented by censors was little compensation to the Moscow bureau chief trying to get his copy back to the West. An exasperating experience, it began at the *Glavlit* – the Department of Literary Supervision – in the cavernous Central Telegraph Office on Gorky Street, a few blocks from Red Square. Six cubbyholes there were reserved for foreign correspondents turning their stories in to be reviewed. A humorless woman wearing a smock would take your copy away, presumably handing it to some faceless bureaucrat with a blue pencil somewhere further inside the bowels of the building. At least that's what she was supposed to do. And there you'd wait. Eventually the copy came back, each page of it approved with a rubber stamp, or with words blacked out, or with entire sentences blacked out, or with whole pages blacked out. Sometimes it didn't come back at all.

Like so many things in the Soviet Union, the system defied logic. A story stopped one week by one censor could be passed in its entirety the next week by the very same censor. Some of the older, wiser correspondents relied on code words they hoped their editors would understand and long-winded sentences they hoped the censor wouldn't. But that didn't always work. One reporter in the 1950s who described a Soviet writer living in Paris as a 'francophile,' had the phrase struck out, the censor objecting that the person never was a supporter of Franco. Protests of any kind were either immediately ignored or, if you filed a written complaint, eventually ignored.

Curiously, the information coming out of the Soviet Union bore no relation in either quantity and quality to the information coming in. Only the Party line got out. How much of the news you saw from the rest of the world depended on how far up the Party ladder you were. The popular media limited the space available for foreign stories, and even then distorted them to suit Party purposes. But there were different channels of information and different levels of news. Just as Party officials were allowed to shop at different types of stores depending on their rank, the news they received was also related to rank. Harrison Salisbury learned during his tenure with the *New York Times* in Moscow that Tass defined news by color, usually referring to the paper it was printed on. There was the Green Tass or Blue Tass, which contained 'treated' stories which were dished out to the proletariat. There was White Tass, which went to government ministries, Party officials and trusted media bosses. And there was Red Tass, which was limited to the highest officials in the land. A train accident or a health epidemic that might not get reported to the public might wind up in White Tass. A provocative statement by the President of the United States that provided some insight into the personality of the Russian leader might be kept out of the White edition and appear only in the Red one. Even this 'limited eyes-only' Red version did not contain classified information. This wasn't about intelligence, it was about news. And Red Tass was, at best, what Western journalists would consider ordinary news.

But then nothing in the Soviet Union was ever ordinary.

For example, Russian leaders, up to the time of Mikhail Gorbachev, never had press secretaries. There was no Soviet press to deal with, and the foreign press was kept on tight reins by bureaucrats in the Foreign Ministry. Nor did Khrushchev ever hold a press conference in the USSR. That too was a Western custom.

Where Khrushchev shined was in the fact that he was generally comfortable with the Western press and was enough of a natural showman to use it to his own advantage.

Early on he developed a rather cunning technique that revolved around cocktail parties. It would be announced that he was going to attend a reception, usually at the invitation of a foreign embassy or trade delegation, and foreign correspondents would be freely admitted. Khrushchev would make himself accessible and say things such as, 'We will bury you.' It didn't matter that he often got a little drunk because he knew he was backed up by Glavlit, which would take out anything he shouldn't have said.

A Western reporter would come up to him, introduce himself, propose a toast to peace and then casually ask if there was a likelihood the USSR would one day abandon Communism. Khrushchev's answer, 'Those who wait for that must wait until a shrimp learns to whistle,' would end up being quoted on front pages around the world.

He quickly mastered the knack of the one-line 'sound bite.' When asked about the prospects of a war with the West, he answered, 'If you start throwing hedgehogs under me, I shall throw two porcupines under you.' When it was noticed at one reception that he'd been very cordial to the Secretary General of the United Nations, Dag Hammarskjöld, Khrushchev explained there was a tradition of the mountain people of the Caucasus. 'When the enemy is inside your home, sharing your bread and salt, you should always treat him with the greatest hospitality. But as soon as he steps outside the door, it is all right to slit his throat.' And when he was asked what the West should do when it came to negotiating an arms treaty, he advised, 'If you cannot catch a bird of paradise, better take a wet hen.'

He also possessed a natural sense of photo opportunities.

The US Secretary of the Interior, Stewart Udall, was in the Black Sea with Khrushchev when the Soviet Premier asked if he wanted to have his picture taken with him. Udall said yes. The two men began to pose and, while the photographer focused, Khrushchev mumbled, 'If it will help you out, you can go ahead and shake your finger in my face.'

It therefore didn't take him long after the launch of Sputnik to realize that there was a lot of mileage to be gained with it. So he set out to conquer the *New York Times*.

Some weeks before Sputnik, Khrushchev had been approached by James Reston of the *New York Times* for an exclusive interview. The Soviet leader granted the request, but in typical fashion insisted that Reston supply him with a list of subjects for discussion. Reston forwarded that to the Kremlin, putting some of the topics down in the form of questions. It was to be a detailed and concise interview revolving around disarmament. Then Sputnik happened. And Khrushchev has seldom been better.

He and Reston met on the Monday after Sputnik, in Khrushchev's office. The interview began with Khrushchev instructing his interpreter to read a series of written replies to Reston's subject list. Reston was, however, permitted to ask supplementary questions as replies to each topic were read. The two men talked, sitting at the table in front of Khrushchev's desk, for 3 hours and 20 minutes.

Two topics stand out from the text of that conversation.

The first revolved around increasing tensions in the Middle East. Turkish troops had been reinforced along the border with Syria and Khrushchev now bluntly accused the United States of trying to stir up a war in the area. He said Deputy Under Secretary of State Loy Henderson had specific instructions from Foster Dulles that, should he fail to obtain Arab cooperation, he should undertake efforts to get Turkey to launch an attack against Syria. 'The instructions Henderson was carrying out are known,' Khrushchev claimed. Reston tried to pin him down to a specific document which suggested such a thing and Khrushchev hinted that the Senate should demand to see Henderson's brief. 'Dulles,' he said, 'was a man who often appealed to God and he should be asked to swear that Henderson did not have such instructions.'

Khrushchev then warned, 'As regards the consequences to which the actions of Dulles and Henderson can lead I can say that it is very easy to start a war but far more difficult to stop it. If Turkey starts hostilities against Syria, this can lead to very grave consequences, and for Turkey too. This spark can set off a great war conflagration.'

He pointed out that the US was a long way away from this region, while the USSR bordered on it. 'If guns start firing there, it will be difficult to stop and events can progress from machine guns to cannons to rockets.'

The essence of his thoughts on the Middle East was that the US and the USSR had either to fight things out or to talk things out. Apparently Washington did not think the time was right for serious new conversations on disarmament, although he indicated that Sputnik might help produce a new approach.

When they spoke about Sputnik, Khrushchev directly linked the success of the satellite to the success of the ICBM that launched it. 'I think I will not be revealing any military secret if I tell you that we now have all the rockets we need.'

He said that, when the USSR announced the successful testing of an intercontinental missile, some American statesmen did not believe it. 'The Soviet Union, they claimed, was saying it had something it did not really have. Now that we have successfully launched an earth satellite, only technically ignorant people can doubt this. The United States does not have an intercontinental ballistic missile, otherwise it would have easily launched a satellite of its own. We can launch satellites because we have a carrier for them, namely the ballistic missile.'

Years later James Reston would wonder if Khrushchev had lied to him. 'I never knew whether or not Khrushchev was telling me the truth. But nobody who ever met Khrushchev forgot him. He was funny, good at making wisecracks, good at making analogies. He was always comparing the United States with a clodhopper and the Soviet Union as a racehorse who would pass it by. There was never any pause with Khrushchev. He was always quick and funny and gave you the impression that he was very natural and kind of honest about things.'

Towards the end of the interview, with the 40th anniversary of the October Revolution less than a month away, Reston asked Khrushchev what he foresaw for his country 40 years down the line. Khrushchev promised, 'The Soviet Union will, in a shorter period than 40 years, by virtue of the difference in the rate of development of our countries, leave the United States of America far behind in the rate of industrial and agricultural production per head of the population.' Then Khrushchev wanted to know how old Reston was. Reston told him, 48.

Khrushchev said that Reston might then expect to live long enough to see the time when a Communist society was built, 'And you will then regret that you have come to understand the advantages of socialism so late.'

In August 1991, 34 years after that interview, James Reston was 82. He'd made it. But Khrushchev's vision was decidedly second best.

Almost as soon as Khrushchev's interview with Reston ended, he summoned Sergei Korolev. The man from the *New York Times* had started him thinking. He firmly believed in the eventual victory of Communism and, as it turns out, he was the last Soviet leader to believe that. Now, the more he thought about Sputnik, the more the satellite reinforced his faith in that final victory. Sputnik confirmed his doctrine. And since Sputnik had created so much attention in the Western press, he wondered, why stop now?

He phoned the Chief Designer in Sochi and told him to come to Moscow immediately. The military arranged transportation and Korolev walked into the First Secretary's office on Tuesday morning. Khrushchev explained to him that the response to Sputnik had been very surprising, so much so that he wanted something like it to celebrate the anniversary of the Bolshevik Revolution in November. He asked Korolev point-blank, what can you do?

Korolev was astounded by the question. Obviously Khrushchev didn't understand how complicated these things were.

But Khrushchev was insistent. He needed Korolev to keep the momentum going.

Thinking fast, trying to invent something off the top of his head, Korolev blurted out, 'We could launch a dog.'

Khrushchev grinned. He liked that, but wanted some time to think about it. Two days later he rang Korolev and told him, all right, go ahead and do it.

In a panic, Korolev radioed Sochi and canceled everyone's holiday. Mishin complained that he was running a fever. Korolev said he didn't care, he wanted everyone back at Baikonour right away. One of the first Tupolev-134 jet transports was sent to pick them up. Korolev joined them there the next day. In the past they'd conducted at least ten experiments with dogs in rockets, but none of those came close to the complexity of this. He had three weeks to figure it out. Putting a living creature into orbit around the earth now became the highest-priority project in the USSR.

That same afternoon, Khrushchev met a delegation of British MPs and signaled to them, 'We have more up our sleeves.' He said, 'The Soviet Union is no longer a peasant country. It is dangerous to take this view. The age of the bombers is over. You might as well throw them on the fire. The ICBM shows that it is no longer feasible to send humanly controlled aircraft against missiles. You cannot send human flesh and blood to fight things like that.'

Later that evening, at a reception hosted by the East Germans to celebrate the seventh anniversary of their 'liberation,' Khrushchev was even more accessible than usual.

'Some people said our ICBM was only psychological warfare,' he told a group of foreign journalists, 'that we were only doing it to impress. Now they see we not only have a rocket which can fly to other continents but a satellite that flies around the world. Any fool can point to it with his finger. Well, if you want, that's real psychological effect.'

He then flung himself into his 'bombers are obsolete' routine. 'Fighter and bomber planes can now be put into museums. We don't want to brag, but we don't want to overlook our scientific superiority. Rockets are terrible, pitiless weapons. Those responsible for the fate of people should seriously think about these things. We are for peaceful competition. Our policy is clear. Our roads are clearly marked. We are sure of the victory of our system.'

Glavlit let it all through.

The next day *Pravda* claimed that Sputnik was sending coded signals that gave temperature data, among other things. They also predicted that the Soviets would launch other satellites in the very near future, this time with animals aboard.

Khrushchev was becoming Russia's first international media star.

If the Russians seemed obsessed with what the Americans thought, it was because America confused the Soviets. The Soviets remembered how they were received as allies by the Americans and how they feted the end of the war together. Now Red Army generals saw America fortifying NATO and shipping missiles to Europe to surround the Soviet Union. Baffled by such naked hostility, they answered the American build-up with a build-up of their own.

At least that's the way the Russians explain it.

Throughout the 1950s, the hostility shared by the Soviets and the Western allied powers was based on what the Central Intelligence Agency used to call 'the objective situation.' It meant that the United

States, Great Britain and sometimes France were the only real obstacles to Russia's global ambitions. At the same time, the Soviet Union deliberately impeded Western goals. But the Soviets' national imperatives were born out of Marxist–Leninist doctrine, which viewed the world as the arena for the struggle between socialism and capitalism. To win that struggle, the socialist forces had to weaken the imperialists to the point that the working classes could rise up and destroy them from within. And the best way to weaken the Western powers – especially the United States, being the main capitalist power and therefore seen as the main enemy – was to destroy their influence around the world. Sitting in his office, watching with some astonishment as the reaction to Sputnik gathered pace, Nikita Khrushchev began to think of ways to use Sputnik to help him attain that end.

In order to assess accurately the blow the Russians had dealt, the KGB were assigned the task of reporting on the damage. Their 85-page document, of which only ten copies were made, became the most complete picture available to the Soviet leader on the effects of the satellite.

'The launch of the artificial earth satellite,' the report observed, 'was accepted in all countries both by the general public and by scientists as being the greatest achievement of mankind.'

Based largely on press reports, they selectively quoted Western newspaper columnists, in large part telling Khrushchev what they thought he wanted to hear, especially underlining how the military and political aspects of the launch had superseded the scientific significance of it. 'The well-known political columnist Walter Lippmann questions the whole American economic system, in which products of wide consumption, created for worldly comfort, play a large role at the same time that other areas of life hold less significance. Scientists and teachers are not only badly provided for materially, in comparison with other sections of the population, but they do not have the social standing that is their right.'

They also found, 'Some analysts have approached the real reasons that the US lags behind the USSR. The root of evil, in their opinion, lies not in actions by individual ministers but in the social structure of the United States.'

Sputnik had, the summary pointed out, automatically raised the Soviet Union's political clout, establishing Russian superiority as a military power and proving that Communism would determine the future. The influence of such assertions on other countries, especially on those that could be categorized as neutral, could be very great. 'One paper has suggested that after the launch of the satellite the Soviet Union will hold a strong position and will not allow itself to be treated as a secondary power, and further will require any negotiations to be carried out on Soviet terms.' They then quoted a British source as saying, 'We are forced to admit that the Soviet Union has managed to overcome the West and to make its own system the most powerful and successful in the world.'

There were statements by Edward Teller, who saw Sputnik as proof that the Soviets were far ahead of the US and predicted, 'If the Russians do not already have an accurate system for guiding intercontinental ballistic missiles, then they will soon create one.'

And there was acclaim from several undisclosed military sources, including someone in the US Army who felt Sputnik had demonstrated that the Soviet Union was successfully fulfilling a wide program of work on long-distance rockets. 'The creation of the satellite is part of that program. It occupies a special place in Soviet military policy and plans for the conquering of the world. Similarly, it must strengthen the belief in the supremacy of Soviet power and fighting capacity.'

Another military source put Russia 'at least two years ahead' of the US in missile development.

The authors of the KGB report hoped that impressionable nations would look at the Soviet Union the way a small boy looks at his hero. 'The triumph is a heavy blow to America's prestige. The idea that a country which produces electronic machinery and cars on such a massive scale must now be satisfied with second place in the battle to conquer the Universe is, for many, unacceptable.' Quoting Britain's *Financial Times*, they stressed, 'All Americans recognize that America has sustained a military, political and psychological defeat.'

The launch of Sputnik, according to the KGB, deeply worried the American public because they'd been confronted with the reality that they could no longer speak of American superiority in every field, that their favorite epitaph, 'The best in the world,' was no longer true. Such pessimism had understandably spilled over to the British. 'Depression reigns in London,' a German source reported. 'There they are trying with all their might to get away from the news that Prometheus has arrived in Communist clothes.'

Quoting *Time* magazine, the report charged that political leaders in the

United States had seriously underestimated the capabilities of the USSR. Searching for excuses to rationalize their defeat, former President Harry Truman had announced, 'McCarthyism carries responsibility for the fact that some scientists were fired, while others were afraid of entering government service.'

They said Eisenhower had been 'reproached for diminishing the danger posed by highly developed Russian rocket technology,' that Congress was demanding an inquiry and that the Democrats were using 'the havoc caused by the situation' as a means to get at the Republicans. 'Practically all politicians and newspapers of the country have called for arms improvement and better organization of the work carried out. Much hostility has been expressed to Eisenhower in relation to this. He had apparently lowered arms expenditure and had allowed unsatisfactory organization of rocket technology.'

Science and technology were now determining world politics, they alleged, and nothing summed that up better than a telegram supposedly sent to the White House by a concerned citizen. It read simply, 'On 4th October political and diplomatic power moved from Washington to Moscow.'

There could be no lingering doubt in Nikita Khrushchev's mind that Korolev's dream had turned into a very rich reality. He saw much to be gained by playing this for all it was worth. And so, with his comments to James Reston reverberating throughout the West, he set out to do just that. He met with Henry Shapiro of United Press International and disclosed, 'We can launch more Sputniks, as many as necessary, for this does not require any new technique. The only thing we need is to replace the hydrogen charge by the necessary apparatus. Our ballistic missiles can function with a hydrogen charge too.'

He reiterated the theme with William Randolph Hearst Jr. 'In the creation of new types of weapons, we have outstripped your country. We now possess the absolute weapon, perfect in every respect and created in a short period of time.'

He told Bob Considine of Hearst Newspapers, 'If we want, we can launch 10 or 20 satellites. All that is required for this is to exchange the hydrogen warhead of an intercontinental ballistic missile with the necessary apparatus.'

He met with American journalists and European journalists and Third World journalists. He bragged, 'The Soviet Sputniks are not a miracle, not an isolated achievement. They are the result of the harmonious development of Soviet society as a whole.' He insisted, 'They show the world that our long-term plans are real.' He lied, 'We have hundreds of ICBMs ready to be launched, hundreds more Sputniks ready to go.'

With each interview, Khrushchev saw himself emerging into the world as an equal to Eisenhower and Macmillan.

His power base at home was strengthening too.

By the end of October he decided the time had come to test it.

He called for a meeting of the Presidium and announced the removal of Marshal Zhukov as Minister of Defense. Zhukov was also removed from the Presidium. The official reason for the firing was Zhukov's vanity where the military's political workers were concerned. He'd reportedly resented these civilian intrusions – the First Departments – and had taken it upon himself to order all political workers in the military to study military tactics alongside his officers. That move, and others like it, had never been approved by the Central Committee and produced enormous discontent within the Defense Ministry's Main Political Directorate.

It was, of course, a pretense. Khrushchev didn't fear any sort of military coup, he wanted to consolidate his own power.

Khrushchev and Zhukov had clashed before, in early 1957, when Khrushchev wanted to split the Ministry of Defense Production and the Ministry of Aviation Industry away from direct control by the Defense Ministry, and Zhukov objected. The military refused to give in and Khrushchev had to back down. Zhukov had also taken a hard line on nuclear weapons in the face of Malenkov's officially sanctioned warning that such weapons could bring about the end of civilization. By the autumn of 1957, Khrushchev was intending to introduce budget cuts to the army and obviously realized that Zhukov would try to fight them. Zhukov's immense popularity around the country and his gradual metamorphosis from military man to politician worried Khrushchev to the point where he now saw the World War II hero becoming a Russian Eisenhower. Getting rid of him was the only logical answer. Zhukov had served his usefulness in eliminating Beria and putting down the 'palace coup.' What Khrushchev wanted to do now was reorganize the Main Political Directorate and bring it directly under the control of the Central Committee. If that meant sacrificing Zhukov, he must have reasoned, then it was simply too bad for Zhukov. Such were the ways of individual loyalties in the Kremlin.

Before long, Khrushchev's other 'Godfather,' Ivan Serov, would be dismissed from his post as chief of the KGB. The official reason had to do with the Queen of Belgium's crown. It was stolen by the Nazis during World War II, and the Belgians had all but abandoned any hope of ever getting it back, when it suddenly turned up in the vast collection of war relics Serov had secretly put together while working as a senior official at Smersh, Russia's wartime counter-intelligence service. Khrushchev heard about it, ordered the crown returned to the Belgian monarchy and immediately fired Serov. But, instead of pensioning him off, the way he'd done with Zhukov, Khrushchev put Serov in charge of the GRU, the army's main intelligence organization. That not only checked Serov's power – he was now working for Khrushchev's wartime chum and Zhukov's replacement as new Defense Minister, Marshal Malinovsky – it gave Khrushchev the opportunity to reorganize the KGB, an important move in fortifying his own position.

Secure at home, Khrushchev turned his attention back to the huge poker game he was playing with Eisenhower and Dulles.

The Soviet leadership was of two minds when it came to John Foster Dulles.

They saw him, first and foremost, as their main ideological enemy in the West. They firmly believed that he was imposing his own foreign policy on Eisenhower. They never knew how far he would try to push them. Nor did they ever know for certain if he always had the full backing of the President.

Khrushchev was convinced that Eisenhower was totally under Dulles' influence. How else, he wondered, could anyone explain the so-called 'Eisenhower Doctrine' – a declaration of intent, designed to put the Soviet Union on notice that, in the aftermath of the Suez crisis, the United States would not allow the Russians to fill the vacuum left by the British and French. Ratified by Congress, thanks to aggressive lobbying by Foster Dulles, this gave the President permission to intervene with military force in order to defend any nation in the Middle East that requested American help against 'overt armed aggression from any nation controlled by International Communism.' Not only did the doctrine not win favor in the Middle East – leading to the crisis with Syria in the fall of 1957 and in the Lebanon the following year – it was proof positive, as far as Khrushchev was concerned, that Dulles was a dangerously tenacious man. He imagined Dulles tormented by 'a physical revulsion against the Soviet Union and an ideological

hatred for anything new, everything Communist, everything socialist.'
Eisenhower was, at this point, still treated with some deference by the
Russians. After all, he'd been, like Zhukov, a celebrated hero and ally
in the fight against the Nazis. Khrushchev wanted to like Eisenhower.
But there was no way he could say the same for John Foster Dulles.

On 29 October, the Turkish Ambassador in Moscow gave a party and,
of course, Khrushchev was invited. He arrived in a cheerful mood, got
drunk and declared magnanimously that there was no longer a threat to
peace along the Turkish–Syrian border. His remarks were soon being
wired to Washington, London and throughout the Middle East.

The crisis that never was, was no longer.

Within a few days the Turks reduced their forces stationed on that
border and the Syrians withdrew their complaint against Turkey in the
UN. Khrushchev walked away looking like the Arabs' savior for having
somehow, magically, averted an imperialist-provoked war.

The Democrats now called for Foster Dulles' resignation.

The more Nikita Khrushchev played this game, the more he liked it.

Chapter Eleven

American Panic

It was five days after Sputnik's launch before the President of the United States addressed the American people.

He arrived at the office earlier than usual on Wednesday morning to approve the final version of his statement. The Dulles brothers' drafts had helped him focus on the tone of what he wanted to say, but he'd ruled out flag waving. Nor would he include any reference to Peenemünde. He'd pruned his statement down to a summary of the facts in America's development of a satellite: that it had first been discussed in 1954, that it was always intended to be part of the IGY, that this was strictly a non-military effort, that it had been deliberately separated from the ballistic missile program, that it had been undertaken solely for the sake of science.

He was going to insist, 'Our satellite program has never been conducted as a race with other nations.'

He would congratulate the Soviets on their achievement and conclude, 'I consider our country's satellite program well designed and properly scheduled to achieve the scientific purpose for which it was initiated. We are, therefore, carrying the program forward in keeping with our arrangements with the international scientific community.'

That done, someone from Jim Hagerty's office rushed it away to be mimeographed.

Among the cuttings in the 'read file' that Hagerty prepared for the President every morning was an Associated Press story out of Madrid noting that two senior US Army officers were claiming America could have launched a satellite two years ago, had there not been any interference from the Navy. The two were named as Major General Holgar Toftoy, commander of the Redstone Arsenal, and Brigadier General John Barclay, Medaris' deputy at ABMA, both of whom were attending an international conference on astronautics in Spain. Toftoy was apparently very angry, because he held nothing back in his criticism of the administration. 'We said we could do it and by God we could. But shortly after our proposal we were told this was not a race. It was not simply a case of getting a satellite going. The idea was to get as much information as possible out of the satellite. So the Vanguard proposal was made and accepted. Quote me as saying that the wisdom of this course of action remains to be evaluated. It did not result in the first world satellite.'

At 9:30, Ike swore in Neil McElroy as the new Secretary of Defense and awarded Charles Wilson the Medal of Freedom, America's highest civilian honor. He conducted the ceremonies in the Cabinet Room, after which the press managed to get some questions to McElroy and the President. One journalist asked about the American response to Sputnik and the President preempted his own statement to say that the Russian success would not cause America to speed up its own missile program. When the same journalist posed the same question to McElroy, he answered that the national program to put a satellite into space would indeed be speeded up.

After coffee and cake, Eisenhower invited the entire Department of Defense contingent to a brief meeting. McElroy and Quarles, plus Secretaries Brucker (Army), Gates (Navy) and Douglas (Air Force), and the Joint Chiefs, Twining (Chairman), Taylor (Army), White (Air Force) and Pate (Navy), joined Hagerty, Goodpaster, presidential aide Robert Cutler and John Eisenhower in the Oval Office. As soon as the door was closed, the President lashed out that the decision to separate the military aspects of the US satellite program from the scientific aspects had been on purpose. Staring directly at McElroy, he said, 'When military people begin to talk about this matter and to assert that other missiles could have been used to launch a US satellite sooner, they tend to make the matter look like a race, which is exactly the wrong impression. I want to enlist the efforts of the whole group on behalf of, "No Comment," on this development.'

In other words, from here on out, he ordered, the entire DoD was to shut up.

Wilbur Brucker decided the President's instructions were aimed at Toftoy and Barclay, and when he got back to the Pentagon he issued a memorandum, a copy of which was dispatched immediately to Huntsville, prohibiting all Army personnel from any further comments on the Russian or American satellite programs.

The President then dismissed the Pentagon bunch and went through a final rehearsal for his press conference with his staff.

Eisenhower was very hands-on when it came to preparing what he'd say in public, having had a lot of speech-writing experience while working for Douglas MacArthur in the Philippines. One of the tricks he picked up from MacArthur was double-speak. More politely referred to in Eisenhower's case as 'amiable incomprehensibility,' it's based on the canon that you can indeed fool some of the people – and sometimes most of the people – at least some of the time. He'd dress up his remarks with his home-town folksy manner, mix in just enough authority, sound good and say nothing. It was a ploy he used over the years and, more often than not, he got away with it.

This morning, he wouldn't.

Hagerty left the meeting before it ended to see that everything in the press room was ready and to hand out copies of the President's two-page statement. Eisenhower continued fielding questions from the rest of his staff as they sat facing him with yellow note pads balanced on their knees, trying to second-guess the media. All the obvious questions were asked, so were a lot of off-beat ones, and all sorts of answers were discussed. When the President felt comfortable with an answer, he went over it several times. At one point, someone suggested he stress that American technology was not behind Russian technology. Eisenhower looked aghast. 'I don't have to tell them that. I said that six months ago.'

The Presidential News Conference, which would be aired in its entirety later in the day on the NBC network, was being filmed at 10:30. With two minutes to go, Eisenhower and the others left the White House and walked next door, to the Old Executive Office Building where Hagerty had already 'warmed up' the audience of 235 accredited reporters waiting in the Indian Treaty Room. After he'd reminded them of the usual ground rules, the President was announced, everyone stood up and Eisenhower took his place behind a pair of microphones. He said, 'Please sit down. Good morning, ladies and gentlemen. Do you have any questions you would like to ask me?'

Merriman Smith of United Press International, as the senior White House correspondent, led off with a simple one. 'Russia has launched an earth satellite. They also claim to have had a successful firing of an intercontinental ballistic missile, none of which this country has done. I ask you, sir, what are we going to do about it?'

Ike fed him a rehearsed answer. He spoke about the background of the US satellite program, about how the nation's interest in this field was strictly scientific and that America had never been in a race.

Next, the correspondent from the *Minneapolis Star and Tribune* threw a little curve, asking if he'd had any advance warning of the Russian launch. Ike admitted he'd been told that whoever launched first would have a great psychological advantage in world politics, but insisted, 'That didn't seem to be a reason, in view of the real scientific character of our development, there didn't seem to be a reason for just trying to grow hysterical about it.'

Someone from the Associated Press tried to pin him down on whether or not any of the other services could have launched by now. Ike sidestepped that one by explaining that the Navy was chosen 'because the scientists agreed upon it.'

Then came a question from NBC. 'Are you saying at this time that with the Russian satellite whirling about the world, you are not more concerned nor overly concerned about our nation's security?'

He took that one in his stride. 'I see nothing at this moment, at this stage of development, that is significant in that development as far as security is concerned.'

When someone wanted to know if the future of satellites included spying, he replied with the heaviest dose yet of amiable incomprehensibility. 'I think that period is a long ways off when you stop to consider that even now, and apparently they have, the Russians under a dictatorial society, where they had some of the finest scientists in the world, who have for many years been working on it, apparently from what they say they have put one small ball in the air. I don't, I wouldn't believe that at this moment you have to fear the intelligence aspects of this.'

For 32 minutes, alone under the television lights, he hit anything they could throw at him. But the best of his double-speak – rehashing those points the Dulles brothers had raised and which he'd originally ruled out – came in an answer to Robert Clark of the International News Service.

'Mr President,' Clark wanted to know, 'do you think our scientists made a mistake in not recognizing that we were, in effect, in a race with Russia in launching this satellite and not asking you for top priority and more money to speed up the program?'

'Well, no I don't because, as, even yet, let's remember this . . .' he switched gears, 'the value of that satellite around the earth, going around the earth, is still problematical, and you must remember the evolution that our people went through and the evolution that the others went through. From 1945, when the Russians captured all of the German scientists in Peenemünde, which was their great laboratory and experimental grounds for the production of the ballistic missiles they used in World War II, they have centered their attention on the ballistic missile. Originally our people were, seemed to be, more interested in the aerodynamic missile, and we have a history of going back for quite a ways in modest research in the Intercontinental Ballistic Missile, but until there were very great developments in the atomic bomb, it did not look profitable and economical to pursue that course very much, and our people did not go into it very earnestly until somewhere along about 1953, I think. Now, so far as the missile, this satellite itself is concerned, if we were doing it for science and not for security, which we were doing, I don't know of any reasons why the scientists should have come in and urged that we do this before anybody else could. Now, quite naturally you will say, "Well, the Soviets gained a great psychological advantage throughout the world," and I think in the political sense that this is possibly true. But in the scientific sense, it is not true, except for the proof of the one thing, that they have got the propellants and the projectors that will put these things in the air.'

Convinced he'd beaten the press at their own game, the President had a good lunch, then headed for Burning Tree. Hagerty, also pleased with the boss's performance, took the afternoon off and went to New York to attend the World Series.

But the American public didn't want double-speak this time.

They were scared.

And when the *Huntsville Times* rang the White House to ask why the President said what he'd said about the German scientists, and to wonder if he'd ever heard of Wernher von Braun, no one was available for comment.

The National Security Council met in the White House the next morning.

The agenda for the meeting had been set the week before. It was to be a fairly standard gathering, to consider such things as US policy on France and civil defense. The schedule was hastily revised Monday morning, the main item now being 'Implications of the Soviet Earth Satellite for US Security.'

Along with the redrafted schedule, Bobby Cutler sent a secret memo to Don Quarles, Allen Dulles and Christian Herter, who was sitting in for Foster Dulles. Obviously at Eisenhower's request, Quarles would outline the latest information on Sputnik, speak about the present status of the US satellite program and discuss the military implications for American security in reference to the Soviet missile program; Dulles would give an intelligence briefing on Sputnik; and Herter would summarize its foreign policy implications. But, Cutler warned, again, obviously at Eisenhower's request, 'In view of the amount of time the President has already spent on the matter, it is hoped that the presentations can be completed in 30 minutes.'

Prophetically, the day before, a Top Secret memorandum was sent from David Beckler, Special Assistant for Scientific Liaison in the President's Office of Defense Mobilization, to his boss, Victor Cooley who was acting head of that office. In it, Beckler put forth several observations he hoped would be brought to the President's attention.

Noting that sometime in the next 10–11 weeks the United States planned to launch a satellite of its own, Beckler was convinced that the launch vehicle was 'marginal' in performance and that the program was underfunded. 'Although there is a good chance of success, there is possibility of failure with its adverse political consequences.'

He said the weight of the Soviet satellite left no doubt that the Russians were using high-thrust multi-staged military rockets. 'Although the satellite is not military, it tends to be identified in the minds of the world with the impressive military and technological strength of the USSR . . . (And) the duration of the satellite in orbit is being cleverly exploited by a continuing stream of publicity from the USSR, so as to give an important time dimension to Soviet claims. This will inevitably be impressed in the minds of the world.'

Having seen the President's laid-back reaction to Sputnik and the spin the administration was putting on the event – playing down the threat to national security while still emphasizing the satellite's scientific merits – Beckler warned that such a strategy would lead to failure. 'This type of information makes sense in terms of overseas climate of opinion. But it is too complacent from the standpoint of national leadership and the American people, who must be made more acutely aware of the serious technological and military competition with which we are faced.'

The Russian satellite, he wrote, highlighted a growing realization that 'all is not well in the technological effort underlying the US military program.'

Among other things, he recommended that inter-service rivalries in rocket development be stopped in favor of a coordinated effort; that the country should adopt a national policy recognizing the continuing importance of space exploration; that a reconnaissance satellite program be developed immediately, 'As a possible psychological as well as physical breakthrough of the Iron Curtain and a means of regaining the prestige lost with the Soviet satellite success'; and that the intermediate range ballistic missile (IRBM) program be given the highest priority, 'To include production and the prompt securing of overseas base arrangements and transfer to selected allies.'

Beckler did not attend NSC meetings and wasn't invited to this one. Cooley was. But Cooley didn't speak at the meeting and Beckler's letter was relegated to an office filing cabinet.

In addition to the usual NSC members – Eisenhower, Nixon, Herter, McElroy, Allen Dulles and selected White House staff – attendance was specially requested of Admiral Lewis Strauss, who was Chairman of the Atomic Energy Commission, Alan Waterman from the National Science Foundation, Detlev Bronk from the National Academy of Sciences and John Hagen, director of Project Vanguard.

The meeting began at 9 o'clock with Allen Dulles' intelligence briefing. Worried about the military implications of a space-nuclear weapon, Dulles maintained that the Soviets had managed it only by combining their ICBM and earth satellite programs. He did not know if the satellite was sending out coded messages and warned that additional launches could be expected during the IGY. He said the Soviets themselves had already announced 6–13 more satellites in the pipeline.

He pointed out that Khrushchev had moved all his propaganda guns into place, as the earth satellite was obviously one of a trilogy of propaganda moves, the other two being the successful ICBM launch in August and this week's atomic bomb test at Novaya Zemlya. However, larded in with Khrushchev's propaganda statements had been a number of remarks Dulles found particularly interesting, such as the one in which Khrushchev confined bombers to museums in the future. Dulles noted, without making any direct reference to the U-2, that US intelligence had not observed as many heavy bombers on Soviet airfields as had been expected. This posed the question, which remained to be answered, were the Soviets de-emphasizing their heavy bomber program? He said he had no doubt the Soviet propaganda effort over the past few days – boasting of the scientific accomplishments which prove the effectiveness of the Communist social system – was aimed mainly at the Middle East in a continuing effort to exercise maximum influence. The Chinese Communists were seconding the Soviet claim, insisting that Sputnik proved Soviet military and scientific supremacy over the United States. 'Such propaganda is making a very wide and deep impact.'

Don Quarles was next. He began by apologizing because much of what he was going to say would be familiar to the President.

Eisenhower cut in, 'I'm beginning to feel somewhat numb on the subject of earth satellites.'

Quarles said there was strong evidence that the main objective of the Russian program was simply to have been first to launch. He recognized Soviet competence in long-range rocketry and then suggested they'd inadvertently been helpful in establishing the principle of the freedom of outer space. 'Their earth satellite has overflown practically every nation on earth and there have thus far been no protests.'

He concluded, the most important implication of this satellite was that it signaled the next step, which would be the development of reconnaissance satellites.

Then it was the turn of the scientists.

Dr Hagen gave a status report on the US program, announcing that one earth satellite had now been completed and that three others were in various stages of completion. Dr Waterman said America could take heart in knowing that solving the problems of launching a satellite required a typical marriage of science and engineering and that the strength of US technology had always depended on that marriage. Dr Bronk warned that America must not put the nation's scientific community into a race against the Russians. 'We must adhere strictly to our stated earth satellite program and not be deflected from our course merely by the fact that the Russians had been the first to launch an earth satellite.'

That was precisely the kind of thing the President wanted to hear.

Now, looking around the table, he cautioned that a number of them could expect to be called to testify before Congress, or make additional statements to the press about all of this. 'I can imagine nothing more important than that anybody so involved should stand firmly by the existing earth satellite program which is, after all, adopted by the

Council after due deliberation as a reasonable program. In short, we should answer inquiries by stating that we have a plan, a good plan, and that we are going to stick to it.'

No one will ever know if Eisenhower would have remained so unruffled about this and spoken the same way, had he seen Beckler's memo.

Herter then got up to admit that there were already some indications of the serious effects of the Soviet success, and warned that there would probably be repercussions in the United Nations. 'The United States may now encounter much greater difficulty in defending our disarmament position.'

By and large, he said, America's allies were standing firm, 'Though even the best of them require assurance that we have not been surpassed scientifically and militarily by the USSR. The neutralist countries are chiefly engaged in patting themselves on the back and insisting that the Soviet feat proves the value and wisdom of the neutralism which these countries have adopted.'

Then, candidly acknowledging that foreign reactions so far were 'Pretty somber,' Herter affirmed that the United States, 'Will have to do a great deal to counteract them and, particularly, to confirm the existence of our own real military and scientific strength.'

Arthur Larson, director of the United States Information Agency (USIA), the government's main propaganda arm, now told the group, 'If we lose repeatedly to the Russians as we have lost with the earth satellite, the accumulated damage would be tremendous.' He wanted America to set out intentionally to beat the Russians with the next great breakthroughs, for example a manned satellite or a landing on the moon. 'If we don't already have such plans, we should begin to think about them.'

The President granted that he could hardly quarrel with Larson's conclusions, yet the fact remained that the US couldn't possibly set up a whole vast scientific program of basic research simply to beat the Russians.

He said, 'Only yesterday I was again asked how much of the delay in our earth satellite program derives from inter-service rivalry. I have always denied the validity of such assertions, but the question shows the widespread belief in our country that we are competing among ourselves rather than with the Russians.'

Nixon now spoke up, referring to numerous press reports about inter-service rivalry and a lack of adequate support for the American satellite and missile programs.

The Vice President admonished, 'We will be in for a very rough time when Congress begins investigating these rumors and reports. The Congressional investigators will light on every shred of evidence indicating undue delay or rivalry among them services. If they think that they have proved the existence of these obstacles, they will force on us a single-missile program whether we like it or not.'

He said that the ICBM had been built up as 'the great ultimate weapon.' The Russians felt they had to have ICBMs to frighten the Americans. But it is the IRBM, he claimed, 'that is much more dangerous to the Russians than the ICBM is to us. Accordingly, the IRBM is of extreme importance in the propaganda of the Cold War.'

The discussion ended with the Chairman of the Joint Chiefs of Staff, Air Force General Nathan Twining, cautioning the Council, 'We should not permit ourselves to become hysterical about the Soviet achievement.'

The President said that's exactly the way he felt, then ended the meeting. Deep down he was hoping he'd finally heard the last of the discussions about the Russian satellite.

It wasn't to be.

That afternoon, General Jerry Persons came into the Oval Office to see the President alone. He said he was worried about the US missile program because there was more than just inter-service rivalry going on. It had gotten to the point where there was fierce rivalry between civilian scientists and the military, and even worse, between American scientists and German scientists.

Eisenhower nodded, 'I know.'

He told Persons how, when he was first elected, he'd wanted to integrate all guided missile research into one service but had been talked out of the idea. The argument against it was that it would have pushed work back by more than a year while the reorganization was taking place. Now there was growing support for a sort of Manhattan Project, the all-out effort that had given America the atomic bomb. It was coming from outside the services and it was something they might have to consider.

At the Pentagon they didn't necessarily see things the President's way. They'd already issued the statement, as the President had ordered, saying that the US satellite program was proceeding according to plan. But, within hours of the NSC meeting, Twining was growing increasingly apprehensive about the effects of the Russian satellite. He'd asked his Chief of Research and Development, William Holaday, to look into the military implications of the satellite and, on Wednesday afternoon, a one-page secret report from the Director of Special Weapons was handed to him.

It consisted of four terse paragraphs.

(1) – The successful launching of a relatively heavy Soviet satellite appears to confirm Soviet ICBM claims. More important to most of our military allies is the apparent confirmation of Soviet inter- mediate and shorter range ballistic missile claims. The above are direct, short term, military implications. In addition, the heavy weight of the Soviet satellite implies an early Soviet capability for satellite reconnaissance of the US.

(2) – With respect to our military position overseas, apparent Soviet possession of ballistic missiles capable of attacking the homelands of our major allies will probably result in an increasing reluctance of those allies to be associated militarily with the United States. From our own viewpoint, Soviet possession of such missiles decreases the value of our overseas air bases and underlines the diminishing value of fighter-interceptors. To restore our military position we need an early US capability to offset the Soviet ballistic missile threat. This increases the importance of early deployment of intermediate range ballistic missiles to positions on the periphery of the USSR in addition to missiles now planned for UK deployment.

(3) – With respect to the security of the Continental US, apparent Soviet ICBM success increases the importance of providing protection for critical areas of the Continental US against ballistic missiles. This heightens the urgency of providing an active anti-ICBM defense.

(4) – In summary, the Soviet satellite success indicates a clear possibility that the USSR leads the US in the development of long range ballistic missiles. The Soviet success increases the importance of early overseas deployment of a US intermediate range ballistic missile and the early completion of development of an ICBM and of an active anti-ICBM system. With respect to an earth satellite, we should see a quick, interim solution to counter Soviet claims, reserving our main effort for the development of an advanced satellite of significant military value.

McElroy and Holaday brought that report to the President the next morning. They saw him for half an hour in the Oval Office before the cabinet met at 9.

It was not mentioned again.

Nor was Sputnik mentioned at the President's cabinet meeting on 11 October. Eisenhower put his foot down. He was going to get on with all the other things that required his attention.

But then came word from Allen Dulles that the Soviets might launch a second satellite any day now. Eisenhower told Goodpaster, we should make a statement saying that we were not surprised by the first satellite and that we anticipate the Soviets will launch another satellite sometime in the next few days. Goodpaster related that to Allen Dulles who added, 'If they send one up, Hagerty can say this is not unusual or unexpected, that when we start ours, we plan on sending several up.' Goodpaster then checked with Christian Herter, who thought it was a good idea because, 'It will soften the effect of it and can be done without any intelligence breach.'

That night Christian Herter sent a telegram to all chiefs of US missions around the world. In view of the propaganda the Russians were getting with Sputnik, the State Department wanted to make some points very clear. First, he stressed, 'Soviet satellite is of military importance only in sense that achievement of science in long run contributes to military technology.'

After presenting a brief history of the way the Russians had exploited the German efforts at Peenemünde, he made a truly startling claim. 'In vital air/atomic area, we believe that Soviet Union now is, and for some time will continue to be, in a position of relative inferiority.'

He justified it by indicating that Khrushchev's remark about putting bombers in museums was a way of covering up Russia's weak long-range bomber position. 'By attempting to jump long-range bomber stage he would avoid bearing at same time expense of a large bomber and missile development. It is unlikely however that he will have for some time an atomic delivery capability in the very long-range missiles which would be an adequate counterpart for the large number of bombers capable of reaching the Soviet Union now in possession of United States.'

Having ventured so far out on such a weak limb, he immediately back-tracked. 'Even if Soviet claims about long-range missiles are fully substantiated, we believe that the time difference between their capability in this area and our own will be minor and that at least in the meantime we will have a distinct superiority with our long-range bomber force.'

He then ordered all of America's foreign service officers not to allow anyone to feel that the US was in a position of relative weakness. 'It is quite the contrary.'

A PS was added for European and Middle East posts only. 'In respect of European and Middle East apprehensions regarding Soviet attack by intermediate range ballistic missiles, this would not occur without immediate overall reaction by United States. Such an attack would be completely unproductive unless US striking power was destroyed simultaneously.'

For an administration claiming to be fully confident, there didn't seem to be a lot of confidence.

Over the weekend Eisenhower managed to get in a round of golf.

But the wire services were still flooding the papers with Sputnik stories. Dr I. M. Levitt of the Fels Planetarium at the Franklin Institute in Philadelphia, who the weekend before had predicted, 'The satellite can remain in the sky a thousand or a million years and there is nothing man can do to bring it down,' now avowed, 'The Pentagon's failure to launch its big Jupiter-C missile as a satellite last year was an astonishing piece of stupidity.' An editorial in Canada asserted, 'If modern military aircraft can bomb with frightening accuracy at supersonic speeds from unbelievable heights, it is not too extravagant a stretch of mental elastic to assume it can be done in time from a height as great as the Russians claim for their artificial moon.' And Evangelist Billy Graham said at a convention in Miami that the 'beep-beep' of the Russian satellite was signaling a national crisis, and that an unnamed 'high Washington official' told him Americans would 'panic' if they knew the truth about the crisis.

On Monday morning, Ike's 67th birthday, Neil McElroy came in to see him. They talked about anti-ICBM defenses, which McElroy said were still in the study stage. Then he showed Eisenhower Wilbur Brucker's memo to Charles Wilson asking permission for the Army to back up Vanguard. Eisenhower said if they could do it at a reasonable cost, they should go ahead. McElroy wrote Brucker that afternoon, 'Vanguard will proceed along current lines but I am willing to look at an Army proposal if it includes time and cost estimates.'

With Congress calling for increased funding for the military, Eisenhower sent a memo to Foster Dulles, sounding slightly exasperated. 'There's a limit to the amount of defense money can buy.'

By Tuesday, it was as if the administration had instructed everyone to water down the fire. The Pentagon confirmed that the Air Force had successfully fired a Thor missile, that the Army had successfully tested its Jupiter and that the Navy had successfully tested its Vanguard. Eisenhower had no choice but to announce that America's missile programs would be speeded up, although there would be no extra funds made available. McElroy now said that, in order to put the missile programs in overdrive, he would personally take control of them.

Foster Dulles had bumped into Richard Nixon a few days after Sputnik and related the story of how, when he was in Moscow in 1947, he'd witnessed the Soviets giving German scientists the VIP treatment. He also said that General Twining had confirmed to him that absolutely nothing was done about missiles by the United States until 1953. America, according to Dulles, had therefore handed the Russians an enormous advantage.

Ever ambitious, one of the qualities which made Nixon unusual was his knack for objectively judging situations and political prospects that concerned him. That sense might have failed him as President, but in the second term of his Vice-Presidency, when he was unmistakably Eisenhower's heir apparent, it was as well honed as any politician's in America's history. He saw Eisenhower's mistaken judgement when it came to Sputnik and instantly translated it into a plan of action that would benefit Dick Nixon. He understood how Sputnik had shaken the public's faith in Eisenhower's leadership of foreign affairs and national defense, and concluded the most effective measure would be if America could pull off some superior space achievement. Now, when Nixon saw Dulles he said he was apprehensive about the way Congress was reacting to Sputnik and missiles, and believed the thing to do would be to pool the country's best brains. Dulles thought it was a good idea, something America would automatically do in the case of a war.

Nixon confided in the Secretary of State, 'I have the data as to the order of magnitude for the missile business. I'll send it over. Between 1946–1952, the spending was for aerodynamics rather than rockets. The economy and inter-service rivalry delayed this business. The satellite program was treated as a fifth cousin because the military were not too keen about it, nor was there any keenness among some people in the executive. We can tear them to pieces. The data is classified and Defense is reluctant to give it, but I have it. While the Soviets were making a big push, we were doing nothing.'

With that in mind, Dulles tried to press Eisenhower to make a major speech on disarmament. But Eisenhower was reluctant. His gut feeling was that the timing for it was wrong, that it had become somewhat 'outdated by events.'

That same day, Arthur Larson at the USIA reported that Sputnik had caused a greater psychological impact overseas than any other Soviet Cold War action. 'Public preoccupation with the subject is virtually universal. It appears likely that the effect in unsophisticated countries will be to increase an impression of Soviet technical and military superiority over the United States; even in more sophisticated areas, such as Europe, the impression may be that the USSR is at least equal.'

He proposed that America demonstrate its 'clean bomb,' a fusion explosive with reduced fallout, 'since even a falloutless H-bomb is a horrible thing to contemplate.' He wanted the Atomic Energy Commission to blow up part of Alaska. His plan was to find a reasonably remote place, and demonstrate the peaceful uses of such a weapon by creating a man-made harbor for the amusement of invited journalists.

At 11 o'clock that Tuesday, Eisenhower met with the Science Advisory Committee, which operated under the Office of Defense Mobilization. He asked, point blank, if they thought American science had been outdistanced by the Soviets. Dr Isidor Rabi, the Nobel Prize winning physicist who chaired the Committee, believed it was only fair to recognize that the Soviet Union had gained impressive momentum by launching the satellite and that, unless the United States took action, the Soviets would pass America, just as America had passed Europe. Edwin Land felt that the science needs of the two countries were different but that American science needed help from the Oval Office. Dr James Killian, President of MIT, was of the impression that American science was missing a sense of urgency and mission. Then Rabi suggested that the President appoint a full-time science adviser. Naturally, all the scientists in the room were in absolute agreement. Eisenhower said he would have to think about it.

The next day Eisenhower named Larson Special Assistant to the President for International Affairs, with special emphasis on Soviet propaganda efforts.

Nixon took a first tiny step in distancing himself from the Eisenhower administration by saying publicly, 'We could make no greater mistake than to brush off this event as a scientific stunt – the Soviet Union has developed a scientific and industrial capacity of great magnitude.'

Foster Dulles got ready for his upcoming press conference by phoning his brother to explain, 'If they ask about Sputnik I'll say it has no military significance but was significant of the intensity of the Soviet effort.' Allen firmly warned him, 'Don't say it has no military significance.'

And Drew Pearson's column highlighted the forthcoming visit to Washington of the Queen of England. He said it had originally been planned to give a lift to sagging Anglo-American friendship and British prestige in the United States. 'Now, thanks to Sputnik and Russia's ICBM, it looks as if it's American prestige that needs bolstering. Prime Minister Harold Macmillan is so worried, not only about American prestige but Allied prestige, that he has offered to fly to the United States immediately to confer with President Eisenhower regarding Russian scientific progress. He considers the Russian advance so serious that he has sent word he's ready to fly to Washington any time Ike says the word.'

What Pearson didn't know was that Ike had already said the word.

Foster Dulles met the press as planned on Wednesday, 16 October, and pretty much stuck to the script he'd drafted for the President. He waved the flag, credited the Germans at Peenemünde for giving the advantage to the Russians, threw in a little Kremlin-bashing and insisted that America was markedly superior to the Soviets in military strength. He stressed America's decided advantage in heavy bombers, 'which are now, and for some years to come will be, the preferred and most effective means for the delivery of missiles.'

It doesn't make a lot of sense today, but he got away with it then.

The President greeted the Queen and Prince Philip in the rain at the end of Thursday morning, then spent the afternoon in the office. The USIA's preliminary evaluation, 'World Opinion and the Soviet Satellite,' showed up on his desk. It reinforced what he'd been hearing for the past week: that Sputnik had given the Russians the opportunity to claim they'd overtaken the United States in a vital field where America was accustomed to counting on its superiority; that the USSR had a clear advantage in the Cold War; that Sputnik had helped to sharply increase Soviet credibility.

★　　★　　★

Sputnik reared its head in front of the cabinet for the first time, despite the President's personal desire to get on with the business of running the country, a full two weeks after the launch was announced.

Eisenhower's cabinet meetings always began on time and rarely lasted more than an hour. All the cabinet officers were assigned a place around the dark wood table in the Cabinet Room, near the Oval Office. The Secretary of State sat on the President's right. The Secretary of Defense sat on the President's left. The Vice President sat directly across the table from the President, with the Secretary of the Treasury on his right and the Attorney General on his left. The White House Chief of Staff sat at the north end of the table.

These weren't formal affairs. Ike would walk in unannounced, everyone would stand, he'd take his place at the center of the table with his back to the windows overlooking the lawn, and there would be a moment of silent prayer. The agenda was prepared by Sherman Adams as Chief of Staff – presentations for the President first, followed by discussions. Members of the staff who did not enjoy cabinet rank sat on chairs against the wall and anyone was welcome to contribute. People would raise their hands and the President would call on them, using their last name – a throwback to 40 years in the Army. Although the meetings could never be described as light-hearted, there were occasional jokes. But Eisenhower was overtly aware of the responsibilities he carried and it showed in a generally serious tone.

For the most part, the meetings were a forum for reporting things to the President. Decisions were taken in the Oval Office.

That morning was no exception. Reports on Sputnik again monopolized the President's time.

Ten years later, Neil McElroy thought back to those late-October cabinet meetings and recalled how some of the men around the table were beginning to worry that the country might find itself so far out of position that it could be seriously exposed to destruction without the ability to retaliate. The theory behind America's defenses was still massive retaliation. But Sputnik proved the existence of a Russian ICBM and the thing about the ICBM was that America had no defense against it. Although no one liked the idea of the Russians possessing a long-range bomber fleet, at least America had the ability to deal with that. The distant early-warning network of radar stations, stretching from the Aleutian Islands, across northern Canada and into the Atlantic towards the Azores, would provide sufficient notice of an

236

attack coming in. But it wouldn't help where missiles were concerned. They could reach North America in under 30 minutes. And no one would see them coming. What was needed, the cabinet began to sense, was an effective anti-ICBM program.

At the cabinet meeting on 18 October, Don Quarles argued that the success of Sputnik did not provide a basis for judging the relative status of Russian versus US military efforts and that, while Russian competence must not be belittled, there was insufficient justification for regarding the Russians ahead of America. Secretary of Commerce Sinclair Weeks questioned Quarles on that point and forced him to admit that a satellite the size of Sputnik could be launched only by military rockets and not by something like America's Vanguard and that considerable time would be necessary to adapt US military rockets to that purpose. The President did not comment.

Drew Pearson's column that Sunday promised that Sputnik was only the first step in the Soviet space program, which aimed at putting the Red Star on the moon, then the planet Venus, and then seizing control of outer space. He even predicted that the Russians could try to send a rocket to the moon on 7 November, the anniversary of the Bolshevik Revolution. 'The Russians might fill the nose cone with red dye and literally splatter a Red Star on the face of the moon.'

He described how US intelligence experts were telling him that the Russians had already built several dozen satellites and that the Soviet timetable eventually called for strapping a dog into one of them. 'It is known that the Soviet Commission on Interplanetary Travel has top priority plus all the money, men and materials it needs. Yet our Defense Department has done its best to block expenditures for space research.'

Then, recalling that Charles Wilson had once snapped, 'The Air Force has no business flying to the moon,' he revealed that the US Air Force had been working on a rocket at a hidden location in the Pacific, had tried to launch four of them with balloons and had failed. 'Reported reason for the failure is that the Defense Department is now pressuring the Air Force so hard to do something spectacular to counter the Soviet Sputnik that the four rockets were fired prematurely.'

Lastly, he broke the news that the Defense Department had issued orders on 9 October telling their officers 'not to speak about space ships.' The military, he said, denied it but he had it on the highest authority.

On Monday, *Aviation Week* magazine, published by McGraw Hill, came out with the two-page story, 'How US Taps Soviet Missile Secrets.' It was filled with highly classified information. Following on the heels as it did by one week of a story, 'USAF Pushes Pied Piper Space Vehicle,' which disclosed that the Air Force had a top secret reconnaissance satellite program in the works, Ike went up the wall.

It constituted such a serious breach of security that he dispatched General Goodpaster to New York to speak personally and behind closed doors with Don McGraw, president of the company. Goodpaster told McGraw he could not discuss specific details, but was permitted to say that the article contained 'some things that were true, some things that were untrue and some things that were in between.' The problem was, those things which were true had never been published before and were not intended to be published. McGraw defended his right to publish and said he'd been informed that the material in the article was known outside defense circles and to the Russians. Goodpaster conveyed to him the President's grave concern that the article intimated further disclosures would be made. McGraw said, please tell the President that, henceforth, any article in *Aviation Week* with a clear national security aspect will be handled with special care. The decision to publish would not be made by the managing editor alone but in consultation with another senior person.

Both of them knew there was nothing the President could do or should dare try to do about such matters. Not only would it create publicity, which in turn would underline in red the secrets he was trying to protect, but the First Amendment to the Constitution is quite direct in prohibiting the government from attempting to restrain the press in any way. It would have been both foolish and illegal. By the same token, responsible news organizations are usually quite strict when it comes to self-censorship of matters pertaining to national security. Goodpaster's accomplished handling of the affair avoided what could easily have become a highly embarrassing situation for the government. At least some of America's secrets would stay out of the aviation press, at least for a while.

After a busy morning on 22 October, making final preparations for Harold Macmillan's visit, the President flew to New York where he spent some time with his friend Bernard Baruch. They talked about the current economic situation, atomic agreements, missiles and Sputnik. Referring to America's satellite program, the White House notes of that meeting say, 'Mr McElroy must drive the program hard, like Jeffers "bulled" the rubber program in WW II. Demonstrating not only that everything possible is being done but that the "impossible" will be done if necessary.'

It was the first real sign that the President was beginning to understand.

Secretary of the Navy Thomas Gates had not been especially pleased with the Pentagon press release of 9 October. It was all well and good for the President to try to keep the nation calm by insisting the American satellite program would continue on schedule, but the schedule as announced by the President – which committed the Navy to launching in December and again in March – wasn't reasonable. He wrote to Neil McElroy on the 22nd, 'There is in fact only a probability, not a certainty, that satellites will be achieved on these first attempts.' He made it perfectly clear that, while the Navy would try its best to meet those dates, 'All experience with experimental rocket programs shows that no one can have confidence that the dates of planned firing attempts will always hold firm.'

McElroy took that letter to Eisenhower, who said flatly that he expected the Department of Defense to meet these commitments. So McElroy wrote to Gates, 'At the time the US satellite program responsibility was assigned to the Navy, the atmosphere of a completely scientific effort in the framework of the International Geo-physical Year prevailed. The Soviets' success with their satellite has changed the situation. We now have the added burden of not only launching a successful satellite but doing it as per our current schedule. The psychological factors in this matter have obviously received a new emphasis. If necessary, a back-up program to insure success will be initiated. We must, therefore, go forward with deliberate speed in this program and meet the dates if at all possible.'

Wilbur Brucker received McElroy's memo of the 14th and immediately got in touch with Medaris and von Braun, asking them to submit cost and time estimates. When the figures came up from Huntsville, Brucker wrote McElroy that, according to ABMA's best estimates, by using a Redstone/ Jupiter rocket as the first stage plus a Jupiter-C three-stage cluster, they could put a small sphere in orbit by June. However, if they could use a small cylindrical satellite, which would still support the scientific experiments called for in the Vanguard program, they could put that up by February.

On Thursday, 24 October, Eisenhower interrupted his meetings with Macmillan to breakfast with James Killian. The President had finally come to a decision about a Science Adviser and he wanted Killian to fill the post.

Ike met on Friday with Gordon Gray, who was then the director of the Office of Defense Mobilization. The only other person present was Andrew Goodpaster. Gray reported on the series of meetings he'd just attended at NATO, characterizing them as having a sense of urgency and purpose not felt before. He attributed this to Sputnik, which was 'having effects far beyond its real significance.'

Army Chief of Staff General Maxwell Taylor was quoted in the *New York Times* on Sunday that Sputnik had signaled the end to America's nuclear superiority. And around the White House it seemed as if everybody was suddenly jumping onto the Sputnik bandwagon. Groups as influential as the National Science Foundation, the National Association of Teachers, the New York State Board of Regents, the United Automobile Workers, the AFL-CIO, the National Association of Manufacturers, the American Institute of Physics, Harvard University and the US Chamber of Commerce were all condemning the administration's 'complacency.' They wanted vast changes in the way science was taught in school, increased funding for higher education, more money for defense. They wanted a national effort aimed at 'preventing the United States from being outdistanced by the Soviet Union in any category of scientific or economic achievement.'

There was no let-up the next week either.

The President swore in Arthur Larson as his Special Assistant, started putting together a set of speeches he wanted to give to reassure the nation that everything was under control, spoke for a while with Foster Dulles, then complained that he wasn't feeling well. He knocked off for the rest of the day.

The National Commander of the American Legion was in the next day, Tuesday, 29 October, to urge the President to restore budget cuts in the guided missile program, 'in view of the Russian launching of the satellite.' Eisenhower's answer was to tell him about the amazed reaction of the Queen and Prince Philip to the 'hysteria in this country generated by a satellite which was a scientific development that imposed no immediate threat to the world.'

Goodpaster then came in with Gray, Dr Rabi, Admiral Strauss and Bobby Cutler, to speak about developing an anti-ICBM system. They agreed it was now necessary to counter Soviet missile supremacy and to protect the Strategic Air Command, even though they were willing to concede that the Soviets did not yet have an effective ICBM system in place.

At the Pentagon, where McElroy had passed Brucker's latest memo to one of his special assistants for further study, the answer came back that the Army program not only was feasible, but should be recommended to the President. So on Wednesday morning, McElroy was the President's first appointment. He repeated the importance of allowing the Army to back up Vanguard and showed Eisenhower the costings. McElroy said he felt this would be the best way 'to make sure we fire a satellite at an early date.' Eisenhower nodded, all right, the Army can do it. But then he snapped, 'When I myself suggested that, as much as 18 months ago, the Defense Department disagreed.' They also talked about the anti-ICBM system. McElroy wondered if it shouldn't be taken out of the services to avoid the kind of rivalry that had impeded the satellite program, and again the President agreed.

He got to hit some golf balls that afternoon and met with the NSC on Thursday. Later he spoke to General Twining about the missile program. He talked to Foster Dulles about how the Democrats in Congress were making points on this Sputnik thing, about the speeches he planned to give to reassure the country that the Russian satellite did not present a threat to the nation's security, about how the Army Jupiter would be ready to back up Vanguard and about how he would announce a federal budget cut but leave military expenditures alone. That he hoped should finally calm things down a bit.

He was wrong.

Each day that the Soviets had a satellite in orbit, and the United States did not, Russian prestige increased in the eyes of the world. The newspapers had pretty much summed up the public mood when they claimed, 'The Soviet first in earth satellites stands as a deserved rebuke to the assumption of superiority that prompted American scientists to give the name of Vanguard to their planned moon, which now in deference to historic accuracy, must be redubbed, "Rearguard."'

If the Russians could out-do America in satellites, even if satellites weren't weapons, then their technology was advanced enough to out-do America in weapons too. It was easy to confuse technical prowess with a military threat, especially where space was concerned. What would happen if the Russians claimed the moon? It was the high ground. Whoever controlled the moon controlled the earth.

The public wanted action and they weren't getting it.

On Friday, 1 November, a beleaguered Eisenhower announced that he would address the nation no fewer than six times over the coming months, 'to stimulate faith and confidence' in America's defenses.

Two nights later, the Russians launched Sputnik II.

Two weeks after that, Eisenhower suffered a stroke.

Chapter Twelve

The Sweetening of Great Britain

Britain entered the 20th century as the greatest power on earth, the greatest Empire the world had ever seen.

Fifty years later the Empire was broke.

The Industrial Revolution had turned parts of the largely agrarian island into smog-filled slums of dark-brick terraced houses. Class didn't simply reign, it dominated. The landed gentry had their clubs and cotillions. The working classes were left to smelly, uncomfortable pubs. And when it came time for those who didn't drop their 'h's to keep those who did in the munitions factories, they voted to shut those pubs – but only those pubs – and left their own clubs open.

The future drowned in a them-and-us struggle that became unwinnable for either side and unmanageable for both.

World War I mobilized the national spirit but, when the war to end all wars ended, the British share of victory cost a staggering three-quarters of a million lives and $35.3 billion. Only the Germans paid a bigger bill.

The Great Depression followed.

So did the build-up to the next war.

For a few weeks, during the late summer and early autumn of 1940, a bunch of kids in Spitfires and Hurricanes showed their true grit in the skies above the Realm, and that may well be forever remembered as Britain's finest hour. But five years later another half million were dead and now the nation's bellies were subjected to the humiliation of rationing.

Churchill was returned to Downing Street in 1951, the Festival of Britain held out some hope that the world was at last changing for the better and Ford Populars cost a mere £390, including tax. Elizabeth the Princess became Elizabeth the Queen. The national census showed that Britons were living longer, marrying earlier, divorcing in greater numbers and working less in traditional manufacturing jobs than they had in 1931. Yet one-third of the nation's households did not have a bathtub, one in twenty did not have running water and only one in ten had a TV set.

The British made it to the top of Everest, and before long there was even a second television channel. On the very night that Independent Television made its debut, BBC Radio kidnapped the entire country by killing off Grace Archer, she of the never-ending soap opera family. The telly fought back by stealing radio's premier disc jockey, Jack Jackson, and making him a star. There was *Dixon of Dock Green* and *The Quatermass Experiment*, Gilbert Harding's utter irascibility on *What's My Line?* and the country's first made-for-television comedy star, Benny Hill.

The Burgess-Maclean-Philby spy scandal broke into the headlines at about the same time that Roger Bannister broke through the mile's 4-minute barrier. Lester Piggot won his first Derby at 18 and British housewives eventually tore up their rationing books. Dylan Thomas delivered *Under Milk Wood*, ten years after he'd promised it to BBC Radio, although he left the country before he could hear it narrated by a youthful Richard Burton. William Golding wrote *Lord of the Flies*, and Ian Fleming invented James Bond. The cinema was alive with *The Lavender Hill Mob* and *The Bridge Over the River Kwai*. An American named Gussie Moran changed British tennis forever by wearing frilly panties at Wimbledon and a Lady named Docker explained why she covered the seats of her limousine with Zebra skin. 'Because everyone knows, mink is too hot to sit on.'

The world's first regularly scheduled jetliner service opened between London and Johannesburg and ICI invented 'Terylene,' which came to be known as Dacron. You made yourself look better with Brylcreem and your kitchen look better with Pyrex Colourware. Adverts promised, 'You Make New Friends at Butlins' and 'A Guinness A Day Is Good For You' and 'Smart's Bedroom Suite – Superb Furniture – Helpful terms – £10-9-11 down, only 13/9 weekly with two years to pay.'

Donald Campbell became the fastest man on water in his Bluebird, Stirling Moss became the first Briton to win the British Grand Prix, Ruth Ellis became the last woman in the Kingdom to be hanged and Princess Margaret was told she couldn't marry Peter Townsend.

Then along came Suez, ending whatever faint hope there was that the map would forever be covered in pink and the sun would never set. By

October 1957, the greatest Empire the world would ever see had sunk beneath the waves it once ruled.

John Hay Whitney, better known as Jock, had only just moved to London.

Born to wealth and social connections, he was the 53-year-old heir to a publishing family which owned the New York *Herald Tribune*, half of the Paris *Herald Tribune* and a chain of magazines. He was urbane, a good golfer, a fine bridge player, a long-standing solid Republican and exactly the kind of person Ike liked to spend time with.

He was also, the President hoped, the perfect man to replace Winthrop Aldrich in America's most prestigious diplomatic posting, as Ambassador to the Court of St James. Aldrich had been closely associated with the American stand on Suez. Eisenhower saw Whitney, coming in fresh, as a step towards renewing the special relationship.

On the night of 4 October, 1957, Whitney was at Winfield House, the Ambassador's official residence in Regent's Park, when the Embassy duty officer phoned with the news about Sputnik. He spent the weekend sorting through the newspapers and on Monday filed a detailed report to Washington.

'Satellite dominated front pages British press Saturday, Sunday, today,' he wrote. 'Headlines proclaiming, "Space Age Is Here" and "Russia Wins Space Race." Story was a natural for Britain's mass circulation Sunday papers and they had field day with it. Front page banner headlines continue today, supplemented by pictures, graphs, maps, etc. Some major treatment accorded by news programs, British radio and TV. BBC news programs featured first recording of "Beep" signals emitted by satellite and later broadcast signals "live".'

This first step to the stars, the British press proclaimed, was a longer stride than expected. It was proof that the Soviets had made rapid advances in rocket technique. It was something the Americans were right to find alarming. 'Prestige and propaganda value to Moscow,' one paper declared, 'prestige and propaganda damage to US.'

Because of Sputnik, Whitney said, the British public now accepted Russia's claims to possess an ICBM. There was also a tendency to pay more attention to Communist political philosophy. Equally worrying was the opposition party's call for agreements with the Soviets. 'Shadow Foreign Secretary Bevan already has deplored exclusion USSR from Middle East settlement. Labour representatives at Brighton conference last week went on record in favor of temporary unilateral suspension of atomic testing in effort to obtain general disarmament agreement. This departure from Western disarmament position may gain increased support.'

He pointed out that post-war Britain had suffered under the constant strain of trying to maintain its status as a great power. America's refusal, therefore, to share technical secrets with the British added a certain touch of relish to whatever regret the British had about the Soviet triumph. He forecast that the Tory government would now increase their efforts to participate in America's atomic weapons program and that their argument would be, unless all Western scientific potential is coordinated, the world will fall behind the Soviets.

It was as if Jock Whitney had read Harold Macmillan's mind.

Harold Macmillan held court in the Cabinet Room at the rear of No. 10 Downing Street. His desk was the 25-foot-long, coffin-shaped, green-baized cabinet table.

Surrounding that table were 23 armless mahogany chairs with dark-red leather seats and backs, the same ones Disraeli and Gladstone used. Macmillan's place was in the middle, on the side with the view of the garden. He sat on the 24th chair, the only one with arms, which is today known as 'Churchill's Chair.' Behind him was a marble fireplace and, above that, the only painting in the room – a mere copy of the Jean Baptiste van Loo portrait of Sir Robert Walpole that hangs in the Hermitage in St Petersburg.

In front of him was a green-shaded brass library lamp and a silver inkwell. Three mahogany letter stands were next to that, with two wooden trays – marked 'In' and 'Out' – on either side. Other letter stands, filled with writing paper, were spread out evenly across the table. So were heavy glass ashtrays. There was a block of buttons on Macmillan's right, like the kind you find in fancy old hotels to hail the maid. Wires from it ran under the table so that he could summon his Principal Private Secretary, whose office was past the pair of Corinthian columns and just beyond the double doors at the very end of the room. Two heavy Bakelite telephones were also within arm's reach.

At 10:30 on Tuesday morning, 8 October, 1957, an apprehensive Macmillan assembled his ministers around that table. The situation was getting worse in the Middle East and Britain was not ready to face another Suez crisis. On top of that, he'd been reading about Sputnik for the past three days and was troubled by the way the American public was reacting to it. The Foreign Minister, Selwyn Lloyd, sat directly across the table from Macmillan. He reported that the Syrians were gaining the advantage because they had Russian help. He saw the Soviet Union clearly embarking on a new campaign of political and economic warfare – witness Sputnik – and thought it was now more important than ever to strengthen Britain's special relationship with America.

Macmillan couldn't have agreed more.

Four hours later, two blocks away at the Ministry of Defence, the Chiefs of Staff gathered. Presiding over the meeting, Field Marshal Sir Gerald Templer, Chief of the Imperial General Staff, said that because of Sputnik he wanted to take another look at British estimates of Russian potential. He wanted to know more about Russian ballistic missiles, when they become fully operational and when they would supersede manned aircraft. He told the assembled Chiefs, who included Lord Mountbatten, those estimates were now vital for planning the defense strategy of Great Britain.

A comment was made that Sputnik had produced a powerful psychological shock in the United States and that this was bound to cast doubts in American minds as to the wisdom of continually refusing to cooperate with the British in the nuclear field. Perhaps, the Chiefs decided, the time was right to reopen the question of American atomic restrictions.

At Templer's request, the Ministry's Joint Intelligence Committee (JIC) was asked to look into the implications of the Russian satellite.

Back in the Cabinet Room, early that same evening, Harold Macmillan read the minutes of the Chiefs of Staff meeting.

As Great Britain does not have a direct equivalent of America's National Security Council, the nation's primary intelligence functions are divided between a group called the Cabinet Committee on Oversea and Defence Policy and the JIC. Together they advise the Prime Minister on intelligence, defense and national security matters by considering input from various intelligence services at home and abroad.

Information from the intelligence directorates – at the Ministry of Defence, the Treasury, the Foreign Office, the Northern Ireland Office, the Home Office, the General Communications Headquarters, Allied Intelligence Services and the Defence Intelligence Staff – is fed into the JIC. Since 1947, intelligence has been regularly pooled between Britain, the United States, Australia and Canada, and those reports also find their way into the JIC.

In turn, the JIC keeps the Cabinet Committee up to date through the highly classified 'Red Book,' which is somewhat similar to an NSC report. However, because of the nature of the JIC's work, it does not always have to deal through the Cabinet Committee and can go directly to the Prime Minister. Only the counter-espionage/counter-terrorist M.I.5, which comes under the Home Office, and the espionage and intelligence-gathering M.I.6, which comes under the Foreign Office, also enjoy that access.

Known in the Whitehall vernacular as 'black box' agencies – because JIC and Cabinet Committee papers are transported in black boxes instead of the familiar red boxes used by the cabinet ministries – their existence is not usually acknowledged by the British. Unlike the United States, where for example the CIA is listed in the phone book and its Virginia headquarters is signposted, when you ring around Whitehall and ask about the JIC, the stock answer is either, I never heard of this agency, or, officially it doesn't exist.

Responding to the Chiefs of Staff, the JIC prepared a top secret one and a half-page report on 9 October and met on it the following day. The report, with the JIC's comments, arrived on Macmillan's table in the Cabinet Room later that afternoon. It supported his contention that the implications of the Russian satellite went far beyond mere scientific achievement. Sputnik was a propaganda coup of the greatest magnitude. It was also proof that Russia's military potential was outstripping allied expectations.

So the Chiefs of Staff were right. This would be the ideal moment to reopen the question of atomic cooperation with the Americans.

He wired Eisenhower, asking if they could meet.

Eisenhower responded right away, inviting Macmillan to Washington, and reassuring him that the special relationship was as important to the United States as it was to Great Britain. Within a week the Foreign Office and the State Department were busy coordinating plans for the visit.

The CIA's man in London, obviously alerted to look for Sputnik intelligence, picked up an odd fact which he sent back to Washington. His telex was processed, along with tens of thousands of other reports from field agents at that period, properly filed and there it sat for the next 40 years.

No action was ever taken and there doesn't seem to have ever been any other reference to his message.

The gist of it was this: In April 1957, the Soviets placed an order with a manufacturer in the West for a small number of mercury battery packs. The operative wrote that he couldn't determine the exact number, but that the small size of the order led executives at the manufacturing plant to suppose that they would be used for some sort of experimental work. Those same executives were now telling the CIA that unless the Soviets had perfected a rechargeable lead or a silver oxide battery – which the CIA theorized they hadn't – then it would have been those mercury batteries that they used to power the transmitters in Sputniks I and II.

If that's true, then long before anything saying 'Made in USA' was thrust into space – at least according to a long-forgotten CIA report – some mercury batteries were, with the labels, 'Manufactured in England.'

That America in 1945 wished to remain the world's only atomic power is certain. But the moment mushroom clouds formed over Hiroshima and Nagasaki, much as the proverbial genie popped out of the bottle, it was sheer fantasy to imagine that charter membership in the nuclear club would forever be exclusively limited to one.

Within four months of the Labour Party's victory over Churchill, Prime Minister Clement Attlee showed up in Washington with his hat in his hand, trying to get restrictions removed on commercial exploitation of atomic energy. Truman refused. Attlee argued that Roosevelt and Churchill had agreed to cooperate on atomic matters, and in practice, until Attlee came along, there was some cooperation. For example, under an accord signed in Quebec in 1943, Truman needed Churchill's consent to drop the atomic bomb on Japan. Churchill duly agreed to the request on 4 July, 1945 and the war ended a month later.

But Attlee wasn't Churchill.

Anyway, the mood on Capitol Hill was shifting away from granting the British everything they wanted to reminding the British how grateful they should be for what they'd already gotten.

With the Cold War taking root, Attlee announced that Britain would develop its own atomic arsenal.

In the meantime, Congress passed the Atomic Energy Act, sponsored by Senator Brian McMahon of Connecticut, which established the principle of civilian control over America's atomic resources and programs. Referred to as the McMahon Act, the 1946 bill gave the military a loud voice in the use of atomic resources for weaponry, but put the final decisions firmly in the hands of civilians appointed by, and reporting directly to, the President. Formation of the Atomic Energy Commission was one result of the bill.

Angering Attlee was another.

He objected to the clause which specifically forbade the United States from any agreements involving nuclear cooperation with other nations. Congress firmly took the stance that science was one thing and could be shared with friends, while nuclear secrets were another. As nuclear secrets were best kept secret, they would not be shared, even with old allies.

Interestingly enough, these days historians of prominence, among them McGeorge Bundy, contend that had Congress known the full extent of Britain's role in developing the bomb – in other words, that without British know-how the bomb might not have become a reality by 1945 – the McMahon Act would have carried an exclusion clause in favor of the United Kingdom. But, as Bundy notes, no one bothered to speak up for Britain's interest or to make that point when the bill was debated.

Within a year, Truman decided he resented having to ask anyone, especially Clement Attlee, for permission to use the bomb and set his mind to getting the 'consent' clause removed from the Quebec Agreement. He had the additional anxiety of raw uranium being in short supply. A major source was the Belgian Congo, but the lion's share of their output was going to none other than the British. So Truman approached Attlee and the two struck a deal. Under the terms of what was then called the 'modus vivendi,' consent was renounced and the British agreed to supply the US with uranium. In exchange, the Americans promised technical cooperation under a vague set of terms that did not violate the McMahon Act. It was only when Attlee tried to get the Americans to help Britain make weapons that he discovered the vaguenesses of the agreement didn't necessarily cover that particular area. Further concessions were arranged in 1948 when, in exchange for American weapons, Britain permitted the United States to station B-29 bombers at RAF bases. However, once the British arrested the atomic spy Klaus Fuchs in 1950, serious doubt was cast on Britain's ability to keep American secrets and hope temporarily faded for any further nuclear cooperation between the two old allies.

The British of course went on to build their own bomb. Almost five years to the day before Sputnik was launched, they exploded an atomic device off the coast of Western Australia. The core of it was plutonium, created in production reactors at Windscale, in Cumbria, in the northwest corner of England. Largely due to that success, Eisenhower was able to convince Congress to relax the McMahon Act's restrictions slightly in 1954. Congress permitted the administration to share with the British certain information of a very general nature about nuclear weapons.

In March 1957, Eisenhower and Macmillan returned to Bermuda. It was their first meeting since Suez, and the first time they'd ever conferred as equals. The two countries came together like a pair of old lovers trying to rekindle the flame where it was once so good. At the end of the four-day summit the President and the Prime Minister declared that their disagreements over Suez were now confined to the history books and that mutual confidence had been restored. The 'Ike-Mac Pact' condemned the Soviets for their intervention in Eastern Europe and heralded NATO as the cornerstone of Western defense policy. It was at Bermuda that Eisenhower agreed to supply guided missiles to the British, although the missiles would have to remain wholly under American control.

Two months later, Britain's first hydrogen bomb demolished Christmas Island in the South Pacific.

Then, on 10 October, a fire destroyed Windscale's Pile No. 1 reactor. The fallout from the accident contaminated milk in a 200-mile radius of the plant. Macmillan immediately ordered that reports of this near-catastrophic disaster be censored. He didn't view it as a matter of national security because it clearly wasn't. What he cared about was how the Americans would look at it. With his trip to Washington less than two weeks away, he didn't want to provide anyone there with any ammunition to oppose a revision of the McMahon Act.

Jock Whitney continued bombarding the State Department with telegrams through the week, keeping Foster Dulles abreast of the British attitude towards Sputnik.

On 9 October, having queried his contacts in Parliament, the Foreign Office, the Ministry of Defence, the Atomic Energy Agency and the British intelligence community, he wrote, 'Principal and immediate impact is largely psychological one which USSR is vigorously exploiting and will certainly continue to exploit.' And those sources were staunchly in favor of greater collaboration between the US and the UK, especially in the development of nuclear weapons and delivery systems. 'This theme ran through all comments.'

It was apparent, he said, referencing the opinion to an unidentified 'high official,' that the great unanswered question in Britain was whether the United States would react with sufficient energy and determination to reestablish its technological superiority. 'Major damage would be if it [Sputnik] creates panic atmosphere in US with issue becoming football party politics and if it starts witch hunts at time when world should be shown US coolness and determination without complacency in face of unpleasant realities.'

The biggest danger, the British saw, lay in the probability that the USSR would increasingly act on the assumption that America would not use nuclear weapons even on a limited scale. In fact, they worried America might not even be willing to employ conventional forces unless the Soviets launched a direct attack on the US. Britain feared the Russian leaders would take a more aggressive presence in areas of tension, like the Middle East, without adequately appreciating the degree to which the United States intended to repel such aggression. Heightened Soviet aggression would, consequently, force Britain and America to make increasingly difficult choices as to the use of force. Two Ministry of Defence officials told Whitney that Sputnik put America in the same boat as Britain, within range of Russia's atomic capabilities. He'd also observed considerable 'wry pleasure' in the fact that the US had taken a jolt to its pride. The prize for Britain could be the ultimate enhancement of Anglo-American relations, restoring the UK to the status it had enjoyed during World War II.

In the long term, Britain might turn to its European partners for mutual defense and call for a reshaping of the Atlantic alliance.

Whitney believed everything now depended on whether the United States showed its will and determination to reassert the preeminence essential to maintain the free world alliance.

Sputnik also became an issue of sorts at the Conservative Party Conference a few days later at Brighton. The Minister of Defence, Duncan Sandys, remarked what a shame it was that Britain was forced to duplicate America's effort in the nuclear field. 'But it does not rest with us,' Sandys indicated. 'Should the Americans decide in the light of recent developments that some change is reasonable, they will find a very ready response over here.'

The next day, Selwyn Lloyd amplified the need to rebuild Anglo-American friendship on the basis of confidence and respect as real partners, and the necessity that Britain be a nuclear military power in order to contribute to the deterrent against Soviet expansionist efforts.

When Macmillan addressed the Conference, he labeled the combined nuclear forces of the US and the UK as the only means available to deter the Soviet Union from open aggression.

Speaking privately to his political contacts, Whitney heard again and again how Sputnik's success meant it was time for the United States to share its atomic secrets with Britain. He reported his contacts were saying to him, 'The West has suffered a severe reverse, and this reverse is due to a failure of determination and leadership in the United States.'

He surmised, 'Since they have no illusion that their fate is irrevocably tied to ours, there is no tendency to disassociate themselves from us, but rather the opposite. The traditional British steadiness and stubbornness in the face of adversity manifests itself here. They are more than ever convinced that the resources and efforts of our two countries in this field should be pooled. They consider that this is the touchstone of US capacity to exert effective leadership of the free world in the new and more critical phase of the Cold War.'

On Monday afternoon, 21 October, Macmillan briefed his cabinet on his upcoming trip.

He said he thought Sputnik had awakened the United States to the reality that, in order to counter the Soviet threat, the whole structure of Western collaboration needed to be reexamined. He said he sensed the Americans were particularly anxious to review the pattern of their relationship with Great Britain. The purpose of the trip was to discuss the methods by which the collective strength of the free world could be more effectively mobilized.

The Soviet Union was a formidable antagonist, he went on. And even though he was sure that Communist ideology would one day crumble in on itself, Russia's resources, its technical efficiency and its system of government might enable it to continue putting real pressure on the Western democracies for a very considerable time. The free world, however, possessed vast resources with which to meet this challenge, provided they were not dissipated and misapplied. His objectives in going to Washington were therefore two-fold. He wanted the technical resources of both countries pooled to create an effective policy of collective defense. The way to do that was by repealing the McMahon Act. He also wanted to establish, unobtrusively and without provoking the suspicion of other nations, a joint Anglo-American machine to implement policy for the political, military and economic issues which confronted both governments, particularly in the Middle East.

He promised to impress upon the Eisenhower administration that the Western democracies would not be able to withstand the Soviet menace unless they developed a greater integration of policy and purpose. He said he was going to Washington because there were 'grounds for hope that we might succeed in re-establishing the close association with them which had been so fruitful in earlier years.'

Eisenhower had also been looking for ways to fortify the special relationship. He and Macmillan had known each other since the war years and few Presidents have matched Ike when it comes to being a natural Anglophile. Meticulously concerned with doing what was right for both countries, Eisenhower sought advice from one of the most trusted men in his inner circle, his friend and sometimes speech writer, C. D. Jackson.

The meeting with Macmillan, Jackson felt, could go a tremendous way to somehow recapturing the international prestige lost to Sputnik, but only if the end product was not 'standard barley water.' He argued, God was on America's side, having provided Sputnik as an excuse for this meeting. However, at the end of it, the two leaders would have to come up with something concrete in order to show the world that the West was united against the Russian threat. It was equally important to make the military aspect of the Anglo-American alliance unmistakably clear and to include appropriate words about NATO. Jackson begged, 'Please, let's not get NATO too cultural. I have a mental picture of some great emergency and a NATO aviator stumbling out to get his plane and falling over some cultural character.' He also hoped progress could be made towards scientific coordination with the British, especially where atomic weapons were concerned. 'If not, every country including Ghana is going to have the hydrogen bomb and the way to avoid that is to get cracking with the only people we really trust and with whom we have and can work.'

Yet it was Foster Dulles' opinion that was the key to Eisenhower's game plan.

When Macmillan's letter first arrived suggesting they meet, Dulles encouraged Eisenhower to accept. Ike then described to Dulles how disappointed he'd been when Truman canceled the Joint Staff Operations at the end of the war. It was a natural forum for maintaining the special relationship. Perhaps, Eisenhower thought, he could take a stronger line with the Joint Chiefs of Staff and get them to accept a greater spirit of cooperation with the British. But there Dulles was skeptical. The President wondered out loud if perhaps they should have a private telephone line going into 10 Downing Street. Dulles promised to check on it. Ever pragmatic, Eisenhower's concern was not whether or not a US-UK hotline could be done, but how much it would cost.

To arrange the meeting without arousing suspicions in the press or among the other Western allies, Dulles felt they needed to announce some sort of reason for it. The President agreed that, without any 'cover,' it would take on a panicky look and they didn't want the world to know how nervous Macmillan was about the Russians.

There was no doubt in Dulles' mind that Macmillan wanted to restore British prestige around the world, and to do that he needed to be seen sharing leadership of the allied effort with the United States, the way it had happened during the war. Wrapped into the middle of this, Dulles agreed with Jock Whitney's assessment from London, that the British were fixing to launch an all-out assault on the McMahon Act. It had been a particularly sore point for too long. That Macmillan would try to take advantage of America's reaction to Sputnik to obtain a modification of the Act seemed only logical.

Accordingly, Dulles listed what he wanted from the British:

(1) The British would have to bring their policy towards Communist China into line with America's. That was very important. Clement Attlee had been the first Western leader officially to recognize Mao's right to China and Dulles was going to demand that the British reverse that by breaking off all relations with the mainland as soon as possible and voting with the US to deny mainland China UN membership.

(2) Adjustments would have to be made to British policy in the Persian Gulf, which included the restoration of normal diplomatic relations with Saudi Arabia.

(3) Dulles wanted a firm commitment from Macmillan that Britain would not obstruct progress towards achievement of a Common Market in Europe. He didn't want to be seen conspiring with the British against the French and Germans.

If the British would agree to those points, then the United States would be in a position to make four specific offers:

(1) The administration would do everything in its power to modify the restrictions of the McMahon Act, allowing Great Britain to purchase weapons-grade uranium from the US for the development of their own independent nuclear deterrent.
(2) In light of the Windscale accident, the US Atomic Energy Commission would sell the British 5000-9000 kg of enriched uranium for power plants, which would save them the huge costs of building new production facilities.
(3) In return for a promise not to interefere with the progress of the Common Market, the US would be willing to support the British in their Free Trade Area proposals. Macmillan would surely go for that because he'd always said that a Free Trade Area was vital if Britain was to maintain its competitive position against a Common Market.
(4) An earlier agreement to deploy intermediate-range ballistic missiles to the UK, which was at the time stuck in the bureaucratic maze of the Defense Department, could now be concluded.

In recommending the plan to the President, Dulles wanted to assure himself that, whatever was agreed, he'd be the one to oversee its implementation. He asked that Eisenhower and Macmillan appoint Selwyn Lloyd and himself as their agents to monitor the progress of the decisions taken. If it was left to Lloyd and himself, he believed, things could get done. Lloyd would not make the same mistake Eden had. Dulles would be able to control the British so that they never again endangered America's position the way they had with Suez.

Selwyn Lloyd was dispatched to Washington as the advance man. His visit coincided with the arrival of Queen Elizabeth and Prince Philip, on Thursday morning, 17 October. They'd come to help celebrate the 350th anniversary of the first British settlers in Virginia and were staying in the White House as Eisenhower's guests. Protocol dictated that Macmillan not do anything to overshadow Her Majesty's visit and therefore he had to wait in London until the Queen came home.

In the build-up to the Queen's visit, the nation's newspapers were filled with 'royalabilia.' For example, it was noted that, according to a former royal chef, Queen Elizabeth did not have any special dietary requirements and would eat anything put before her, which the paper asserted, made her no different from the average American housewife who would do the same thing, 'as long as she doesn't have to cook it.'

During their stay, every step they took was covered by the press and no detail was overlooked. Every meal they ate, every dress she wore, every man she danced with, was described in print. It was even noted that while at the White House Her Majesty would occupy the Queen's Bedroom – the one Churchill preferred – while His Royal Highness would sleep alone in the Lincoln Bedroom, across the hall.

But not even the Queen of England could move Sputnik off the front pages. Eisenhower mentioned the Russian satellite to the Queen and Philip at separate times and was interested to hear them both say, independently of the other, how amazed they were at the American press reaction to the satellite. According to Ike, they told him that people in London just gave it one day of excitement, then went about their business. Unfortunately, this wasn't true.

The visit was an overwhelming success and, when Ike said goodbye to the couple on their way home, he told them, 'I wish you could stay a little longer.'

The Queen smiled and is said to have responded, 'I wish I could, but you see, the Prime Minister needs the aeroplane.'

Macmillan left the UK on the night of 22 October, arriving at Washington's National Airport just after 9 the next morning. Foster Dulles was there to greet him.

Once the Prime Minister's party were installed at the British Embassy on Massachusetts Avenue, just off Observatory Circle – a 15-minute drive through traffic from the White House – Macmillan, Dulles and Lloyd went into a private meeting.

Under the heading, 'The Present Political Situation,' they talked in general terms about nuclear power and how it had become necessary to come up with new arrangements for their mutual security. Macmillan echoed the concern among some Western allies that the United States might not be willing to use nuclear power to defend its allies. When Dulles suggested they move NATO headquarters from Europe to Washington, Macmillan confessed he often thought of trying to create an entirely new organization which might become a substitute for the United Nations, leaving the UN in the somewhat titular role of a House of Lords. Dulles said he too had gone through much the same mental process, envisioning an organization of about 50 allies who would guarantee world peace.

After lunch, Dulles returned to the British Embassy with Christian Herter, Jock Whitney and a few close aides. Macmillan and Lloyd were joined by the British Ambassador, Sir Harold Caccia, and some of their aides. The designated topic was, 'Closer US–UK Relations and Free World Cooperation.'

Macmillan pointed out that he viewed these meeting as 'taking counsel together and not embarking on a negotiation.' He was of the conviction that Sputnik had revealed just how formidable an adversary they faced. He accepted the fact that no one wanted a war but saw the Soviets hoping and expecting to dominate the world. The Western allies had found themselves in the midst of a long, secular struggle, and the question had to be asked, 'Can we last the course?' Looking 50 or 60 years in the future, Macmillan doubted that the US and the UK would still be existing in a separate and independently sovereign relationship. 'We must unite and use our assets effectively or we will lose them all.'

Foster Dulles was in complete agreement.

Macmillan said he was hoping for 'a marriage of heart as well as worldly goods.'

Again Dulles agreed, and now brought up the irritating business of Britain's UN stance on China.

Macmillan assured him that Britain would stand by America, then got back onto the subject of assets. 'What are our assets? First of all, they consist of two countries. The problem is, however, to put them to the best use. I'm not thinking of the creation of boards or committees, I'm thinking more of rationally pooling, for common use, our brains, experience and resources.'

And Dulles assured him that America would stand by Britain.

It's probably just as well neither of them had a used car for sale.

The scene cut to the White House that evening and for the next two days, where Macmillan repeated to Eisenhower much of what he'd said to Dulles and where Dulles brought up China again, only to hear Macmillan affirm, 'As long as I am Prime Minister, I would never agree to anything which might bring the Communists into the United Nations. We have enough trouble with the Soviets there and do not want to compound it.'

Almost as if Dulles didn't trust the British, he somehow got Lloyd to put their pledge in writing. In a one-page, top secret, personal letter, Lloyd wrote, 'My dear Foster, I write to confirm what I said to you last night about China's representation in the United Nations. The present Government of the United Kingdom will not seek or support, without prior agreement with the United States Government, any change in regard to the representation of China in the United Nations, its dependent agencies and other international organizations in which this question may arise. Yours ever, Selwyn.'

The letter was never discussed again and when it came time to compose the 'Declaration of Common Purpose,' which would be held up as the conclusion of the conference, there was no mention whatsoever of China.

While Macmillan was in Washington, Foster Dulles and Christian Herter took it upon themselves to ring various influential Senators at home and keep them abreast of the meetings. Dulles wanted them to know that, 'We are not trying to work out any exclusive US-UK relationship but rather ways of bringing more closely together all of our allies.'

It wasn't exactly the truth, but that obviously didn't matter to Dulles, who realized that the administration would need friends on the Hill if the McMahon Act was to be repealed or amended. Letting influential law makers think they were being kept informed was a way of doing that.

Only one minor incident came close to marring the warmth of understanding that had been successfully reestablished between the two countries. On Friday afternoon, 25 October, during his talks with Macmillan, Eisenhower had somehow given the British the impression that he would clear the way with Congress for them to have all the nuclear weapons they wanted. Dulles was horrified. Convinced that the President never intended to turn everything over to the British, irrespective of whether or not it involved classified information that the British did not need to know, Dulles did some fast back-tracking. He got McElroy at the Defense Department and Admiral Strauss at the Atomic Energy Commission to help him put together a definition of just what the program should be so that there could be no serious misunderstandings. In the end, Macmillan and Lloyd had no choice but to accept Dulles' version of events.

The Declaration of Common Purpose, issued by Jim Hagerty's office acting for the President and the Prime Minister, was a three-page, single-spaced lesson in double-speak. It spoke of trusted friends and historic ties. It spoke of the assets of free nations and the dreams of world domination by the Communists.

It referred to Sputnik by saying, 'We do not ignore the fact that the Soviet rulers can achieve formidable material accomplishments by concentrating upon selected developments and scientific achievements, and by yoking their people to this effort. Despotisms have often been able to produce monuments. But the price has been heavy. For all peoples yearn for intellectual and economic freedom, the more so if from their bondage they see others manifest the glory of freedom.'

What the rhetoric boiled down to was that the President would request an amendment of the McMahon Act from Congress in order to 'permit the close and fruitful collaboration of scientists and engineers of Great Britain, the United States and other friendly nations.'

Together they would seek to establish a sound basis for disarmament negotiations with the Soviets and at the same time reinforce various organizations designed for mutual security, such as NATO, the Southeast Asia Collective Defense Treaty and the Baghdad Pact, the British Commonwealth and the Organization of American States – collectives representing the 50 allies Macmillan had spoken to Dulles about when he first arrived.

As soon as Macmillan headed home, Foster Dulles held a 'background only' press conference. The rules were strict: no direct quotes, no attribution to either the Secretary of State or the United States government.

It was one of those 'according to informed sources' affairs.

'In any civilized community,' Dulles said, 'you move away from the kind of society where each fellow protects himself and his own house, as you do at a primitive frontier place, with his own gun, with his own dog, with his own water buckets to put out fires, and you rely more and more upon a central collective force. But that is possible only because of these three qualities we speak about here. First, you have a knowledge about what the force is and how it is going to operate. Secondly, you have confidence that in fact it will be used to protect you if you are attacked. And in the third place, the policemen aren't going to go around beating the heads of law-abiding citizens just because they are being erratic or feel like blowing off steam in that way.'

He continued, 'Now, in order to get acceptability of this new concept of a community force which is going to be for the protection of people, you have enough knowledge about it to feel that it is capable of protecting them; they have got to be confident that it will be used to protect them; and, third, they have got to be confident that it will not be misused to bring about their unnecessary destruction.'

In other words, 50 allies would be brought together into some sort of loosely defined global police force, beyond the reach of the United Nations and a Soviet veto. And that global police force would be armed by the one nation capable of assuring that there would be enough fire power to counter the Russian menace.

Britain would stand at America's side and the world would think they were equal.

Back at Downing Street, on Monday afternoon, 28 October, Macmillan defined the Declaration of Common Purpose as a declaration of interdependence. He said the impact of Sputnik had shown the Americans that no single country, however powerful, could stand alone against the Soviet threat and that all the resources of the free world must now be marshaled to meet it.

He outlined what had been agreed upon. He said the two governments would take steps to concert a common policy for countering Soviet encroachment, not only by military preparations but also by political, economic and propaganda means. Resources would be pooled in the development of new weapons. Ike would ask Congress to amend the McMahon Act, allowing for greater cooperation with the UK. And the two countries would regard their possession of nuclear weapons as a trust for the defense of the free world.

He said these undertakings represented substantial and valuable concessions on the part of the United States and in return agreed to give a private undertaking that the UK would not, without the agreement of the US, press for a change in the representation of China in the UN. The US also agreed to a joint study with the UK on the threat to Hong Kong and steps which might be taken to meet it.

Selwyn Lloyd concluded, 'Largely as a result of the personal friendship between the Prime Minister and President Eisenhower, we had now succeeded in regaining the special relationship with the United States which we had previously enjoyed.'

The following day, a wire arrived for 'Harold' from 'Ike.' 'There never has been any doubt in my mind that in an emergency we would, as we have done before, find ourselves shoulder to shoulder. But it is reassuring to know that in the more difficult job of waging the peace we are, all of us, again working toward a common goal.'

Sputnik had placed Macmillan in a position to get something the British had passionately wanted ever since the end of the war – full membership in the nuclear club. It had also given him the chance to wash away, once and for all, the bitter taste left by Anthony Eden's adventure at Suez.

The special relationship was working again. Great Britain would be sweetened with atomic weapons. But the heady days of World War II were long gone. The special relationship, post-Sputnik, would work only as long as Britain played the dutiful wife.

Chapter Thirteen

Yankee Determination

The first Sputnik opened a wound.

The second Sputnik, with a dog named Leika sealed inside it, was a half ton tablespoon of salt.

'The Soviets have increased their lead,' reported America's Ambassador to West Germany, where the second launching was received with greater excitement than the first. 'US will be even harder put to catch up. Sov. success also great political significance in Cold War. Arms race probably will be transferred from earth to space.'

The world was 'stupefied,' said the Ambassador to the Netherlands. 'Russians have solved problem of "ultimate weapon,"' wrote his counterpart in Sweden. And the Prime Minister of Luxembourg commented, 'There are many who will not regain their full confidence in the United States leadership until the United States launches a satellite.'

In Spain, the evening newspaper *Madrid* accused both the United States and Great Britain of being humiliated and threatened by the Russians. 'The disillusionment was brusque and brutal.' At the morning daily *ABC*, a story had been scheduled strongly criticizing the US for losing the space race and jeopardizing the security of Europe. But the Spanish Foreign Office suppressed it. Franco's men would not permit the paper to say that the two Sputniks made America so jittery its European allies could no longer count on US intervention should war come with the Soviets. The paper was prohibited from demanding that America either commit itself to defending Europe with medium-range ballistic missiles or abandon its bases so that Spain could claim neutrality and, it was hoped, avoid being attacked.

The French continued to gloat. One paper claimed, 'Americans have at last discovered they cannot be stronger than the Soviets.' It was much the same in South America, where the Ambassador to Chile observed, 'Cynics derive satisfaction from the fact that rich Uncle Shylock is getting his dose of humiliation. Our friends, though remaining polite, are truly distressed. They believe we have been beaten to the draw and fear the undecided countries are now bound to turn to Communism.'

Arab governments saw the second launching as a further deterioration of US prestige. While in Japan, the socialist opposition used Sputnik to attack the government's security arrangements with the United States. The Prime Minister of Australia felt Khrushchev was exploiting satellites specifically to create a climate of fear. And the government in Thailand expressed alarm that the USSR was now in a position to attack any country in the world with guided missiles.

The *Lausanne Gazette* in Switzerland was almost unique in the world in not casting a shadow of doom. 'As the surprise attack on Pearl Harbor proved, the Americans, when they feel themselves in danger, are capable of prodigious efforts. They have invariably beaten rivals who have stolen an advance on them. In this respect, we may well witness some astonishing things in the near future.'

If the rise and fall of great civilizations can be charted by their ability to respond to challenge, then there should have been some hope for the future because a lot of supposedly astonishing things had been in the works ever since Sputnik I.

Ten days after the first launch, the Rand Corporation, one of America's premier think tanks, published a secret report for the Defense Department. In 'Proposal for Manned Satellite,' Rand labeled Vanguard 'weak-kneed,' and counted on America's sudden sense of inadequacy to get the country moving towards lunar rockets and manned satellites, 'immediately and vigorously.'

A week later, the American Rocket Society forwarded to Neil McElroy their monograph, 'Space Flight Program,' which was originally written in August but now hastily revised. Because 'Astronautics can no longer be considered as an appendage of the Science of Aeronautics,' they wanted a national space flight program and the creation of an independent agency to manage it. They were looking for American satellites to be orbiting the moon and Venus in 5–10 years, manned orbital vehicles within 10 years, manned orbiting of the moon within 15 years and manned landings on the moon within 20 years.

On 23 October, the CIA Advisory Committee reported to Allen Dulles on the Soviet ICBM. They concluded, the Russians had 'an orderly and progressive program which is being prosecuted in an aggressive and intelligent manner.' They calculated that America was behind the Russians by two to three years. Perceiving no short-term remedies for such a critical difference, they told Dulles the country was 'in a period of grave national emergency' and emphasized, 'increased efforts by the intelligence community, both overt and covertly, are mandatory to counter this threat.'

Allen Dulles obviously discussed this with his brother, who obviously discussed it with General Twining, because on Friday morning, 1 November, Foster Dulles met with the Joint Chiefs of Staff and the topic was, 'Steps That Might Be Taken to Counter Sputnik.'

In this case, the State Department–JCS alliance was a marriage of convenience. Dulles needed the military because satellites did not recognize borders and Sputnik had pretty much shut the door on his theory of containment. The JCS needed the State Department because the military saw satellites as potential bases for launching missiles with atomic warheads. They envisioned manned space stations orbiting the earth as surveillance weapons, and believed the next step had to be the moon. Whichever nation got there first, and with the most hardware, would possess an overwhelming advantage. If you could fire missiles from the moon down to earth, you would drastically alter the military balance of power. Having as contentious an anti-Communist as Foster Dulles on their side reassured the JCS of a foreign policy that relied on a build-up of forces.

The men at that meeting pledged, 'The United States will not allow itself to be outdone.' They wanted a US rocket to hit the moon within 12–18 months, a manned orbital satellite within two years, an unmanned landing on the moon within five years and a manned landing there within 10. The JCS sought rapid progress on the development of reconnaissance satellites. Dulles looked to find ways to force the Soviets into a disarmament position on American terms. Together they committed themselves to work for the establishment of a top secret scientific laboratory to develop weapons that could operate above the earth's atmosphere and other weapons to defend against those weapons.

The first seeds of the 'Star Wars' Strategic Defense Initiative had been planted.

In the House, the Armed Services Committee hosted 'An Investigation of National Defense and Missiles,' then formed the Select Committee on Astronautics and Space Exploration to put the administration under a magnifying glass. In the Senate, Lyndon Johnson made this his personal *cause célèbre*. His attack on Eisenhower's management of the national defenses was forged in cynicism. 'The Roman Empire controlled the world because it could build roads. Later, when men moved to the sea, the British Empire was dominant because it had ships. Now the Communists have established a foothold in outer space. It is not very reassuring to be told that next year we will put a better satellite into the air. Perhaps it will even have chrome trim and automatic windshield wipers.'

Solicited by the Pentagon, he was given a detailed briefing on their version of the events. In explaining the military consequences of the satellites and how America had been beaten in the space race, they plainly hoped to convince him – and like-minded men – that if the US was ever going to catch the Russians, they'd need a lot more money. For the blatantly ambitious Johnson, this was a golden opportunity.

Having failed to gain his party's nomination for President in 1956, and with an eye to putting his name at the top of the ticket in 1960, he masterminded an elaborate Senate hearing on the shortcomings of the administration's military policies. For nearly eight months, his Preparedness Investigating Sub-committee called witness after witness to explain how America had suffered such a humiliating defeat. Siding with the military and the scientists, Johnson then had little trouble securing the chairmanship of the Senate's new Committee on Aeronautical and Space Sciences, giving himself yet another platform from which to launch assaults on the White House.

The parade of witnesses was headed by the father of the H-bomb, Edward Teller, who debunked the story that captured Germans had put the Soviets into space. Teller insisted, the Russians had managed it on their own. He was followed by Vannevar Bush, who found Sputnik to be 'one of the finest things that Russia ever did for us. It has waked this country up.' General Jimmy Doolittle, who was serving on the board of the National Advisory Committee for Aeronautics, feared that the USSR was poised to surpass the United States in just about every field and that the only way to prevent it was by sinking huge amounts of money into military research and development. McElroy appeared to rationalize the lower priority given to Vanguard than to the nation's ICBM program. Quarles showed up, only to do a fast shuffle when asked why von Braun's program was kept in a hangar. Wilbur Brucker appeared, so did Generals Gavin and Taylor, all arguing how vital it was to be first on the moon. Medaris testified and, of course, von Braun did too, advancing the position that the best way to overtake the Russians in space was through the centralized efforts of a national space agency.

With each general, scientist and political pundit, President Eisenhower's stewardship of the national pride looked less trustworthy. With each general, scientist and political pundit, Lyndon Johnson took a step closer to the Oval Office.

As Johnson turned up the heat, some people in Washington advanced the argument that the two Sputniks had been an even greater achievement for the Russians than they would have been for the United States. From what America's intelligence sources were saying, to get those satellites into space the Soviets had to stretch their technology a lot further than the United States would have had to. In other words, they beat America not because they were technically superior but because of their technological weakness. Not capable of building small, light missiles like America's, they needed big, powerful military boosters to get into space. It's a rare case of sophistication becoming a drawback.

It was also a difficult pill to swallow.

The National Security Council took it upon themselves to become the focal point of a program designated 'Regaining the Initiative.' They saw the crisis in these very stark terms. 'Now that Communism has shown a material superiority or equality, Americans are hell-bent to surpass them where progress can be measured or demonstrated. The Executive Branch and the Congress are ready to expend new billions on gadgets – claimed to be necessary for our national existence – to show our technical and materialistic superiority. What these new proposals will accomplish in solving the basic controversy between International Communism and the free world has been lost in the foggy fears of comic-strip variety: weather control of sections of the world, space stations, extension of world rivalry into the galaxies of the universe. And while we spend mightily, and wastefully expend our national sustenance, gazing upwards at our Vanguards, Thors, moon rockets, etc. the land we live on will be lost to us because we do nothing positive to reduce the power and appeal of International Communism.'

The most important question before the American leadership was, therefore, what to do about Communism. 'Our current national policy is not only negative and clearly ineffective, it is worst of all, old and out of date. War will not favor American objectives. War will not end Communism any more than water will put out a gasoline fire.'

All sorts of suggestions poured into the NSC, including the organization of an International Medical Year, the establishment of processing plants to help feed the Third World, funding research on synthetic foods and foods from sea water, foreign medical aid, allowing the two Germanies to negotiate directly on reunification, announcing a unilateral suspension of atomic and hydrogen weapons tests, promoting cultural exchanges between the US and the USSR, replacing Nationalist China on the United Nations Security Council with India and admitting Red China to the UN.

But none came close to a proposal from the Department of Defense, where someone suggested they fight the spread of International Communism with a 'Space Train.' The idea was to send an exhibition of American rockets, missiles and futuristic space suits around the country in specially equipped railroad cars.

'Some Pentagon strategists believe World War III has already begun,' the inventor of the concept said in his proposal to Don Quarles. 'It is not a war of screaming missiles and city-busting bombs that might have been expected. The weapons are so terrible that neither side wants to use them. Rather it is a technological war, a struggle for scientific supremacy. Russia can win the world without firing a missile, these strategists believe, if she can gain scientific superiority. They claim the Sputnik launching was the first shot in this new technological war. Already Russia has followed up her victory by bluffing and bullying her neighbors. She is boasting of her coming conquest of space and, at the same time, shaking the ICBM like a big stick in the background.'

How would the Space Train help fight the Red menace?

He outlined the answer: '1) The railroads would be performing a valuable patriotic service. 2) The Space Train will make front page news every place it stops. 3) The Space Train is sure to draw tremendous crowds to railroad stations and remind the public of the part railroads have played in pioneering America and the integral part they continue to play.'

Two days after Sputnik II, the Russians pulled out of the talks at the UN Disarmament Commission. Dulles warned that the United States could no longer expect to enjoy the predominance of power it had held a decade before. It was a startling remark for him to make, all the more so because he'd been maintaining the public position that there was no great political significance to Sputnik.

'The launching of an earth satellite by the Soviets,' Dulles was finally willing to concede, 'may mark a decisive turn in the worldwide struggle between Communist imperialism and the free world. No doubt the Communist rulers gained a success. They have an opportunity to gloat, an opportunity they have not neglected.' But then he put the Soviets on notice. 'Sputnik, mocking the American people with its "beep-beep," may go down in history as Mr Khrushchev's boomerang.'

As 'Mutnik' circled overhead, Neil McElroy phoned Wilbur Brucker to say what Medaris and von Braun had been waiting five weeks to hear. 'You'll back up Vanguard. Go ahead and get your Redstone project off the shelf.' When Brucker phoned Huntsville, Medaris never mentioned that fact that von Braun had started weeks ago.

By 6 November, Dulles had turned his attention to the upcoming NATO meeting, which because of the Russian satellites, Eisenhower had agreed to attend. Taking into account Khrushchev's remark about bombers becoming obsolete, he decided NATO required both 'a shield and a sword.' Harold Macmillan had forwarded to him a White Paper he'd commissioned that concentrated on the sword. Dulles rejected that. The British would take what they were given. What they were given would depend entirely on what the United States needed them to have. And that would be decided on three basic points:

(1) NATO's capabilities for a general war, which in reality, were America's capabilities for a general war.
(2) Allied confidence that the US will not hold back in the event of local aggression, and therefore start giving way to the Russians a little at a time.
(3) Allied confidence that the US will use atomic weapons if necessary.

Dulles reckoned the Europeans didn't understand what went on in other regional groups, and that Macmillan's vision was not the answer. It didn't matter that he'd played up to Macmillan two weeks ago. It was one thing to make a visiting head of state feel welcome. It was another to let him dictate American foreign policy. Anyway, it was difficult to trust those allies where opposition leaders expressed views wholly contrary to the alliance system. He was particularly worried about the British Labour Party and men like Aneurin Bevan.

He wanted Eisenhower to say, there is no subject the United States isn't prepared to discuss with NATO. But all the time to keep it clear in his own mind that this did not mean America was prepared to give in to the Europeans.

The following day, newspapers around the world carried a boast from Nikita Khrushchev that the Soviet Union would soon out-produce the United States in consumer goods and the building of heavy industries. That afternoon, the President, Foster Dulles, Allen Dulles and Andrew Goodpaster met to discuss ways of bolstering the nation's ever-dwindling confidence, and Foster Dulles wondered if the President should use his speech that night to mention the U-2.

It was precisely the kind of revelation that would stir up the public and show that the administration had taken the bull by the horns. He suggested the President say, 'The United States has a capability in the way of aerial photography which could, in the event of need, be used to photograph with accuracy and precision the Soviet Union without its capability of interference. This is through the use of very high altitudes.' It wasn't necessary to be more specific than that.

The four men talked about it for quite a while. And Ike was almost persuaded. He came very close to doing it. In the end, he decided against it.

Addressing the American people in the first of what he intended to be six 'chin-up' speeches, he exulted in America's military prowess. He spoke of submarines carrying nuclear warheads cruising under the Polar ice caps, of successful ICBM tests, of IRBMs in forward positions ringing the USSR, of an enormous early-warning defense system, and of ground and naval forces stationed throughout the world, always on the ready. 'We are well ahead of the Soviets in the nuclear field both in quantity and in quality. We intend to stay ahead.' He put less value on the Russian ability to launch a satellite than on the overall military strength of the free world. He said he'd appointed James Killian to be his Science Adviser and explained how he'd instructed the Secretary of Defense to see that no inter-service rivalries could get in the way of missile development. He understood the national sense of urgency, but didn't think that was reason enough to mount the charger and ride off in all directions at once. What the country needed and what the country might desire were not always the same thing. The critical needs of the country would be met. He was promising a sound defense and a sound economy.

Eisenhower made a strong case for confidence and sane direction. But America wanted action.

Maybe he should have pulled the wraps off the U-2 that night. If nothing else he would have unknowingly changed the course of history.

His insistence that Sputnik was not a military program probably accounts for the comment often attributed to him, 'I don't have any enemies on the moon.' He said, 'You could have a Sputnik up in the air and one day we might be able to put a man on the moon, but our problem is enemies on earth. Our problem is the defense of democracy against the thrust of Communism around the world.' Then again, it was totally characteristic of Ike to be more interested in substance than in appearances, and the need to be first to circle the globe just didn't move him.

That's when the Gaither Report landed on his desk.

In the spring of 1957, Eisenhower had asked the chairman of the board of the Ford Foundation, H. Rowan Gaither Jr, to oversee a committee of civilians to report on the nation's state of defense readiness. Although Gaither fell ill and had to pass the job on to Robert Sprague, chairman of the Sprague Electric Company, the committee's work is forever known by his name.

The Gaither Report could not possibly have come at a worse time, nor could it have possibly contained worse news. The committee found the United States in the midst of the gravest danger in its history. It depicted a nation tumbling into second-class status with the ever-increasing evidence of the Soviet Union's ICBM capability. The report estimated that the Soviet Union had enough fissionable material for at least 1500 nuclear weapons, 4500 bombers and 300 long-range submarines. It cautioned, the Russians could possibly launch an attack against the United States sometime within the next two years using as many as 100 ICBMs equipped with megaton nuclear warheads and, if that happened, the civilian population would find itself unprotected. Just as frightening, America's main retaliatory army, the Strategic Air Command (SAC), would be highly vulnerable to destruction. Soviet military might had reached the stage where America's survival over the next few years could depend solely on Russian benevolence. The committee's conclusions were so severe that at least three of the members decided the only hope for the nation's future lay in a preemptive strike against the USSR.

271

It was such a damning condemnation that Eisenhower, exactly as Harry Truman did with Clark Clifford's report 11 years previously, locked it away. While he didn't necessarily agree with everything it said, he didn't want anyone to see it.

Unfortunately for the President, parts of the report leaked out. The *Washington Post* revealed that it 'strips away the complacency and lays bare the highly unpleasant realities in what is the first across-the-board survey of the relative postures of the United States and the Free World and the Soviet Union and the Communist orbit.'

Eisenhower told General Goodpaster on 9 November, he'd come to the conclusion that if there was a great big major war right now, both sides would be smashed to the point where they could not recover for a long time, and that another power would emerge as the greatest in the world. That power would be Germany.

Goodpaster, who'd also read the Gaither Report, stressed the need for the US to work towards 'instant retaliation.' SAC, he said, must realize we simply cannot allow the enemy to strike the first blow.

Eisenhower now admitted to Foster Dulles, 'America is scared.'

The British Labour Party's Shadow Foreign Secretary Aneurin Bevan showed up on 12 November 1957, and tried to lecture Eisenhower and Dulles on foreign policy. He'd come to the US to say that Jawaharlal Nehru had disclosed to him that the US was selling bombers to India's neighboring enemy, Pakistan. Eisenhower denied it. Bevan conceded Dulles had also denied it but said that before he believed either of them he'd have to check the point again with Nehru. Next, Bevan related how Khrushchev told him he'd been willing to accept the vital importance of oil to the West until the formation of the Baghdad Pact. After that, he could no longer ignore the situation in the Middle East. Khrushchev had also reacted sharply to Western complaints about Soviet arms being shipped into the region when the United States had been arming Israel for years. Bevan said his plan was to impose an arms embargo on the Middle East, with the US, the UK, France and the USSR guaranteeing the borders in the region, and hoped the President would endorse it.

Eisenhower needed to remind Bevan that the US, the UK and France had declared in favor of such a pact in 1950, and had repeated it several times since, but the Russians would never agree.

Thinking there was always the possibility he might have to do business with men like Bevan and the British Labour Party, Eisenhower requested

Dulles to ask Jock Whitney what he thought. A few days later Whitney cabled back, reassuringly, 'No question at this time of Britain's loyalty as ally. Their attitude might be summed up by statement, Suez taught them they have no future except in close association with us and they believe Sputniks have taught us we have no future except in close association with free world, especially in West, and have thus provided opportunity to make close association a reality.'

The same day he saw the note from Whitney, Eisenhower wrote to a friend, 'Since July 25th of 1956, when Nasser announced the nationalization of Suez, I cannot remember a day that has not brought its major or minor crisis.'

For the President of the United States, crisis had now become normalcy.

In the past he didn't usually show the physical stress that went with the job. He was a very controlled man. But as November moved on, he became more easily angered and irritated. He showed his temper whenever anyone talked about a crash program to rival the Russians. He was openly annoyed with Congress when they called for great increases in funding. And he took on the military, especially the Air Force, when he caught them trying to deal behind his back. Up to then, he'd had a fairly good relationship with them. But they started taking out full-color ads in magazines to show off their new weapons systems and he blew up. He accused them of generating public pressure to increase spending on programs that he didn't think were necessary. He also felt they were deliberately trying to focus public attention on a military confrontation with the Soviets, which is what he thought they should be working to avoid.

Ann Whitman, Eisenhower's secretary, alluded to the pressure in the diary she kept for the President. 'November 7: One of the most dreadful days. November 11: Checkup at Walter Reed. General physical condition is excellent. November 12: The days seemingly get longer and fuller.'

That week disquieting news arrived from Allen Dulles.

On November 9, the CIA circulated a Top Secret-Priority report – basically a scientific assessment of the massive thrust needed to launch the second Sputnik – which stated, flatly, that putting two earth satellites into orbit had to be considered 'a stupendous achievement.' And while the Agency's experts were fast to reassure the President, 'It does not appear that these satellites can be employed for war purposes' –

supporting Eisenhower's own publicly stated contentions – they wanted the President and his Cabinet to understand, 'The successful launching of these satellites does indicate, however, that the USSR has perfected an ICBM which they can put on any desired target with accuracy.'

The next day, Dulles chaired a meeting in his conference room at CIA headquarters which included the intelligence directors from each branch of the military, the Joint Chiefs, the State Department and the Atomic Energy Commission. Their conclusions were sent to the President. That Top Secret report – Special National Intelligence Estimate submitted by the Director of National Intelligence – noted several items which, clearly, they believed the public could not be told.

Among them:

*Since mid-1953, the Russians had tested some 300 ballistic missiles. On one day, they'd launched 4; in another 24-hour period, they'd launched 5; in August 1957, they'd launched 22.

*Putting a satellite into orbit did not necessarily mean that the Russians had solved the intricate problems otherwise associated with the complicated guidance control systems needed to send an ICBM to a target, but from what was known of those ballistic missile tests, the Russians were capable of solving critical guidance problems.

*Their first fully operational ICBM system would probably consist of 50 railroad trains, each carrying 10 missiles. Each train would be made up of 110–120 cars, requiring 400 miles of sidings, the preparation of 500 or more launch pads and an allocation of 25,000 personnel. The total initial costs for this deployment would be on the order of $2.5 billion.

*The second fully operational ICBM system would consist of 50 fixed launch sites, underground control centers, crew quarters and fuel storage tanks. The cost of that would come to $3.5 billion.

*High-yield nuclear warheads, suitable for deployment in an ICBM, could be readily available to them as early as 1958 and the Soviet Union would have nuclear warheads in serial production by the following year.

Eisenhower went to Georgia on 15 November to play golf at Augusta for a few days, although he didn't find the warm welcome he was accustomed to. The South wasn't about to forget about those federal troops going into Little Rock. There the diary entries read, 'The President didn't relax' and 'Too many interruptions.'

Back at the White House, Whitman recorded, 'November 22: Just about the worst day . . . full of gloom and doom.'

On Saturday, 23 November she wrote, 'President had worked late last night.'

There is no entry for Sunday.

On Monday morning, the President went to the airport to greet King Muhammad V of Morocco. It was a cold day and though he normally wore a hat, this morning he didn't. On Monday afternoon, while signing papers, he got very dizzy. He rang for Ann Whitman but when she came into the Oval Office he was unable to tell her what was wrong because he couldn't speak. She called for Andrew Goodpaster, who brought Eisenhower back to his private apartments and summoned the President's personal physician. Dr Howard Snyder spent the next day sitting vigil. He diagnosed the problem as a vascular spasm, making certain that no one confused it with a blocked artery type of stroke. But it was a stroke nonetheless, probably triggered by Eisenhower having stayed out in the cold with his hat off waiting for the King. Looking deeper, there was little doubt that it had come about as a result of the increased stress he'd been under for the past 18 months, capped off by the added strain on him since 4 October. Foster Dulles and Richard Nixon decided between themselves that post-Sputnik criticism was the real cause.

Eisenhower spent the next 72 hours in the private apartments, resting, watching westerns on television, reading and working on a portrait he was painting of Princess Anne. He regained his speech facilities and Snyder said he could go back to work. But his recovery was, in fact, never total. For the rest of his life, Eisenhower always had a little more trouble than usual finding his exact words.

Now the public had even more reason to worry.

'There's no doubt that America over-reacted,' says John Eisenhower, who spent many of those post-Sputnik days in the White House at his father's side. 'Public opinion is not always cool and considered and it wasn't this time. There was no imminent danger posed by Sputnik. But I think that's where Dad made an error. I think he misread the American people. He was astonished at their reaction to Sputnik. He thought he'd pulled out a reasoned argument and it amazed him that nobody paid any attention to it. I think Dad miscalculated.'

Andrew Goodpaster had also come to be convinced that Sputnik was no 'mere bauble,' and that the public reaction to it was presenting serious problems. Eisenhower never denied that the satellite documented the reality of the Soviet ICBM. But he already knew about their rocket capability. The CIA and the U-2 had been keeping an eye on them for nearly two years. The President was also regularly briefed on the development of American rocket guidance systems which were being designed to deliver a thermonuclear warhead to any spot on the globe. When it became evident that the US could do it, Eisenhower assumed it was equally evident the Soviets could do it too.

But Eisenhower had always prided himself on his ability to judge the feelings of the American people. And this time he totally mis-read them.

'I never knew Eisenhower to be wrong in his assessment of public opinion,' Goodpaster claims, 'with the exception of Sputnik.' He insists, 'Sputnik is the only mistake I know of.'

The hope of the nation was riding on the Navy.

With enormous fanfare, the Pentagon said that Project Vanguard was ready, and set the launch date for Wednesday, 4 December.

The slender three-stage, 72-foot rocket was assembled on the simple launching platform at the far end of the Long Range Proving Ground at Cape Canaveral. The aluminum satellite, just 6.4 inches in diameter and weighing a mere 3½ lb, was loaded into the nose cone. Security patrols took up positions along the base perimeter fence while crash boats patrolled off shore and along the Banana River boundary. The bright yellow ball that announced all launchings was hauled to the top of the 90-foot pole at the Cape Canaveral beach. As curious onlookers gathered along the shoreline – they were known to the launch technicians as 'bird watchers' – the huge gantry crane, sitting on railed track at the side of the launch platform, was wheeled away.

Then the weather changed. A storm front rolled in from the ocean, the sky darkened, the wind picked up and mission control halted the launch.

On Thursday, they hoisted the yellow ball again. This time technical problems stopped the countdown.

They cranked up for the third time on Friday. The weather held and the order came to move the gantry away. When the countdown went from minutes to seconds, all the various electrical and pneumatic cables that made up the rocket's umbilical cord were yanked from it.

Then the countdown reached zero.

The mission controller pushed the launch button.

It was 11:45 in the morning.

The United States was finally heading into space.

But only for 2 seconds.

The rocket rose majestically to the height of 3 feet before falling back onto the launch pad, toppling over, snapping into three pieces, and blowing up. The third stage was thrown clear of the fire ball, setting off the satellite's radio transmitters.

The nation's pride went up in smoke while Vanguard beeped.

The press called it 'Kaputnik.'

The day after Vanguard blew up, an Army three-star general casually remarked to Eisenhower, 'This is a great day for the Army because the Navy has fallen flat on its face.' Eisenhower went wild. It was precisely the kind of remark that triggered his temper. And for the next 30 seconds, expletives flew from his mouth.

A few days after that, John Foster Dulles walked into the Oval Office and told Ike that he was thinking the time had come to offer his resignation. He was only a few months shy of his 70th birthday, and was being treated for cancer. He'd been operated on a year before and the doctors told him he'd make it. But he was no longer as optimistic about his career as his doctors were about his health. Criticism, which over the past few months had been mounting both at home and abroad, had finally given way to shouts of 'Dulles Must Go.' What's more, the United States had just suffered a staggering blow to its national pride. He said he thought it was time for him to step down.

This shocked Eisenhower, who by now had a wonderful understanding of Dulles. In the first years of his Presidency, Eisenhower would sit talking with Dulles for hours on end, trying to get to know the inside of his mind as well as Ike knew his own. He regarded Foster Dulles as a highly experienced diplomat, someone very well qualified to conduct the operations of diplomacy. He also saw Dulles as a man who always looked to his President for policy and unceasingly deferred to his President on matters of public opinion.

He started out with a traditional job description. But over the years Eisenhower grew more and more dependent on him. The relationship matured, professionally and personally. He defended Dulles by telling people, 'You have to realize what kind of man Foster is.'

No, Eisenhower told Dulles that day in December 1957, there was no question of resignation. He wouldn't entertain the idea at all.

A month later, at the first press conference since his stroke, Eisenhower publicly reiterated his support of John Foster Dulles. 'He is the wisest, most dedicated man that I know . . . he stays right squarely on the job and that is where he belongs!'

It appeared to be a fine testimonial to the President's deep-seated sense of loyalty to his trusted Secretary of State. But it's probably closer to the truth to say that Eisenhower simply couldn't summon up the courage to let him quit.

An old friend put a bug in Ike's ear that Sputnik was part of a Communist plot to force the United States into a bankrupting space race.

It was an intriguing thought and not something the President would easily dismiss. In his 1953 State of the Union address, Eisenhower said one of the nation's priorities was to 'achieve adequate military strength within the limits of endurable strain upon our economy. To amass military power without regard to our economic capacity would be to defend ourselves against one kind of disaster by inviting another.'

Even if the Russians hadn't purposely conspired to ruin the American economy, he had no intention of doing it for them by plunging into a frantic build-up of military strength.

When James Killian moved into the White House, he immediately set out to solve the problems Sputnik had exposed. His first recommendation of note was for the establishment of a single new agency which could amalgamate the varied and often conflicting efforts being made in the name of space technology. As Eisenhower had, right from the beginning, tried to keep the fledgling American space program away from the military, the idea of a civilian agency was enormously appealing to him. Killian helped write the National Aeronautics and Space Act of 1958, which took the National Advisory Committee for Aeronautics and turned it into the mission-oriented National Aeronautics and Space Administration (NASA). The idea was, over time, to fold into it the Jet Propulsion Laboratory at Cal-Tech and the ABMA at Huntsville. NASA was then charged with the development of the vehicles and equipment necessary to explore space. And, while there might always be some military input, space policy would no longer be set in the Pentagon.

Killian's next notable contribution came out of his belief that the nation's educational system was inadequate for the scientific and technological challenges it was suddenly facing. That led to a massive campaign to upgrade science programs in the nation's schools.

The National Defense Education Act (NDEA) was, up to that time, the most important federal education bill ever submitted to Congress. It was also, according to Elliot Richardson, who was then serving as Assistant Secretary of Health, Education and Welfare, one of the most satisfying pieces of legislation anyone in government could have dealt with.

The nation was mobilizing its brain power.

The NDEA created a boom in academia which opened a great debate on what should be taught and how it should be taught and changed the very look of education, turning black boards into green boards and classrooms into modular learning centers. Audiovisuals were stressed, and so were subjects so brand-new that they had to be called New Math and New Social Studies. The federal government threw money at education to encourage science, math and eventually language teaching at all levels. Scholarships meant that many youngsters who might not otherwise have attended university were able to do so. Colleges and universities opened places and there was a surge of entrants from the minorities and inner-city youths.

The great surge of enthusiasm carried through for most of the 1960s. Then, with the Russians out of surprises and the nation short on Sputnik-shock, it gradually faded away.

The Science Advisory Committee, under Killian, became a group of 15 outstanding scientists, including Isidor Rabi and Edwin Land. Meeting once a month, they focused their attention on any area that caught their fancy, with a primary interest in space, warfare, disarmament, education, medicine and the environment. When pesticide manufacturers and the Department of Agriculture denounced Rachel Carson's book, *Silent Spring*, as being inaccurate, Killian and his colleagues convened a special panel to look into the question of pesticide pollution. Their report proved Carson right.

Not that everyone mobilized for the Sputnik response effort was fast or with the kind of team spirit Killian would have wanted. Early on he asked the military to help obtain Soviet scientific journals which could then be translated and passed along to US scientists. For some odd reason, his request was sent all the way up to the Joint Chiefs, who discussed it in that meeting with the State Department on 1 November 1957. They then sent it to the Joint Intelligence Committee for an opinion. After studying the matter, the JIC reported back that there were no statutory or policy restrictions on such publications, that translation facilities were adequate and anyway, this wasn't a matter for the DoD. All Killian wanted were some magazines. But the Pentagon washed their hands of it and suggested that the Department of Commerce worry about it.

Killian did however ignite a spark in the Pentagon when he said he wanted a special research and development organization formed to foresee future trends and make certain that America was geared up to meet them. The answer became the Defense Advanced Research Projects Agency (DARPA).

At about the same time, a small group of research scientists working at the Naval Ordnance Test Station (NOTS) at China Lake, California, were studying the possibility of launching a satellite from an airplane. NOTS, now known as the China Lake Naval Weapons Center, is a chunk of heavily guarded Mojave Desert, about half the size of England, some 120 miles northeast of Los Angeles. Assigned the mission of preparing the fleet for war, technicians in the 1970s actually built, somewhere in the middle of that desert, a mock-up of the entire Soviet Baltic Fleet.

In November 1957, just after that Joint Chiefs of Staff-State Department meeting, the Navy proposed a 'top secret – need to know' operation they called the Naval Observational Television Satellite Project, or NOTS-nik for short. They believed that, by taking a rocket up to 50,000 feet, they not only saved the cost of a first stage, but they could put a heavier payload into orbit using smaller rockets. So China Lake designers came up with a multi-staged $14\frac{1}{2}$-foot rocket that easily fit under the wing of a stripped-down Navy F4D fighter. When the State Department raised objections to the use of TV cameras, claiming they'd turned NOTS-nik into a spy satellite and that wasn't the Navy's business, the cameras were taken out. The Atomic Energy Commission was somehow secretly involved and requisitioned three of the six scheduled launches for experiments of their own, under the name Project Argus. By the time the Navy was ready, in April 1958, DARPA came along to assume overall responsibility. They were the ones who bathed everything in secrecy. Demanding that all press queries at China Lake be directed to DARPA at the Pentagon, their stock answer became, 'Certain high-altitude experiments involving both aircraft and guided missiles' were taking place.

These days an aura of mystery still surrounds what did or did not eventually happen there.

The first NOTS-nik launch took place over the Pacific Ocean on 25 July 1958. The rocket disintegrated. The second time they tried it, 18 days later, the rocket motor blew up. The same thing happened for the fourth try on 25 August. The rocket did not ignote on 26 August, and failed totally two days later on attempt six.

However, no one can agree on the results of the third attempt.

The Office of the Naval Historian in Washington couldn't find anything about it. No one at the Atomic Energy Commission knew. Nor was there anything conclusive to be found at China Lake. The pilot who fired the rocket on 22 August reported that it fell away from his plane, hung for a moment in mid-air, ignited and sped off skyward. The second stage apparently also ignited, as did the third stage. But at that point the pilot lost visual contact. His official log says the missile 'disappeared over the horizon.'

For the next 90 minutes or so, nothing happened. Then a tracking station in New Zealand reported a possible contact. They said it came quickly and disappeared just as quickly. If a satellite had been put into orbit there should have been a second contact 90 minutes later. There wasn't. However, 90 minutes after that, a contact was reported. But that was the last one. There was never anything else.

The men who worked at China Lake in those days swear they put a satellite into orbit. If they didn't, it was a good try. But if they did, even if it lasted only a couple of orbits, then America might not have been as far behind the Russians as everyone seemed to think. The thing is, at a time when the country needed every success it could muster, DARPA cancelled NOTS-nik and no one will ever know for sure.

John Medaris and Wernher von Braun also had dealings with DARPA. In January 1958, they'd begun putting together a proposal called 'The Man Very High Program,' or 'Project Adam.' They believed they had enough technical ability at Redstone to send a manned space capsule up to 150 miles above the earth in an Army rocket and bring it back safely by parachute to an ocean landing. But because of the way ABMA was funded, they knew they'd have to get input from at least one of the other services. Suppressing what bitterness remained from the days of the Orbiter project, they approached the Air Force and were initially received with some enthusiasm. At first it appeared as if the two Sputniks had swept away inter-service rivalries. But within a month the Air Force dropped out, forcing Medaris and von Braun to look for a new backer.

The Secretary of the Army, who liked what Redstone had to offer, arranged for von Braun to pitch the idea to the newly created DARPA.

Allen Dulles heard about it and began wondering if this might not be the perfect way to put his undercover agents into foreign countries. When he let the Army know that the CIA might be willing to become their benefactor, von Braun abandoned DARPA in favor of the Agency. But Dulles wanted to see Project Adam happen much faster than von Braun could make it happen and, when von Braun balked, Dulles backed out. So von Braun returned to DARPA. But their attitude had changed and they now said, no thanks.

Without an angel, von Braun packed Project Adam in cardboard boxes which soon disappeared into some storage hangar. The Army program to put a man in space went the same way as the original Project Orbiter. Had anybody been willing to take a punt, it's possible von Braun might have put a man into space at least six months before Sergei Korolev made a hero out of Yuri Gagarin.

On Wednesday, 29 January 1958, the final countdown began at Cape Canaveral. The Jupiter-C with the 18-lb Explorer satellite in its nose cone was ready. So were Medaris and most of the former Peenemünde team in Mission Control in Huntsville. So was von Braun, in a special communications room at the Pentagon, purposely sent to Washington to be easily accessible to the international press corps the moment the satellite was confirmed in orbit.

But the weather was wrong and high winds stopped the flight.

They tried again the next day.

Everyone was in place. And the weather closed them down a second time.

They restarted the countdown on Friday.

At 5:30 that afternoon, Andrew Goodpaster took a call from the Pentagon communications room, saying the weather at Canaveral was improving. The White House switchboard immediately put him through to Jim Hagerty, who was with the President at Augusta. Goodpaster relayed the message that all systems were go and that the estimated launch time was 10:34 p.m. Hagerty informed Eisenhower, who'd just come off the golf course and was settling into a game of bridge.

Exactly three hours later, the Pentagon called Goodpaster at home to report the weather was holding and the missile was being fueled. Goodpaster used the White House switchboard again to patch him through to Hagerty, who walked over to the cottage where the President was staying and interrupted him at dinner to give him the latest news.

The Pentagon's communications center was already overcrowded at 9:30 when Wilbur Brucker arrived in his tuxedo, having left a formal reception to be there. He took his place next to von Braun.

At 9:45, someone in the block house at Canaveral happened to spot something mysterious on one of the closed-circuit television monitors that was focused on the launch pad. It appeared as if there was a small pool of liquid on the ground just beneath the rocket. Nothing like that should have been there. The countdown was immediately halted as everybody crowded in front of the TV monitor trying to figure out what it was.

At best, a fuel leak would abort the mission. At worst, the rocket could blow up at any moment.

No one in Huntsville knew what to do about it. Neither did von Braun. There was no way anybody in Florida could make an accurate assessment of the problem without seeing it up close, which meant – if they were going to have any chance of launching – someone would have to go to the rocket. It was a propulsion expert who volunteered. He literally risked his life to run out from the block house to the pad, to stick his head under the ready-to-launch missile, then race back to the block house to announce, it's a fuel spill, not a fuel leak.

So the countdown resumed.

It was 9:50 when Goodpaster was informed. He told Hagerty the firing was a virtual certainty. He then left home for the White House, ringing Hagerty from there at 10:25 to inform the President that the status at Canaveral was T minus 20 minutes and counting.

Fifteen minutes later there was another crisis.

A caution light came on at one of the control positions, suggesting that something was wrong with part of the second stage. Everything stopped while mission controllers scrambled around to check what they could. The countdown stayed stopped for several minutes until, almost out of sheer desperation, someone decided the fault was in the control panel, not on the rocket.

From minutes, they were now down to seconds.

Goodpaster listened to the countdown on a loudspeaker at the Pentagon over one phone while he repeated it to Hagerty on another.

At exactly 10:48 p.m., the launch commander in Mission Control ignited the engines.

And the rocket lifted off exactly the way it was supposed to.

Although the satellite deployment system was set for automatic, when the time came, one of the German scientists at Huntsville was given permission to manually fire the final stage. Ernst Stuhlinger and his 'golden finger' pressed the button so hard that around Redstone he was forever after known as the man who 'pushed America's payload into orbit.'

For the next 100 minutes, everyone at Cape Canaveral and everyone at Huntsville and everyone at the special communications center in the Pentagon waited. So did Goodpaster at the White House and the President at Augusta. Von Braun kept looking at his watch and, when he realized they should have heard something by now, he asked why they hadn't.

Thirty seconds later it was there.

Explorer's signals came in loud and clear.

The President told Goodpaster, 'That's wonderful,' and went to bed.

The Pentagon celebration continued well into the night. It was the same thing at Cape Canaveral. In Huntsville, the mayor ordered the town's sirens turned on, calling thousands of people onto the streets. They waved American flags and Confederate flags and sported signs that read, 'Move Over Sputnik,' 'Our Missiles Never Miss' and 'We Dood It.'

Someone even remembered to burn Charlie Wilson in effigy.

The United States had finally crossed the finish line.

But second place still means you lost.

Chapter Fourteen

Khrushchev's Bluff

Sputnik-mania reigned.

The Soviet Embassy in Washington received an irate letter from a physician in upstate New York protesting that Sputnik's signals kept opening his remote-controlled garage doors. In Times Square, a billboard advertising whiskey was connected to the RCA laboratories on Long Island and rigged so that, every time the satellite passed by, lights flashed. At Lloyds of London, at least one insurance policy was sold to a woman worried that Sputnik could fall down on her.

The first verified sighting of the satellite was logged by Larry Ochs of Columbus, Ohio, who spotted it on 5 October at 10:28 p.m. moving slowly across the night sky from west to east. 'It had a sort of yellowish color,' he said. Newspapers reported their readers seeing red flashes and silver streaks and one hearing the satellite go by as it made a clicking noise. The BBC in London laid claim to the West's first reception of the satellite's radio signals.

On Tuesday, 7 October, Mr James T. Mangen of Chicago, Illinois announced that he had, some years ago, established a priority claim on outer space, which the Russians were now violating. No details were given as to exactly how his claim had been staked, but the Mangen announcement sparked a sharp rebuttal from one Mr A. F. Ettinger of Halifax, Nova Scotia. The way Ettinger saw it, he and he alone had a priority claim on outer space, having already organized the first expedition to the moon. Calling Mangen 'a thorn in my side' and a 'Johnny-come-lately to space,' Ettinger said that, in November 1950, he'd formed the Interplanetary Transportation Company specifically to supply scientists on earth with data brought back from the moon. Unfortunately, he couldn't seem to locate any of the company documents. But a small matter like paperwork wasn't going to stop him from putting the Soviets on notice that they had better keep their satellites out of his territory.

Before long there was a magazine named *Sputnik*, a travel agency named Sputnik and a perfume named Sputnik. There were also countless cafes, restaurants and nightclubs named Sputnik. And on 7 October, at a hairdressers' convention in Lansing, Michigan, the Sputnik hairdo was born. A lady's hair was wrapped around her head with an upward emphasis, covering her ears and most of her forehead. On top of that sat a four-inch model satellite, complete with radio antennae arching in all directions.

Binocular manufacturers were swamped with orders and a New York toy manufacturer rushed out a launcher that could hurl a toy Sputnik to an altitude of 75 feet. He promised the satellite would return to earth without disintegrating.

In Berlin, Germans were invited to dial the local telephone number 255 to hear a tape-recorded 'beep' from Sputnik. In Vienna, Austrians were invited to phone 1563 to hear one as well. In Moscow, the local radio station introduced its news programs with Sputnik beeps. And the post office was swamped as tens of thousands of cards and letters began arriving at the 'Moscow-Satellite' box. Mail came in from all over the Soviet Union and much of the rest of the world. A disproportionate number of cards and letters were received from Japan.

The Japanese, it seems, were extremely impressed with Sputnik. They turned out a whole range of tin rockets and Sputnik toys, some of which were manufactured in the small town of Usa, which meant they could stamp on the bottom, 'Made in USA.' What's more, a non-profit organization calling itself the Japanese Astronautical Society, which specialized in selling land on Mars, used Sputnik as their excuse for raising the price of Martian real estate from 55 cents an acre to $2.78.

At Jodrell Bank, near Manchester, England, work was speeded up on the giant radio telescope center so that scientists could train on it, using the Soviet satellite.

In Kelowna, British Columbia, radio station CKOV followed their daily special summary of Sputnik news with an un-introduced recording of Orson Welles' famous radio-drama *The War of the Worlds*. Originally broadcast in 1938, it was the story of a Martian invasion of earth and sounded so real to the millions of people who tuned in, that panic broke out in several cities. Nineteen years later, the radio station received 60 calls within a couple of minutes from local citizens who honestly believed that Sputnik had landed and hostile Russians were taking over in North America.

Protests poured into the White House, Congress, the State Department, No. 10 Downing Street, Buckingham Palace, Soviet embassies around the world and the Kremlin from animal rights activists. The Anti-Vivisection League, the Humane Society and the Society for the Prevention of Cruelty to Animals all formally voiced their objections to sending a dog into space. But Corinne Griffith, who noted she'd been deputized as a special representative of the Tailwaggers Foundation of America, went beyond mere protest, she categorically demanded the Russians bring Leika down immediately.

By December, an American dictionary publisher had already included the word 'Sputnik' in a standard lexicon. 'Some new words take years to get into the language,' the editor Clarence Barnhart said. 'Sputnik made the grade overnight. She's a record-breaking word.'

Shortly after that, San Francisco columnist Herb Caen took the 'nik' from Sputnik and tagged it on to Jack Kerouac's 'Beat' generation, to coin the word 'Beatnik.'

Keeping the record straight, the National Geographic Society put out a press release asking people not to say that Sputnik was in 'outer space,' because that term meant, 'incredibly distant reaches among the stars and galaxies.' They wanted it understood that Sputnik was only in 'inter-planetary' space, or the local space of our own solar system.

Also keeping the record straight, Britain's former Astronomer Royal, Sir Harold Spencer Jones, guaranteed that in spite of Sputnik, it would still take generations before man landed on the moon. 'Should he eventually succeed in doing so, there would be little hope of his succeeding in returning to the earth and telling us of his experiences.'

The Federation of American Scientists urged the government to begin negotiations immediately with the Russians for the international control of space weapons. And the Vatican issued a statement officially denouncing Sputnik as 'a frightening toy in the hands of childlike men who are without religion or morals.'

A Russian officer on duty at the Berlin Air Safety Center filed a flight plan for Sputnik and passed it along to his American counterpart. In the proper format, he listed: Identifying Call Sign – USSR; Type – Artificial Satellite; Fuel – Forever; Departing – Moscow; Route – Round the earth; and Alternate Destination – The moon.

The Governor of Michigan, a fellow named G. Mennan Williams, broke into print with a poem about Sputnik.

Oh little Sputnik, flying high
With made-in-Moscow beep,
You tell the world it's a Commie sky
And Uncle Sam's asleep.

And every Soviet comedian had at least two jokes about Sputnik. More often than not they were: Did you know that the Americans have invented a Sputnik cocktail? It's a mixture of vodka and sour grapes. And, did you know your wife was in bed with another man? No I didn't, I was watching Sputnik.

Five days after the first Sputnik launch, the Soviet Ambassador in Washington, Georgi Zaroubin, received orders from the Foreign Office in Moscow to send senior members of his staff into the hinterlands of America. Their instructions were to contact local school groups, civic organizations and newspaper editors and to make themselves available for interviews. Concerned with the stories he was now seeing in the American press, Khrushchev wanted to counter the media's apparently aggressive attitude towards the USSR by having people work at propaganda on the local level. He wanted to make the Russians look more human, less menacing.

Two of the men assigned to the embassy in those days as political counsellors were V. S. Lavrov and A. M. Ledovski.

The summer before Sputnik, Lavrov had traveled to Iowa and, when he met a group of students, asked if any of them were studying Russian. Their answer was an assertive, 'We're Americans, we don't need to study Russian.'

Now, immediately after Sputnik, he saw a nation overtaken with fear. 'Paranoia is a result of politics. But the fear the Americans felt was real. People kept saying to me, if we sit down together we can solve our problems. Sputnik had produced a revolution in the national psyche. Americans saw for the first time they were not the most advanced nation on earth. In some ways that was good. It caused America to look at the world with a more realistic approach. Overnight, Russian language lessons appeared on television. Russian studies were offered in high schools and universities. Three weeks after Sputnik, the US and the USSR began negotiating agreements for cultural and educational exchanges. The first group of 30 American students went to Moscow and 30 Russian students came to the States. An American was also invited to compete in the prestigious Tchaikovsky Prize competition. He was a brilliant young pianist named Van Cliburn, and he won the prize. But except for him, the American media seemed preoccupied with representing Russia as a hostile, military power.'

Ledovski says he was sent to Milwaukee, where people didn't know what to make of him. 'The editor of a local newspaper got up enough nerve to ask for an interview and when I said yes right away, he was shocked. He said he thought Russians needed permission to do interviews.'

The embassy's men had been thoroughly briefed to play up the angle that America and the Soviet Union were equally advanced and shared a common destiny. Moscow wanted Lavrov and Ledovski and all the others to make frequent allusions to World War II, which was still fresh in so many minds, and always to refer to the two nations that defeated the Nazis as 'Comrades in arms.'

'People kept introducing me as "a real Russian,"' Ledovski recalls. 'Not a Russian immigrant to the USA but a representative of the Soviet Union and the socialist system. They were surprised to discover that real Russians looked exactly like real Americans. It was confusing for them because they thought Russians had long beards and wore red shirts with knives and swords stuck into our belts. I sometimes felt that when we didn't turn up looking like Cossacks, Americans were disappointed. The creation of that image however was as much our fault as anyone's. Americans thought of Russia as a backward country filled with people who rode horses or pushed wheelbarrows and wore old peasant shoes. It was Sputnik which caused them to see things differently. It shocked them to discover the Soviet Union was a highly developed country, even more advanced than the US in science and technology. And yes, they were afraid. When you combine the popular image of a backward, illiterate country, with the political caricature of the Soviet Union as a threat to American security, it's easy to see how so many Americans feared that the USSR could only solve its problems by capturing a rich country.'

The embassy's men were cautioned to stay away from political subjects but, if asked, were told to keep in mind that John Foster Dulles was their primary target.

'We referred to him as Secretary of State for the Cold War,' Ledovski continues. 'He was a stiff and formal man who obviously played a bigger role in the formulation of policy than Eisenhower. We never said that the Cold War was the personal policy of Mr Dulles. But we did say it was the policy of the Conservative circles that had imposed him on Eisenhower. You see, we never considered Eisenhower a great politician. And we understood that the right wing in America needed someone like Dulles to compensate for that. We knew that whenever there was any serious confrontation between the US and the USSR that it wasn't Eisenhower's fault, it was down to Dulles.'

One night at a party, Ledovski found himself talking to Supreme Court Justice William O. Douglas. He asked Douglas, 'How can a subordinate be permitted to publicly contradict his boss?' Douglas supposedly responded, 'Ike didn't appoint Dulles, it was Dulles who was imposed on Ike.'

The Russian line was, they'd hear Eisenhower say one thing and the next day Dulles would say something different. Whether or not it was true hardly mattered. Here were 'real' Russians who looked like real Americans, speaking quietly, calmly and directly to grass-roots America about how to end the Cold War. If anyone believed them, it was because people wanted to believe them.

'Eisenhower was highly respected in the Soviet Union as Commander in Chief of the Allied forces during World War II,' Lavrov says. 'He received the highest honor in the Soviet Union and many people expected him to be the one American statesman who could make real progress in disarmament. We expected him to go to Congress and say, "I know what's needed to defend the US." But he didn't. That was a disappointment to us and we never hesitated to say so. We wanted the Americans to understand where our differences lay. The bad influence on him was Dulles. He was a very tough man who was never able to accept the realities of the world. It's interesting that when Eisenhower finally made a significant contribution, it was after Dulles died. It was in his last message as President when he warned America about the danger of the military–industrial complex. Unfortunately, it came too late.'

In those days they had to toe the party line, especially when anyone mentioned Nikita Khrushchev. These days they're more frank.

'He was a relaxed, easy-going man with a somewhat vulgar sense of humor,' Ledovski says. 'He used to exaggerate a lot, especially with the Americans. He was a great actor. He was always acting. He was always exaggerating our superiority. Everyone in the Soviet Union knew that but the Americans didn't. And we liked that. We also wanted to believe him. Russians are born optimists. However, he made a very foolish mistake when he came up with that comment, "We will bury you."

It was a bad blunder. Of course he meant it in the political sense. He meant that, politically, our system would see yours out. But America took it to mean something else.'

Lavrov agrees. 'The remark was clearly misunderstood. But Khrushchev should have known better than to allow such a mistake to happen, because it set back relations with the USA. The thing about him was that he sincerely believed the future belonged to socialism. He was a very human, instinctively clever man. Yet in spite of his good intentions, it's perfectly fair to say that the results were not always good.'

After Sputnik, the embassy men found themselves regularly invited to all sorts of social occasions, cocktail parties, dinners, receptions and even luncheons on Capitol Hill. 'Russians became celebrities,' Ledovski says. 'Everyone wanted to hear what we had to say about everything.'

What the Russians didn't tell the Americans was the joke going around the embassy: Over the rest of the world Sputnik's radio signal goes 'beep-beep-beep,' but over the United States it changes to 'hah, hah, hah!'

Riding high on his two successes, Korolev lost interest in just launching simple satellites. He saw the time growing closer when more complex instrumentation in space might control the weather. He saw space flight as transportation too, which might cut the 11-hour journey between Moscow and New York down to under 2 hours. Outer space might even be turned into a sort of health resort, where periods of weightlessness could be used to treat heart disease and pulmonary ailments. However, the ultimate goal had to be interplanetary travel, 'to enable earth dwellers to set foot upon the surface of these mysterious planets, to learn their essence and, in the final analysis, to increase the knowledge of the surrounding universe and our own planet.'

Knowing that putting a man into space required a huge financial commitment, he convinced Khrushchev of the political value of such a move. And one of the very first signs Korolev had of Khrushchev's interest was when he ordered special phone links installed connecting Baikonour directly with the Kremlin.

Throughout this Korolev remained anonymous. No one knew his name. His work was considered top secret and his name was never used in connection with it. Years later he supposedly confided to friends that he didn't mind the anonymity. 'It helped keep the newspaper and television people away.' But he wasn't telling the truth. He did mind the anonymity, and resented it enormously when Blagonravov started taking credit for Sputnik. He complained about that directly to Khrushchev and Blagonravov was instructed, in no uncertain terms, to keep his mouth shut. There was also talk, at one point in 1958, that the Nobel Prize Committee wanted to give their science award to the chief designer of the Sputniks. Rumor had it they approached the Kremlin asking for the name of the man responsible, but when the Kremlin was not forthcoming they gave their prize to someone else.

Publicly anonymous, it was still with the full authority of Khrushchev's office that Korolev built himself an empire. He commandeered an old aircraft factory near the Byelorussian railway station in Moscow and turned it into a center for research on maintaining life in space. He handpicked the staff, and charged one of his trusted engineers, a man named Voronin, with making certain that, by the time a rocket and space capsule were ready to put a man into space, this center would have everything ready that was necessary to keep him alive. For the next two years, Voronin and his staff did almost nothing but study American patents and scientific publications on that single subject.

To put a man into space, Korolev knew he needed a rocket with nearly five times the thrust of the R-7. The quickest way of designing one was to copy American engines. The KGB came up with plans for the Vanguard, Atlas and Thor rockets, and Korolev ordered prototypes built. The problem was, however, the Russians didn't have similar materials to work with and, even using American plans, they couldn't match American technical quality. Much to Korolev's immense frustration, every one of the American rocket engines built in the USSR burned out in the testing stages.

Sputnik ignited Khrushchev's passion for rockets. He instinctively understood that they must become the key element in the defense of the Soviet Union, and used his draconian powers to smooth the way for the various design bureaus. The men working for him might have been Stalin's designers, but Stalin didn't have the same interest in rocket development that Khrushchev did. Stalin was an office man. Khrushchev got out of the office and met the designers and found out what they were doing. His own son Sergei was an engineer who worked for V. N. Chelomei, one of Korolev's rival designers, and he kept his father informed on a daily basis of what was happening with rocket and space technology.

'He made a point of keeping up to date with the latest improvements,'

Sergei Khrushchev wrote about his father, 'knowing the types of rockets and missiles that were coming into the Soviet arsenal, comparing their characteristics with earlier models and the information he was being supplied by the KGB on American rockets and missiles. He took great pride in the fact that Soviet rocketry had kept pace with American rocketry.'

Khrushchev had come to understand that rockets and missiles and artificial earth satellites could be used for more than just destruction, that they were the Soviet Union's most powerful weapons in the propaganda battle for global influence. He canceled the production of certain bombers and put that money into submarines and rockets. Sputnik became the banner for a new military doctrine. There couldn't be an arms race with the usual arms any more. Anyway, rockets were ten times cheaper to build than cruisers and bombers. He saw the link between strategic military operations and space, and was smart enough to leave space technology in the hands of his military rocket forces. He displayed considerable skill in emphasizing the political significance of space, rallied national pride and sent a message to the uncommitted world that Soviet leadership would produce further successes in many fields. Whatever those first two Sputniks cost, they more than paid for themselves in sales of Soviet machinery and technical goods to the Third World.

In late October 1957, a motorist was driving through some mountains near Los Angeles when he spotted a crudely machined metal object, 3 feet long with fins and a spinner, on the side of the road. Cyrillic writing on the bottom translated to read, 'Russian Government.' He turned it in to the police and they turned it over to the Air Force. Investigators dubbed it 'Whatnik,' and refused to comment on the object, other than to say, 'We are taking no chances.' Two days later, the government broke silence to announce that 'Whatnik' was a 'Fakenik,' as American as the corner Army–Navy surplus store from where the parts came.

Like many fads that originate in California then head east, 'fakeniks' began popping up all over the country.

The joke took on new dimensions when Nikita Khrushchev showed up at the Finnish Embassy in Moscow for a cocktail party on 5 December. A reporter sidled up to him and asked if he had anything to say about the two Sputniks. Khrushchev gave him an earful. 'We know the carrier rocket that launched Sputnik I fell over the United States but they do not want to give it back to us. We relied on their decency but they did not live up to it. We know it fell somewhere in the United States and will announce it publicly soon with a request that they return it to us.'

He didn't have to announce it soon, he'd just done it.

United Press International carried the story. So did Tass and Radio Moscow, both of which specified that the carrier rocket had fallen to earth over the United States on the night of 30 November. The American IGY Committee confirmed the last US sighting of the rocket at 7:11 p.m. EST on Saturday the 30th. As it had not been seen on schedule over England the next morning, they estimated it fell somewhere in Southeast Asia. However, the US Naval Research Lab calculated the rocket had fallen over Soviet territory, specifically in Outer Mongolia. After checking radar tracking reports, the Defense Department said categorically that, if the Russian rocket had crashed to earth, it didn't land in the US.

But the Russians knew a good thing when they saw one, so they kept the story alive. Academician Alexander Nesmeyanov cabled his American counterpart Detlev Bronk, insisting that the United States had the Russian rocket and asking, please send it back. Bronk answered that there was nothing to suggest the remnants fell in the United States, nor had there been any reports of finding any such objects.

That's when Alan Waterman at the National Science Foundation dropped Jim Hagerty a line with a proposition to give the Russians a helping hand. 'Advertise for anyone finding an object which might be a stray piece of rocket casing to send it to the Soviet Embassy in Washington for examination. Upon the Embassy identifying the object, the finder would receive a reward which Science Service would be pleased to donate for the purpose. The American public would certainly catch on to this one and really give the Embassy a time.'

It's doubtful the Russians would have found it quite as funny as most of America.

On 5 November 1957, unable to stem the tide of discontent that was sweeping the country three days after Sputnik II, John Foster Dulles dropped the hint that the United States would be shipping intermediate-range ballistic missiles to bases in Europe, ringing the Soviet Union with them, just in case anyone in the Kremlin believed their ICBMs gave them an advantage in threatening American security.

The following day, Nikita Khrushchev accused the US and Britain of having reached an agreement to further intensify the Cold War. He called for a summit meeting. But neither Eisenhower nor Macmillan was anxious to oblige. Ten days later, Khrushchev repeated his demand for a summit, adding this time that his military had enough bombs and missiles to smash NATO and destroy American cities.

In Washington, two camps formed, both reaching the same conclusion from different directions. One refused to negotiate away whatever advantage America still possessed. The second refused to negotiate from a position of weakness.

A telling comment on the times came from the political cartoonist Herblock when he drew a caricature of Foster Dulles sitting on the lid of a box. One side of the box said, 'When we're strong we don't need to negotiate.' The other read, 'And when we're weak we're afraid to.' Uncle Sam, who is trying to push himself out from under the lid, is saying, 'How did I get in this box?'

In Canada, future Prime Minister Lester Pearson warned, if the West did not proceed with an effort towards peace, only two options remained. He saw the world heading towards nuclear war. Short of that, the world would sit on the knife edge of terror, somewhere between war and peace. And, he said, history proved that the second option ultimately leads to the first. He expanded on that theme a few weeks later in Oslo, when he accepted the Nobel Peace Prize. 'We face the inescapable fact that we cannot defend our society by war. Yet we prepare for war like precocious giants and for peace like retarded pygmies.'

Nikolai Bulganin threw oil onto the fire in a letter to Konrad Adenauer that he copied to various news agencies, which saw it published throughout the world. With great dexterity, Bulganin put forward his case that the Soviets were anxious to end the Cold War while the Americans were just as anxious to continue it.

George Kennan, then a visiting lecturer at Oxford, joined Pearson's call for negotiations. But Dulles, attending the NATO conference in Paris, told the BBC that he opposed talks with the Russians at this point.

Khrushchev now announced that he wanted to turn much of Europe into a nuclear-free zone. Dulles rejected the proposal outright. But then the Norwegian Ambassador to NATO stunned his allied partners by declaring that Norway would not allow atomic weapons to be stockpiled on its territory, nor would it permit any of America's IRBMs to be stationed there. The Canadian and Dutch Prime Ministers showed support for their Norwegian colleague, putting pressure on Harold Macmillan to try to cool things down by saying that negotiations with the Soviets should be considered. Dulles was forced into the position of agreeing that there could be negotiations, but only on the understanding that Europe would eventually accept IRBM bases. As the missiles wouldn't be ready for another few years, the Europeans said all right.

On 10 December, Nikolai Bulganin wrote to Eisenhower. He lamented the atmosphere of nervousness and fear created by an 'imaginary threat' from the USSR, and all the propaganda being spread around America about Sputnik in an effort to maintain that atmosphere. 'The launching of artificial earth satellites bears witness to the great achievements of the USSR, both in the field of peaceful scientific research and in the field of military technology. However, it is well known that the USSR has insisted and still insists that neither ballistic missiles nor hydrogen bombs should ever be used for purposes of destruction, and that so great an achievement of the human mind as the discovery of atomic energy should be put to use entirely for the peaceful development of society.'

Believing that the tense and almost hostile state of Soviet–American relations could not give any satisfaction to either the Soviet people or the American people, he called on the President to undertake joint efforts to put an end to the Cold War. He wanted the US, the UK and the USSR to announce a test-ban treaty on the use of nuclear weapons. Next he proposed that no nuclear weapons be stationed in either Germany. From there he suggested that a non-aggression agreement be signed between NATO and the Warsaw Pact, that America and Britain abandon their support of Israel so that the independence of nations in the Middle East might be assured, and that trade agreements be negotiated between the US and the USSR. He proclaimed Eisenhower a peace-loving man of great breadth of vision, and hoped that he would join the Soviets in trying to find a durable peace.

He then wrote to Harold Macmillan, saying he was deeply concerned at recent events, as they were developing in a manner which was dangerous to the cause of peace. 'The Soviet Government cannot fail to take into account the fact that the elaboration of all these military plans and preparations by the NATO countries is accompanied by systematic propaganda designed to spread the idea that war is inevitable, and that the elaboration of these plans is taking place in an atmosphere created by an artificial and deliberately conducted campaign to frighten the population of the western states with the idea that they are threatened by the Soviet Union.' Bulganin said that, in order to create an atmosphere of fear and suspicion, 'Attempts are being made to frighten people with the fact that the Soviet Union possesses intercontinental ballistic rockets, and even the fact that the USSR has launched artificial earth satellites for scientific purposes.' At the same time, the West had stubbornly suppressed the Soviet Union's repeated proposals for the prohibition of all types of nuclear weapons, the ending of thermonuclear weapons production and the total destruction of existing atom bombs, hydrogen bombs and rockets with nuclear warheads of all ranges, including ICBMs.

It was all grist for the mill and despite the fact that both Eisenhower and Macmillan answered Bulganin's letters with firm pledges to work for peace – and stern reminders that it was the Soviets who had continually rebuffed American and British efforts to put an end to the Cold War – Khrushchev's star kept rising.

Public opinion in the United States continued to turn against Dulles and his intransigence when it came to negotiating with the Russians. He went on television to defend his position, but only made matters worse because the country did not want to be pushed to the brink of war. Instead, they pushed for Dulles' removal.

Khrushchev's power was now such that he could at last consolidate his victory in the succession to ultimate power in the USSR by assuming the office of Chairman of the Council of Ministers, combining, as Lenin and Stalin had done before him, leadership of both Party and government. For all intents and purposes, the Soviet Union had returned to a Stalin-model full dictatorship. The terror aspect was gone but the three branches of the Soviet system were firmly united through Khrushchev. As First Secretary of the Communist Party, he controlled the Central Committee, which in turn controlled the various regional parties which oversaw almost all aspects of life in the country. As Premier and Chairman of the Council of Ministers, he controlled the day-to-day working functions of the government. Laws were proposed by Khrushchev's government, ratified and approved by Khrushchev's Politburo, and rubber-stamped by the Supreme Soviet, which was run by Khrushchev's Communist Party. It is significant to note that minutes of Politburo meetings were not kept in those days. It wasn't until Yuri Andropov came along in the 1980s that stenographers were invited in. Khrushchev, like the men who preceded him, had no interest in leaving records to show how decisions were made. Great public ignorance was one of the necessary ingredients in making this sort of rule work.

Time magazine put Khrushchev on the cover of their January 6, 1958 issue – describing him as stubby, bald, garrulous and a brilliant peasant, 'As extraordinary a dictator as the world has ever seen' – and named him 'Man of the Year.'

Their decision was based largely on, 'Two pale, clear streaks of light that slashed across the world's night skies' – in other words, the launch of the Sputniks, at least one of which he never believed in – and in so doing, for 'hurling mankind into the space age,' ironically, an act he had little, if anything, to do with.

'Whatever the future might bring,' *Time* explained, 'in 1957 the US had been challenged and bested.'

The editors continued, 'The shock wave from that reversal ran, perceptibly and profoundly, through the world's watching millions, disturbing the US's friends, cheering its enemies, swaying the uncommitted, as eyes in African jungles and Asian market places, in European town squares and American suburbs strained skyward for a glimpse of Russia's tiny moons. In 1957, under the orbits of a horned sphere and a half-ton tomb for dead dog, the world's balance of power lurched and swung toward the free world's enemies.'

And while *Time* was fast to note, 'Not since Alexander the Great had mankind seen a despot so willingly, so frequently, and so publicly drunk,' they could not deny that in 1957, Khrushchev had 'outrun, outfoxed, outbragged, outworked and outdrank' all the others.

Domestically, Khrushchev's philosophy was a simple one. 'People must first of all eat, drink, have homes and clothe themselves before they are in a position to engage in politics, science and art. The people took power into their own hands precisely to develop the forces of production, to multiply society's wealth, to improve their well-being and to create better living conditions as rapidly as possible.' By mixing in just enough fear, with loaves of bread, plenty of fish and a roof that doesn't let the snow in during the winter, he intended to wind up with a stable populace.

To help him manipulate the nation's foreign policy, he ordered the KGB to furnish him with all sorts of cuttings from the Western press. He wanted to learn everything he could about the differences within the leadership of the NATO powers, and in particular, how those differences expressed themselves in American politics. He'd seen how

Stalin's hostile line served to help the West more clearly define the Soviet threat and rally their side. What he wanted to attempt was a transformation, to signal a less aggressive style – call it a kinder, gentler face of Communism – in order to ease the military and political pressures aimed at the USSR. He also sought to help Europe's Communist parties, like the ones in France and Italy, make real advances.

Insidiously, Khrushchev set out to exploit whatever differences arose between Europe and the United States. One of the areas where he saw the possibility of European independence from Washington was in disarmament. After all, if a hot war was to break out of the Cold War, much of it would be fought in the fields and skies of Europe. If he could cast a spell of uncertainty among the member states of NATO, he could quite clearly limit America's alternatives.

Having seen his faith in Korolev rewarded – the world apparently believed the Soviet Union was in a position of nuclear parity with the United States – Khrushchev's instincts told him his opponents were on the ropes. So he called for a moratorium on all atomic testing.

James Reston reported in the *New York Times* that America did not want to give in to the Russians now because the Russians were ahead. He said Washington did not want to cease atomic weapons testing before a balance could be achieved between offensive and defensive weapons. The Rockefeller Foundation issued a report by a panel they'd set up – which included Edward Teller and Henry Kissinger – calling for a $3 billion increase in arms spending over the next several years. Lyndon Johnson insisted that America must win control of outer space, because whoever controls space controls the earth.

A beleaguered Foster Dulles could not have been more pleased.

But his complacency was shaken by Harold Macmillan's call for 'a solemn pact of non-aggression' with the Soviets.

Bulganin now wrote a 19-page letter to Eisenhower, with copies to all the NATO leaders, restating the Soviet position on the Cold War and offering advice on how to end it. Eisenhower answered, he would be willing to meet the Russians as soon as they allowed free elections to settle the German problem, allowed self-determination in Eastern Europe, were willing to limit the use of their UN veto and acknowledged the United Nations charter as an already existing non-aggression pact.

A day later, 9235 scientists from around the world presented a petition to the Secretary General of the United Nations calling for an end to atomic testing. By now, even the British were beginning to lose their patience with America.

Khrushchev was pulling every trick he had out of his hat. He was determined to force the United States into an agreement to ban atomic weapons testing. But Eisenhower and Dulles held their ground. Bulganin kept writing letters and Khrushchev went on the stumps, making speeches condemning the war-mongering imperialists and warning them that Soviet technology was moving at an incredible pace. 'We can double and more than double the weight of our Sputniks, since Soviet ICBMs posses such enormous power, allowing us to launch sputniks weighing still more to still greater heights.'

As the years 1955–1957 were a peak period for atmospheric weapons tests – the United States conducted 79 atomic and thermonuclear tests, the Soviet Union 39 and Great Britain 2 – it looked as though Khrushchev had come up with a grandstand play when on 27 March 1958 he announced that the Soviet Union would set the example for the rest of the world and unilaterally cease all tests on atomic weapons.

'One of the most urgent international problems of our time,' he said, 'of special concern to millions of people in all countries of the world, is the need to discontinue immediately atomic and hydrogen weapons tests.' He pointed out, as there were only three atomic powers, America, Britain and the Soviet Union should find it relatively easy to reach an agreement. He said the Soviet Union's motivation for the cessation of atomic weapons testing was its sincere desire 'to make a practical beginning for the general discontinuance of atomic and hydrogen weapons testing, and thus make the first step toward the final release of mankind from the threat of an atomic war of annihilation.'

If the countries now possessing nuclear weapons supported his proposal and discontinued their own tests, he promised, 'a problem that is of deep concern to the nations of the world will at last be solved, and important progress made towards the establishment of genuine confidence among nations and the strengthening of peace.'

Dulles called the announcement 'nothing but propaganda.' Eisenhower labeled it 'a gimmick.' But around much of the rest of the world, Khrushchev scored heavy points.

Nobody knew that Khrushchev was not being overly magnanimous. He stopped testing atomic bombs because he didn't have a choice. He'd run out of bombs to test.

Until the mid-1950s, the Soviet Union's main atomic bomb production and waste storage center was concentrated at a single site on the eastern slopes of the Ural Mountains, between the two towns of Kyshtym and Kasli, some 40 miles or so from Chelyabinsk, a stop along the Trans-Siberian Railway. Igor Kurchatov had placed the USSR's first plutonium-producing facility there in 1948. Nine years later, the plant known as 'Post Box 40' consisted of five reactors and a radiochemical reprocessing plant. But because Stalin put such a high priority on building a bomb, little attention was paid to disposing of nuclear waste. The system consisted of 60 stainless-steel cauldrons sunk into individual underground concrete tanks that had been filled with water to cool them down. The method was, to say the least, primitive.

Sometime in 1956, one of those cisterns began leaking. Scientists thought they'd stopped the leak and expected the wastes to remain stable. But the surrounding water had been contaminated. The water temperature rose, failing to keep in check the temperature of the waste. Nothing was done about it. By late September the waste was boiling. By then it was too late. On 29 September 1957, the waste exploded.

The force of the blast was the equivalent of 100 tons of TNT. There were broken windows in villages seven miles away. Huge amounts of strontium-90 and caesium-137 contaminated an area of nearly 1200 square miles, which had to be evacuated. Strong winds blew radioactive clouds for dozens more miles, affecting the safety of tens of thousands of people. More long-lived radio isotopes were released by the explosion at Chelyabinsk-40 than at Chernobyl.

Yet no mention of the accident was made.

Orders came from the Kremlin that this was to remain a state secret of the highest priority. No casualty figures were forthcoming, although estimates put the death toll by contamination in the thousands. The only official indication that something had happened was a sign posted along a 20-mile stretch of road going through the area warning people not to stop.

It took the dissident geneticist Dr Zhores Medvedev to write about it in 1976. When he did, some prominent scientists, including Sir John Hall, then chairman of the United Kingdom Atomic Energy Authority, dismissed the story as science fiction and accused Medvedev of having invented it. In response, Medvedev presented further proof of the accident. And still the Russians denied it. Even Andrei Sakharov lied, saying he knew nothing about it. But Medvedev had piqued the interest

301

of the Ralph Nader organization in America, which petitioned the US government under the Freedom of Information Act for whatever they had, which by that point was enough to confirm Medvedev's original claims.

Faced with undeniable proof, the Soviets officially acknowledged the accident in July 1989, some 32 years after the event.

According to the CIA's files, the earliest the Agency knew of the disaster was February 1961, when it was mentioned in a dossier on nuclear installations in the USSR. A source inside the Soviet Union had informed them that swimming in the numerous lakes and rivers throughout the area was considered a health hazard, that food brought to the market was checked for radioactivity, that passengers were stopped at the Kyshtym railway station, that no one without a special pass was allowed into the town, and that several villages in the area had been burned down. Furthermore, in late 1960, signs started appearing along the banks of the Techa River warning that the water was polluted and was not suitable for drinking, bathing, washing or fishing.

More details became available to the Agency once Medvedev published his original article on the disaster. But, at the time the accident occurred, the CIA had – arguably – been caught napping. Their March 1958 report on Soviet atomic weapons capabilities made no mention of it at all. General Goodpaster does not recall ever having seen anything come across the President's desk about it. Nor do the White House files show that the President knew.

That Khrushchev called for a test ban treaty because he had nothing left to test actually amuses Goodpaster. 'I wouldn't put that past him. That's just the kind of innate cleverness and cunning he had.'

It hardly mattered that Sputnik II's nose cone stayed too close to the satellite and inhibited the working of the ultra-violet detection device. The success of the second satellite became the green light for the launch of a 3000-lb, instrument-laden Sputnik III. The success of that meant the Russians would try to put a man into space. If they managed that, it was obvious the next step would be to land him on the moon.

Korolev wanted to do it but the Kremlin said no.

During the first full calendar year after Sputnik, the USSR and the USA launched a combined total of eight spacecraft. Over the next two years the competition intensified. Within four years of Sputnik, United States reconnaissance satellites had photographed and completely mapped the Soviet Union's main ICBM sites. By this time, the CIA had finally figured out that the Soviets were lying whenever they spoke about the number of revolutions their satellites had made around the earth. They would claim that orbit number three was either number two or number four. The reason being, if the Americans could determine the correct orbit number, they could then plot the satellite's trajectory back to the launch point. And in a country obsessed with secrecy – to the point of paranoia where they did not include large towns on maps or they deliberately put them in the wrong place – the Soviets did not want to give the Americans any advantage in the search for their missile sites. So they lied about the number of orbits to conceal the launch point, which in the end didn't accomplish much, first because of the overflights by the U-2 and then because of the spy satellites. The Americans had proof that the Russians were lying and the Russians knew that the Americans knew, but they continued to lie because that's the way the game was played.

In 1961, Korolev put Yuri Gagarin into orbit. Over the next six weeks, the new President, John Kennedy, considered an American response. There was talk of a huge space station and an unmanned mission to Mars. He turned them both down and opted for something that would truly stretch man's imagination. On 25 May 1961, a full nine months before John Glenn made America's first orbital flight, Kennedy committed the nation 'to achieving the goal, before this decade is out, of landing a man on the moon and returning him safely to Earth.'

He determined the end of the decade timetable with two things in mind. First, that the National Security Council was estimating that the earliest date the Soviets could put a man on the moon was 1970. Second, when he asked NASA if they could do it before 1970, they said yes. So he announced the race for the moon.

What he never knew was that the race was already over.

It looked at first as if the Soviets were trying to answer Kennedy's challenge. They constructed bigger and bigger boosters and embarked on a long series of unmanned missions. They more than proved the capability of their scientists. But the system couldn't stand the weight of its own inefficiency. Khrushchev squandered so much money trying to impress the Americans that, by 25 May 1961, the Russians were, for practical purposes, already beaten.

It wasn't until three years later that the Russians even seriously discussed putting a man on the moon. By then they were not only three years behind the Americans, they were also severely under-funded.

'The success of the Sputniks and of Yuri Gagarin's flight,' explains Vasily Mishin, who inherited Korolev's job as Chief Designer, 'were very much based on colossal self-sacrifice and on the leadership qualities of Korolev. But eventually our lack of organization and our general technical level betrayed us. The rocket that might have put a Russian on the moon was being made by 500 organizations in 26 departments. Of these, only nine fell within the competence of the military-industrial complex. The rest had to be begged for. Resolutions from the Council of Ministers did not help at all. The tasks were just outside their competence and delivery schedules were not met. We failed to agree with minister after minister. The Americans had invested $25 billion in their program. We had a tenth of that and had to extract each million one by one.'

The story is confirmed by Boris Chertok, who worked with Mishin. 'There was never a single Soviet program to land a man on the moon. Instead, we had several ideas we wanted to pursue. The main program died when Khrushchev was pensioned off in 1964. When Korolev died in 1966, the other possibilities simply dissipated. Anyway, by then we were much too far behind. We knew we couldn't catch up. We simply didn't have the resources. We were beaten, so we gave up.'

But they didn't tell the Americans.

Sputnik had allowed Khrushchev to claim that his leadership was capable of great achievement, even though the technical breakthroughs that made it possible had come before his leadership. Sputnik also gave him the opportunity to say to the world, look at how the USSR is using its military potential for the good of all mankind. But Sputnik couldn't stop a succession of crop failures and Sputnik couldn't save his latest Five-Year Plan from ruin. Money disappeared down the black hole of the space program while the economy went into a tailspin. The men at Baikonour started to get sloppy and accidents started killing people. Khrushchev remained stubbornly committed to staying ahead of the Americans. And with things at home turning so sour so fast, he came to believe that his own future depended on another achievement in space. He emptied the coffers and threw that money down the drain too.

Stalin left the country suffering. By mid-1958, Khrushchev had bankrupted it.

★   ★   ★

On 9 February 1959, John Foster Dulles entered Walter Reed Military Hospital outside Washington for a hernia operation. Three days later his doctors diagnosed terminal cancer. He'd been in remission for nearly two years, since they first treated him. Now the disease had begun to spread again.

Eisenhower asked Dulles what he wanted to do.

Dulles said he would like to keep working.

He stayed on the job, as best he could, until mid-April. The President accepted his resignation with enormous sadness. But, in a typical show of Eisenhower loyalty, four days after Dulles' resignation, Ike named him Special Advisor on Foreign Affairs and awarded him cabinet rank.

Five weeks later Dulles was dead.

Such was the respect he commanded that his funeral would be an official state event and even Andrei Gromyko would attend. Later the main international airport serving Washington and its environs would be named in honor of him.

But on that day, when the President was told, he admitted to some very close friends that this was the second saddest day of his life. The saddest, he explained, was the day his own first son died.

Rumors spread throughout the late spring and early summer of 1959 that Nikita Khrushchev would accept an invitation to come to the United States if one were to be offered. On the likely chance that Eisenhower would soon extend an invitation, *Life* magazine dispatched Averell Harriman to Moscow to interview Khrushchev.

Harriman, one of America's most distinguished statesmen, was a former ambassador to both the USSR and the United Kingdom and at the time the outgoing Governor of New York. He met Khrushchev in early July and was perhaps the first person in America to openly suggest that Khrushchev was a fake.

'I could not escape the impression that at least some of his more bellicose threats were mere acting,' he wrote. 'Khrushchev is a superb actor and obviously enjoys making an impression on his listeners, whether they are peasants he is cajoling into growing more corn or diplomats he is trying to influence.'

Comparing Khrushchev with Stalin, whom Harriman knew well, he said Khrushchev lacked Stalin's caution and calculating shrewdness. Khrushchev's frequent outbursts contrasted with the colder, more sinister personality of Stalin. And it struck Harriman that, while the West must pay attention to Khrushchev's brashness, and that even his most pugnacious claims must not be underestimated, the West should keep in mind with whom they were dealing and not overreact.

Although that issue of *Life* was dated Monday, 13 July, it hit the news-stands at the end of the previous week, the same day that Eisenhower decided to extend the invitation.

Khrushchev's first thought was that public opinion in the US had begun to shift in favor of improved relations with the Soviet Union. Christian Herter was now Secretary of State and Khrushchev believed it was just possible that Eisenhower, out from under the Dulles influence, was being forced to listen to more reasonable arguments. On top of that, Khrushchev was intrinsically curious about America. As Russia's strongest opponent in the capitalist world, the United States occupied a special position in the way the Soviets thought and viewed the world. So Khrushchev accepted – 'We were interested in a first-hand look at our number one capitalist enemy' – and the long run-up to the visit began.

Embassies on both ends, the US State Department, the Soviet Foreign Ministry, the Kremlin and the White House all got involved with the myriad of problems that had to be settled, planning down to the minutest detail what would amount to be a 13-day, 7-city tour.

Two weeks after Harriman's interview appeared, the Vice-President of the United States, Richard Nixon, arrived in Moscow.

At the time the Russians considered Nixon to be directly out of the Dulles mould, a man of the Cold War, a hardliner, inflexible. The official reason for his visit was to open an exhibition of American life and culture. But Nixon, with his future staked on the 1960 presidential election, had come prepared for a confrontation.

Having agreed sometime in April to go to Moscow, he began calling and writing everyone he could think of who'd ever met Khrushchev. He read every file at the NSC, the JCS, the State Department and the CIA on the Russian Premier. Dulles had assured him from his hospital bed that he could hold his own with Khrushchev and hoped he might 'expose at least some segment of the Russian people to the reasonableness and justice of the American position on world issues.'

By the time his plane landed in Moscow, Richard Nixon was ready for Nikita Khrushchev.

The two men met the next day. The Vice-President went to the Kremlin where he and Khrushchev instantly disliked each other. Although they smiled together for the cameras, once they were alone Khrushchev accused Nixon of perpetuating the spirit of Joe McCarthy. In 1953, Eisenhower had proposed, and Congress had passed, something called the Captive Nations Resolution, which on the surface seemed innocent enough. It gave the President the right to declare Captive Nations Week, during which the American people were asked to pray for the freedom of people living under Communism. An annual event, Eisenhower had invoked it a few days before Nixon left for Moscow. Khrushchev now resented having the Vice-President talking peace out of one side of his mouth, while his country – and presumably he too – was praying to God for the overthrow of Communist tyranny. 'People should not go to the toilet where they eat. This resolution stinks. It stinks like fresh horse shit, and nothing smells worse than that.'

Nixon said Khrushchev was mistaken. 'There is something that smells worse than horse shit, and that is pig shit.'

Their relationship was off to a fine start.

From the Kremlin they went to the exhibition grounds where workmen were preparing for the official opening that evening. Khrushchev and Nixon walked around together, with Khruschhev telling Nixon that he didn't much like what he saw. Stopping at a model television studio, where cameras were rolling, a fed-up Nixon thought he'd let Khrushchev have it with both barrels. He accused the Soviet leader of keeping the Russian people down, of keeping the truth from them. 'There must be a free exchange of ideas.'

Khrushchev responded, 'America has been in existence 150 years and this is the level she has reached. We have existed not quite 42 years and in another seven years we will be on the same level as America. When we catch you up, in passing you by, we will wave to you . . .' And he waved to the camera.

With an idiotic grin, Nixon tried to interject, 'You don't know everything . . .'

But Khrushchev was in great form. 'If I don't know everything, you don't know anything about Communism except fear of it.'

Nixon was willing to concede that the Russians might be ahead of America with rockets, but that was all. America was, he suggested, ahead in such things as color television.

'No,' Khrushchev barked, 'we are up with you on this too. We have bested you in one technique and also in the other.'

'You never concede anything,' Nixon snapped.

'I don't give up,' Khrushchev responded.

They left the studio and, with a huge press contingent fighting to get their tape recorders in between the two men, they stepped into a model American kitchen. The argument continued as Nixon pointed to all the latest gadgets. 'Anything that makes women work less is good.'

Khrushchev shook his head. 'We don't think of women in terms of capitalism. We think of them better.'

Nixon said that a prefabricated home like this one cost only $14,000 in America, well within reach of the average worker.

Khrushchev retorted, they were built to last no more than 20 years so that capitalists could sell more homes. 'We build for our children and our grandchildren.' He said, in Russia everyone had a house and in America only people who could afford houses had them, otherwise they had to sleep on the pavement.

Now the Vice-President tried, 'To us diversity, the right to choose, the fact that we have a thousand different builders, that's the spice of life. We don't want to have a decision made at the top by one government official saying that we will have one type of house. That's the difference.'

Khrushchev answered, 'It's inefficient to produce so many types of houses and washing machines.' Anyway, he added, Soviet products are superior.

'Isn't it better,' Nixon asked, 'to be talking about the relative merits of our washing machines than the relative strength of our rockets? Isn't this the kind of competition you want?'

'Yes,' Khrushchev admitted, 'but our generals say we want to compete in rockets. We can beat you.'

Because both nations were strong, Nixon said, neither should put the other in a position where they had to face an ultimatum.

Khrushchev wondered who was giving whom ultimatums. Jabbing his finger into Nixon's chest he warned, if America intended to threaten the Soviet Union, they were prepared to answer that threat.

Nixon jabbed back. 'We will never engage in threats.'

The press loved every minute of it.

Khrushchev's version of the famous kitchen debate with Nixon is slightly different. Completely disregarding anything said in the television studio, he claimed that when they got to the kitchen he picked up a lemon squeezer and muttered what a silly thing it was. 'All you need for tea is a couple of drops of lemon juice. I think it would take a housewife longer to use this gadget than it would for her to do what our housewives do, which is slice a piece of lemon, drop it into a glass of tea, then squeeze a few drops out with a spoon. That's the way we always did it when I was a child, and I don't think this appliance of yours is an improvement in any way. It's not really a time saver or a labor saver at all. In fact, you can squeeze a lemon faster by hand. This kind of nonsense is an insult to our intelligence.' Nixon disagreed and, according to Khrushchev, the 'great kitchen debate' centered around how the abundance or lack of lemon squeezers proved the merits of capitalism over socialism.

Khrushchev then claimed that, during their tour of the exhibition, Nixon asked what type of fuel Soviet ICBMs used. He found the question wholly inappropriate. 'He didn't act like a statesman in that kitchen,' Khrushchev told his son, 'but like a second-rate spy.'

What neither of them ever went into detail about is that the debate continued the following afternoon at Khrushchev's dacha. But now, without the media to impress, Khrushchev's tone noticeably changed.

Luncheon was served at 3:30. Somewhere around 5, Khrushchev confided in Nixon that he'd met the day before with his rocket scientists – no names were mentioned – who presented plans to him to put a satellite into orbit that weighed 100 tons. He said it was equipped to carry a man into space and return him to earth. He also bragged that Soviet missiles had proven accurate enough to land within 1.7 km of their target 7000 km away.

In this connection, he said, he wanted to tell the Vice-President a secret. Krushchev confided, a month ago they'd launched an ICBM that malfunctioned and overflew its target by 2000 km. The launch technicians worried that it might land in Alaska. Luckily it fell short and crashed into the ocean. It did not carry a warhead but could have created a serious international incident. The point was, the USSR had enough ICBMs to paralyze vital centers in the US. They also had more than enough IRBMs to use against the UK and Germany.

Khrushchev and Nixon talked for more than three and a half hours, covering nearly every subject of mutual interest, moving on from missiles and bombers to submarines and Germany.

It was here that Nixon says he mentioned rocket fuel. He broached the subject of solid fuels and Khrushchev, far from accusing Nixon of being a second-rate spy, replied that the Soviets had attained some successes in the development of rocket fuels but it was a technical subject he didn't know much about and was not qualified to discuss. Suddenly Pat Nixon, the Vice-President's wife, jumped in, telling Khrushchev how surprised she was that in a system of one-man government, there was a subject that one man wasn't prepared to discuss.

First Deputy Chairman Anastas Mikoyan defended Khrushchev, saying he couldn't be expected to deal with every aspect of everything.

They then spoke about World War III.

Khrushchev insisted, American bases in Europe and Turkey, and all those American missiles surrounding the USSR, gave him the distinct impression that the United States wanted a war. He warned that the Soviet Union could destroy Germany, France and England on the very first day of a war. There would be Russian losses too, he conceded, but the other countries would become deserts. The Soviet Union did not want war but would not be threatened by American military might. The Soviets, he reiterated, had all the weapons they needed to defend themselves.

'You know what they tell me about England?' he asked Nixon. 'They tell me that in England there are optimists and pessimists. The pessimists think only six atomic bombs would be enough to wipe out the UK. The optimists think it would take nine or ten.'

Chapter Fifteen

To the Brink of World War III

For his trip to the United States, Khrushchev came up with a pair of surprises.

First, he did something no Soviet leader before him had ever dared. He brought his family along. Stalin had frowned on such things and even Khrushchev usually considered it unbusinesslike, a bourgeois luxury. But Mikoyan managed to convince him that being seen with his family would give him a more human face. So, for the first time since 1917, the wife of a Russian ruler was visible. Khrushchev's son Sergei came along too, and his daughter Rada also emerged from the shadows. Along with her came her husband, Alexei Adjoubei. A journalist by trade, the Premier's son-in-law had been elevated to editor-in-chief of the newspaper *Izvestia*. As such blatant nepotism was not the norm in the USSR, Adjoubei's appointment had raised eyebrows. There is an old Russian expression that goes, 'Don't have a hundred roubles, but have a hunded friends.' It was now changed to, 'Don't have a hundred friends, get married like Adjoubei.'

Khrushchev understood the sense of Mikoyan's argument and agreed to use his family to appeal directly to the public. He was going to say to the average American on the street, look, I have a wife and children and grandchildren, I am someone you can relate to.

The second surprise was Korolev's doing. Once the dates of the trip were settled, Khrushchev told Korolev he wanted to organize his own welcoming celebration. In January 1959, Korolev's Lunik I spacecraft had missed landing on the moon and gone into an unexpected solar orbit. To keep his patron happy, Korolev set out again to land a Russian rocket on the moon. And, three days before Khrushchev's arrival in Washington, Korolev had already captured the front pages for him. Lunik II impacted on the moon, the first man-made object ever to do so.

No sooner had the Tupolev-114 landed at Andrews Air Force base, than Khrushchev was telling Eisenhower all about the Russian moon shot. He'd even brought with him a gift for Eisenhower, a scale model of Lunik II.

After an initial stay in Washington, Khrushchev began traveling. For 13 days, he showed off his family and he spoke about the moon, turning both into purely political happenings. He visited New York and he visited Hollywood. He went to San Francisco and to Pittsburgh. But he really demonstrated to the American public that he was in his element when he arrived at Roswell Garst's farm in Iowa. Surrounded by animals and mud, the traditionally bellicose Communist leader from Moscow suddenly didn't look quite so menacing.

'He had that earthy touch,' James Reston recalls. 'No doubt about that. He was in his glory wandering through the pig pens. He was in touch with the people, close to the people. He should have been the Senator from Iowa.'

Over the course of 13 days, hardly ever out of the media's eye, Khrushchev managed to pull off what, for a Soviet leader in the middle of the Cold War, had to be the most difficult stunt of all. The man who'd once threatened to bury the capitalists proved to America that he had a human side. And America responded to that. The people opened up to him. He might have been embarrassed by the dancing girls when he visited the set of the film *Can Can* and there might have been some awkward moments when Russian-born Americans castigated him for perpetuating a Communist dictatorship, but wherever he went hundreds of thousands of people lined the streets to greet him. And he liked that. He saw the ultimate consumer society, and he liked that too. He realized there were things to learn in America. He was a realist, a practical man, and he admitted to his family that he was impressed with what he saw.

However, it was what happened at the presidential retreat in the Maryland mountains, that held promise for the future. Left alone with Eisenhower, with only Adjoubei there to translate, the two leaders found time to talk privately, to get to know each other on a one-to-one basis.

It was the first time that a leader of the West and a leader of the Communist bloc had ever dared stake the future of the world on personal understanding.

They spoke about Berlin and they spoke about disarmament. They discussed space – 'Sputnik was my star trip,' Khrushchev confessed to

Ike – and they talked about their grandchildren. Khrushchev asked Eisenhower all sorts of questions about consumer goods and wondered if American know-how and American techniques could be applied to Russian manufacturing. He wanted to know how much a house cost, how much an automobile cost and how much a suit of clothes cost. And he asked about salaries.

At one point, Eisenhower wanted to know, 'How do you budget for your military?'

Khrushchev answered, 'When the military comes to me and says, the US has everything and we have nothing, I have to give them money.'

Eisenhower laughed. 'We have the same system. The Pentagon comes to me and says, we need more money because the Russians have so much.'

Later, Eisenhower confided in Hagerty that Khrushchev was a very reasonable man when the two of them were alone like that. It was only when another Russian walked into the room that Khrushchev switched back to hardnosed, hardline arguments, back to traditional Communist banter.

'In many ways,' Andrew Goodpaster says, thinking back to Khrushchev's stay at Camp David, 'we were living through an era of great paranoia. But I felt Khrushchev was starting to see beyond that. He said to the President, "My generals come to me and tell me what forces you're building up and I imagine your generals come to you and tell you the same thing. Isn't there some way we can break through all of this?" Now, he was mercurial and could fly off the handle. He said what was on his mind. Sure, he might try to deceive you. But there's no doubt that he was genuine about the policies he was trying to put forward.'

As the two men grew more confident in each other's company, similarities in their personalities began to show. Having both seen World War II, they spent time telling each other war stories.

One morning over breakfast, Khrushchev explained to Eisenhower how he'd been a 'political commander' – a Party position that paralleled a military commander – in a field army on the southern front near the cherished city of Kiev. He said that, during the German advance, they were about to be surrounded when he and the military commander agreed orders to retreat. When Stalin learned of the orders, he revoked them. Realizing that no one in the chain of command had the nerve to argue with Stalin, Khrushchev picked up the phone, but Stalin refused to take his call. Stalin had a tendency, he said, to make military decisions primarily in terms of prestige considerations, without taking into account the actual military situation, and had more than once unfavorably affected the course of the war.

He also told Ike about Hitler's great mistake at Stalingrad. He said the Russians were strong only inside the city and that Field Marshal von Paulus could have crossed the river to take the Soviet forces with a flanking maneuver. The Soviet lines could have been broken. However, Hitler gave orders that the city had to be taken with a frontal attack. It was a matter of German honor and prestige. It was also impossible. By the time Hitler permitted von Paulus to attempt a western movement, Soviet reinforcements had been brought up and it was too late for von Paulus to escape.

Eisenhower explained to Khrushchev how Hitler had continually reinforced the North African front with excellent fighting units long after the Germans were contained in Tunisia and the complete destruction of their forces had become inevitable. He reinforced them practically to the date of surrender, Eisenhower said, while his own method had been to reinforce success and turn an advance into exploitation.

Military experience came up again later that afternoon. Eisenhower wanted to make a point, so he leaned forward and reminded Khrushchev, 'You must not forget, Comrade Lieutenant General, that I am a five-star general, and General of the Army.'

'Ah,' Khrushchev responded with a huge grin. 'I am not just a Lieutenant General. I am also First Secretary of the Communist Party and I am the Premier.'

And the two began to laugh.

Khrushchev even told Eisenhower a joke. He said, 'There are three defense ministers in a plane. One is American, one is British and one is Marshal Zhukov. They're flying over Europe and the British defense minister points to some planes on the ground and says, "That's our Air Force defending Britain." The plane flies further, now over the sea and the American points to some ships. "That's our Navy defending America." They fly further and now Zhukov points to some bubbles in the sea. "And that's our infantry marching to the United States."'

It was the beginning of a relationship.

No sooner had a triumphant Khrushchev returned to Moscow when Korolev came up with the icing on the cake. Lunik III was launched from Baikonour into lunar orbit and sent back to earth with the first-ever pictures of the moon's dark side.

There couldn't have been many people left in America who doubted that the Russians were way ahead of the United States, except perhaps in the White House.

It became known as the missile gap.

The essense of strategic planning, according to former Secretary of Defense Robert McNamara, is conservative calculations. You never prepare for the most probable case, you always prepare for the worst case. In the wake of Sputnik and the Gaither Report, combined with inaccurate and unsubstantiated intelligence about the Soviet build-up, the worst case – a successful all-out thermonuclear attack against the United States – now became a believable case.

That it was possible was beyond doubt. That it was believable was, in large part, because of America's 'Pearl Harbor psychosis.' Japan's surprise attack on Hawaii in December 1941 left US defense planners with the fear that, if it happened once, it could happen again. In the ten years between 1947 and 1957, there'd been Clark Clifford's report to Harry Truman, NSC-68, the JCS plan for World War III, and now the Gaither Report, all making it abundantly clear that the Soviet Union was an inherently evil enemy, intent on ending the American way of life as that was the one thing standing in the way of the ultimate Communist victory.

Given the parameters of the game, American planners could not rule out that the Russians might be willing to submit themselves to an 'acceptable level of retaliatory damage' as long as the odds favored their victory in a first strike. And when planners sat down to put estimates to that first-strike capability, the figures they came up with were so overwhelmingly in favor of the USSR that it appeared America might at last be doomed. They warned it could happen sometime around 1961.

In those days, each service had its own intelligence system. Geared to the specific needs of that service, they produced only a fragment of the overall picture. When the CIA pasted them all together, they wound up with a confusing pot pourri of what the Russians were up to. The Air Force led the field in overestimating the number of missiles the Soviets had. This was probably done on purpose because it helped reinforce the Air Force case for increased funding. The Army did much the same thing, in many instances using the same data, although their estimates of the Soviet build-up were the lowest of the three services. The Navy's figures tended to fall in between those of the Air Force and the Army. It turns out, all three were way off.

But that didn't stop the Democrats from picking up on those figures and running with them. While Senator Henry 'Scoop' Jackson concentrated on what he called the creeping and groaning national security structure, and Lyndon Johnson pursued the space program, it was Stewart Symington who, as father of the bomber gap, was the ring leader of this thing too. 'The launching of the earth satellite by the Russians was further proof of Communist superiority in the all-important field of missiles and if this advance develops into supremacy, it would not be well for the free world.'

He was backed up by the newspapers, which categorically refuted Eisenhower's claim that Sputnik was merely a scientific achievement. 'From a military standpoint, it is nonsense to dismiss the Russian launching as being without significance for defense.'

Using his solid connections with the Air Force, Symington built a good issue on which to stake his presidential ambitions.

A troubled Eisenhower asked General Goodpaster to look into Symington's claims. Goodpaster discovered that, like the bomber gap, the missile gap too was based on estimates of potential missile production and not on actual missile production. Symington argued that estimates must always be made on the basis of capability. The Soviets were capable of creating additional production facilities and, if they created those additional production facilities, this would be the rate of production. But the U-2 didn't confirm those claims. Eisenhower knew the dangers of negative information and never discounted the possibility that there was something out there beyond the range of the U-2's camera. The worst case estimates suggested that by 1961 the USSR would have perhaps as many as 1500 missiles, ten times as many as the US. With such a staggering imbalance, the argument went, the Soviet Union would feel confident enough to launch a surprise attack on the United States. But as long as Symington's estimates were about a future missile gap and until Eisenhower was shown hard evidence that Symington's figures were right, the President remained highly skeptical.

With hindsight, he was rightfully skeptical. He knew the military well, knew what a bunch of liars they were and knew how they'd exaggerate the enemy threat in order to increase their own budgets. He even used to say, 'God help the nation when it has a President who doesn't know as much about the military as I do.'

★   ★   ★

Over the summer of 1957, Eisenhower had managed to convince Harold Macmillan to bring the British back into the U-2 program.

Royal Air Force pilots officially resigned their commissions, although they remained on British payrolls. A small group of them, possibly as few as six, were brought to the United States where they were trained on the airplane, then sent to supplement the squadron already in place in Adana, Turkey. Allen Dulles and Richard Bissell had worked out the details of the joint mission agreement, allowing flights to the USSR upon approval of either the President or the Prime Minister. On at least two occasions, Macmillan approved flights and British pilots flew U-2 missions over the USSR.

Two other operational U-2 squadrons served the program at its height. One flew out of Wiesbaden, Germany, the other out of a base near Tokyo.

If the U-2 started life as one of the best-kept secrets in the world, it didn't stay that way very long. By mid-1958, a good cross-section of the Washington press corps had heard about it. Amidst some government cajoling but largely of their own volition, the story did not make the papers.

But then Khrushchev didn't need to read about it in the *Washington Post* or the *New York Times*. He already knew.

Although he never learned that British pilots were flying the plane as well, his radar had been tracking the flights from the very beginning. There wasn't much he could do about it, though. The plane flew at 70,000 feet, an altitude untouchable by either fighter interceptors or Soviet surface-to-air missiles. As early as July 1957, the Soviets had made formal, albeit secret, protests to the United States about U-2 overflights. They even, quite accurately, described the plane. But Dulles was willing to tell half-truths for the cause and responded that there were no US military planes violating Soviet airspace. Apparently, the reason Khrushchev never publicly protested the overflights was because he didn't want to admit that Soviet defenses were incapable of stopping them. There's little doubt that he also heard more about the U-2 when a young American marine who'd been stationed at a radar station next to the operational base in Japan defected to the USSR. The soldier probably didn't have any information about the plane or its mission that the Soviets didn't already know. But from an historical perspective, it's interesting to note that the American defector's name was Lee Harvey Oswald.

In April 1960, Eisenhower personally approved a U-2 mission which would take the pilot from Peshwar, Pakistan, past the Aral Sea and Chelyabinsk, straight through the heart of the Ural Mountains, 3800 miles north to Bodo, Norway. Accompanying the 31-year-old, Kentucky-born Francis Gary Powers on that flight were a hunting knife, a .22 calibre pistol with a silencer, a parachute, an inflatable life raft, a compass, signal flares, matches, a first-aid kit and a silk scarf with a message in 14 languages that read, 'I am an American and I do not speak your language. I need food, shelter, assistance. I will not harm you. I bear no malice toward your people. If you help me, you will be rewarded.'

He also had with him one 'silver dollar.'

A coin worn on a chain around the pilot's neck, it split in half revealing a needle contaminated with a shellfish poison that, in the event of capture, would bring about instant death. Suicide, the pilots knew, was almost always preferable to the torture they would invariably undergo if captured.

The plane was also said to be equipped with a time-bomb device that was to be activated manually by the pilot in the event that he had to bail out. It gave him 70 seconds to get clear before the U-2 self-destructed.

At 6:26 a.m. local time, on 1 May, word was received in Peshwar from Washington that the mission was go.

Four and a half hours later, the Soviets shot that U-2 down.

One of the things that Powers never knew on his flight over Chelyabinsk that morning was that, following the nuclear accident there in September 1957, Khrushchev had taken the totally uncharacteristic Soviet step of decentralizing nuclear weapons production and the testing facilities for bombs and warheads. He'd insisted, amidst great controversy, that major installations be relocated as far apart as possible from one another for sound strategic reasons.

Another thing Powers never knew was how, after the Russians had shot him down, the Red Army went on general mobilization for three days, scouring the area looking for the second pilot. They initiated a massive man hunt which – obviously – ended in vain. The reason they were looking for the second pilot was because, in Russia, everything came in pairs. There were always two train drivers for each train, two bus drivers for each bus, and they naturally assumed, two pilots for each U-2.

As soon as word reached Washington that the plane was overdue, action was required. When the program was first conceived, Bissell and

Dulles considered cover stories for just such an event. The cover story they settled on had been approved by the President himself. Because of its special characteristics, the plane was ideal for use by the National Weather Service and NASA. There had even been stories planted in the press that both the NWS and NASA were flying the planes for scientific research. So an initial statement was issued on 2 May by the base commander at Adana that a U-2 engaged in upper air studies had been lost. The statement said oxygen difficulties had been reported and a search for the plane was taking place in the remote areas of eastern Turkey.

Khrushchev now played his first card. He reported on 5 May that the plane had been shot down over Soviet territory.

In the Oval Office, the question was asked, what about the pilot? Nobody knew his fate but Eisenhower knew about the 'silver dollar.' Bissell and Allen Dulles had to make a recommendation. They wanted to gamble that Powers was dead.

Besides the President, only three men in the White House knew about the mission – Goodpaster, John Eisenhower and Gordon Gray. Allen Dulles gave them categorical assurances that no man would be taken alive. What he failed to say was that the pilot had a parachute.

On 6 May, Khrushchev released photos of wreckage. But he was too clever by half because CIA experts immediately recognized that the wreckage in the photos was not the U-2. NASA then released a statement written for them by the CIA, following along the lines of the original cover story. So did the State Department.

Then Khrushchev claimed he had the pilot. Allen Dulles' cover story had been outflanked, creating a major dilemma in the Oval Office.

From time to time a President has to decide whether to duck responsibility for something or accept it. Eisenhower was faced with the choice of saying, yes I did it, I authorized it, I told them to do it, or, I have so little control over my government that this was done without my knowledge. The President chose to hedge his bet. It was a rare case where a reasonably competent and honest Chief Executive preferred to be seen to be out of control of the government than to take responsibility.

Christian Herter issued a statement on 9 May, acknowledging the fact that the President had put into effect directives to gather information that would protect the United States from a surprise attack, but insisting that specific missions 'have not been subject to Presidential authorization.'

Admitting a lie with another lie would soon prove to be the worst of all possible solutions.

People close to the President suggested that he fire Allen Dulles. The original cover story would have held up if Powers had not been taken alive. But he had a parachute. He hadn't used the 'silver dollar.' Overall responsibility fell squarely on Allen Dulles.

Khrushchev knew Eisenhower was lying.

He was extremely upset about the U-2 incident and took it personally. He felt that Ike had betrayed him. For the very first time, a Russian leader had attempted to put a relationship with an American leader on a personal basis. That had never happened before. And it wasn't an easy thing to do because there were so many problems, political and military, dividing the two super-powers. Now he couldn't get over the fact that he'd so badly misjudged Eisenhower.

Compounding matters, Eisenhower's betrayal was seen by some men in the Kremlin as undermining Khrushchev's power. Years later Khrushchev would confess, 'From the time Gary Powers was shot down in a U-2 over the Soviet Union, I was no longer in full control. Those who felt America had imperialist intentions and that military strength was the most important thing, had the evidence they needed, and when the U-2 incident occurred, I no longer had the ability to overcome that feeling.'

The two men met in Paris a few months later, at a summit that had been organized before the U-2 went down and would end in disaster because of it. There, Khrushchev tried to give Eisenhower a way out. He said the incident could be overlooked if Eisenhower would do three things: apologize for it, say he didn't know anything about it, and promise there would be no repetition, that the U-2 would never again violate Soviet air space.

Eisenhower refused and the Paris summit broke up.

Only one minor thing came out of the meeting. Charles de Gaulle inadvertently managed to get Khrushchev to concede a point he'd previously refused to make for Eisenhower. In discussing the U-2 incident, de Gaulle challenged Khrushchev about a Russian spy satellite that was crossing over French territory 18 times a day, at altitudes much higher than airplanes. Khrushchev responded that satellites and airplanes weren't the same thing and even went so far as to say that the USSR had no objections to satellite reconnaissance. He noted that the Americans had put reconnaissance satellites over the USSR and shrugged them off with, 'Let them take as many pictures as they want.'

Without thinking, he'd finally accepted in practice Eisenhower's Open Skies proposal of 1955. Unfortunately, the personal rapport Eisenhower and Khrushchev shared at Camp David was erased. 'The U-2,' Khrushchev told his son-in-law, 'stopped everything.' And because it did, there is a slightly bitter-sweet postscript to the U-2 story.

Khrushchev had hoped to welcome Eisenhower to the Soviet Union before he retired from the Presidency. The trip was under discussion and Khrushchev was planning to escort him to Lake Baikal in Siberia where a few surprises awaited. First, Khrushchev had built a guest cottage on the edge of the lake just for Eisenhower. Next, he'd arranged to give him a Russian hovercraft as a gift. Finally, knowing how much Eisenhower loved golf and because he thought Ike might like to play in Russia, Khrushchev personally ordered a golf course built at Lake Baikal.

When it was finished, it was the only golf course in the USSR.

After the visit was canceled, the golf course was abandoned and never used.

Thirteen months after his first trip to the United States, Khrushchev came up with an encore.

He announced he'd attend an October 1960 meeting of the General Assembly of the United Nations and told Korolev that he wanted to celebrate the occasion with something spectacular. This time Korolev tried to put a Soviet rocket on Mars. He failed on his first two attempts and on the third the rocket exploded, killing several people, including Marshal Mitrovan Nedelin, commander of the newly created Strategic Rocket Forces. At the government's insistence, word of the failure was not to be released, and the cover story of an aircraft accident was used to explain Nedelin's death.

Khrushchev compensated for the lack of a Martian spectacular with his shoe.

Attending the General Assembly meeting supposedly to bring attention to his disarmament position, he took his place behind the desk with the metal plaque marked USSR. Because he was there, an inordinate press contingent was there too, including television cameras.

A Third World delegate speaking from the platform was in the midst of charging the Soviet Union with grievous faults, when Khrushchev took offense. He decided he'd heard enough and turned to Andrei

THE COLD WAR AND OTHER GAMES

Gromyko, who was sitting next to him. Having no knowledge of the local rules of parliamentary order, Khrushchev whispered to Gromyko that he wanted to answer the delegate's charges immediately. Gromyko explained he should take the USSR plaque in front of him, and hold it up to show the President of the General Assembly he wanted to speak. Obligingly, Khrushchev waved the plaque. But the President didn't pay any attention to him. Khrushchev kept waving it back and forth, clearly asking for the floor. Still nothing happened. Originally annoyed at the delegate, he grew furious at being disregarded like that. If waving the sign failed to get their attention, he thought, I know a better way.

Khrushchev reached down, took off his shoe and started pounding it on the table.

At first no one in the room understood what was happening. Then all eyes turned to him. Then the photographers spotted him. So did the television cameras. Once he had the world's attention, he kept on banging his shoe.

The Russian leader's primitive party mentality was the lead story on the news that night, and accounted for a lot of newspaper ink over the next few days. Khrushchev might not have gotten the message across that he was a tribune of the people, but he definitely touched a chord with a lot of Americans. Every morning for weeks to follow, the Soviet delegation at the UN was inundated with packages and envelopes filled with old shoes.

There's no way to be certain how history would have changed had the United States been first to launch a satellite. It's possible that the Soviet Union would not have joined in the space race for the simple reason that there would not have been any propaganda benefit to be derived from it. Without Soviet competition, it's equally likely that John Kennedy would not have felt any need to push the country into a race for the moon.

Had an American satellite gone into orbit first, beeping or blinking, or at least doing something to attract attention, it's a good bet the world would have taken a few minutes to say, hey look at that. It would have made the papers. And just as quickly, the novelty might have worn off. The richest, most powerful, most scientifically advanced nation in the history of man was expected to come up with such stunts. The world viewed the US as a place where the difficult became a distinct possibility and the impossible became a maybe. So, if an American satellite had been first, that could have been the end of that. And even if the Soviets had eventually followed with one of their own, the world would likely have said, okay, both super-powers can do it, so what?

One reason Sputnik was so momentous an event was because it was Russian and not American. And in America, there were two very obvious casualties.

Late in the summer of 1957, the Ford Motor Company introduced a new car to their stable called the Edsel. Named for Henry Ford's only son, the company hyped it as a product of America's most advanced technology. Because Sputnik put such a serious doubt in the minds of American consumers about American technology, the Edsel failed so miserably that the name instantly became synonymous with the term 'white elephant.' To be perfectly honest, the car was probably doomed to failure anyway. It was too blatantly a symbol of the chrome trim and shiny baubles America realized it had to cast aside in order to get back to basics. Sales were slow right from the beginning, even before Sputnik. But if slow sales were just one battle, Sputnik marked the day the war was lost.

A second big loser was Richard Nixon.

When Eisenhower told the American people that Sputnik did not raise his apprehensions about the national security 'one iota,' he was making a military assessment. But within a few months he'd ordered the Army Jupiter and the Air Force Thor medium-range missiles into production and had accelerated the Navy's Polaris submarine program. He'd increased the Atlas and Titan ICBM programs and, before the ink had dried on those edicts, he'd stepped up production of the Minuteman ICBM. To many outsiders, for someone who said he hadn't been worried 'one iota,' he had a very worried look.

Sputnik had also caught him in the midst of an economy drive at the Defense Department. The public wanted him to spend money on defense, and even if it was not the right course of action – which Eisenhower firmly believed it was not – the voters gave Nixon a hint of things to come in November 1958. The Democrats made a clean sweep of the mid-term elections, producing the biggest majority for themselves in both the House and the Senate since Franklin Roosevelt thrashed the Republicans in 1936.

By November 1960, Richard Nixon had a lot to live down.

It was generally acknowledged that he would succeed Eisenhower. Once the second term began, Nixon was also more than just confident about it. He expected to win and took on the airs of a President in waiting. Nobody in the White House ever anticipated that Nixon would not win. Eisenhower was said to have preferred Robert Anderson, his Treasury Secretary, but Nixon had too many IOUs in his pocket. He went to the Republican convention in Chicago that July and, despite Eisenhower's lackluster endorsement, he beat Nelson Rockefeller and Barry Goldwater on the first ballot. Nixon chose as his running mate Henry Cabot Lodge, the Bostonian whom John Kennedy had defeated in 1952 for his Senate seat.

At the Democrats' convention that same month in Los Angeles, a number of fairly strong candidates appeared. Symington and Johnson were both there. So was Hubert Humphrey. But Kennedy was young and spoke in that accent of his about the 'vigah' needed to rally the national spirit.

He had the magic.

This was the beginning of Camelot.

And he beat the others on the first ballot.

A northern, big-city Catholic in a largely rural Protestant land, he brought Lyndon Johnson, a ten-galloned-hat Texan, onto the ticket to assure himself of the southern WASP vote. He was also assuring himself that the Eisenhower–Nixon handling of the national defenses would remain at the forefront of the campaign.

John Kennedy had already used Sputnik as an opening salvo in the attack on Nixon's right to the succession in the build-up to his nomination. 'The United States has less to fear,' he said at a women's club luncheon in Virginia in January 1958, 'from Russian military advances, than from the gains the Soviet Union has made through Sputnik diplomacy.'

By August 1958, he'd hooked his own bandwagon alongside Johnson's and Symington's, promoting the missile gap by warning that Soviet supremacy in the ICBM field during the 1960–64 period might 'open to them a new shortcut to world domination.'

Even if the Russians stopped short of launching a surprise attack, there was still a real threat to deal with. 'The Soviets may be expected to use their superior striking ability to achieve their objectives in ways which may not require launching an actual attack. Their missile power will be the shield from behind which they will slowly but surely advance – through Sputnik diplomacy, limited brushfire wars, indirect non-overt aggression, intimidation and subversion, internal revolution, increased prestige or influence, and the vicious blackmail of our allies. The periphery of the free world will slowly be nibbled away. The balance of power will gradually shift against us.'

The Eisenhower Doctrine preached finite deterrence. Sputnik raised serious questions about the validity of that. Kennedy knew he had to avoid personal criticism of Ike because the man was much too popular for that. But he realized, once Nixon took the position that Eisenhower had not gone far enough and tried to enlarge on the basic concept of the Doctrine, he could be beaten. He would not only be overemphasizing nuclear retaliatory might, he'd be exposing the United States to anything from rocket blackmail to a preventive Soviet strike.

Kennedy's alternative became a strategy of assured superiority and a willingness to fight limited wars.

It forced Nixon into an untenable corner.

Eisenhower presided over eight years of relative peace. At least he'd managed to avoid a global confrontation with the Soviets. But Nixon couldn't swing that to his ultimate advantage because in 1960 the world was even scarier than it had been in 1957.

His campaign crisis was simple. Khrushchev-bashing was clearly a vote winner. But screaming, 'The Russians are coming,' meant playing up to the missile gap. Doing that, even if the missile gap didn't exist, was Ike-bashing. He needed to find an alternative, a way around it. The tack he chose was to go public with praise for Eisenhower, and private with damnation.

On the stumps, Nixon proclaimed Ike a national hero. A vote for the Democrats, he said, was a personal affront to such a great world statesman. A vote for Kennedy made you an ingrate.

But once the rallies ended and the handshaking was finished for the night, he pulled the press aside and spoke off the record, confiding in them how he was dismayed by the Republican leadership, how he'd been the lone hawkish voice of dissension in the White House when it came to defense policy, how he was now anxious to offer the nation a younger, more coherent leadership.

It was typical Nixon, political footwork at its best. And he almost managed it.

There were those reporters following the campaign who claimed there was never much to choose between the two, except perhaps Kennedy's good looks and sense of humor. Kennedy's handling of the first televised debate certainly gave him the edge. He looked young and healthy. Nixon looked unshaven and jowly. Kennedy preached it was time for a new generation of leadership as America moved into a 'new frontier.' The reference to space did not go unnoticed. Nixon argued that 'the kitchen debate' more than proved he was experienced in international diplomacy and could handle Khrushchev. Kennedy burst that balloon by saying that, while Mr Nixon had experience in kitchen debates, so did most married men.

The outcome of that first debate is wonderfully described in a now much-quoted syllogism. Nixon says he can handle Khrushchev. The debate proved Kennedy could handle Nixon. Therefore, Kennedy could handle Khrushchev.

The Republicans subtly pointed out that Kennedy was a Catholic, reminding voters that the national secrets could never be safe because any Catholic would have to confess them to the Pope. The Democrats made allusions to 'Tricky Dick,' and asked, 'Would you buy a used car from this man?'

In the end, the voters decided they needed to redress the balance of power and didn't believe that Nixon would or could do that. At least, some of the voters felt that way. Kennedy crossed the finish line with a popular majority of only 112,881 votes out of the nearly 69 million cast. His electoral victory – the one that really counts – appeared to be more substantial, 303 to 219. Yet, if a mere 12,000 people in five states had voted for Nixon instead of Kennedy, the result would have been different. And there were apparent irregularities in the vote count in Illinois and Texas, both of which had gone to Kennedy.

In a footnote to his book *Robert Kennedy and His Times*, Arthur Schlesinger says that even if Illinois had gone to Nixon, Kennedy would still have won by 276 to 246, meaning that Nixon would have had to carry Texas as well. In spite of irregularities in Texas, Schlesinger contends Kennedy's margin of 47,000 votes was probably too great to be attributed to fraud. As for Illinois, he assumes, 'One party stole as many votes as the other. When the Illinois vote was challenged, the state electoral board, which was 4–1 Republican, voted unanimously to certify the Kennedy electors.'

Accepting the fact that Schlesinger's affection clearly rests with John Kennedy, there probably were sufficient grounds for Nixon to have demanded a series of recounts and investigations. That, however, would almost certainly have thrown the election into the House of Representatives. And, while 1960 saw the Democrats hold on to the Senate, the Republicans had taken back the House. Nixon might have been elected there, but the process would have tied up the government for perhaps as much as a year. The confusion that might have caused, especially in view of the Soviet threat, would have been incalculable. Nixon refused to go that route. He conceded to Kennedy and the 'New Frontier' had begun.

Had Sputnik not come along, Richard Nixon would not have had to bear the burden of Eisenhower's misjudgement of public opinion in the wake of Sputnik. Free of that albatross, Kennedy campaign artillery would have been much less effective. Sputnik didn't win the election for John Kennedy, but the after-effects of Sputnik might be the single most important contribution to Richard Nixon's defeat. Without Sputnik, he almost certainly could have ridden on the back of Eisenhower's immense personal popularity to become the 35th President.

That, in turn, would have changed a lot of things – the Bay of Pigs, the Cuban missile crisis, the war in Vietnam, Watergate. Perhaps none of them would have happened at all. Or, at least, they would have happened differently. And the world today would be a different place.

Then too, without Camelot, 22 November 1963 would forever be just another Friday.

John Kennedy initiated the largest military build-up in the peacetime history of the United States. He wanted Khrushchev to know that America would assure itself of nuclear superiority.

And Khrushchev feared Kennedy's policy of strength.

He tested it in Berlin, blockading the city, then building a wall through the middle of it.

In the autumn of 1962, he tested it again off the coast of Florida. Unable to match Kennedy with ICBMs, Khrushchev delivered intermediate-range nuclear weapons to Cuba.

On Tuesday, 16 October, the President saw for the first time U-2 photos that proved the Russians were installing ballistic missiles in Cuba. It was in direct contradiction to a Khrushchev statement earlier in September that no missiles would be placed in Cuba. It was in direct contradiction to assurances from Andrei Gromyko that there were no Soviet missiles there.

On Friday, 19 October, the CIA presented Kennedy with their estimate of probable Soviet reactions to certain courses of action.

'A major Soviet objective in their military buildup in Cuba,' the CIA suggested, 'is to demonstrate that the world balance of forces has shifted so far in their favor that the US can no longer prevent the advance of Soviet offensive power even into its own hemisphere.'

They warned that unless strong action was taken, 'there would be a loss of confidence in US power and determination and a serious decline of US influence generally.'

The CIA also said, 'We believe that whatever course of retaliation the USSR elected, the Soviet leaders would not deliberately initiate general war or take military measures which, in their calculation, would run the gravest risks of general war.'

This time they were wrong.

After six days of wondering what to do, Kennedy publicly accused the Soviets of lying about their intentions in Cuba and ordered a blockade of the island. He said, any missiles launched from Cuba against the United States or any of its allies would be considered a direct attack on the United States by the Soviet Union and that would bring about a full response upon the USSR. 'I call upon Chairman Khrushchev,' Kennedy said, 'to halt and eliminate this clandestine, reckless, provocative threat to world peace and to stable relations between our two nations.'

Both militaries mobilized. Kennedy deployed 180 ships into the Caribbean. B-52s were armed with atomic weapons and put on full alert status. Some 18 Soviet ships, many of them bringing missiles to Cuba, were now joined by Soviet subs and continued on their heading towards Cuba. 'We were on the edge of a precipice,' Bobby Kennedy said later, 'with no way off.'

Satellite spying had advanced to such a state that the CIA was able to provide the President with proof positive that the US held the advantage, putting Kennedy in a position to make a calculated stand against Khrushchev. He'd learned the truth about the missile gap, discovered that the Soviets had very few missiles, knew that he could act with complete assurance that it was not possible for the Soviets to launch an all-out attack against the United States.

What John Kennedy didn't know was that Khrushchev was fully prepared to launch what he had.

At Baikonour, on the very same pad that Korolev had used to launch Sputnik, a modernized version of the R-7, equipped with a space station, was waiting to be sent to Mars. Korolev was in Moscow and Boris Chertok was in charge at Baikonour. On Tuesday night, 23 October, orders came from Moscow to take down the space station and refit the rocket with a nuclear warhead. The guidance system was also to be reset to aim the rocket at the United States.

Chertok now says he did everything possible not to fulfill his orders. He says he tried to find Korolev in Moscow, but telephone connections were not good. He says he argued about it with the head of the State Commission, who said that if they didn't fit the rocket the way they'd been ordered to, every one of them would face a military tribunal. In the end, he shrugs, he didn't have a choice.

Whether Chertok resisted or not, one thing is perfectly clear – Khrushchev was making the Soviet Union ready for war.

The American invasion of Cuba came closer with each day. This time, Kennedy would allow the military to plan it, and not give the CIA another chance to repeat the debacle at the Bay of Pigs which had been a major cause of this crisis. Kennedy even asked the State Department to proceed with plans for establishing a puppet civilian government in Cuba once Castro was overthrown.

On Saturday morning, the President received word that an American U-2 had been shot down over Cuba. The military wanted to react with a surgical strike against Fidel Castro's surface-to-air missile installation. Kennedy held them back, although he permitted the build-up towards war to continue.

Later that night, Khrushchev sat down to write a letter directly to John Kennedy. At the dining-room table in the dacha outside Moscow, he penned a long, emotional note in which he repeated several times that nuclear war had to be avoided. 'If indeed war should break out, then it would not be in our power to stop it, for such is the logic of war. I have participated in two wars and know that war ends when it has rolled through cities and villages, everywhere sowing death and destruction.'

He wrote, 'If assurances were given that the President of the United States would not participate in an attack on Cuba and the blockade lifted, then the question of the removal or the destruction of the missile sites in Cuba would then be an entirely different question. Armaments bring only disasters. When one accumulates them, this damages the economy, and if one puts them to use, then they destroy people on both sides. Consequently, only a madman can believe that armaments are the principal means in the life of a society. No, they are an enforced loss of human energy, and what is more are for the destruction of man himself. If people do not show wisdom, then in the final analysis they will come to a clash, like blind moles, and then reciprocal extermination will begin.'

The parallel he drew was of two men holding a rope with a knot tied in the middle. 'We and you ought not to pull on the ends of the rope in which you have tied the knot of war, because the more the two of us pull, the tighter the knot will be tied. And the moment may come when the knot will be tied so tight that even he who tied it will not have the strength to untie it, and then it will be necessary to cut the knot, and what that would mean is not for me to explain to you, because you yourself understand perfectly of what terrible forces our countries dispose. Consequently, if there is no intention to tighten the knot, and thereby to doom the world to the catastrophe of thermonuclear war, then let us not only relax the forces pulling on the ends of the rope, let us take measures to untie that knot. We are ready for this.'

Another thing John Kennedy did not know was that Khrushchev saw himself boxed into a corner. He didn't want to have to open up a second front in Berlin. He supposed the Americans had a contingency plan in that event. And then it would be too late. This, Khrushchev concluded, was probably their last chance for an honorable settlement. If Kennedy and his advisers refused to let him out of this corner, the Russians would have no choice but to force their way out, with all the consequences that entailed.

The letter arrived at the White House at around 6 p.m. Saturday evening. That made it 2 a.m. Sunday morning in Moscow.

Kennedy didn't know what to make of it.

Then a second letter arrived. This one was much more businesslike, basically restating that the missiles would be removed if the Americans would promise not to invade Cuba.

In the first, Khrushchev appeared emotionally strained, perhaps even nearing the point of irrationality. The stricter, more reasoned tone of the second letter suggested to some that it had not been written by the same man. The President's advisers debated the two letters, questioned whether the Russian Premier had written either or both, and wanted Kennedy to write back, asking for a clarification. Bobby Kennedy then suggested that his brother respond only to the first note, as if the second one had never been received.

So Kennedy wrote to Khrushchev, 'The United States is very much interested in reducing tensions and halting the arms race; and if your letter signifies you are prepared to discuss a detente affecting NATO and the Warsaw Pact, we are quite prepared to consider with our allies any useful proposals. But the first ingredient, let me emphasize, is the cessation of work on missile sites in Cuba and measures to render such weapons inoperable . . .'

The wire was delivered to Khrushchev before dawn on Sunday morning, 28 October. He read it and decided he did in fact have an honorable way out. He would later explain that Kennedy was the one to back down.

He ordered the missiles removed.

Then he sent word to Baikonour. Chertok was told he could refit the space station. But, instead of doing that, Chertok and everyone else went out and got very drunk. They emptied every bottle of cognac in Baikonour. They found every single bottle and drank the town dry.

The order to step down had come from Moscow with only 60 minutes to spare.

Epilogue

There is something very haunting about Moscow in the dead of winter when snow blankets the city and traffic vanishes and parks filled with silver birch trees are deserted and Red Square is absolutely silent.

But the romance of it quickly fades.

Old cars in dark colors and older trucks with grinding gears and dilapidated buses overcrowded with people turn the streets to slush and the real Moscow reappears.

It is a grim and morbid place.

The winter before August 1991, food shortages brought the Russians to the verge of utter desperation. The winter after the coup, things were even worse. At one point there was no milk. When there was milk, there was no meat. Then there were no eggs. For a while there were no sanitary napkins, no tomatoes, no dried meats, no shoes. When there was fruit juice, there was no toilet paper. When there were cigarettes, there was no soap. Planes stopped flying because there was no fuel. Factories closed because there was no heat.

Communism turned out to be the worst economic disaster in the history of mankind.

The decrepit infrastructure that the Party had always propped up to keep the country alive finally imploded. It toppled in on itself, brought down by the massive weight of its own inefficiency.

With it came the Union.

We in the West saw Mikhail Gorbachev's peace initiatives change the course of the 20th century. But at home he granted himself draconian presidential powers, made himself near-omnipotent – a born-again Czar – and tried to leave much of the old system intact. Like the promises of *perestroika*, he too was doomed to failure. For people standing in queues all day because that was their only chance to keep their families alive, he'd not only deprived them of food, he'd also deprived them of their dignity.

Some of them, of course, have very short memories. The 18 Brezhnev years were ones of flourishing stagnation. The only thing to be said for Comrades Andropov and Chernenko is that they somehow gave way to Mr Gorbachev. You don't have to spend years in Moscow to understand that, because the country never really emerged from feudal times, the Union was always ill-fated. A totally artificial conglomeration of conflicting peoples, religions, traditions, languages and cultures, the only thing that ever kept it together was intimidation, fear and force. The men who held the reins were right to surmise that without the Thought Police the people would begin to think, is this all there is?

The Union was simply too big ever to be manageable. Eleven time zones put the east coast as far from the west coast as Moscow is from Beverly Hills, with 160 nationalities in between, as dissimilar in every way as the deserted Gorkyskaya is from the over-neoned Rodeo Drive. The Estonians had nothing whatsoever in common with anyone in Vladivostok, who never had anything at all in common with anyone in Azerbaijan.

What they needed was the one thing Communism never could have delivered – an economic miracle.

One McDonald's does not a boom-time make.

October 1957 brought the Soviets as near as they would ever be to the eventual triumph they'd been waiting for like a Second Coming. They were infected with enthusiasm. They had drive. They had credibility. They had international recognition and they had desire. They simply didn't have anything to build on. Because the foundation was basically flawed, the more they tried to build, the deeper they found their pylons sinking into the construction-site mud.

With hindsight, they never stood a chance.

George Orwell wrote, 'Whoever controls the past controls the future.' Under Gorbachev, the Communists either relinquished control of the past, or more likely, had it taken away from them. There is no defense against fax machines and jet planes and televisions and – ironically – satellites. The truth arrived on the very technology they used to think would bring them the ultimate victory.

Once the Soviet people saw the realities of the past, once they confirmed what many had long suspected, they knew they had no future.

It's almost impossible for Westerners who have never been there to imagine what life has been like. It's not much easier for someone who has been there to believe it. In some parts of the country there's still no electricity. Yet this was for so long the world's second-greatest nuclear force. They had computers to soft-land probes on other planets but in most stores they still count on an abacus. They may now have bread, meat, fish, frozen TV dinners, baby food, roasted peanuts and Paul Newman Popcorn, yet there are school children in central Moscow suffering from malnutrition.

Until recently, everything was always sold at a loss. A loaf of bread used to cost 20 kopeks to buy but 60 kopeks to bake. At those prices, it didn't take long before farmers decided it was easier to feed bread to their livestock than to purchase the grain that went into the bread. By raising the price of bread just to meet its cost, inflation jumped 300%.

Capitalism, they used to say at official Party functions whenever a visitor was within earshot, is the exploitation of man by man. Socialism, they would then explain, is the opposite!

Now they want to be capitalists and now we want them to be capitalists, but it's foolhardy to have ever believed that one system would automatically fill the vacuum left by the other. Explaining a market economy to people who have no basis for understanding the concept is like talking calculus to a five year old. He's happy to listen for a few minutes, but doesn't know enough basic arithmetic to get beyond counting to 109. Metaphorically, neither do the Russians. Bored and frustrated, he soon gives up. So do they.

One afternoon, when my interpreter in Moscow saw me paying for goods with a credit card, he asked how it worked. I explained that my piece of plastic allowed at least three people to use the same money. I might as well have been speaking in tongues. After all, this is a country where, when you order a Russian beer in a rouble-only restaurant, you're asked to pay for it in dollars – as preposterous as having to pay for a glass of wine in the middle of Texas with French francs.

The mentality you find there is as obtuse as the Third World can get. In the old days, the government promised everyone a job. If you were trained as a draughtsman, you had a good chance of being sent to some factory actually to be a draughtsman. Except the factory, which might have gainfully employed three draughtsmen, already had 85 on the payroll. The government has since stopped guaranteeing jobs, but offices and factories are still outrageously overmanned. In theory, you could fire everybody and start again. Except the concept of a work ethic is as extraterrestrial to most ex-Soviets as the alien notions of competition, service, credit, profit, loss, and basic cost accounting.

This is a land of enormous wealth. They've got more oil and natural gas than Saudi Arabia. They've got more diamonds than South Africa. They've probably got more gold than anyone. They've certainly got more forests than anyone. Those forests, if properly harvested, could transform Russia into an economy similar to Sweden's. But even if they knew what they were doing, it would take them 50 years to become a world player in pulp and paper. The trees are inaccessible. Worse, there's no infrastructure. They need roads, pulping plants and hydropower. They need new laws to encourage investors. They need to understand the philosophy behind investment, incentive and motivation. They need to erase 74 years of ingrained, obsolete thought-processing.

It will take at least one, if not two generations, to undo what the Party has done.

For nearly three-quarters of the 20th century, these people lived in a system that offered no real rewards for initiative, while meting out draconian penalties for failure. They learned how to survive, but not how to prosper.

The seeds of August 1991 were planted 36 years before, ironically almost exactly half-way between the 1917 Revolution and Boris Yeltsin's Tuesday night stand. It was Sputnik that gave birth to the beanstalk. But before they knew it, the beanstalk overran the garden and eventually buried it.

Arriving in Moscow for the first time is an exhilarating experience.

Especially if there is fresh snow on the ground.

Sadly, the only time you sense that same exhilaration again is every time you leave.

/JR

Notes

Abbreviations used in notes:

AP   Associated Press
DDEL   Dwight D. Eisenhower Library, Abilene, Kansas
EOHP   Eisenhower Oral History Project, Columbia University, New York
FOIA   Freedom of Information Act
FRUS   *Foreign Relations of the United States* 1955–1957, US Government Printing Office, Washington, DC
HSTL   Harry S. Truman Library, Independence, Missouri
JFDP   John Foster Dulles Papers, Princeton University, Princeton, NJ
JFKL   John Fitzgerald Kennedy Library, Boston, Mass.
LBJL   Lyndon Baines Johnson Library, Austin, Texas
NARC   National Archives, Washington, DC
PRO   Public Record Office, Kew, London, England
UPI   United Press International

Prologue

['It happened on . . . back to sleep.'] Various sources, including interviews with and some private documents of men in the bunker at Baikonour, plus Khrushchev's own description of that night in his memoirs and an interview with his son-in-law, Alexei Adjoubei.

1 *Opening Moves*

['The heavy folder . . . White House safe.'] The story of the Clifford report is compiled from several sources, including

Daniel Yergin, *Shattered Peace*, and Arthur Krock, *Memoirs*. Copies of the original document can be found in the Truman Library and the National Archives.

['He usually read . . . like official documents.'] Kenneth Leish, *The White House*, p. 117.

['The declaration of World War III.'] Ed Cray, *General of the Army*, p. 592.

['He'd helped to . . . as the enemy.'] ibid.

['On 5 March . . . across the continent.'] Robert Hendrickson, *Encyclopedia of Word and Phrase Origins*, Facts on File Publications, New York, 1987, pp. 277–8.

['Proclaiming the Communists . . . America's atomic monopoly.'] Churchill, Fulton, Missouri, speech.

['Some Americans felt . . . real danger existed.'] John Sharnik, *Inside the Cold War*, p. 26.

['Harry Truman among . . . calling for war.'] James MacGregor Burns, *Crosswinds of Freedom*, pp. 228–9.

['It was journalist . . . the following year.'] William Manchester, *The Glory and the Dream*, p. 436.

['And it was . . . American–Soviet relations.'] Hendrickson, *Encyclopedia of Word and Phrase Origins*, op. cit., p. 127.

['Unbeknownst to the . . . to be secure.'] George Kennan, *Memoirs*. The Telegraphic Message from Moscow of 22 February, 1946 (Moscow Embassy Telegram No. 511) is excerpted as Appendix C, pp. 547–59.

['Soviet leaders believe . . . restrain the Soviet Union.'] Clark Clifford, 'American Relations with the Soviet Union – A Report to the President by the Special Counsel to the President,' September 1946. Top Secret. Reprinted in its entirety as Appendix A in Arthur Krock's *Memoirs*.

['Throughout the year . . . Atomic Energy Commission.'] Walter LaFeber, *America, Russia and the Cold War*, pp. 29–48.

['At the end . . . of intelligence information.'] Nathan Miller, *Spying for America*, pp. 355–7.

['Electronic spying was . . . also highly unreliable.'] Sir Frank Roberts, *Dealing with Dictators*, p.93, and Miller, *Spying for America*.

['In the short . . . the growing tension.'] LaFeber, *America, Russia and the Cold War*.

NOTES

['With 'Uncle Joe's' . . . past each other.'] John Diggins, *The Proud Decades*, p. 73.

['The struggle against . . . heritage and ideals.'] Robert Kennedy, *Thirteen Days*, p. 39.

['The United Kingdom . . . a rebuilt Germany.'] Harold Macmillan, *Tides of Fortune*.

['Under Secretary of . . . own national security.'] Manchester, *The Glory and the Dream*, pp. 438–9.

['That became the . . . of Western Europe.'] Several sources, including Manchester, *The Glory and the Dream*, Cray, *General of the Army*, Paul Kennedy, *The Rise and Fall of the Great Powers*, and Burns, *Crosswinds of Freedom*. Also Felix Belair, Jr of the *New York Times* in a private oral history, cited by Arthur Krock in *Memoirs*. The comment 'one of the most brilliant successes' comes from the *Manchester Guardian*'s assessment of the Marshall Plan, cited by Manchester, op. cit., p. 440.

['Superimposing that over . . . more than 15,000.'] Victor Marchetti and John Marks, *The CIA and the Cult of Intelligence*, pp. 19–24.

['Kennan, who'd been . . . could be contained.'] Manchester, *The Glory and the Dream*, p. 436.

['The CIA was now . . . accident or miscalculation.'] Central Intelligence Agency, 'Threats to the Security of the United States,' 28 September, 1948.

['Having hit the . . . of the Universe.'] Related by Truman's Secretary of the Army, Kenneth Royall, to Arthur Krock of the *New York Times* and retold by Krock in *Memoirs*, pp. 242–3. Also, Manchester, *The Glory and the Dream*, pp. 446–8.

['There is nothing . . . of our country.'] Top secret telegram, US Embassy Moscow to Secretary of State, 23 September, 1945, NARC.

['When the National . . . interests were threatened.'] NSC-68, 'United States Objectives and Programs for National Security,' 14 April, 1950, Top Secret, NARC. See also, Kennan, *Memoirs*, Burns, *Crosswinds of Freedom*, LaFeber, *America, Russia and the Cold War*, Daniel Yergin, *Shattered Peace*, Manchester, *The Glory and the Dream*, and John Gaddis, *Russia, the Soviet Union and the United States*.

['Not that Acheson . . . five years away.'] US Department

338

of Defense, 'Report by the Joint Intelligence Committee to the Joint Chiefs of Staff on the Implications of Soviet Possession of Atomic Weapons,' Top Secret, 23 February, 1950, NARC.

2 The Soviet Challenge

['Despite the ill-informed . . . said it was.'] Robert C. Tucker, writing in Ivo Lederer (ed.), *Russian Foreign Policy*, p. 190.

['He ruled with . . . failures necessitated "retreat".'] Seweryn Bialer, *Stalin's Successors*, p. 22.

['In January 1953 . . . agents were everywhere.'] Confidential Report, 'Soviet Policies after Stalin's Death,' the Foreign Office, London, 9 April, 1953, PRO.

['Although Stalin's illness . . . as a possibility.'] Confidential telegram, Gascoigne to Eden, 4 March, 1953, PRO.

['Within a few . . . First Deputy Premier.'] Roy and Zhores Medvedev, *Khrushchev – The Years in Power*, pp. 2–7.

['Malenkov at 52 . . . shoulder to shoulder.'] Robert Conquest, *Power and Policy in the USSR*, pp. 202–3.

['Gascoigne described him . . . as Foreign Minister.'] 'Analysis of the Changes in the Government of the USSR,' Confidential Telegram, 16 March, 1953, from Sir A. Gascoigne (UK Ambassador, Moscow) to A. Eden, Foreign Office. Also quoted from 'Soviet Union, Quarterly Report, January – March 1953,' Confidential Telegram, 13 April, 1953, from Sir A. Gascoigne to W. Churchill, PRO.

['Molotov had a . . . in Stalin's presence.'] Nikita Khrushchev, *Khrushchev Remembers – The Glasnost Tapes*, p. 17.

['Winston Churchill described . . . cold-blooded ruthlessness.'] Winston Churchill, *The Gathering Storm*, p. 599.

['Harold Macmillan was . . . and even softness.'] Macmillan, *Tides of Fortune*, p. 610.

['Just plain thick.'] N. Khrushchev, *Khrushchev Remembers – The Glasnost Tapes*, pp. 86–7.

['During the war . . . a loaded pistol.'] Kenneth Leish, *The White House*, p. 114.

['The weakest link . . . was without protection.'] Nikita Khrushchev, *Khrushchev Remembers*, see notes by translator

Edward Crankshaw, 'Khrushchev's Kremlin Colleagues,' pp. 540–1.

['Yet, as such . . . negotiated with Malenkov.'] Roy Medvedev, *Khrushchev*, p. 56. The Khrushchev remark to Bulganin about Beria is from Alexei Adjoubei, *A l'Ombre du Khrouchtchev*, p. 105.

['The speed with . . . not functioning correctly.'] Sir A. Gascoigne to Mr Eden, 'Analysis of the Changes in the Government of the USSR Following the Death of Marshall Stalin on 5 March, 1953,' Confidential Telegram from the British Ambassador in Moscow to the Foreign Minister, London, 16 March, 1953, PRO.

['Sometime during the . . . his military commanders.'] This story was recounted by British diplomat Paul Mason, who heard it from a Swedish counterpart on 10 July, 1953. The Swede told Mason he'd heard it directly from the East German. PRO.

['At the National . . . avoiding general war'.'] Special Estimate of the CIA, 'Probable Consequences of the Death of Stalin and the Elevation of Malenkov to Leadership in the USSR,' SE-39, Top Secret, presented to the NSC, 11 March, 1953, FOIA.

['Churchill tried in . . . lot of things.'] Churchill letter to Eisenhower, 25 December, 1953, Top Secret, PRO.

['Within a week . . . becoming too close.'] Letter in PRO, 30 January, 1954.

['The Soviets were . . . Stalin since 1946.'] Confidential Report, 'Soviet Policies after Stalin's Death,' the Foreign Office, London, 9 April, 1953, PRO.

['Nikita Sergeievitch Khrushchev . . . It went unfulfilled.'] Adjoubei, *A l'Ombre du Khrouchtchev*, p. 161.

['At the age . . . down at night.'] Nikita Khrushchev, *Khrushchev Remembers*. The comment about the mining college being the Cambridge of Russia's disinherited is from Adjoubei, *A l'Ombre du Khrouchtchev*, p. 162. Khrushchev's conversation with Stalin is also from Adjoubei, p. 163.

['the Butcher of the Ukraine'] Sir Frank Roberts, *Dealing with Dictators*, pp. 208–9.

['On a personal . . . to quit smoking.'] Adjoubei interview and *A l'Ombre de Khrouchtchev*, pp. 93–6 & pp. 142–4.

['Throughout those years . . . always faithfully follow.'] R. &
Z. Medvedev, *Khrushchev – The Years in Power*, pp. 4–6.
['"Without me," Stalin . . . us all up."'] Adjoubei, *A l'Ombre
de Khrouchtchev*, p. 100.
['You'll see, when . . . necks like chickens.'] Khrushchev,
Khrushchev Remembers, p. 392.
['Knowing how universally . . . his wholehearted support.']
Medvedev, *Khrushchev*, pp. 58–62.
['In July, a . . . Beria was seized.'] There are several versions of
what actually happened inside the meeting. The first account
was the official news release. The second, filling in some of the
blanks, appeared shortly thereafter in the Soviet newspaper,
Novy Mir. Khrushchev's own description is in his autobiography. A particularly dramatic reconstruction of events that day
appears in Roy Medvedev's *Khrushchev*. See also Adjoubei, *A
l'Ombre du Khrouchtchev*, for a full chapter on the Beria affair.
['A formal trial . . . left on time.'] Medvedev, *Khrushchev*,
pp. 65–8.

3 *The American Century*

['A largely empty . . . could do anything.'] Several sources,
including *Chronicle of the* 20th Century, the *World Almanac*,
Timetables of History, *Encyclopedia Britannica*, *New American Desk
Encyclopedia*, J. K. Galbraith, *Affluent Society*, William Manchester,
The Glory and the Dream, William O'Neill, *American High*,
John Diggins, *The Proud Decades*, and J. Ronald Oakley,
God's Country. The term 'American Century' was coined by
Henry R. Luce of Time-Life Corporation in *Life* magazine, 17
February, 1941.
['A tall, large-framed . . . to detective stories.'] Townsend
Hoopes, *The Devil and John Foster Dulles*, p. 40.
['Eisenhower and Dulles . . . state of collapse.'] Several sources,
including Elie Abel, EOHP, Andrew Berding, *Dulles on Diplo-
macy*, Richard Goold-Adams, *The Time of Power*, Eleanor
Lansing Dulles, *John Foster Dulles – The Last Year*, and
Townsend Hoopes, *The Devil and John Foster Dulles*.
['the highest-paid corporate lawyer'] Goold-Adams, *The Time
of Power*, pp. 16–17.

['Anyone else but Dulles.'] See David Carlton, *Anthony Eden*, p. 323 and also Dwight Eisenhower, *Mandate for Change*.

['technical competence in the diplomatic field'] Eisenhower Diaries, 10 January, 1956, DDEL.

['It didn't take . . . out of him.'] Eisenhower Diaries, 14 May, 1953, DDEL.

['Foster's a bit . . . to know him.'] Eisenhower to Macmillan, 20 June, 1955. Cited by Harold Macmillan, *Tides of Fortune*, p. 608.

['Harold Macmillan found . . . the Secretary of State.'] Macmillan, *Tides of Fortune*, p. 634.

['It's perfectly true . . . Secretary of State.'] Marquis Childs, *Eisenhower*, pp. 188–90.

['Yet it wasn't . . . be particularly difficult.'] The story of the Mossadeq telegram is related by Eleanor Lansing Dulles, *John Foster Dulles*. The 'restlessly uneasy' quote comes from Emmet Hughes, as cited in Hoopes, *The Devil and John Foster Dulles*, p. 137. The conclusions are my own.

['Every American President . . . the Presidency worked.'] There are several sources, including Kenneth Leish, *The White House*, plus Eisenhower's, *Crusade in Europe* and *Mandate for Change*.

['Eisenhower having refused . . . was forever doomed.'] Stephen Ambrose, *Ike's Spies*, pp. 157–8.

['the monolithic mass of Communist Imperialism'] Eisenhower Diaries, 27 January, 1949, DDEL.

['He was an . . . them do it.'] Raymond Saulnier interview.

['But, like so . . . of his character.'] Harrison Salisbury, EOHP.

['As President, not . . . suspicious of newspapermen.'] Elie Abel, EOHP.

['One day early . . . you than me.'] Paul Boller, *Presidential Anecdotes*, p. 296.

['Televised coverage of . . . grandson, Camp David.'] Several sources, including Eisenhower, *Mandate For Change*, Emmet Hughes, *The Ordeal of Power*, and personal interviews, including Andrew Goodpaster, John Eisenhower and Raymond Saulnier.

['He'd pledged during . . . substitute for war.'] Arthur Krock, *Memoirs*, p. 272.

['Stalin had great . . . the Red Army.'] Harrison Salisbury, EOHP.

['Of course, long . . . already been shot'.'] Adjoubei interview.

['Yet Eisenhower was . . . the Soviet Union.'] Eisenhower, *Mandate for Change*, pp. 143–5.

['His much-quoted excuse . . . such a meeting'.'] ibid.

['They'd first met . . . that moment on.'] ibid., pp. 258–9.

['The reason I . . . no glory-hopper.'] Boller, *Presidential Anecdotes*, p. 290.

['While making arrangements . . . cold for me'.'] Letter from the Prime Minister to the President, 8 November, 1953, PRO.

['Eisenhower responded in . . . much admiring son.'] James Hagerty, EOHP.

['As President-elect, just . . . is completely fatuous.'] Eisenhower Diaries, 5 January, 1953, DDEL.

['Now that Stalin . . . frustration and delusion.'] The *Economist*, 2 June, 1990, p. 19.

['Eisenhower and Dulles . . . the same treatment.'] Carlton, *Anthony Eden*, p. 300.

['uninstructed'] W. Scott Lucas, *Divided We Stand*, p. 23.

['And their relationship . . . had for Churchill.'] Carlton, *Anthony Eden*, pp. 323–4.

['Then again, Churchill . . . to the Premiership.' The *Economist*, 2 June, 1990, p. 22.

['Once with Dean . . . impatience to show.'] Carlton, *Anthony Eden*, pp. 294–9.

['Like Churchill, he . . . in the world.'] The *Economist*, 2 June, 1990, p. 19.

['A year later . . . the United States.'] Salisbury Dispatch, 3 July, 1953, PRO.

['At least in . . . their own views.'] Eisenhower, *Mandate for Change*, pp. 252–3.

['The two old . . . than good government.'] Sir John Colville, *The Fringes of Power*, pp. 683–6.

['He constantly impressed . . . typical British understatement.'] James Hagerty, EOHP.

['The story told . . . hard of hearing.'] Interview with Lord Boyd-Carpenter.

['Just how hard . . . off the machine.'] Hagerty, EOHP.

['One of the . . . were acting together.'] Anthony Eden, Draft Cabinet Paper, 19 November, 1953, PRO.

['Making matters worse . . . a third one.'] Hagerty, EOHP.

['Churchill's contempt for . . . south of France.'] Carlton, *Anthony Eden*, p. 336.

['In 1949, the . . . the United States.'] Victor Rothwell, 'Britain and the First Cold War,' in Richard Crockatt and Steve Smith (eds) *The Cold War*, pp. 58–75.

['Considering that, Churchill . . . lies and corruption'.'] Meeting notes, 'Policy of the Soviet Union,' PRO.

['Eisenhower saw Britain's . . . the 49th state.' Rothwell, 'Britain and the First Cold War.'

4 *Drawing the Boundaries*

['Josef Stalin was . . . America's atomic arsenal.'] Compiled from Nikita Khrushchev, *Khrushchev Remembers – The Glasnost Tapes*, pp. 100–1, and Alexei Adjoubei, *A l'Ombre du Khrouchtchev*, pp. 140–5.

['At the start . . . importance to us.'] J. V. Reistrup, 'With Sputnik Soviets Began Plucking Many Easy Fruits,' *Washington Post* article reprinted in *Huntsville Times*, 1 October, 1967.

['In fact, Stalin . . . at any minute".'] N. Khrushchev, *Khrushchev Remembers – The Last Testament*, pp. 63–4.

['As early as . . . first-strike preventative attack.'] References to all these plans can be found in Michael Kaku and Daniel Axelrod, *To Win a Nuclear War*, pp. 10–40. The July and September conclusions of the Chiefs of Staff are in JCS 1496, Top Secret, 19 July, 1945, and the revised JCS 1496, 30 September, 1945. Operations Totality, Pincher, Broiler and Bushwacker are all NARC. 'Strategic Vulnerability' is JIC 329/1, Top Secret, November 1945, NARC.

['Summarizing their case . . . the world revolution.'] 'Evaluation of Malenkov's Resignation, Bulganin's Appointment and Molotov's Foreign Policy Speech, 8 February 1955.' Joint Intelligence Committee of the Joint Chiefs of Staff, 15 February, 1955, Washington DC, Top Secret, NARC.

['That was not . . . the Soviet Arsenal.'] Khrushchev, *Khrushchev Remembers – The Glasnost Tapes*, pp. 68–9.

['Forty years after . . . World War III.'] 'Who Started the Cold War,' *Pravda*, 29 August, 1988.

NOTES

['The strength of . . . up over Canada.'] Edgar Bottome, 'Balance of Terror.'

['Through NATO, the . . . the capitalistic threat.'] A. M. Ledovski interview.

['By the middle . . . they are themselves.'] Prime Minister's personal telegram, 27 January, 1954, Foreign Office to UK Delegation, Berlin, Top Secret, PRO.

['He thought it . . . off the Russians.'] McGeorge Bundy, *Danger and Survival*, p. 301.

['On 8 April . . . value that immensely.'] Prime Minister's correspondence with the President of the United States. PRO.

['The year 1955 . . . international foreign relations.'] Edgar Bottome, 'Balance of Terror,' p. xiii.

['If we are . . . from the earth.'] *New York Times*, 22 July, 1954.

['In the spring . . . by the mid-1960s.'] Charles J. V. Murphy, 'Khrushchev's Paper Bear,' *Fortune* magazine, December 1964. Bomber designations from Jane's interview.

['The following year . . . of 18 Bisons.'] John Newhouse, *War and Peace in the Nuclear Age*, p. 110. Bomber characteristics from Jane's interview.

['"US estimates of . . . much too high".'] Memorandum of Discussion at the 289th Meeting of the National Security Council, Washington, 28 June, 1956, *Foreign Relations of the United States*, 1955–1957, Volume XXIV, item No. 55.

['The U-2 divulged . . . a second time.'] The story of the Bisons in 1954 was confirmed by Murphy, 'Khrushchev's Paper Bear,' while the story of the 1955 Red Air Force Day is confirmed by Newhouse, *War and Peace in the Nuclear Age*.

['The truth of . . . strike against them.'] Edgar Bottome, *Balance of Terror*, p. 42.

['As the term . . . to remain confrontational.'] Sir Frank Roberts writing in Richard Crockatt and Steve Smith (eds), *The Cold War – Past and Present*, pp. xv-xvi.

['Where Soviet foreign . . . lack of resistance.'] Adam B. Ulam, writing in Ivo Lederer (ed.), *Russian Foreign Policy*, p. 57.

['Eden hardly had . . . caused by them.'] David Carlton, *Anthony Eden*, pp. 348-9.

['That Eden and . . . and small points.'] John Colville, *The Fringes of Power*, p. 700.

['A calmer, more . . . times downright devious.'] Harold Macmillan, *Tides of Fortune*, goes into great detail about Geneva and Dulles, pp. 587–651.

['Had Dulles been . . . such a maneuver.'] John Foster Dulles, 'Soviet Goals at Geneva,' State Department Notes, 6 July, 1955, NARC.

['A weighty US . . . concealed iron will.'] Eisenhower, *Mandate for Change*, pp. 517–18.

['Macmillan likened Bulganin . . . this vast country?'] Macmillan, *Tides of Fortune*, pp. 619–22.

['Until the Russian . . . Palais des Nations.'] *The Times* (London), 28 July, 1955.

['Yet it was . . . of the talking.'] James Hagerty, EOHP.

['Khrushchev himself claimed . . . had liked Eisenhower.'] Khrushchev, *Khrushchev Remembers*, pp. 220–2.

['That said, Geneva was . . . favorably to them.'] General Andrew Goodpaster interview.

['Unfortunately, Zhukov's presence . . . and portable radio.'] Eisenhower, *Mandate for Change*, p. 518.

['Seeing Zhukov for . . . never to be.'] ibid., p. 525.

['Eisenhower later told . . . lost on Eisenhower.'] Goodpaster interview.

['The two were . . . about his kidneys.'] John Eisenhower interview.

['In any case, . . . were never reunited.'] Macmillan, *Tides of Fortune*, pp. 617–23.

['Eisenhower tried to . . . the Western alliance.'] Eisenhower, *Mandate for Change*, p. 523.

['The same man . . . we were denied".'] John Eisenhower, *Strictly Personal*, p. 177.

['But as the . . . into our bedrooms".'] Goodpaster interview.

['Later that evening . . . could be arranged.'] Michael Beschloss, *Mayday*, p. 105, Anthony Eden, *Full Circle*, p. 307, and the President's memo to Congress, 25 July, 1955, DDEL.

['That the Russians . . . election of 1956.'] William Manchester, *The Glory and the Dream*, pp. 747–51. Also Hagerty, EOHP.

['Harold Macmillan believed . . . bases in Europe.'] Macmillan, *Tides of Fortune*, p. 610.

['He believed that . . . to live with.'] Hagerty, EOHP.

['Without knowing that . . . important man there'] Adjoubei, *A l'Ombre de Khrouchtchev*, p. 149.

['when Dulles got . . . and devious ways".'] Andrew Berding, *Dulles on Diplomacy*, pp. 52–3.

5 The General, the Lawyer and the Spy

['Three days after . . . balance of terror.'] John Newhouse, *War and Peace in the Nuclear Age*, p. 801.

['Eisenhower inherited Truman's . . . between the services.'] Sherman Adams, *First-Hand Report*, p. 398.

['On 12 January . . . a world war.' Eleanor Lansing Dulles, *John Foster Dulles – The Last Year*, pp. 52–3, and *Foreign Affairs* magazine, March 1954.

['"We need allies . . . our own choosing.'] Dulles address to Council on Foreign Relations, the State Department, NARC and Dulles Papers, JFDP.

['The following day . . . preserve our freedom.'] McGeorge Bundy, *Danger and Survival*, pp. 255–60.

['The very fact . . . Politburo know that.'] Bundy, *Danger and Survival*, p. 259.

['While the possibility. . . of the dice.'] Henry Kissinger, *Nuclear Weapons and Foreign Policy*, pp. 133–4.

['A draft of . . . never saw it.'] Eleanor Lansing Dulles, *John Foster Dulles*, p. 52.

['Some people thought . . . an edgy gambler.'] Townsend Hoopes, *The Devil and John Foster Dulles*, pp. 308–11.

['The Soviets joined . . . Cold War approach.'] Charles Bohlen, EOHP.

['Dulles the man . . . the atheistic Marxists.'] Arthur Krock, *Memoirs*, p. 323.

['neutrality as immoral'] William O'Neill, *American High*, p. 220.

['A militant Presbyterian'] Paul Boller, *Presidential Anecdotes*, p. 293.

['Eisenhower felt that . . . was always skeptical.'] Andrew Goodpaster interview.

['"I'll say this . . . us too far".'] Nikita Khrushchev, *Khrushchev Remembers*, p. 398.

['A man of . . . and unimpeachable character.'] Dwight Eisenhower, *Mandate for Change*, p. 86.
['A few years . . . and just thing.'] Eisenhower Diaries, 24 January, 1958, DDEL.
['Yet in his . . . arise between us.'] Dwight Eisenhower, *Waging Peace*, p. 364.
['When the brinkmanship . . . meant to him.'] Eleanor Lansing Dulles, *John Foster Dulles*, pp. 51–2.
['a planned mistake'] *New York Times*, 15 January, 1956.
['Where John Foster . . . conquered the world.'] Leonard Mosley, *Dulles*, pp. 32–5.
['His uncle, Robert . . . on its side.'] Hoopes, *The Devil and John Foster Dulles*, p. 31.
['Foster spoke with . . . gregarious, more relaxed.'] Raymond Saulnier interview.
['Allen also displayed . . . many people's eyes.'] Richard Bissell interview.
['Eisenhower shared their . . . Conference of 1945'.'] Eisenhower, *Mandate for Change*, p. 504.
['Still, however much . . . even more intense.'] Stephen Ambrose, *Ike's Spies*, p. 239.
['And the Joint . . . layers of bureaucrats.'] Based on interviews with Bissell and Goodpaster, and on Killian, *Sputnik, Scientists and Eisenhower*, and Michael Beschloss, *Mayday*.
['The Killian group . . . protect against it.'] Bissell interview and James Killian, *Sputnik, Scientists and Eisenhower*, p. 68.
['non-tendentious'] Confidential Foreign Service Dispatch, 12 August, 1955, from US Ambassador Charles Bohlen in Moscow to the State Department, Washington DC, NARC.
['A few days . . . comparatively near future".'] As translated in confidential Foreign Service Dispatch, 12 August, 1955, from US Ambassador Charles Bohlen in Moscow to the State Department, Washington DC, NARC.
['That was followed . . . US Information Agency.'] Foreign Service Dispatch No. 78, 18 August, 1955, from Amembassy, Moscow to the Department of State, Washington, FOIA, US State Department.
['As it happened . . . his leaking secrets.'] Vladimir Stabnikov fax, 14 August, 1991.

['In September 1955, . . . in this field.'] Current Intelligence Weekly Summary, Central Intelligence Agency, Washington, 27 June, 1957, Secret, FOIA.

['It wasn't until . . . back to the Presidium.'] Private notes of V. E. Luppo.

['Then too, the . . . a satellite in space.'] Yaroslav Golovanov interview.

['It still exists . . . such an activity.'] Victor Marchetti and John Marks, *The CIA and the Cult of Intelligence*, pp. 279–81.

['Especially when it . . . influence over Eisenhower.'] Bissell interview.

['In Allen's case . . . a role model.'] Ambrose, *Ike's Spies*, p. 242–4.

['Based on his . . . and clandestine operations.'] Goodpaster interview.

['Before long, the . . . wouldn't have it.'] Ambrose, *Ike's Spies*.

['Then again, he . . . else I know'.'] United States Senate, *Final Report of the Select Committee to Study Government Operations with Respect to Intelligence Activities* (Church Committee Report), Senate Report 94–755, 94th Congress, Second Session, US Government Printing Office, Washington DC, 1974.

6 *Paranoia and Confrontation*

['On a warm . . . facing the nation.'] Operation Alert is described by James McGregor Burns, *The Crosswinds of Freedom, p.* 256, Stephen Ambrose, *Eisenhower – the President*, pp. 256–7, and Peter Lyon, *Eisenhower – Portrait of the Hero*, p. 655. Further references, DDEL.

['Seven months later . . . no significant difference.'] Compiled from 'An Evaluation of the Anticipated Damage in the Initial Stages of a Nuclear War with the Russians – A Report to the President,' Top Secret, DDEL. Also, Eisenhower Diaries, 23 January, 1956, DDEL.

['Risking cries of . . . less capricious, etc.''] Alexei Adjoubei, *A l'Ombre du Khrouchtchev*, pp. 158–9.

['Once Lenin was . . . with Lenin alone.'] Seweryn Bialer, *Stalin's Successors*, pp. 29–30.

['Stalin was a . . . one's own will.'] From a reprint of the speech in 'The Anti-Stalin Campaign and International Communism,' The Russian Institute, Columbia University.

['Khrushchev reproached Stalin . . . his own person.'] The Russian Institute, Columbia University.

['The men and . . . was a pretense.'] R. Medvedev, *Khrushchev*, pp. 86–7.

['Realizing that he . . . afraid of Stalin.'] Adjoubei interview.

['Although 1 million . . . printed, then destroyed,'] Roy and Zhores Medvedev, *Khrushchev*, p. 70.

['Allan Dulles ordered . . . text was acquired.'] Allen Dulles, *The Craft of Intelligence*, pp. 81–2.

['Once his men . . . 4 June, 1956.'] Stephen Ambrose, *Ike's Spies*, p. 238.

['Over the next . . . without police recrimination.'] US Department of State, Intelligence Brief, 'Current Status of the Anti-Stalin Campaign in the Soviet Bloc,' Official Use Only, 24 April, 1956, NARC.

['Still, by being . . . of his life.'] Medvedev, *Khrushchev*, pp. 87–92.

['At the June . . . rid of him.'] Memorandum of Discussion at the 289th Meeting of the National Security Council, Washington, 28 June, 1956, FRUS, Volume XXIV.

['Unable to assure . . . which ridiculed Stalin.'] Report of OCB Special Working Group on Stalinism, Operations Coordinating Board, Secret, 17 May, 1956, NARC.

['In June he . . . enemies of Communism".'] Medvedev, *Khrushchev*, p. 71 and p. 96.

['It was not . . . you know why".'] Clifton Fadiman, *Little Brown Book of Anecdotes*, Little Brown, New York, 1985, p. 330.

['Trapped to some . . . never come easily.'] Medvedev, *Khrushchev*, p. 114.

['Khrushchev was hardly . . . ever get done.'] R. and Z. Medvedev, *Khrushchev*, pp. vii–ix.

['Although he remained . . . one contradicted him.'] Note by William Taubman, editor of Sergei Khrushchev, *Khrushchev on Khrushchev*, p. 152.

['He wanted the . . . challenge his own.'] Merle Fainsod, *How Russia Is Ruled*, pp. 581–3.

['Years later, John . . . of Stalin's mistakes'.'] Fadiman, *Little Brown Book of Anecdotes*.

['Eisenhower suffered a . . . of presidential duties.'] Raymond Saulnier interview.

['By the middle . . . if they attacked.'] Douglas Kinnard, 'President Eisenhower and the Defense Budget,' *Journal of Politics*, 1977, p. 603.

['Until someone found . . . of such weapons.'] Eisenhower Diaries, 30 March, 1956, DDEL.

['The same evening . . . into Eastern Europe.'] Michael Beschloss, *Mayday*, p. 112, and Nathan Miller, *Spying for America*, pp. 406–10. Also, U-2 Files, PRO.

['His first trip . . . a silent movie.'] Nikita Khrushchev, *Khrushchev Remembers*, pp. 392–400.

['Khrushchev continued to . . . found too distant.'] Adjoubei interview.

['Eden hosted a . . . his de-Stalinization reforms.'] Sergei Khrushchev, *Khrushchev on Khrushchev*, pp. 4–5.

['a smart man but exceedingly rude'] Khrushchev, *Khrushchev Remembers – The Glasnost Tapes*, p. 97.

['fat and doddering'] Khrushchev, *Khrushchev Remembers*, p. 410.

['If I lived . . . I'd vote Conservative.'] John Boyd-Carpenter interview.

['Bulganin can vote . . . to vote Conservative.'] Kennett Love, *Suez*, p. 259.

['Their visit to . . . couldn't help smiling'.'] Khrushchev, *Khrushchev Remembers*, p. 411.

['enough vodka and caviar for 4000 people.'] Interview with Claridge's manager Michael Bentley.

['A few days . . . a week ago".'] British Admiralty official statement, 29 April, 1956, PRO.

['Five days later . . . not to happen.'] Robert Rhodes James, *Anthony Eden*, pp. 435–8.

['But if he . . . before getting involved.'] Conclusion is mine.

['Not being one . . . Moscow and Leningrad.'] Beschloss, *Mayday*, pp. 113–23, Miller, *Spying for America*, and PRO.

['In a cable . . . it can last.'] Top Secret Telegram, Prime Minister to the President, 1 May, 1956, PRO. It should be noted that the more general descriptions of the Soviet visit to

Britain were found in newspaper and magazine articles written at the time.

['The help given . . . the Soviet Union.'] Andrei Gromyko, *Memoirs*, p. 231.

['The help we . . . throughout the world.'] Khrushchev, *Khrushchev Remembers*, p. 429.

Description of the Suez conflict compiled from several sources, including Keith Kyle, *Suez*, W. Scott Lucas, *Divided We Stand*, Harold Macmillan, *Riding the Storm*, Dwight Eisenhower, *Waging Peace*, Anthony Eden, *Full Circle*, Sergei Khrushchev, *Khrushchev on Khrushchev*, and Nikita Khrushchev, *Khrushchev Remembers*.

['Anthony Eden was . . . his own demise.'] The descriptions of Eden come from several sources, including David Carlton, *Anthony Eden*, p. 376, Frank Roberts, *Dealing with Dictators*, pp. 155–63, and personal interviews.

['If we take . . . be finally destroyed.'] Emergency Secret Telegram, Prime Minister to the President, 27 July, 1956, PRO.

['The response from . . . our Western allies".'] Top Secret Telegram, the President to the Prime Minister, 31 July, 1956, PRO.

['Now Eden tried . . . among our objectives".'] Immediate Secret Telegram, the Prime Minister to the President, 5 August, 1956, PRO.

['In Eisenhower's opinion . . . Near East oil.'] Top Secret Telegram, the President to the Prime Minister, 3 September, 1956, PRO.

['Eden answered by . . . perish by degrees".'] Emergency Secret Telegram, the Prime Minister to the President, 6 September, 1956, PRO.

['He agreed with . . . most distressing results.'] Emergency Secret Telegram, the President to the Prime Minister, 9 September, 1956, PRO.

['The US cannot . . . somewhat independent role.'] *Washington Post*, 3 October, 1956.

['The British Ambassador . . . I ever read".'] Note on copy in the PRO.

['The growing split . . . into his study.'] Robert Divine, *Eisenhower and the Cold War*, pp. 85–6. See also, Emmet Hughes, *The Ordeal of Power*, Eisenhower, *Waging Peace*, and Robert Rhodes James, *Anthony Eden*.

['Andrew Goodpaster was . . . leaving Eden isolated.'] Goodpaster interview.

['Did you know . . . of the Canal.'] Fadiman, *Little Brown Book of Anecdotes*, p. 330.

['Eisenhower couldn't believe . . . height of folly.'] James Hagerty, EOHP.

['I believe as . . . all the world.'] Emergency Secret Telegram, the Prime Minister to the President, 5 November, 1956, PRO.

['Thirteen years after . . . the weaker partner.'] Eden, *Full Circle*, p. 64.

['That empire mattered . . . second-class power.'] The *Economist*, 2 June, 1990, p. 22.

['A wave of . . . in the UK.'] Kyle, *Suez*, p. 509.

['He'd opened the . . . the Middle East.'] Richard Aliano, *American Defense Policy*, pp. 268–9.

['So was his golf . . . just been bombed.'] Paul Boller, *Presidential Anecdotes*, pp. 297–8.

['Whether or not . . . will bury you.'] Quoted in *The Times*, 19 November, 1956.

7 *The Nazi Connection*

['It was, however . . . a valid one.'] Willy Ley, *Rockets, Missiles and Space Travel*, pp. 108–9.

['Three years after . . . across the Alps.'] Willy Ley's introduction to *V-2* by Walter Dornberger, pp. 9–10 and Ley, *Rockets, Missiles and Space Travel*, pp. 110–16.

['At the end . . . Wernher von Braun.'] US Army Ballistic Missile Agency, 'Historical Monograph, US Army Ordinance Satellite Program,' November 1958, Secret, ABMA, Redstone Arsenal (hereafter ABMA 'Historical Monograph').

['We needed money . . . milked most successfully.'] Daniel Lang, 'Interview with von Braun,' the *New Yorker*, 21 April, 1951.

['Dornberger's crew at . . . more advanced A-4.'] The War Office, 'German Long-Range Rocket Programme,' p. 11, Imperial War Museum.

['Construction of the . . . havoc on England.'] ibid., pp. 12–15.

['65,000 alterations'] David Johnson, *V for Vengeance*, p. 113.

['One version of . . . about the A-4.'] David Irving, *The Mare's Nest*, pp. 70–4.

['Begun in March . . . onto its target.'] 'Handbook on Guided Missiles of Germany and Japan,' Military Intelligence Division, War Department, Washington DC, Confidential, 1 February, 1946.

['But not all . . . at Peenemünde-East.'] Irving, *The Mare's Nest*, p. 74.

['They met him . . . were SS guards.'] The War Office, 'German Long-Range Rocket Programme,' p. 16, Imperial War Museum.

['Not surprisingly, so . . . the A-4 facilities.'] Frederick Ordway and Mitchell Sharpe, *The Rocket Team*, pp. 113–24.

['Unbeknownst to the . . . a fortnight later.'] Irving, *The Mare's Nest*, pp. 205–7.

['Over the 24 . . . the launches failed.'] 'Handbook on Guided Missiles of Germany and Japan,' Military Intelligence Division, War Department, Washington DC, Confidential, 1 February, 1946.

['When a report . . . attacks per week.'] 'Handbook on Guided Missiles of Germany and Japan,' Military Intelligence Division, War Department, Washington DC, Confidential, 1 February, 1946. The comparison with the SCUD-B comes from an interview with Jane's.

['The impact of . . . been banking on.'] Ordway and Sharpe, *The Rocket Team*, pp. 248–9.

['However, Eisenhower saw . . . been written off.'] See Dwight Eisenhower, *Crusade in Europe*.

['In early April . . . service was excellent.'] ABMA, 'Historical Monograph.'

['With the foresight . . . and then discarded".'] Ordway and Sharpe, *The Rocket Team*, pp. 256–74. See also ABMA, 'Historical Monograph.'

['The bulk of . . . of the A-9.'] *Secret Report On Operation Backfire*, Vols I-V, The War Office, January 1946, Secret, Vol. I, p. 27, PRO.

['The Americans located . . . the Peenemüde files.'] Brian Johnson, *The Secret War*, pp. 185–7.

['While the Germans . . . it's too late.'] Van Slingerland, 'How

We Let the Missile Secrets Get Away,' *Look* magazine, 4 February, 1958, and ABMA, 'Historical Monograph.'

['Back in Washington . . . returned to Germany.'] Memo from Assistant Secretary of War, 'Military Exploitation of German Scientists,' 1 February, 1946, NARC.

['More interested in . . . camp in Wales.'] Tom Bower, *The Paperclip Conspiracy*, pp. 122–4.

['Even highly respected . . . period to come.'] Edwin Diamond, *The Rise and Fall of the Space Age*, p. 16.

['Some years later . . . military expenditures curtailed.'] Daniel Lang, 'Interview with Wernher von Braun,' the *New Yorker*, 21 April, 1951.

['They were, he . . . prisoners of peace.'] ABMA, 'Historical Monograph.'

['General Omar Bradley . . . and funding battles.'] Maj.-Gen. H. N. Toftoy, 'Army Missile Development,' *Army Information Digest*, December 1956, pp. 10–35.

['In 1952, the . . . high-priority project.'] Charles Alexander, 'Pathway to the Moon,' paper delivered to the Organization of American Historians, Chicago, 30 April, 1967.

['By the middle . . . do it first'.'] Von Braun report, 'A Minimum Satellite Vehicle Based on Components Available from Developments of the Army Ordinance Corps,' Secret, US Army, Redstone Arsenal.

['Eisenhower had recruited . . . and procurement problems.'] Dwight Eisenhower, *Mandate for Change*, p. 86.

['His mistake was . . . ends to pare.'] Marquis Childs, *Eisenhower – Captive Hero*, pp. 171–2.

['Described by an . . . overlap and "boondoggling".'] ibid.

['a man who . . . than he knows.'] Eisenhower is quoted by Childs, *Eisenhower*, p. 183.

['During briefings, Wilson . . . the assembly line.'] James Gavin, *War and Peace in the Space Age*, pp. 152–3.

['Unbeknownst to anyone . . . by the military.'] Statement of Policy prepared by the NSC Planning Board on US Scientific Satellite Program, NSC 5520, Washington DC, 20 May, 1955, NARC.

['Annexed to NSC . . . afford to lose".'] Memorandum for James Lay, Executive Secretary, National Security Council,

from Nelson Rockefeller, Special Assistant to the President, 17 May, 1955, NARC.
['With the benefit . . . seem to matter.'] Several sources, including John Medaris, *Countdown for Decision*, ABMA, 'Historical Monograph,' Andrew Goodpaster interview and private papers of members of the Stewart Committee.
['For instance, in . . . returned to Germany.'] Ordway and Sharpe, *Rocket Team*, pp. 378–9.
['The Army decided . . . America into space.'] ABMA, 'Historical Monograph.'
['In March 1956 . . . heard of it.'] John Eisenhower, EOHP.
['Next came the . . . just in case.'] Ordway and Sharpe, *Rocket Team*, pp. 377–8.
['The NSC continued . . . rocket that worked.'] Memoranda of discussions of meetings of the NSC (Numbers 283, 310, 322), as described in FRUS, Volume XI. Also, 'A Progress Report on the US Scientific Satellite Program (NSC 5520) 3 October, 1956,' Secret, NARC.
['Charles Wilson was . . . any future speeches.'] Bernard Schriever quoted in Allan Needell, *The First 25 Years in Space – A Symposium*, p. 28.
['On 9 April . . . do with satellites.'] ABMA, 'Historical Monograph.'
['In various languages . . . the satellite problem.'] Medaris testimony during the 'Inquiry into Satellite and Missile Programs,' Committee on Armed Forces, United States Senate, Part II, Washington, 1958.
['On 20 June . . . cosmic ray particles.'] Max Frankel, 'Soviet to Launch First Moon in '58,' *New York Times*, 20 June, 1957.
['The press secretary . . . 1955 and 1956.'] Proposed News Release from the National Academy of Sciences, 18 June, 1957.
['Except for Bronk's . . . announcement "old hat".'] Administrative-Confidential memorandum from the head office of the IGY, Washington to the director, re: Publicity on USSR Satellite, 21 June, 1957, NARC.
['So did the . . . end is expected.'] Current Intelligence Weekly Summary, Central Intelligence Agency, Washington, 27 June, 1957, Secret.

['When Richard Bissell . . . the Vanguard project.'] Bissell interview.

['On 20 July . . . against the Russians.'] Diary Note, Alan Waterman phone conversation with Hugh Odishaw, Administrative Confidential, NARC.

['Towards the middle . . . to believe it.'] Several sources, including John Ranelagh, *The Agency – The Rise and Decline of the CIA*, Michael Beschloss, *Mayday*, Jeffrey Richelson, *American Espionage and the Soviet Target*, Charles J.V. Murphy, 'Khrushchev's Paper Bear,' *Fortune* magazine, December 1964, interviews with Bissell and Goodpaster; plus White House minute meetings and briefing papers, DDEL.

['Few people in . . . Wilson was leaving.'] Medaris, *Countdown for Decision*, p. 152.

['McElroy – who was . . . list of priorities.'] Compiled from several oral histories, including Lyman Lemnitzer and Neil McElroy, EOHP. Also notes from Brucker, Gavin and Medaris.

8 *The Day the World Changed*

['Our planet is . . . in a cradle.'] *Moscow News*, 11 November, 1957.

['Interplanetary Communications'] is the literal translation of the Russian for space travel.

['Very much a . . . his bank account.'] Several sources have been used, including Yaroslav Golovanov and Boris Chertok interviews. Also, *Soviet Russia* magazine, 10 January, 1982, which includes comments and recollections from Korolev's colleagues, among them V. V. Chernov, K. P. Feoktistov, K. S. Shustin, S. O. Okhapkin, A. N. Voltsifin, A.A. Zlotnikova, V. A. Koshelev and N. D. Bondarenko.

Korolev's background comes from Golovanov, Nathalie Korolova and Georgi Vetrov interviews, plus written sources, among them Golovanov, *Sergei Korolev*, James Oberg, *Uncovering Soviet Disasters*, and Walter McDougall, *The Heavens and the Earth*. The line 'vanish without a trace' comes from Leonid Vladimirov, *The Russian Space Bluff*, p. 146. The reference to his eyes and other facts about his imprisonment come from comments of fellow inmates made in *Soviet Russia* magazine, 10 January, 1982.

['He was released . . . until January 1947.'] Korolev's official state records, KGB, Moscow, and Vetrov interview.

['One story that . . . the parking lot.'] Golovanov and Vetrov interviews. Also Vladimir Stabnikov Fax No. 2.

['One summer afternoon . . . to Korolev's rescue.'] The information in this section was compiled through interviews with Golovanov, G. Yu Maximov, Dr Boris Rauchenbach, Chertok, Dr Vasily Mishin and Vetrov, plus documents obtained in Moscow.

['Pyotr Leonidovich Kapitza . . . 30 July, 1955.'] Several sources, including *Current Biography; Moscow News*, 15 April, 1955; the *New York Times*, 20 August, 1953, 30 July, 1955, 18 October, 1978; L. Badash, *Kapitza, Rutherford and the Kremlin*; N. Khrushchev, *Khrushchev Remembers – The Last Testament*; and A. Parry, *The Russian Scientist*.

['Invited by Mstislav . . . him do it.'] Chertok, Maximov and Mishin interviews.

['In May 1957 . . . so did Bulganin.'] Roy and Zhores Medvedev, *Khrushchev*, pp. 757–76.

['The group decided . . . himself First Secretary.'] R. Medvedev, *Khrushchev*, p. 117.

['But Nikita Khrushchev . . . to give in.'] Several sources, including N. Khrushchev, *Khrushchev Remembers*, Mikhail Heller and Aleksandr Nekrich, *Utopia in Power*, and R. Medvedev, *Khrushchev*.

['It may mean . . . conflict of policies.'] Macmillan diary, 5 July, 1957, in H. Macmillan, *Riding the Storm*, p. 308.

['Mr Khrushchev appeared . . . from his own.'] Minutes of the Cabinet Meeting, 9 July, 1957, PRO.

['Eisenhower look on . . . for us all.'] Memorandum of discussion of 329th meeting of the National Security Council, 3 July, 1957, DDEL.

['There were times . . . for Khrushchev's attention.'] Several sources, including Vetrov, Chertok and Mishin interviews.

['Something that struck . . . was about all.'] Mishin interview, and KGB documents, Moscow.

['What he never . . . with his title.'] 'Scientific Intelligence

Research Aid – Scientific Research Institute and Experimental Factory 88 for Guided Missile Development – Moscow/ Kaliningrad,' CIA, Office of Scientific Intelligence, 4 March, 1960, Top Secret.

['Korolev saw the . . . that infuriated him.'] Rauchenbach interview.

['Punish the Americans'] Vetrov interview.

['A severe taskmaster . . . before 11:30 a.m.'] *Soviet Russia*, 10 January, 1982, includes comments and recollections from Korolev's colleagues, among them V. V. Chernov, K. P. Feoktistov, K. S. Shustin, S. O. Okhapkin, A. N. Voltsifin, A. A. Zlotnikova, V. A. Koshelev and N. D. Bondarenko.

['In late 1956 . . . how it tasted.'] Text is from Vetro interview. Quote is from Khrushchev, *Khrushchev Remembers – The Last Testament*, p. 46.

['He was hampered . . . the R-7 engine.'] Vladimirov, *Russian Space Bluff*, p. 61.

['That engine was . . . took another month.'] Several sources, including Vetrov, Rauchenbach, Mishin and Maximov interviews.

['When the rocket . . . tested its ICBM.'] Several sources, including Mishin, Rauchenbach, Vetrov, Luppo, Maximov interviews and Tass.

['In the third . . . him launch it.'] Chertok interview.

['The original design . . . would see him.'] Several sources, including Luppo, Mishin, Vetrov and Rauchenbach interviews.

The description of the Kremlin comes from personal interviews, plus the description of Sir W. Hayter in a telegram to Anthony Eden, 8 December, 1953, reporting on his conversation with Malenkov on 28 November, 1953, Confidential, PRO.

['That Khrushchev didn't . . . believed in it.'] Mishin interview.

['But Khrushchev appreciated . . . He liked that.'] Khrushchev, *Khrushchev Remembers – The Last Testament*, p. 46.

['Most of all . . . an after-thought.'] Mishin interview.

['In Korolev's mind . . . to be reworked.'] Maximov interview.

['For Vyacheslav Luppo . . . took this seriously.'] Luppo interview. The magazine article appeared in *Radio* magazine, issue no. 6, July 1957.

['On 23 August . . . up American cities.'] Chertok interview.

['When that day . . . never their own.'] Parry, *The Russian Scientist*, p. 187.

['In fact, Korolev . . . the most pleasing.'] Vetrov interview.

['Once that was . . . and nose cone.'] Maximov interview.

['At least that . . . Sergei Pavolovich, backwards.'] Luppo interview.

['Blueprints were drawn . . . copies for museums.'] Korolova, Rauchenbach and Golovanov interviews.

['On 23 September . . . Friday, 4 October.'] Vetrov interview.

['The next day . . . carried his news.'] Rauchenbach interview.

['On 3 October . . . final countdown began.'] Luppo interview.

['The military filmed . . . of Soviet history.'] Golovanov interview.

9 *The First Shock*

['The formal dinner . . . out the window.'] There are several versions of what happened at Redstone that evening, all agreeing in tone, the differences being in minor detail only. The best of those descriptions is probably in John Medaris' book, *Countdown for Decision*. The dialogue is reconstructed from the various sources.

['In the end . . . "ahead. Get started."'] Several sources, including Medaris, *Countdown for Decision*, and US Army Ballistic Missile Agency, 'Historical Monograph, US Army Ordinance Satellite Program', November 1958.

['The President returned . . . a military escort.'] Dwight Eisenhower, *Waging Peace*, pp. 162–76.

['Now in early . . . a golfing weekend.'] Eisenhower Diaries, October 1957, DDEL.

['Andrew Goodpaster was . . . is about science.'] Andrew Goodpaster interview.

['Born in the . . . exception of Lenin.'] Text and quotes have been compiled from various obituaries of Andrei Gromyko, appearing in the *Philadelphia Inquirer*, the *Miami Herald*, the *San Francisco Chronicle*, the *Los Angeles Times* and the Knight-Rider News Service, 3 July, 1989. Other comments

from Khrushchev, *Khrushchev Remembers*, Eisenhower, *Waging Peace*, and Sir William Hayter, *The Kremlin and the Embassy*.
['Congratulate me, . . . a second time.'] Albert Parry, *Russia's Rockets and Missiles*, p. 50.
['He was at . . . it at all.'] Andrei Gromyko, *Memoirs*, p. 324.
['Walter Sullivan, the . . . to his story.'] Personal correspondence, 22 September, 1991. Berkner quote is from Sullivan's story in the *New York Times*, 5 October, 1957, p. 3.
['The Saturday edition . . . crossing over US.'] *New York Times*, 5 October, 1957.
['With news services . . . into orbit. Period.'] Papers of James Hagerty, DDEL.
['He was at . . . write one too.'] Papers of John Foster Dulles, JFDL.
['These two originally . . . another very well.'] Gromyko, *Memoirs*, pp. 222–3.
['In that same . . . very forthright, "Yes."'] Department of State, Memorandum of Conversation, 5 October, 1957, Secret, DDEL.
['The satellite was . . . as fellow traveler.'] *New York Times*, 6 October, 1957.
['Senate Majority Leader . . . our own game.'] *New York Times*, 5 October, 1957.
['Political columnist Joseph . . . the vanishing point.'] Also column in the *Nashville Tennessean*, 15 October, 1957.
['Calling Sputnik 'a . . . the earth's surface.'] *Chicago Daily News*, 5 and 7 October, 1957.
['The *New York* . . . past national policies.'] *New York Times*, 7 October, 1957.
['Dr Edward Teller . . . of mortal danger.'] The *Washingtonian*, September 1982.
['If the intercontinental . . . Henry once expressed.'] Eric Sevareid, CBS Evening News, 7 October, 1957.
['At the Redstone . . . of inter-service rivalries.'] *Huntsville Times*, 8 and 9 October, 1957.
['Hermann Oberth, who . . . to the Navy.'] *Huntsville Times*, 6 October, 1957.
['Much the same . . . the Redstone proposal.'] Cited by Hanle in *Smithsonian* magazine, July, 1982.

['In England, the . . . wins space race,'] *Daily Express* and *News Chronicle*, both 5 October, 1957.

['Science fiction writer . . . have colossal repercussions.'] Associated Press, 6 October, 1957.

['Sir Bernard Lovell . . . more reasonable figure.'] *The Times* and Associated Press, 7 October, 1957.

['No one can . . . a Russian ICBM.'] Richard Aliano, *American Defense Policy*, p. 48.

['What strikes a . . . the ultimate weapon.'] *The Times*, 7 October, 1957.

['In Paris, where . . . the government crisis,'] *New York Times*, 6 October, 1957.

['As Jim Hagerty . . . with the Soviets.'] *New York Times*, 6 October, 1957.

['Senator Stewart Symington . . . right to know.'] Associated Press, 5 October, 1957.

['Senator Henry Scoop . . . are to survive.'] *New York Times*, 6 October, 1957.

['A hunk of . . . anybody could launch.'] *New York Times*, 5 October, 1957.

['White House Chief . . . space basketball game.'] *New York Times*, 16 October, 1957.

['Presidential adviser Clarence . . . worry about it.'] Cited in *The Washingtonian*, September 1982.

['The real danger . . . balance and proportion.'] *New York Times*, 7 October, 1957.

['When James Reston . . . and containing it.'] *New York Times*, 11 November, 1957.

Ottawa, Canada: Amembassy Ottawa to Secretary of State, 7 October, 1957, NARC.

Cairo, Egypt: Amembassy to Secretary of State, 6 October, 1957, NARC.

The Hague, Holland: Amembassy to Secretary of State, 7 October, 10 October, and 15 October, 1957, NARC.

Bucharest, Romania: Amembassy to Secretary of State, 7 October, 1957, NARC.

Damascus, Syria: Amembassy to Secretary of State, 7 October and 16 October, 1957, NARC.

Tunis, Tunisia: Amembassy to Secretary of State, 23 October,

1957, NARC.

Quito, Ecuador: Amembassy to Secretary of State, 22 October, 1957, NARC.

Buenos Aires, Argentina: Amembassy to Secretary of State, 8 October, 1957, NARC.

Pretoria, South Africa: Amembassy to Secretary of State, 17 October, 1957, NARC.

Bern, Switzerland: Amembassy to Secretary of State, 17 October, 1957, NARC.

Dublin, Ireland: Amembassy to Secretary of State, 17 October, 1957, NARC.

Montevideo, Uruguay: Amembassy to Secretary of State, 15 October, 1957, NARC.

Taipei, Taiwan (then Nationalist China): Amembassy to Secretary of State, 15 October, 1957, NARC.

Lagos, Nigeria: American Consul General to Secretary of State, 11 October 1957, NARC.

Manila, Philippines: Amembassy to Secretary of State, 9 October, 1957, NARC.

Tokyo, Japan: Amembassy to Secretary of State, 17 October, 1957, NARC.

West Berlin: Amembassy Bonn to Secretary of State, 9 October, 1957, NARC.

Paris, France: Amembassy to Secretary of State, 18 October, 1957, NARC.

['William Randolph Hearst . . . a boom boom,'] Hearst Newspapers, 6 October, 1957.

['Some stories expressed . . . was Peter Kapitza.'] Associated Press, 5 October, 1957.

['However, the stories . . . the United States.'] United Press International, 5 October, 1957.

['The *New York* . . . back to earth,'] *New York Times*, 7 October, 1957.

['The *Washington Post* . . . a brilliant victory.'] *Washington Post*, 7 October, 1957.

['The Russians have . . . vulnerable to attack.'] *Atlanta Constitution*, 7 October, 1957.

['Walter Sullivan called . . . forget the experience.'] Allan Needell, *The First 25 Years in Space*, p. 49.

['One of Charles . . . without military significance.'] Memorandum for the President from the Secretary of Defense, 'Earth Satellite,' Top Secret, 7 October, 1957, DDEL.
['Later that morning . . . the next day.'] Minutes of meeting in the White House, 7 October, 1957, Secret, DDEL.
['At 2 o'clock . . . of the IGY.'] Memorandum of meetings, 5 October, 1957 and 7 October, 1957, OCB Working Group on Certain Aspects of NSC 5520 (Scientific Earth Satellite), Confidential, 8 October, 1957, NARC.
['At about the . . . earliest possible moment.'] Secret memorandum, Secretary of the Army to Secretary of Defense, 7 October, 1957, NARC.
['When Foster Dulles . . . Hagerty said, no.'] Diary notes of telephone calls for the Secretary of State, 7 October, 1957, DDEL.
['The President and . . . some golf balls.'] Eisenhower Diaries, 7 October, 1957, DDEL.
['But by Tuesday . . . couldn't understand why.'] Goodpaster interview.
['play down the whole thing.'] Aliano, *American Defense Policy*, p. 50.
['Three of the . . . of the IGY.'] The White House, Staff Notes No. 210, 7 October, 1957, Secret, DDEL.
['The purpose of this . . . satellite in orbit.'] Fact Sheet, 'Army Satellite Capability.' From the Secretary of the Army to the Secretary of Defense and on to the President, 7 October, 1957, Secret, DDEL.
['The front page . . . the next Sputnik.'] *Washington Post* and *New York Times*, 8 October, 1957.
['Hagerty's telephones rang . . . lightly its obligations.'] Several sources, including Eisenhower Diaries and Staff Notes, DDEL. Plus, Eisenhower, *Waging Peace*, pp. 203-4, Hagerty Oral History and Goodpaster Oral History, both EOHP, and Goodpaster interview.
['Just after 8:30 . . . lost another round.'] Memorandum of Conference with the President, 8 October, 1957, Secret, DDEL, and FRUS, Volume XI, pp. 755-6.
['Just before lunch . . . Eisenhower that afternoon.'] Diary notes of telephone calls for the Secretary of State, 8 October, 1957, DDEL.
['Eisenhower, Dulles and . . . Eisenhower about Sputnik.']

Eisenhower Diaries, 8 October, 1957, DDEL.

['Announcing it the . . . more than that.'] *New York Times*, 10 October, 1957.

['Foster Dulles particularly . . . produce spectacular accomplishments.'] Draft statements on the Soviet satellite, 8 October, 1957, DDEL.

['Allen Dulles took . . . dreamed of using.'] Draft statement by Allen Dulles, DDEL. Notes penciled on the draft in Eisenhower's hand.

['At the last . . . that first week.'] Questions for Don Quarles, attached to Hagerty's copy of the statement by the President, DDEL.

['He then got . . . of his head.'] Eisenhower Diaries, 8 October, 1957, DDEL.

10 *The Russian Offensive*

['It was just . . . *Pravda's* front page.'] Translated text from Soviet radio, *Pravda* and Tass, 5 October, 1957.

['The first indication . . . made it happen.'] Alexei Adjoubei, Yaroslav Golovanov and Leonid Zamyatin interviews.

['The Russian press . . . the arms race.'] Described in a classified telegram from US Ambassador Llewellyn Thompson, Moscow, to the Secretary of State, 9 October, 1957, NARC.

['At last, *Pravda* . . . signed, Peter Kapitza.'] *Pravda*, 7 October, 1957.

['Late Saturday night . . . most important priority,'] Vasily Mishin, V. E. Luppo, Nathalie Korolova and Georgi Vetrov interviews.

['Reluctantly, Korolev had . . . any other satellites.'] Golovanov interview.

['On that Sunday . . . would be safe.'] *New York Times*, 7 October, 1957.

['The next day . . . a future Sputnik.'] *New York Times*, 8 October, 1957.

['The bulk of . . . V-2 production plans.'] US Army Ballistic Missile Agency, 'Historical Monograph, US Army Ordinance Satellite Program', November 1958.

['It was hardly . . . them into space.'] Boris Chertok interview.

['Perhaps their single . . . and Boris Chertok.'] Mishin interview.

['Those few Germans . . . those programs forward.'] John Medaris, *Countdown for Decision*, p. 42.

['As Wernher von . . . copies of V-2s.'] Peter Van Slingerland, 'How We Let the Missile Secrets Get Away,' *Look* magazine, 4 February, 1958.

['Once that was . . . end of that.'] Related to Dr Geoffrey Pardoe by some German engineers after the war.

['The world's biggest story,'] Max Frankel, cited in Ruth Adler (ed.), *The Working Press*, p. 66.

['Secrecy presides over . . . truth from foreigners.'] From the diary of Astolphe Louis Leonard, writing as the Marquis de Custine.

['The fetish for . . . any other plant.'] Matthew Evangelista, 'How Technology Fuels the Arms Race,' *Technology Review*, July 1988.

['But then, for . . . its correct position.'] Leonid Vladimirov, *The Russian Space Bluff*, p. 49.

['Khrushchev refined the . . . as the press.'] Douglas Cater, *The Fourth Branch of Government*, p. 180.

['Hypocrisy in Russia . . . time to leave.'] Max Frankel, quoted in Adler, *The Working Press*, p. 72.

['One reporter in . . . were eventually ignored.'] Harrison Salisbury, 'The Freeze and the Thaw,' reprinted in Adler, *The Working Press*, pp. 61–4.

['Curiously, the information . . . consider ordinary news.'] Hedrick Smith, *The Russians*, pp. 474–5.

['Those who wait . . . learns to whistle.'] Clifton Fadiman, *Little Brown Book of Anecdotes*, Little Brown, New York, 1985.

['If you start . . . porcupines under you.'] *Observer*, 10 November, 1963.

['If you cannot . . . in my face.'] Fadiman, *Little Brown Book of Anecdotes*.

['He and Reston . . . have such instructions.'] Secret, eyes-only telegram from Moscow to Secretary of State, 8 October, 1957, DDEL.

['Years later, James . . . honest about things.'] James Reston interview.

['Almost as soon . . . in the USSR.'] Golovanov and Mishin interviews.

['That same afternoon . . . things like this.'] *The Times*, 9 October, 1957.

['Later that evening . . . of our system.'] Several sources, including Reuters, International News Service, the *Washington Post* and the *Daily Express* (UK), 8 October, 1957.

['The next day . . . with animals aboard.'] *Pravda*, 9 October, 1957.

['If the Russians . . . Russians explain it.'] Korolova interview.

['Throughout the 1950s . . . around the world.'] Richard Helms, 'Intelligence in American Society,' speech before Council on Foreign Relations, Washington DC, 17 April, 1967.

['In order to . . . Washington to Moscow.'] Committee for State Security (KGB) of the USSR, 'Evaluation of the Launch by the Soviet Union of the Artificial Earth Satellite,' Top Secret, limited distribution, 1957.

['He met with . . . ready to go.'] *Moscow News*, 20, 23, 30 November plus 4 and 18 December, 1957.

['Khrushchev and Zhukov . . . only logical answer.'] Carl Linden, *Khrushchev and the Soviet Leadership*, pp. 49–57.

['Zhukov had served . . . in the Kremlin.'] R. Medvedev, *Khrushchev*, pp. 122–3.

['Before long, Khrushchev's . . . his own position.'] ibid., pp. 132–3.

['The Soviet leadership . . . in the West.'] Nikita Khrushchev, *Khrushchev Remembers – The Last Testament*, p. 362.

['They firmly believed . . . of the President.'] Zamyatin interview.

['Eisenhower Doctrine . . . by International Communism.'] Eleanor Lansing Dulles, *John Foster Dulles*, p. 67; *State Department Bulletin*, XXXVI, 21 January, 1957, p. 86; and John Lewis Gaddis, *Russia, the Soviet Union and the United States*, p. 221.

['it was proof . . . Communist, everything socialist.'] Khrushchev, *Khrushchev Remembers – The Last Testament*.

['Khrushchev wanted to . . . John Foster Dulles.'] Adjoubei and Zamyatin interviews.

['On 29 October . . . imperialist-provoked war.'] Townsend Hoopes, *The Devil and John Foster Dulles*, p. 414.

11 *American Panic*

['He'd pruned his . . . international scientific community.']
Statement by the President, 9 October, 1957, DDEL.
['Among the cuttings . . . first world satellite.'] Associated Press,
8 October, 1957.
['After coffee and . . . to shut up.'] Several sources, including
Douglas Kinnard, *President Eisenhower and Strategy Manage-
ment*, p. 606, Eisenhower's Diaries and minutes of the meeting,
DDEL.
['Wilbur Brucker decided . . . American satellite programs.']
New York Times, 10 October, 1957.
['Amiable incomprehensibility.'] James Reston, *The Artillery of
the Press*, p. 52.
['He'd dress up . . . away with it.'] Paul Boller, *Presidential
Anecdotes*, pp. 296–7.
['Eisenhower continued fielding . . . six months ago.'] John
Eisenhower interview.
['The Presidential News . . . things in the air.'] Transcript
of the President's Press Conference, *New York Times*, 10
October, 1957.
['And when the . . . available for comment.'] *Huntsville Times*,
10 October, 1957.
['The agenda for . . . of Project Vanguard.'] National Security
Council, Revised Agenda, 7 October, 1957, Secret, NARC.
['The meeting began . . . about the Soviet achievement.']
Discussion at the 339th Meeting of the National Security
Council, 10 October, 1957, Top Secret, DDEL.
['Worried about the . . . space-nuclear weapon.'] Elmer Staats
correspondence, 26 January, 1990.
['That afternoon, General . . . have to consider.'] Eisenhower's
Diaries, 10 October, 1957, DDEL.
['At the Pentagon . . . significant military value.'] Memorandum
for the Secretary of the General Staff, 'Military Implications of
the Soviet Satellite.' Secret, 9 October, 1957, NARC.
['Nor was Sputnik . . . required his attention.'] Notes of the
President's Cabinet Meeting, 11 October, 1957, DDEL.
['But then came . . . any intelligence breach.'] Eisenhower's
Diaries and Goodpaster notes, 11 October, 1957, DDEL.

NOTES

['That night Christian . . . was destroyed simultaneously.']
Official Use Only telegram from Acting Secretary of State
Herter to Chiefs of all Missions, 10 October, 1957, NARC.
['But the wire . . . about the crisis.'] Associated Press, 13 October,
1957, and United Press International, 11–13 October, 1957.
['On Monday morning . . . and cost estimates.'] Eisenhower's
Diaries, and memorandum from the Deputy Secretary of
Defense, Don Quarles, for the President, 'The Vanguard –
Jupiter-C Program.' Secret, 7 January, 1958, DDEL.
['With Congress calling . . . money can buy.'] Memorandum
to the Secretary of State, 14 October, 1957, NARC.
['Foster Dulles had . . . an enormous advantage.'] Stephen
Ambrose, *Nixon*, pp. 442–3.
['Ever ambitious, one . . . superior space achievement.'] Raymond
Saulnier interview and Arthur Krock, *Memoirs*, pp. 317–18.
['Now when Nixon . . . were doing nothing.'] Dulles notes on
meeting with Nixon, 15 October, 1957, DDEL.
['With that in . . . outdated by events.'] Eisenhower's Diaries,
15 October, 1957, DDEL.
['That same day . . . of invited journalists.'] Memorandum
from Larson to Lewis Strauss, Chairman of the Atomic Energy
Commission, Secret, 15 October, 1957, DDEL.
['At 11 o'clock . . . think about it.'] Eisenhower's Diaries and
memorandum of the meeting, Top Secret, 15 October, 1957,
DDEL. Also, James Killian, *Sputnik, Scientists and Eisenhower*,
pp. 12–17.
['Nixon took a . . . of great magnitude.'] Michael Stoiko, *Soviet
Rocketry*, p. ix.
['Foster Dulles got . . . no military significance.'] John Foster
Dulles' notes of conversation with Allen Dulles, 15 October,
1957, DDEL.
['And Drew Pearson's . . . says the word.'] Drew Pearson,
'Merry Go Round' syndicated column, 15 October, 1957.
['Foster Dulles met . . . delivery of missiles.'] Transcript of the
News Conference of 16 October, 1957, Department of State,
NARC.
['The USIA's preliminary . . . increase Soviet credibility.'] USIA
Report, 'World Opinion and the Soviet Satellite.' Confidential,
17 October, 1957, DDEL.

['Eisenhower's cabinet meetings . . . generally serious tone.']
Saulnier interview.
['For the most. . . the Oval Office.'] Neil McElroy Oral History,
EOHP.
['Ten years later . . . anti-ICBM program.'] McElroy Oral
History, EOHP.
['At the cabinet . . . did not comment.'] Minutes of meeting,
DDEL.
['Drew Pearson's column . . . the highest authority.'] 'Merry
Go Round' syndicated column, 20 October, 1957.
['On Monday, *Aviation* . . . for a while.'] Memorandum of
conversation, 29 October, 1957, included in Eisenhower's Dia-
ries, October 1957, DDEL. Also, Jeffrey Richelson, *American
Espionage and the Soviet Target*, p. 176, and *Aviation Week*
magazine, 14 October and 21 October, 1957.
['After a busy . . . done if necessary.'] Eisenhower's Diaries and
notes on subjects discussed with Bernard Baruch, 22 October,
1957, DDEL.
['Secretary of the . . . at all possible.'] Memorandum from the
Secretary of the Navy to the Secretary of Defense, 22 October,
1957, NARC. And, Memorandum from the Secretary of Defense
to the Secretary of the Navy, 29 October, 1957, *Foreign Relations
of the United States, 1955–1957*, Volume XI, pp. 766–7.
['When Wilbur Brucker . . . up by February.'] Memorandum
from the Deputy Secretary of Defense, Don Quarles, for
the President, 'The Vanguard–Jupiter-C Program.' Secret, 7
January, 1958, DDEL.
['On Thursday, October. . . its real significance.'] Eisenhower's
Diaries and notes of meeting, 25 October, 1957, DDEL.
['Army Chief of . . . America's nuclear superiority.'] *New York
Times*, 27 October, 1957.
['And around the . . . or economic achievement.'] Richard
Aliano, *American Defense Policy*, pp. 57–9.
['There was no . . . system in place.'] Eisenhower's diaries and
notes of meetings, DDEL.
['At the Pentagon . . . to the President.'] Memorandum from
the Deputy Secretary of Defense, Don Quarles, for the President,
'The Vanguard–Jupiter-C Program.' Secret, 7 January, 1958,
DDEL.

['So on Wednesday . . . the President agreed.'] Minutes of the meeting, 30 October, 1957, DDEL.

['He got to . . . down a bit.'] Eisenhower's Diaries and notes of meeting with Dulles, 31 October, 1957, DDEL.

['Each day that . . . of the world.'] Donald Cox and Michael Stoiko, *Spacepower*, p. 13.

['The Soviet first . . . be redubbed, "Rearguard."'] *Providence Journal*, 8 October, 1957.

['If the Russians . . . controlled the earth.'] Simon Ramo cited in Allan Needell, *The First 25 Years in Space*, pp. 51–3.

12 *The Sweetening of Great Britain*

['Britain entered the . . . it once ruled.'] Several sources, including *Chronicle of the 20th Century, Timetables of History*, Paul Kennedy, *The Rise and Fall of the Great Powers*, and Edith Horsely, *The 1950s*.

['Satellite dominated front . . . behind the Soviets.'] Confidential telegram, Amembassy London to Secretary of State, 7 October, 1957, NARC.

['Harold Macmillan held . . . within arm's reach.'] Several sources, including Harold Macmillan, *Tides of Fortune* and *Riding the Storm*, John Charlton, *No. 10 Downing Street*, Christopher Jones, *No. 10 Downing Street*, and No. 10 Press Office interview.

['At 10:30 on . . . have agreed more.'] Minutes of the Cabinet Meeting, 8 October, 1957, PRO.

['Four hours later . . . the Rusian satellite.'] Chiefs of Staff meeting, 8 October, 1957, PRO.

['As Great Britain . . . outstripping allied expectations.'] Several sources, including Peter Hennessey, *Whitehall*, Peter Hennessey interview, plus interviews with press officers at the Ministry of Defence, the Foreign Office, the Home Office and the Cabinet Office, and other sources.

['That America in . . . with old allies.'] Several sources, including John Newhouse, *War and Peace in the Nuclear Age*, McGeorge Bundy, *Danger and Survival*, and Dwight Eisenhower, *Waging Peace*.

['Interestingly enough, these . . . bill was debated.'] McGeorge Bundy, *Danger and Survival*, pp. 468–9.

['Within a year . . . two old allies.'] Newhouse, *War and Peace in the Nuclear Age*, and Bundy, *Danger and Survival*, pp. 469–71.
['Two months later . . . the McMahon Act.'] Several sources, including Leslie Freeman, *Nuclear Witness*, Walter Patterson, *The Plutonium Business*, and Christopher Hitchens, *Blood, Class and Nostalgia.*
['Jock Whitney continued . . . free world alliance.'] Confidential telegram in two sections, from US Embassy London to Secretary of State, 9 October, 1957, NARC.
['Sputnik also became . . . the Cold War.'] American Embassy, London to Secretary of State, Confidential, 16 October, 1957, NARC.
['On Monday afternoon . . . in earlier years.'] Minutes of Cabinet Meeting, 21 October, 1957, PRO.
['The meeting with . . . and can work.'] Minutes of a phone conversation between C. D. Jackson and General Goodpaster, 21 October, 1957, DDEL.
['When Macmillan's letter . . . about the Russians.'] Secretary of State's memorandum of conversation with the President, 15 October, 1957, Personal and Private, JFDL.
['There was no . . . had with Suez.'] Secret memorandum for the President from John Foster Dulles, 21 October, 1957. Includes a summary briefing paper and tentative schedule of agenda items for the President's talks with Prime Minister Macmillan, DDEL. Conclusion is mine.
['For example, it . . . to cook it.'] *Chigaco Daily News*, 7 October, 1957.
['But not even . . . it wasn't true.'] Emmet John Hughes, *The Ordeal of Power*, p. 249.
['The visit was . . . needs the aeroplane.'] Associated Press, 23 October, 1957.
['Under the heading . . . guarantee world peace.'] Memorandum of conversation, 10 a.m., 23 October, 1957, at the British Embassy, Top Secret, Eyes Only, DDEL.
['After lunch, Dulles . . . stand by Britain.'] Memorandum of conversation, 'Closer US-UK Relations and Free World Cooperation,' 23 October, 1957, the British Embassy, Secret, NARC.
['My dear Foster . . . yours ever, Selwyn.'] Top Secret letter from Lloyd to Dulles, 25 October, 1957, NARC.

['While Macmillan was . . . of our allies.'] Memoranda of telephone conversations between the Secretary of State and Under Secretary of State and Senators Knowland and Johnson, and Representatives Rayburn and Martin, 23–25 October, 1957, DDEL.

['Only one minor . . . version of events.'] Memorandum for the Secretary of State from David W. K. Peacock, Jr, outlining Dulles' discussions with Admiral Strauss on Eisenhower's having gone too far with Macmillan, Top Secret, limited circulation, 29 October, 1957, NARC.

['The Declaration of . . . he first arrived.'] The Declaration of Common Purpose, The White House, 25 October, 1957, DDEL.

['In any civilized . . . they were equal.'] Text of the background news conference held by Secretary of State John Foster Dulles, 25 October, 1957, DDEL.

13 *Yankee Determination*

['The Soviets have . . . earth to space.'] Amembassy Bonn to Secretary of State, Limited Official Use, 4 November, 1957, NARC.

['The world was . . . counterpart in Sweden.'] Amembassy The Hague and Amembassy Stockholm to Secretary of State, 4 November, 1957, NARC.

['In the final . . . launches a satellite.'] Amembassy Luxembourg to Secretary of State, 'Impact of Sputnik,' Official Use Only, 18 November, 1957, NARC.

['In Spain, the . . . brusque and brutal.'] Amembassy Madrid to Secretary of State, 'Reactions in Spain to second Soviet Satellite,' Official Use Only, 18 November, 1957, NARC.

['At the morning . . . avoid being attacked.'] Amembassy Madrid to Secretary of State, 'Further Reaction to Sputniks,' Confidential, 2 December, 1957, NARC.

['The French continued . . . than the Soviets.'] Amembassy Paris to Secretary of State, Confidential, 5 November and 10 November, 1957, NARC.

['It was much . . . turn to Communism.'] Amembassy Santiago to Secretary of State, Official Use Only, 9 November, 1957, NARC.

['Arab governments saw . . . of US prestige.'] Amembassy Damascus to Secretary of State, Official Use Only, 4 November, 1957, NARC.

['While in Japan . . . the United States.'] Douglas MacArthur in two wires to the Secretary of State, Confidential, 6 November and 9 November, 1957, NARC.

['The Prime Minister . . . climate of fear,'] Amembassy Canberra to Secretary of State, Confidential, 14 November, 1957, NARC.

['And the government . . . with guided missiles.'] Amembassy Bangkok to Secretary of State, 'Implications and Effects of Soviet Satellites,' Confidential, 13 November, 1957, NARC.

['As the surprise . . . the near future.'] Cited in Confidential telegram from Amembassy Bern to Secretary of State, 15 November, 1957, NARC.

['Ten days after . . . immediately and vigorously.'] Rand Report, 'Proposal for Manned Satellite,' Secret, 14 October, 1957, Rand Corporation.

['A week later . . . within 20 years.'] 'Space Flight Program,' Report by the Space Flight Technical Committee of the American Rocket Society, 23 August, 1957, revised 10 October, 1957, NARC.

['On 23 October . . . counter this threat.'] CIA Advisory Committee letter to Allen Dulles, Top Secret, 23 October, 1957, NARC.

['Allen Dulles obviously . . . had been planted.'] Several sources, including Agenda, State-JCS Meeting, Top Secret; notes on 'Space Weapon Concept,' and 'Working Paper on United States Initiatives in Outer Space,' Secret; all dated 1 November, 1957, NARC.

['In this case . . . build-up of forces.'] Donald Cox and Michael Stoiko, *Spacepower*, pp. 15–16.

['The Roman Empire . . . automatic windshield wipers.'] William Manchester, *The Glory and the Dream*, p. 788.

['Solicited by the . . . the Oval Office.'] Several sources, including Manchester, *The Glory and the Dream*, Walter McDougall, *The Heavens and the Earth*, the *New York Times*, the *Washington Post*, and the US Senate Committee on Armed Services, 'Inquiry into Satellite and Missile Programs,' Hearings Before the

Preparedness Investigating Sub-committee, 85th Congress, First and Second Sessions, Volumes 1–3.

['From what America's . . . have had to.'] Robert Seamans interview.

['In other words . . . becoming a drawback.'] Raymond Saulnier interview.

['The National Security . . . a gasoline fire.'] Memo to OCB Staff, 'Regaining the Initiative,' Confidential, 7 January, 1958, DDEL.

['All sorts of . . . to the UN.'] White House memo, 'Suggestions for Regaining the Psychological Initiative,' 30 January, 1958, Secret, NARC.

['But none came . . . continue to play.'] A Space Train proposal, attached to a Don Quarles memorandum to Sherman Adams, 31 October, 1957, DDEL.

['Two days after . . . significance to Sputnik.'] Cox and Stoiko, *Spacepower*, p. 14.

['The launching of . . . Mr Khrushchev's boomerang.'] John Foster Dulles, National Press Club, Washington, 16 January, 1958.

['As "Mutnik" circled . . . started weeks ago.'] Memorandum from the Deputy Secretary of Defense, Don Quarles, for the President, 'The Vanguard–Jupiter-C Program,' Secret, 7 January, 1958; and Redstone Arsenal archives.

['By 6 November . . . to the Europeans.'] Memorandum of discussion at the State Department, Confidential Use Only, 6 November, 1957, NARC.

['That afternoon, the . . . decided against it.'] Dwight Eisenhower, *Waging Peace*, p. 225, plus Andrew Goodpaster and Richard Bissell interviews.

['Addressing the American . . . the same thing.'] Transcript of the President's speech, 7 November, 1957, DDEL, and Eisenhower, *Waging Peace*.

['Eisenhower made a . . . didn't move him.'] Saulnier interview.

['In the Spring . . . against the USSR.'] Several sources, including Eisenhower, *Waging Peace*, pp. 220–3, the *New York Times*, the *Washington Post* and the *New Statesman*; the Gaither Report to the President, November 1957, NARC; Arthur Schlesinger interview.

['It was such . . . to see it.'] Manchester, *The Glory and the Dream*, p. 796.

['The *Washington Post* . . . the Communist orbit.'] *Washington Post*, 20 December, 1957.

['Eisenhower told General . . . the first blow.'] Eisenhower's Diaries, 9 November, 1957, DDEL.

['For the first . . . America is scared.'] James McGregor Burns, *The Crosswinds of Freedom*, p. 259.

['The British Labour . . . would never agree.'] Memorandum of conversation between the President and Aneurin Bevan, 12 November, 1957, Confidential, DDEL.

['Thinking there was . . . association a reality.'] American Ambassador to the UK to the Secretary of State, Secret, 18 November, 1957, DDEL.

['The same day . . . now become normalcy.'] Eisenhower, *Waging Peace*, p. 226.

['In the past . . . working to avoid.'] Goodpaster and John Eisenhower interviews.

['Ann Whitman, Eisenhower's . . . entry for Sunday.'] Eisenhower's Diaries, DDEL.

['On Monday morning . . . his exact words.'] Goodpaster and John Eisenhower interviews. Also Manchester, *The Glory and the Dream*, pp. 811–12, and John Newhouse, *War and Peace in the Nuclear Age*, p. 118.

['There's no doubt . . . think Dad miscalculated.'] John Eisenhower interview.

['By the end . . . I know of.'] Goodpaster interview.

['The hope of . . . called it "Kaputnik."'] Several sources, including the *New York Times*, the *Washington Post* and the Associated Press, all dated 6 December, 1957.

['The day after . . . from his mouth.'] Paul Boller, *Presidential Anecdotes*, p. 292.

['A few days . . . to step down.'] Marquis Childs, *Eisenhower – Captive Hero*, pp. 188–9.

['This shocked Eisenhower . . . man Foster is.'] Goodpaster interview.

['No, Eisenhower told . . . where he belongs.'] Childs, *Eisenhower*.

['An old friend . . . bankrupting space race.'] The old friend turned out to be George Humphrey, Eisenhower's first Secretary of the Treasury who'd stepped down earlier that year. See Edwin Diamond, *The Rise and Fall of the Space Age*, pp. 8–9.

['Even if the . . . of military strength.' Sherman Adams quoted in Richard Alaino, *American Defense Policy from Eisenhower to Kennedy*, pp. 59–60.

['When James Killian . . . in the Pentagon.'] Several sources, including Lloyd Swenson, 'The Megamachine behind the Mercury Spacecraft,' *American Quarterly*, Summer 1969, Eugene Emme, 'The Historical Origins of NASA,' *Airpower Historian*, January 1963, James Killian, *Sputnik, Scientists and Eisenhower*, George Kistiakowsky, *A Scientist at the White House*, and Robert Seamans interview.

['Killian's next notable . . . gradually faded away.'] Killian, *Sputnik, Scientists and Eisenhower*, Kistiakowsky, *A Scientist at the White House*, Landon Jones, *Great Expectations – America and the Baby Boom Generation*, Robert Cowan, 'Sputnik's Splash, Space-age Fizzle,' *Technology Review*, January 1983; and Elliot Richardson correspondence.

['The Science Advisory . . . proved Carson right.'] Jerome Wiesner, 'On Science Advice to the President,' *Scientific American*, January 1989.

['Not that everyone . . . worry about it.'] Joint Chiefs of Staff Report on Importation of Soviet Scientific Publications, Confidential, 2 April, 1958, NARC.

['By the time . . . were taking place.'] DARPA Press Policy. Administrative Confidential, contains the note, 'No comments of any kind authorized,' 21 August, 1958, NARC.

['These days an . . . know for sure.'] Several sources, including Howard Wilcox, John Nicolides and Leroy Doig interviews, plus 'A Summary of Informal Interviews,' a restricted access summary of oral histories with scientists and engineers who worked on the project; also *Newsweek*, 4 August, 1958.

['In January 1958 . . . of Yuri Gagarin.'] Frederick Ordway and Mitchell Sharpe, *The Rocket Team*, pp. 383–4.

['On Wednesday, January . . . went to bed.'] The description comes from several sources, including the *Huntsville Times*, the *New York Times* and the *Washington Post*, all dated 1 February, 1958, and Hagerty's version of the events as related to the Associated Press, datelined Augusta, Georgia, 1 February, 1958.

['The Pentagon celebration . . . Wilson in effigy.'] *Huntsville Times*, Satellite Extra, 1 February, 1958.

14 *Khrushchev's Bluff*

['The first verified . . . color,' he said.'] United Press International (UPI), 5 October, 1957.
['On Tuesday October . . . of his territory.'] *Halifax Mail-Star*, 8 October, 1957.
['And on October . . . in all directions.'] UPI, 7 October, 1957.
['Binocular manufacturers were . . . earth without disintegrating.'] Associated Press (AP), 7 October, 1957.
['In Berlin, Germans . . . the Soviet satellite.'] *New York Times*, 8 October, 1957.
['The Japanese, in . . . acre to $2.78.'] UPI, 9 October, 1957.
['In Kelowna, British . . . in North America,'] AP, 9 October, 1957.
['Protests poured into . . . him down immediately.'] Several sources, including newspaper clippings from New York, Washington, London and Moscow, in addition to copies of letters and telegrams received at the White House, Congress and the State Department, November 1957, State Department files, NARC.
['By December, an . . . record-breaking word.'] AP, 18 December, 1957.
['Keeping the record . . . religion or morals.'] AP, 9 October, 1957.
['A Russian officer . . . Destination – the moon.'] Foreign Service Dispatch, US Mission Berlin to Department of State, 9 October, 1957, NARC.
['The Governor of . . . Uncle Sam's asleep.'"] Quoted in *Washingtonian*, September 1982.
['And every Soviet, ever . . . was watching Sputnik.'] Alexei Adjoubei interview.
['Five days after . . . hah, hah, hah!'] Andrei Ledovski and V. S. Lavrov interviews.
['Riding high on . . . our own planet.'"] From an unpublished Tass interview with Korolev, 30 November, 1963.

['Throughout this Korolev . . . to someone else.'] Yaroslav Golovanov interview.

['Publicly anonymous, it . . . the testing stages.'] Leonid Vladimirov, *The Russian Space Bluff*, pp. 75–8.

['Sputnik ignited Khrushchev's . . . and space technology.'] Adjoubei interview.

['He made a . . . with American rocketry.'] Sergei Khrushchev, *Khrushchev on Khrushchev*, p. 106.

['Khrushchev had come . . . the Third World.'] Charles Sheldon, 'An American Sputnik for the Russians?' *Bulletin of the Atomic Scientists*, September, 1969, pp. 23–7.

['In late October . . . over the country.'] AP, 30 October and 1 November, 1957.

['The joke took . . . Embassy a time.'] Statement by Hugh Odishaw, USNC-IGY, 6 December, 1957, with attachments, including telegrams from Nesmeyanov and Bronk, with letter from Waterman to Hagerty. Also outgoing telegram, Secretary of State to Amembassy Moscow, with Defense Department reply to Dulles, 12 December, 1957, NARC.

['On 5 November . . . scored heavy points.'] Compiled from D. F. Fleming, *The Cold War and its Origins*, William Manchester, *The Glory and the Dream*, James MacGregor Burns, *The Crosswinds of Freedom*. Quotes from the *New York Times*, *Nashville Tennessean* and Manchester *Guardian*.

['On 10 December . . . a durable peace.'] Letter from Nikolai Bulganin to Dwight Eisenhower, 10 December, 1957, DDEL.

['The next day . . . ranges, including ICBMs.'] Letter from Nikolai Bulganin to Harold Macmillan, 11 December, 1957, PRO.

['Public opinion in . . . party and government.'] Robert C. Tucker, writing in *Russian Foreign Policy* (Ivo Lederer, ed.), p. 191.

['It's significant to . . . of rule work.'] Zhores Medvedev interview.

['Domestically, Khrushchev's philosophy . . . a stable populace.'] Julian Towster, 'Changing Russian Politics,' *Current History*, January, 1958.

['Insidiously, Khrushchev set . . . limit America's alternatives.'] L. Bloomfield, *Khrushchev and the Arms Race*, pp. 65–6.

['We can double . . . still greater heights.' Text of Khrushchev speech at Minsk, 11 January, 1958. Quoted by US Ambassador to USSR, Llewellyn Thompson, in telegram to Dulles, 15 April, 1958, Confidential, NARC.

['As the years . . . Great Britain 2.'] Zhores Medvedev, *Nuclear Disaster in the Urals*, p. 145.

['One of the . . . strengthening of peace.'] Letter from Khrushchev to Konrad Adenauer explaining his decision to announce a unilateral nuclear weapons test ban, 10 April, 1958, NARC.

['Until the mid-1950s . . . after the event.'] Several sources, including Zhores Medvedev interview and Medvedev, *Nuclear Disaster in the Urals*, also *New Scientist*, 4 November, 1976 and 30 June, 1977, *New York Times*, 14 February, 1980; *Science* magazine, 26 October, 1979, *Washington Post*, 25 May, 1979, *Discovery*, June 1986, and *Nuclear Engineering International*, November 1990.

['According to the . . . washing or fishing.'] Several CIA sources, including 'Miscellaneous Information on Nuclear Installations in the USSR,' 16 February, 1961, Weekly Surveyor report, 'USSR–Nuclear Accident,' 25 June, 1977; 'Foreign Intelligence Information Report,' 16 March, 1978, 'An Intelligence Assessment – USSR: Nuclear Accident near Kyshtym in 1957–1958,' October 1981, and 'An Analysis of the Soviet Nuclear Accident near Kyshtym in 1957–1958,' January 1982. All are designated Top Secret, and were obtained under FOIA.

['Their March 1958 . . . it at all.'] CIA, 'Impact of a September 1958 Nuclear Test Moratorium on Soviet Nuclear Weapons Capabilities,' 18 March, 1958, Top Secret, FOIA.

['General Goodpaster does . . . cunning he had.'] Andrew Goodpaster interview.

['Within four years . . . main ICBM sites.'] Andrew Wilson, 'Eyes in the Sky,' *Interavia Aerospace Review*, 1 September, 1988.

['For the next . . . safely to Earth.'''] Thomas Paine, 'Who Will Lead the World's Next Age of Discovery?' *Aviation Week & Space Technology*, 21 September, 1987.

['He determined the . . . for the moon.'] National Security Council paper 5918, 'US Policy on Outer Space.' Secret, 17 December, 1959, DDEL.

['The success of . . . one by one.'"] Vasily Mishin interview and *Pravda*, 20 October, 1989.

['There was never . . . tell the Americans.'] Boris Chertok interview.

['Sputnik had allowed . . . of all mankind.'] Medvedev interview.

['But Sputnik couldn't . . . had bankrupted it.'] Several sources, including Golovanov, Mishin, Adjoubei and Medvedev interviews.

['Such was the . . . first son died.'] Goodpaster interview.

['"I could not . . . not overreact either.'] Averell Harriman, 'My Alarming Interview with Khrushchev,' *Life* magazine, 13 July, 1959.

['Khrushchev's first thought . . . the visit began.'] N. S. Khrushchev, *Khrushchev Remembers – The Last Testament*, pp. 368–9.

['At the time . . . a hardliner, inflexible.'] Ledovski interview.

['The official reason . . . engage in threats.'"] Several sources, including the *New York Times*, 25 July, 1957, Stephen Ambrose, *Nixon*, pp. 521–7, and Richard Nixon, *The Memoirs of Richard Nixon*, pp. 206–7.

['Khrushchev's version of . . . capitalism over socialism.'] Khrushchev, *Khrushchev Remembers – The Last Testament*, pp. 364–7.

['Khrushchev then claimed . . . second-rate spy.'] Sergei Khrushchev, *Khrushchev on Khrushchev, p.* 224.

['What neither of . . . nine or ten.'] Memo of Vice-President's dacha conversation with Premier Khrushchev, Confidential, Limited Distribution, 26 July 1959, FOIA.

15 *To the Brink of World War III*

['First, he did . . . can relate to.'] N. S. Khrushchev, *Khrushchev Remembers – The Last Testament*, pp. 368–416. Also, Alexei Adjoubei interview.

['Don't have a hundred . . . married like Adjoubei.'] Alexander Werth, *The Khrushchev Phase*, p. 28.

['He had that . . . Senator from Iowa.'] James Reston interview.

['Over the course . . . what he saw.'] Adjoubei interview.
['They spoke about . . . asked about salaries.'] Andrew Good-
paster interview.
['At one point . . . have so much.'] Adjoubei interview.
['Later, Eisenhower confided . . . traditional Communist line.']
James Hagerty, Oral History, Columbia University.
['In many ways . . . other war stories.'] Goodpaster interview.
['One morning over . . . advance into exploitation.'] Memoran-
dum of conversation, breakfast at Camp David, 26 September,
1959, 'Khrushchev's Wartime Experiences,' Secret, Limited
Distribution, NARC.
['Military experience came . . . the United States".'] Adjoubei
interview.
['The essence of . . . the worst case.'] Robert McNamara, *The
Essence of Security: Reflections in Office*, pp. 57–9.
['In the wake . . . sometime around 1961.'] Edgar Bottome,
Balance of Terror, p. 41.
['In those days . . . running with them.'] Admiral Arleigh Burke,
EOHP.
['The launching of . . . significance for defense.'] *The Times*, 7
October, 1957.
['A troubled Eisenhower . . . remained highly skeptical.'] Good-
paster interview.
['He even used . . . as I do.'] John Newhouse, *War and Peace
in the Nuclear Age*, p. 122.
['Over the summer . . . base outside Tokyo.'] Michael Beschloss,
Mayday, pp. 146–8.
['If the U-2 . . . Lee Harvey Oswald.'] ibid., pp. 234–6.
['Accompanying the 31-year-old . . . U-2 self-destructed.']
Beschloss, *Mayday*, pp. 14–16.
['One of the . . . for each U-2.'] Zhores Medvedev interview.
['As soon as . . . over Soviet territory.'] Statement by Allen
Dulles to US Senate, NARC.
['In the Oval . . . Powers was dead.'] Richard Bissell inter-
view.
['Besides the President . . . had a parachute.'] John Eisenhower
interview.
['On 6 May . . . the Oval Office.'] Allen Dulles' statement to
US Senate, NARC.

['From time to . . . to take responsibility.'] Bissell interview.

['Christian Herter issued . . . to Presidential authorization.'] Statement by the Secretary of State, 9 May, 1960, NARC.

['People close to . . . on Allen Dulles.'] A White House source.

['He was extremely . . . had betrayed him.'] Adjoubei interview.

['For the very . . . badly misjudged Eisenhower.'] Adjoubei interview.

['Compounding matters, Eisenhower's . . . overcome that feeling".'] Khrushchev to Dr Harvey McGehee, quoted in *Life* magazine, 18 December, 1973.

['The two men . . . Soviet air space.'] Adjoubei interview.

['Eisenhower refused and . . . proposal of 1955.'] McGeorge Bundy, *Danger and Survival*, p. 351.

['But where Eisenhower . . . son-in-law, stopped everything.'] Adjoubei interview.

['Khrushchev had hoped . . . and never used.'] Leonid Zamyatin interview.

['the rocket exploded . . . explain Nedelin's death.'] *New Scientist*, 4 November, 1976.

['Attending the General . . . banging his shoe.'] Zamyatin interview.

['Every morning for . . . with old shoes.'] Zamyatin interview.

['There's no way . . . for the moon.'] Leonid Vladimirov, *The Russian Space Bluff*, p. 55.

['Late in the . . . war was lost.'] John Brooks, *The Fate of the Edsel and Other Business Adventures*, pp. 53–75, and William Manchester, *The Glory and the Dream*, pp. 814–17.

['When Eisenhower told . . . very worried look.'] Edwin Diamond, *The Rise and Fall of the Space Age*, p. 26.

['Sputnik had also . . . Republicans in 1936.'] Richard Aliano, *American Defense Policy*, p. 264.

['It was generally . . . would not win.'] Raymond Saulnier interview.

['He went to . . . of the campaign.'] Several sources, including J. Ronald Oakley, *God's Country*, Landon Jones, *Great Expectations*, James MacGregor Burns, *The Crosswinds of Freedom*, and William O'Neill, *American High*.

['In August 1958 . . . shift against us".'] John F. Kennedy, House and Senate Speeches, 14 August, 1958.

['The Eisenhower Doctrine . . . fight limited wars.'] Aliano, *American Defense Policy*, p. 275.

['His campaign crisis . . . almost managed it.'] ibid., p. 243.

['There were those . . . Frontier" had begun.'] Several sources, including Oakley, *God's Country*, Manchester, *The Glory and the Dream*, and Burns, *The Crosswinds of Freedom*. Also Arthur Schlesinger, *Robert Kennedy and His Times*, and Don McLeod, 'Did Democrats Steal it in 1960?', Associated Press, 12 July, 1973.

['The outcome of. . . can handle Khrushchev.'] Bundy, *Danger and Survival*, p. 345.

['John Kennedy initiated . . . of nuclear superiority.'] Aliano, *American Defense Policy*, p. 227.

['And Khrushchev feared . . . policy of strength.'] Adjoubei interview.

['On Friday October. . . of general war".'] Central Intelligence Agency, 'Soviet Reactions to Certain US Courses of Action on Cuba,' 19 October, 1962, Top Secret.

['After six days . . . no way off.'] Several sources, including S. R. Gibbons, *The Cold War*, Schlesinger, *Robert Kennedy and His Times*, Robert Kennedy, *Thirteen Days*, and Bundy, *Danger and Survival*.

['Satellite spying had . . . stand against Khrushchev.'] Andrew Wilson, 'Eyes in the Sky,' *Intervia Aerospace Review*, 1 September, 1988.

['He'd learned the . . . the United States.'] Arthur Schlesinger interview.

['At Baikonour, on . . . ready for war.'] Boris Chertok interview.

['The American invasion . . . to invade Cuba.'] Robert Kennedy, *Thirteen Days*, pp. 85–91.

['Later that night'] . . . Description of Khrushchev writing the first letter is from the Zamyatin interview. Khrushchev letters are in Robert Kennedy, *Thirteen Days*.

['On Saturday morning . . . such weapons inoperable.'] Robert Kennedy, *Thirteen Days*, pp. 93–9.

['Another thing John . . . consequences that entailed.'] Zamyatin interview.

['The wire was . . . minutes to spare.'] Chertok and Zamyatin interviews. It must be pointed out that Zamyatin was at the dacha near Moscow with Khrushchev throughout the entire crisis. The story of the 60-minute deadline was told by both Chertok and Zamyatin, independently of each other.

Bibliography

Interviews and Correspondence

The following interviews were conducted by me:

Adjoubei, Alexei: Moscow, 19 April 1990
Banks, Tony: Jane's *Defence Weekly*: by phone, London, 5 June 1991
Bissell, Richard: Farmington, Connecticut, 14 May 1990
Bourges-Maunory, Maurice: by phone, Paris, 14 January 1991
Boyd-Carpenter, John: London, 20 March 1991
Bundy, McGeorge: by phone, New York, 7 March 1991
Chertok, Dr Boris: Moscow, 13 December 1990
Doig, Leroy III: China Lake, California, 28 March 1991
Eisenhower, John S. D.: by phone to Kimberton, Pennsylvania, 17 May 1990
Golovanov, Yaroslav: Peredelkino near Moscow, 17 April 1990
Goodpaster, General Andrew: Washington DC, 5 March 1991
Korolova, Dr Nathalie: Moscow, 13 December 1990
Lavrov, Ambassador V.S.: Moscow, 11 December 1990
Ledovski, Ambassador Andrei M.: Moscow, 11 December 1990
Luppo, V.E.: Moscow, 16 April 1990
Maximov, G. Yu: Moscow, 11 December 1990
Medvedev, Dr Zhores: London, 15 February 1991
Mishin, Dr Vasily: Moscow, 13 December 1990
Neufeld, Dr Michael: Washington DC, 5 March 1990
Nicolides, Dr John: by phone, San Diego, California, 1 April 1991
Pardoe, Dr Geoffrey: by phone, London, 29 August 1991
Pineau, Christian: by phone, Paris, 14 January 1991
Rauchenbach, Dr Boris V.: Moscow, 16 April 1990
Reston, James: by phone, Washington DC, 5 March 1991

Saulnier, Dr Raymond: New York, 16 May 1990
Schlesinger, Arthur M. Jr: by phone, New York, 27 February 1991
Seamans, Dr Robert: by phone, Cambridge, Mass., 5 April 1991
Vetrov, Georgi: Moscow, 13 December 1990, and also Stabnikov: fax, August 1991
Wilcox, Dr Howard: by phone, San Diego, California, 31 March 1991
Zamyatin, Ambassador Leonid: London, 7 August 1991

Seven further interviews were conducted on my behalf in Moscow by Vladimir and Irina Stabnikov. They included: Mrs Rada Khrushchev Adjoubei, Mr F. Berlatsky, Dr Chomyakov, Dr Koutirkin, Sergei Khrushchev, and the two Mrs Korolev. The Stabnikovs also did follow-up interviews on my behalf with B. Chertok, Y. Golovanov, V. Luppo, G. Maximov, B. Rauchenbach, G. Vetrov.

Personal correspondence includes:

Areeda, Phillip: Cambridge, Mass., 6 February 1990
Benson, Ezra Taft: Salt Lake City, Utah, 1 February 1990
Brownell, Herbert: New York, 8 March 1990
Chaban-Delmas, Jacques: Paris, France, 24 January 1991
Dillon, Douglas: New York, 1 February 1990
Pflimlin, Pierre: Strasbourg, France, 21 January 1991
Rabb, Maxwell: New York, 26 February 1990
Richardson, Elliot L.: Washington DC, 21 May 1991
Saulnier, Raymond J.: New York, 16 February 1990
Staats, Elmer B.: Washington DC, 26 January 1990
Stabnikov, Vladimir: Moscow, Fax No. 1, 14 August 1991, Fax No. 2, 24 January 1992
Sullivan, Walter: Connecticut, 22 September 1991

Books

Adams, Sherman, *First-Hand Report – The Story of the Eisenhower Administration*, Harper Brothers, New York, 1961
Adjoubei, Alexei, *A l'Ombre de Khruchtchev*, La Table Ronde, Paris, 1989
Adler, Ruth (ed.), *The Working Press*, Putnam, New York, 1966
Alexandrov, Victor, *The Tukhachevsky Affair*, Macdonald, London, 1963

Aliano, Richard A., *American Defense Policy from Eisenhower to Kennedy: The Politics of Changing Military Requirements – 1957–1961*, Ohio University Press, Athens, Ohio, 1975

Ambrose, Stephen E., *Eisenhower – The President*, Simon & Schuster, New York, 1984

Ambrose, Stephen E., *Ike's Spies – Eisenhower and the Espionage Establishment*, Doubleday, New York, 1981

Ambrose, Stephen E., *Nixon – The Education of a Politician*, Simon & Schuster, New York, 1987

Ambrose, Stephen E., *Rise To Globalism – American Foreign Policy Since 1938*, Penguin Books, London, 1991

Anonymous, *Soviet Writings on Earth Satellites and Space Travel*, MacGibbon & Kee, London, 1959

Armstrong, John, *The Politics of Totalitarianism – The Communist Party of the Soviet Union from 1934 to the Present*, Random House, New York, 1961

Badash, L., *Kapitza, Rutherford and the Kremlin*, Yale University Press, New Haven, 1985

Bamford, James, *The Puzzle Palace*, Houghton Mifflin, New York, 1982

Bar-Zohar, Michel, *The Hunt for German Scientists*, Arthur Barker, London, 1965

Belfrage, Cedric, *The American Inquisition 1945–1960 – A Profile of the McCarthy Era*, Thunder's Mouth Press, New York, 1989

Berding, Andrew W., *Dulles on Diplomacy*, Van Nostrand, Princeton, New Jersey, 1965

Bergaust, Erik, *Wernher von Braun*, National Space Institute, Washington DC, 1976

Bergaust, Erik and Beller, William, *Satellite – The First Step into the Last Frontier – The Full Facts about Man's Coming Exploration of Space*, Hanover House, New York, 1956

Bergaust, Erik and Hull, Seabrook, *Rocket to the Moon*, Van Nostrand, Princeton, New Jersey, 1958

Beschloss, Michael R., *Kennedy v. Khrushchev – The Crisis Years 1960–1963*, Faber & Faber, London, 1991

Beschloss, Michael R., *Mayday – Eisenhower, Khrushchev and the U-2 Affair*, Harper & Row, New York, 1986

Bialer, Seweryn (ed.), *Russia at the Crossroads*, Allen & Unwin, London, 1982

Bialer, Seweryn, *Stalin's Successors – Leadership, Stability and Change in the Soviet Union*, Columbia University Press, New York, 1980

Blagonravov, A. A., *Soviet Rocketry – Some Contributions to its History*, Academy of Sciences, Moscow, 1964

Bloomfield, L., *Khrushchev and the Arms Race*, MIT Press, Cambridge, Mass., 1966

Boffa, Giuseppe, *Inside the Khrushchev Era*, Allen & Unwin, London, 1959

Boller, Paul F., *Presidential Anecdotes*, Oxford University Press, Oxford, 1981

Bottome, Edgar M., *Balance of Terror*, Houghton Mifflin, Boston, 1986

Bottome, Edgar M., *The Missile Gap*, Fairleigh Dickenson University Press, New Jersey, 1971

Bower, Tom, *The Paperclip Conspiracy – The Battle for the Spoils and Secrets of Nazi Germany*, Michael Joseph, London, 1987

Branley, Franklyn M., *From Sputnik to Space Shuttle – Into the New Space Age*, Harper, New York, 1986

Breslauer, George, *Khrushchev and Brezhnev as Leaders – Building Authority in Soviet Politics*, Allen and Unwin, London, 1982

Brinkley, David, *A Memoir*, Ballentine Books, New York, 1995

Brogan, Patrick, *The Captive Nations – Eastern Europe 1945–1990*, Avon Books, New York, 1990

Brooks, John, *The Fate of the Edsel and Other Business Adventures*, Gollancz, London, 1963

Bulkeley, Rip, *The Sputnik Crisis and Early United States Space Policy*, Macmillan, London, 1991

Bundy, McGeorge, *Danger and Survival – Choices about the Bomb in the First Fifty Years*, Vintage Books, New York, 1988

Burns, James MacGregor, *The Crosswinds of Freedom – From Roosevelt to Reagan – America in the Last Half-Century*, Vintage, New York, 1990

Caidin, Martin, *Countdown for Tomorrow*, Dutton, New York, 1958

Caidin, Martin, *Man Into Space*, Pyramid Books, New York, 1961

Calvocoressi, Peter and Wint, Guy, *Total War*, Penguin, London, 1972

Carlton, David, *Anthony Eden – A Biography*, Allen Lane, London, 1981

Carlton, David, *Britain and the Suez Crisis*, Basil Blackwell, Oxford, 1988

Cater, Douglas, *The Fourth Branch of Government*, Vintage Books, New York, 1959

Charlton, John, *No. 10 Downing Street*, HMSO, London, 1990

Childs, Marquis, *Eisenhower – Captive Hero – A Critical Study of the General and the President*, Harcourt Brace, New York, 1958

Churchill, Winston, *The Gathering Storm*, Cassell, London, 1948

Clowse, Barbara B. (ed.), *Brainpower for the Cold War – The Sputnik Crisis and the National Defense Education Act of 1958*, Greenwood, North Carolina, 1981

Colville, John, *The Fringes of Power – Downing Street Diaries 1939–1955*, Hodder & Stoughton, London, 1985

Conquest, Robert, *Power and Policy in the USSR*, Macmillan, London, 1961

Conquest, Robert, *Russia after Khrushchev*, Praeger, New York, 1965

Cornell, James (ed.), *Astronomy from Space – Sputnik to Space Telescope*, MIT Press, Cambridge, Mass., 1983

Cox, Donald and Stoiko, Michael, *Spacepower – What It Means to You*, Winston, New York, 1958

Crankshaw, Edward, *Khrushchev – A Career*, Viking, New York, 1966

Cray, Ed, *General of the Army – George C. Marshall – Soldier and Statesman*, W. W. Norton, New York, 1990

Crockatt, Richard and Smith, Steve (eds), *The Cold War – Past and Present*, Allen & Unwin, London, 1987

D'Agostino, Anthony, *Soviet Succession Struggles – Kremlinology and the Russian Question from Lenin to Gorbachev*, Allen and Unwin, London, 1987

Daniloff, Nicholas, *The Kremlin and the Cosmos*, Knopf, New York, 1972

Diamond, Edwin, *The Rise and Fall of the Space Age*, Doubleday, New York, 1964

Diggins, John Patrick, *The Proud Decades – America in War and Peace 1941–1960*, W. W. Norton, New York, 1989

Divine, Robert A., *Eisenhower and the Cold War*, Oxford University Press, Oxford, 1981

Dmitriyev, A., *From Spaceships to Orbiting Stations*, Moscow, 1971, NASA Translation, 1973

Dornberger, Walter, *V-2*, Hurst & Blackett, London, 1954

Drummond, Roscoe and Coblentz, Gaston, *Duel at the Brink – John*

Foster Dulles' Command of American Power, Doubleday, New York, 1960

Dulles, Allen, *The Craft of Intelligence*, Harper & Row, New York, 1963

Dulles, Eleanor Lansing, *John Foster Dulles – The Last Year*, Harcourt Brace, New York, 1963

Durant, Frederick C. III (ed.), *Between Sputnik and the Shuttle – New Perspectives on American Astronautics, 1957–1980*, American Astronautical Society, Washington DC, 1981

Eden, Anthony, *Full Circle*, Cassell, London, 1960

Eisenhower, Dwight D., *Crusade in Europe*, Doubleday, New York, 1948

Eisenhower, Dwight D., *Mandate for Change – The White House Years 1953–1956*, Heinemann, London, 1963

Eisenhower, Dwight D., *Waging Peace – The White House Years – A Personal Account 1956–1961*, Doubleday, New York, 1965

Eisenhower, John S. D., *Strictly Personal – A Memoir*, Doubleday, New York, 1974

Fainsod, Merle, *How Russia Is Ruled*, Harvard University Press, Cambridge, Mass., 1963

Ferrell, Robert H. (ed.), *America in a Divided World 1942–1972*, University of South Carolina Press, Columbia, 1975

Ferrell, Robert, H. (ed.), *The Eisenhower Diaries*, Norton, New York, 1981

Finer, Herman, *Dulles over Suez – The Theory and Practice of His Diplomacy*, Quadrangle Books, New York, 1964

Fleming, D. W., *The Cold War and its Origins*, Doubleday, New York, 1961

Fortune Magazine, *The Space Industry – America's Newest Giant*, Time/Prentice Hall, New York, 1962

Frankland, Mark, *Khrushchev*, Stein and Day, New York, 1967

Freeman, Leslie J., *Nuclear Witness*, Norton, New York, 1982

Frutkin, Arnold W., *International Cooperation in Space*, Prentice Hall, New York, 1965

Gaddis, John Lewis, *Russia, the Soviet Union, and the United States – An Interpretive History*, Wiley and Sons, New York, 1978

Galbraith, John Kenneth, *The Affluent Society*, Mentor Books, New York, 1984

Gatland, Kenneth W., *Development of the Guided Missile*, Iliffe & Sons, London, 1954

Gatland, Kenneth W., *Project Satellite*, British Book Centre, London, 1958

Gavin, James, *War and Peace in the Space Age*, Hutchinson, London, 1959

Gibbons, S. R., *The Cold War*, Longman, London, 1986

Golovanov, Yaroslav, *Sergei Korolev – The Apprenticeship of a Space Pioneer*, Mir, Moscow, 1975

Goodwin, Harold Leland, *The Images of Space*, Holt Rinehart & Winston, New York, 1965

Goold-Adams, Richard, *The Time of Power – A Reappraisal of John Foster Dulles*, Weidenfeld & Nicolson, London, 1962

Gromyko, Andrei, *Memoirs*, Arrow Books, London, 1989

Grottrup, Irmgard, *Rocket Wife*, Andre Deutsch, London, 1959

Gurney, Gene: *The Launching of Sputnik – October 4, 1957*, Watts, New York, 1975

Halberstram, David, *The Fifties*, Ballentine Books, New York, 1993

Harvey, M., Harvey, D. and Ciccoritti, L., *US-Soviet Cooperation in Space*, Center for Advanced International Studies, Washington, DC, 1975

Hayter, Sir William, *The Kremlin and the Embassy*, Hodder & Stoughton, London, 1966

Heller, Mikhail and Nekrich, Aleksandr, *Utopia in Power – A History of the USSR from 1917 to the Present*, Hutchinson, London, 1986

Hennessy, Peter, *Whitehall*, Secker & Warburg, London, 1989

Hitchens, Christopher, *Blood, Class and Nostalgia – Anglo-American Ironies*, Vintage, London, 1991

Hodnett, Grey (ed.), *The Khrushchev Years – 1953–1964*, University of Toronto Press, Toronto, 1974

Hoopes, Townsend, *The Devil and John Foster Dulles*, Atlantic Monthly Press, New York, 1973

Horsley, Edith, *The 1950s*, Bison Group, London, 1990

Hughes, Emmet John, *The Ordeal of Power – A Political Memoir of the Eisenhower Years*, Atheneum, New York, 1963

Hughes, Gwyneth and Welfare, Simon, *Red Empire – Forbidden History of the USSR*, Weidenfeld, London, 1990

Huzel, Dieter, *Peenemünde to Canaveral*, Prentice Hall, New Jersey, 1962

Hyland, William G., *The Cold War Is Over*, Random House, New York, 1990

Hyland, William G., *The Fall of Khrushchev*, Funk and Wagnalls, New York, 1968

International Herald Tribune (ed.), *The Front Page 1887–1980*; International Herald Tribune Publishing, Paris, 1980

Irving, David, *The Mare's Nest*, William Kimber, London, 1964

Ishlinsky, A. Yu. (ed.), *The Great Engineer Korolev*, Nauka, Moscow, 1982

James, Peter, *Soviet Conquest from Space*, Arlington House, New York, 1974

James, Robert Rhodes, *Anthony Eden*, Papermac, London, 1987

Johnson, Brian, *The Secret War*, BBC Books, London, 1978

Johnson, David, *V for Vengeance*, William Kimber, London, 1981

Jones, Christopher, *No. 10 Downing Street – The Story of a House*, BBC Books, London, 1985

Jones, Landon Y., *Great Expectations – America and the Baby Boom Generation*, Ballantine Books, New York, 1980

Kaku, Michael and Axelrod, Daniel, *To Win a Nuclear War – The Pentagon's Secret War Plans*, Black Rose Books, Montreal, 1987

Keldish, Mstislav (ed.), *Korolev's Research – A Collection of Works and Documents*, Nauka Publishing, Moscow, 1980

Kennan, George F., *Memoirs 1925–1950*, Hutchinson, London, 1968

Kennedy, Paul, *The Rise and Fall of the Great Powers*, Fontana, London, 1989

Kennedy, Robert F., *Thirteen Days – A Memoir of the Cuban Missile Crisis*, New American Library, New York, 1969

Khrushchev, N. S., *Khrushchev Remembers*, Little Brown, Boston, 1970

Khrushchev, N. S., *Khrushchev Remembers – The Last Testament*, Little Brown, Boston, 1974

Khrushchev, N. S., *Khrushchev Remembers – The Glasnost Tapes*, Little Brown, Boston, 1990

Khrushchev, Sergei, *Khrushchev on Khrushchev*, Little Brown, Boston, 1990

Killian, James R. Jr, *Sputnik, Scientists and Eisenhower – A Memoir of the First Special Assistant to the President for Science and Technology*, MIT Press, Cambridge, Mass., 1977

Kinnard, Douglas, *President Eisenhower and Strategy Management: A Study in Defense Politics*, University of Kentucky Press, Lexington, Kentucky, 1977

Kissinger, Henry, *Nuclear Weapons and Foreign Policy*, Harper Brothers, New York, 1957

Kistiakowsky, George B., *A Scientist at the White House: The Private Diary of President Eisenhower's Special Assistant for Science and Technology*, Harvard University Press, Cambridge, Mass., 1976

Klee, Ernst and Merk, Otto, *The Birth of the Missile – Secrets of Peenemünde*, Harrop, London, 1965

Krieger, F. J., *Behind the Sputniks*, The Rand Corporation, Santa Monica, California, 1958

Krock, Arthur, *Memoirs – Intimate Recollections of Twelve American Presidents from Theodore Roosevelt to Richard Nixon*, Cassell, London, 1968

Kyle, Keith, *Suez*, Weidenfeld & Nicolson, London, 1991

LaFeber, Walter (ed.), *America in the Cold War*, Wiley and Sons, New York, 1969

LaFeber, Walter (ed.), *America, Russia and the Cold War – 1945–1984*, Knopf, New York, 1985

Lasby, Clarence, *Project Paperclip*, Atheneum, New York, 1971

Lederer, Ivo J. (ed.), *Russian Foreign Policy – Essays in Historical Perspective*, Yale University Press, New Haven, 1962

Leish, Kenneth, *The White House*, Newsweek, New York, 1978

Leonhard, Wolfgang, *The Kremlin Since Stalin*, Oxford University Press, Oxford, 1962

Lewis, John S. and Ruth A., *Space Resources – Breaking the Bonds of Earth*, Columbia University Press, New York, 1987

Lewis, Richard, *Appointment on the Moon*, Viking, New York, 1968

Ley, Willy, *Rockets, Missiles and Space Travel*, Viking, New York, 1958

Library of Congress, *Soviet Space Programs: Unmanned Space Activities*, Parts 1,2,3, US Government Printing Office, Washington, DC, 1985

Linden, Carl A., *Khrushchev and the Soviet Leadership*, Johns Hopkins University Press, Baltimore, 1990

Love, Kennett, *Suez – The Twice-Fought War*, Longman, London, 1969

Lucas, W. Scott, *Divided We Stand – Britain and the United States in the Suez Crisis*, Hodder & Stoughton, London, 1991

Lyon, Peter, *Eisenhower – Portrait of the Hero*, Little Brown, New York, 1974

MacCauley, Martin (ed.), *Khrushchev and Khrushchevism*, Indiana University Press, Bloomington, 1988

McDougall, Walter A., *The Heavens and the Earth – A Political History of the Space Age*, Basic Books, New York, 1985

McGovern, James, *Crossbow and Overcast*, Hutchinson, London, 1965

Macmillan, Harold, *Tides of Fortune – 1945–1955*, Macmillan, London, 1969

Macmillan, Harold, *Riding the Storm – 1956–1959*, Macmillan, London, 1971

McNamara, Robert S., *The Essence of Security:Reflections in Office*, Harper & Row, New York, 1968

Magill, Frank N. (ed.), *Magill's Survey of Science, Space, Exploration Series*, Salem Press, Boston, 1989

Mailer, Norman, *Of Fire on the Moon*, Little Brown, New York, 1969

Manchester, William, *The Glory and the Dream – A Narrative History of America 1932–1972*, Bantam Books, New York, 1985

Mansfield, Peter, *The Arabs*, Penguin Books, London, 1985

Marchetti, Victor and Marks, John D., *The CIA and the Cult of Intelligence*, Dell, New York, 1980

Medaris, General John B., *Countdown For Decision*, Putnam, New York, 1960

Medvedev, Roy, *Khrushchev*, Blackwell, Oxford, 1982

Medvedev, Roy and Zhores, *Khrushchev – The Years in Power*, Oxford University Press, Oxford, 1977

Medvedev, Zhores, *Nuclear Disaster in the Urals*, Angus & Robertson, London, 1979

Medvedev, Zhores, *Soviet Science*, Norton, New York, 1978

Miller, David W. and Moore, Clark D. (eds), *The Middle East Yesterday and Today – The George School Readings on Developing Lands*, Bantam Books, New York, 1970

Miller, Nathan, *Spying for America – The Hidden History of US Intelligence*, Dell Publishing, New York, 1989

Miller, R. and Feher F. (eds), *Khrushchev and the Communist World*, Barnes and Noble Books, New York, 1983

Millis, Walter (ed.), *The Forrestal Diaries*, Viking Press, New York, 1951

Moorehead, Alan, *The Traitors*, Hamish Hamilton, London, 1957

Mosley, Leonard, *Dulles – A Biography of Eleanor, Allen and John Foster Dulles and their Family Network*, Dial Press, New York, 1978

Needell, Allan A. (ed.), *The First 25 Years in Space – A Symposium*, Smithsonian Institute Press, Washington DC, 1983

Newhouse, John, *War and Peace in the Nuclear Age*, Vintage Books, New York, 1990

Nicolson, Iain, *Sputnik to Space Shuttle – The Complete Story of Space Flight*, Dodd, New York, 1985

Nixon, Richard, *The Memories of Richard Nixon*, Grosset & Dunlop, New York, 1978

Oakley, J. Ronald, *God's Country – America in the Fifties*, Dembner Books, New York, 1990

Oberg, James E., *Red Star in Orbit*, Random House, New York, 1981

Oberg, James E., *Uncovering Soviet Disasters – Exploring the Limits of Glasnost*, Robert Hale, London, 1989

O'Neill, William L., *American High – The Years of Confidence, 1945–60*, Free Press, New York, 1987

Ordway, Frederick and Sharpe, Mitchell, *The Rocket Team*, Heinemann, London, 1979

Parmet, Herbert S., *Eisenhower and the American Crusades*, Macmillan, New York, 1972

Parry, A., *Russia's Rockets and Missiles*, Doubleday, New York, 1960

Parry, A. (ed.), *The Russian Scientist*, Collier, London, 1973

Patterson, Walter C., *The Plutonium Business – And the Spread of the Bomb*, Paladin Books, London, 1984

Pethybridge, Roger, *A Key to Soviet Politics – The Crisis of the Anti-Party Group*, Praeger, New York, 1962
Pilat, Oliver, *The Atom Spies*, Putnam, New York, 1952
Pistrak, Lazar, *The Grand Tactician – Khrushchev's Rise to Power*, Praeger, New York, 1961

Rabinowitch, Eugene and Lewis, Richard S. (eds), *Man on the Moon – The Impact on Science, Technology and International Cooperation*, Basic Books, New York, 1969
Ranelagh, John, *The Agency – The Rise and Decline of the CIA*, Simon & Schuster, New York, 1986
Reston, James, *The Artillery of the Press – Its Influence on American Foreign Policy*, Harper & Row, New York, 1967
Riabchikov, Eugeny, *Russians in Space*, Weidenfeld & Nicolson, London, 1971
Richelson, Jeffrey, *American Espionage and the Soviet Target*, Morrow, New York, 1987
Roberts, Sir Frank, *Dealing with Dictators – The Destruction and Revival of Europe 1930–1970*, Weidenfeld & Nicolson, London, 1991
Romonov, A., *A Spacecraft Designer*, Novosti, Moscow, 1976
Rothschild, Eric (ed.), *The Korean War, Civil Rights and Sputnik*, New York Times Microfilming Collection, New York, 1978
Rothwell, Victor, *Britain and the Cold War*, Cape, London, 1982

Schauer, William, *The Politics of Space – A Comparison of the Soviet and American Space Programs*, Holmes & Meier, New York, 1976
Schlesinger, Arthur M. Jr, *The Cycles of American History*, Deutsch, London, 1987
Schlesinger, Arthur M. Jr, *Robert Kennedy and His Times*, Houghton Mifflin, Boston, 1978
Sharnik, John, *Inside the Cold War*, Arbor House, New York, 1987
Shelton, William, *Soviet Space Exploration – The First Decade*, Washington Square Press, New York, 1968
Simpson, Christopher, *Blowback – America's Recruitment of Nazis and Its Effects on the Cold War*, Weidenfeld & Nicolson, London, 1988
Slukhai, I. A., *Russian Rocketry – An Historical Survey*, Academy of Sciences, Moscow, 1965
Smith, Hedrick, *The Power Game*, Ballantine Books, New York, 1988

Smith, Hedrick, *The Russians*, Ballantine Books, New York, 1976

Smolders, Peter, *Soviets in Space*, Taplinger, New York, 1974

Sokolsky, V. N., *A Short Outline of the Development of Rocket Research in the USSR*, Academy of Sciences, Moscow, 1960

Speer, Albert, *Inside the Third Reich*, Macmillan, New York, 1970

Stevenson, William, *A Man Called Intrepid*, Macmillan, London, 1976

Stoiko, Michael, *Soviet Rocketry*, Holt, Rinehart, Winston, New York, 1970

Talese, Gay, *The Kingdom and the Power*, Bantam, New York, 1970

Tatu, Michel, *Power in the Kremlin – From Khrushchev to Kosygin*, Viking Press, New York, 1969

Trux, Jon, *The Space Race – From Sputnik to Shuttle – The Battle for the Heavens*, New English Library, London, 1985

Tsiolkovsky, K.E., *Works on Rocket Technology*, Publishing House of the Defense Industry, Moscow, 1947

Tucker, Robert C., *Political Culture and Leadership in Soviet Russia – From Lenin to Gorbachev*, W.W. Norton, New York, 1987

Tucker, Robert C., *The Soviet Political Mind – Stalinism and Post-Stalin Change*, Praeger, New York, 1971

Vladimirov, Leonid, *The Russian Space Bluff*, Tom Stacey Ltd, London, 1971

Voslensky, Michael, *Nomenklatura – The Soviet Ruling Class*, Doubleday, New York, 1984

Werth, Alexander, *The Khrushchev Phase*, Hale, London, 1961

Wicker, Tom, *On Press*, Viking, 1978

Wolfe, Tom, *The Right Stuff*, Farrar, Straus & Giroux, New York, 1979

Yergin, Daniel, *Shattered Peace – The Origins of the Cold War*, Penguin Books, London, 1990

Young, Peter, *World War – 1939–1945*, Pan Books, London, 1966

Zaehringer, Alfred J., *Soviet Space Technology*, Harper, New York, 1961

Zhukov, G.K., *The Memories of Marshal Zhukov*, Cape, London, 1971

General reference books include:

Chronicle of the 20th Century
Current Biography
Dictionary of Nobel Prize Winners
Encyclopedia Britannica
Grolier's American Academic Encyclopedia, On Line edition
International Who's Who?
Jane's Aircraft of the World
Jane's Space Programmes
New American Desk Encyclopedia
Timetables of History
Who's Who?

World Biography

Magazine articles

Alexander, Dr Charles C., 'Pathway to the Moon,' *Aerospace Historian*, Vol. 14 No. 4, Winter 1967

Allward, Maurice, 'The Space Age Is Here,' *Spaceflight*, January 1958

Asher, Lee, 'The Soviet Air Debt to Germany,' *Air University Quarterly Review*, Spring 1952

Astashenkov, Pyotr, 'Academician Korolev: The Life and Works of the Chief Designer of Soviet Spaceships,' *Sputnik*, March 1972

Banks, Peter M. and Ride, Sally K., 'Soviets in Space,' *Scientific American*, February 1989

Boyer, Ernest L., 'The Third Wave of School Reform,' *Christianity Today*, 22 September 1989

Bradley, General Omar, 'This Way Lies Peace,' *Saturday Evening Post*, 15 October 1949

Brown, Kenneth E., 'The Lively Third R,' *American Education*, February 1966

Brune, Lester H., 'The Eisenhower Administration and Defense Policy,' *Armed Forces and Society*, March 1980

Carey, Michael J., 'The Schools and Civil Defense: The Fifties Revisited,' *Teachers College Record*, January 1982

Chalmers, Roberts, 'The Day We Didn't Go To War,' *The Reporter*, 14 September 1954

Clarke, Arthur C., 'Visit to Vanguard,' *Spaceflight*, July 1957

Covault, Craig, 'Soviet Space Records Mark Opening of International Forum,' *Aviation Week & Space Technology*, 5 October 1987

Cowan, Robert, 'Sputnik's Splash, Space-age Fizzle,' *Technology Review*, January 1983

Daniloff, Nicholas A., 'Space Race: Russia Takes Shocks in Stride,' *US News & World Report*, 31 October 1983

Delmas, Claude, 'Il y a Vingt Ans – Le Spoutnik,' *La Défense Nationale* (France), October 1977

Dickson, Paul, 'How a Little Beep-Beep-Beep Scared America Half to Death,' *The Washingtonian*, September 1982

Downing, John, 'The Intersputnik System and Soviet Television,' *Soviet Studies*, October 1985

Dulles, John Foster, 'Challenge and Response in US Foreign Policy,' *Foreign Affairs*, October 1957

Dulles, John Foster, 'A Policy of Boldness,' *Life* magazine, 19 May 1952

Dulles, John Foster, 'A Policy for Security and Peace,' *Foreign Affairs*, April 1954

Easterbrook, Gregg, 'From Sputnik to the Flying Submarine: How Pentagon Rivalries Gave Us the MX,' *Washington Monthly*, August 1981

Eberhart, Jonathan, 'The Day the Sky Was Opened,' *Science News*, 2 October 1982

Emme, Dr Eugene, 'The Historical Origins of NASA,' *Airpower Historian*, January 1963

Evangelista, Matthew, 'How Technology Fuels the Arms Race,' *Technology Review*, July 1988

Fantini, Mario D. and Weinstein, Gerald, 'Taking Advantage of the Disadvantaged,' *Teachers College Record*, February 1967

Feulner, Edwin, 'Sifting through the Rubble,' *Washington Times*, 24 November 1989

Fink, Donald E., 'Moscow Space Forum,' *Aviation Week & Space Technology*, 12 October 1987

Furnas, Dr Clifford C., 'Birthpangs of the First Satellite,' *Research Trends*, Cornell Aeronautical Laboratory, Spring 1970

Gale, Oliver M., 'Post-Sputnik Washington from an Inside Office,' *Cincinnati Historical Society Bulletin*, April 1973

Gatland, Kenneth W., 'Rockets and Artificial Satellites in the IGY,' *Spaceflight*, January 1958

Gatland, Kenneth W., 'Russia's Second Satellite,' *Spaceflight*, February 1958

Gimbel, John, 'US and German Scientists,' *Political Science Quarterly*, Vol. 3, 1986

Hailwood, Ed and Bishop, Carol, 'The Future Isn't What It Used to Be,' *Canadian Business*, January 1984

Hall, R. Cargill, 'Origins and Development of the Vanguard and Explorer Satellite Programs,' *Airpower Historian*, April 1964

Hammond, Paul Y., 'Presidents, Politics and International Intervention,' *Annual of the American Academy of Political and Social Sciences*, 1969

Hanle, Paul A., 'The Beeping Ball That Started a Dash into Outer Space,' *Smithsonian* magazine, July 1982

Harriman, Averell, 'My Alarming Interview with Khrushchev,' *Life* magazine, 13 July 1959

Harvey, Mose L., 'The Lunar Landing and the US-Soviet Equation,' *Bulletin of the Atomic Scientists*, July 1969

Haynal, Kornel, 'Counterrevolution, the Strategy of Imperialism,' *Tarsadalmi Szemle* (Hungary), August – September 1981

Herbst, Jurgen, 'High School and Youth in America,' *Journal of Contemporary History* (Great Britain), March 1967

Higgins, John M., 'Social Studies for Today's Needs,' *Social Studies*, February 1964

Jeffries, John W., 'The Quest for National Purpose of 1960,' *American Quarterly*, Vol. 4, 1978

Johnson, Nicholas, L., 'Soviet Space: 2000th Earth Orbit,' *Jane's Defence Weekly*, 28 November 1987

Jones, R. V., 'The Scientific Intelligencer,' *Studies in Intelligence*, Fall, 1962

Kennan, George, 'Flashbacks,' *New Yorker*, 25 February 1985

Kennan, George, 'The Sources of Soviet Conduct,' *Foreign Affairs*, July 1947

Kenney, Stephen C., 'US Product Liability Law – Its Impact on Commercial Space Activities,' *Interavia Space Matters*, 1 June 1986

Kerr-Tener, Janet, 'Eisenhower and Federal Aid to Higher Education,' *Presidential Studies Quarterly*, Vol. 3, 1987

Kinnard, Douglas, 'President Eisenhower and the Defense Budget,' *Journal of Politics*, Vol. 39, 1977

Knight, Charlotte, 'German Rocketeers,' *AAF Review*, July 1946

Kolesnikov, A., 'Grechko Reveals Efforts to Conceal Soviet Space Failures,' *Spaceflight*, June 1989

Krylov, M., 'The Sputnik Link,' *Morskoi Sbornik* (USSR), October 1982

Landers, Clifford E. and Nudelman, Arthur E., 'Professors, Politics and the Government,' *Midwest Quarterly*, Vol. 1, 1972

Lang, Daniel, 'Interview with Wernher von Braun,' *New Yorker*, 21 April 1951

Lear, John, 'Ike and the Peaceful Atom,' *The Reporter*, 12 January 1956

Leavitt, William, 'The Air Force and Space,' *Air Force and Space Digest*, September 1970

Leavitt, William, 'Bringing Space-Age Education to the Other America – A Challenge for Industry,' *Air Force and Space Digest*, August 1966

Leavitt, William, 'Bringing the Space Program down to Earth,' *Air Force and Space Digest*, September 1967

Lenorovitz, Jeffrey M., 'Soviets' Vast Space Launch Facility Supports Manned, Unmanned Programs,' *Aviation Week & Space Technology*, 16 October 1989

Lovell, Bernard, 'The Great Competition in Space,' *Foreign Affairs*, January 1972

Lubell, Samuel, 'Sputnik and American Public Opinion,' *Columbia University Forum*, Winter 1957

Lubkin, Gloria B., 'Soviet Space Research Flies High 30 Years after Sputnik Launch,' *Physics Today*, February 1988

Luce, Henry R., 'The American Century,' *Life* magazine, 17 February 1941

McDougall, Walter A., 'Space-Age Europe: Gaullism, Euro-Gaullism and the American Dilemma,' *Technology and Culture*, February 1985

McDougall, Walter A., 'Sputnik, the Space Race and the Cold War,' *Bulletin of the Atomic Scientists*, May 1985

McGehee, Dr Harvey A., 'A 1969 Conversation with Khrushchev – The Beginning of his Fall from Power,' *Life* magazine, 18 December 1973

McLeod, Don, 'Did Democrats Steal it in 1960?' Associated Press, 12 July 1973

McLuhan, Marshall, 'At the Moment of Sputnik the Planet Became a

Global Theater in Which There Are No Spectators but Only Actors,' *Journal of Communication*, January 1974

Maddox, John, 'Space Science Celebrated on Sputnik's Thirtieth Birthday,' *Nature*, 8 October 1987

Marty, Martin E., 'A Humanist's View of Space Research,' *Chicago Today*, March 1966

Medvedev, Zhores, 'Bringing the Skeleton out of the Closet,' *Nuclear Engineering International*, November 1990

Medvedev, Zhores, 'Facts behind the Soviet Nuclear Disaster,' *New Scientist*, 30 June 1977

Medvedev, Zhores, 'Two Decades of Dissidence,' *New Scientist*, 4 November 1976

Moore, Otis C., 'Twenty Years in Space: No Hiding Place in Space,' *Air Force* magazine, August 1974

Murphy, Charles J. V., 'Khrushchev's Paper Bear,' *Fortune*, December 1964

Oberg, James, 'Space: Inside the House of Sputnik,' *Omni*, March 1989

Oberg, James, 'Red Star in Orbit,' Transcript of three-part *Horizon Special* for the British Broadcasting Company, aired on BBC2, December 1990

Oberg, James, 'The Why of Sputnik,' *Space World*, December 1977

Paine, Thomas O., 'Who Will Lead the World's Next Age of Discovery?' *Aviation Week & Space Technology*, 21 September 1987

Pattie, Sir Geoffrey, 'Exploring the Idea of a Euro DARPA,' *Jane's Defence Weekly*, 25 July 1987

Pesavento, Peter, 'Sputnik's Heirs: What the Soviets Are Doing in Space,' *Technology Review*, October 1987

Petri, Winfried, 'Space Travel in the Soviet Union: Historical-Ideological Perspectives and Practical Expectations,' *Studies in Soviet Thought* (Netherlands), January 1978

Pollard, Frank, 'US Satellites (Failure And Success), Artificial Meteors and Project Farside,' *Spaceflight*, January 1958

Reed, Fred, 'The Day the Rocket Died,' *Air & Space*, April 1987

Reichek, Morton A., 'A Whistle-stop Tour of the Cold War Years,' *Business Week*, 26 January 1987

Roche, William M., 'Better Understanding through Change and Involvement,' *Catholic Education Review*, May 1966

Rousseau, Pierre, 'Les Avatars de la Fusée: Des V-2 aux Spoutniks,' *Miroir de l'Histoire* (France), Vol. 99, 1958

Saito, Makoto, 'A New Beginning for American Diplomacy,' *Journal of Social and Political Ideas in Japan* (Japan), January 1963

Schorr, Daniel, 'Focus on the Kremlin's Secrecy Obsession,' *New York Times* magazine, 17 August 1958

Sheldon, Charles S. II, 'An American Sputnik for the Russians?' *Bulletin of the Atomic Scientists*, August 1969

Sheldon, Ken, 'Probing Space by Camera: The development of image processing at NASA's Jet Propulsion Laboratory,' *BYTE*, March 1987

Shepley, James, 'How Dulles Averted War,' *Life* magazine, 16 January 1956

Spiro, Thomas, 'Science and the Relevance of Relevance,' *Antioch Review*, Vol. 3, 1969

Stratton, W., Stillman, D., Barr, S., and Agnew, H., 'Are Portions of the Urals Really Contaminated?' *Science*, 26 October 1979

Swenson, Lloyd S. Jr, 'The Megamachine behind the Mercury Spacecraft,' *American Quarterly*, Vol. 2 (Part 1), 1969

Thomas, Phillip Drennon, 'The Teaching of History in the United States in the Era since Sputnik,' *Teaching History* (Great Britain), Vol. 4, 1970

Toftoy, Maj. Gen. H. N., 'Army Missile Development,' *Army Information Digest*, December 1956

Towster, Julian, 'Changing Russian Politics,' *Current History*, January 1958

Tyack, David B. with Kirst, Michael W. and Hansot, Elizabeth, 'Educational Reform: Retrospect and Prospect,' *Teachers College Record*, March 1980

Van Slingerland, Peter, 'How We Let the Missile Secrets Get Away,' *Look* magazine, 4 February 1958

Varennikov, Vladimir Sergeivich, 'Liudi I Tekhnika Kosmicheskoi Ery,' *Voprosy Istorii* (USSR), February 1988

Wellborn, Stanley, 'How Sputnik Turned the World Upside Down,' *US News & World Report*, 5 October 1982

Whipple, Fred and Hyneck, J. Allen, 'Observations of Satellite I,' *Scientific American*, December 1957

Wiesner, Jerome B., 'On Science Advice to the President,' *Scientific American*, January 1989

Wilford, John Noble, 'Riding High,' *Wilson Quarterly*, Vol. 4, 1980

Williams, William A., 'American Century – 1941–1957,' *The Nation*, 2 November 1957

Wilson, Andrew, 'Close Encounters of a Dangerous Kind,' *Interavia Aerospace Review*, 1 November 1988

Wilson, Andrew, 'Eyes in the Sky,' *Interavia Aerospace Review*, 1 September 1988

Wilson, Andrew, 'Thirty Years of Spaceflight – If There Is a Space Race, the USSR Seems to Be Winning It,' *Interavia Space Markets*, 1 September 1987

Zaloga, Steven J., 'Soviet Strategic Missile Development and Production,' *Jane's Defence Weekly*, 6 June 1987

Zhukov, N., 'Military-Naval Forces of the USA: The Postwar Period,' *Morskoi Sbernik* (USSR), Vol. 1, 1979

Unsigned periodicals include:

Aerospace Intelligence: 'Mark Sees US Space Program as Being in Worst Trouble Since Sputnik,' 12 May 1986

Aerospace Intelligence: 'RCA Celebrates 25 Years in Space,' 24 March 1983

Aviation Week & Space Technology: 'A Special Report on the China Lake Naval Weapons Center,' 20 January 1986

Aviation Week & Space Technology: 'How US Taps Soviet Missile Secrets,' 21 October 1957

Aviation Week & Space Technology: 'Preserving the Legacy,' 16 October 1989

Aviation Week & Space Technology: 'Soviets Stress Cooperative Ventures at Space Forum,' 12 October 1987

Aviation Week & Space Technology: 'USAF Pushes Pied Piper Space Vehicle,' 14 October 1957

The *Economist*: 'The Old Order Changes,' 2 June 1990

Interavia Aerospace Review: 'Soviet Union Celebrates Sputnik 1,' 1 November 1987

Interavia Space Markets: 'Spacewatch,' 1 December 1987

National Geographic World: 'Servants in the Sky,' February 1990

Soviet Life: 'Up . . . Up . . . and Away! Soviet Boosters,' April 1988

Soviet Russia: 'Sergei Korolev,' 10 January 1982

Studies in Intelligence: 'The Question of National Defense,' Summer, 1960

US News & World Report: 'Interview with Top Rocket Expert –

Dr Wernher von Braun,' 9 September 1955; reprinted 18 October 1957

Newspapers and news agency sources

Individual articles are referenced in the Notes. This is a general list of newspapers and news agencies used:

United States

Atlanta Constitution
Boston Globe
Chicago Daily News
Chicago Tribune
Cleveland Plain Dealer
Columbia (Missouri) Daily Tribune
Columbia (Washington) Columbian
Dallas Morning News
Detroit News
Flint Journal
Fresno Bee
Gulfport Daily Herald
Halifax Mail-Star
Huntsville Times
Jersey City Journal
Los Angeles Times
Lynchburg News and Daily Advance
Miami Herald
Milwaukee Journal
New Orleans Times-Picayune
New York Journal American
New York Post
New York Times
Providence Journal
Reading Eagle
Richmond Times Dispatch
San Antonio Light
San Antonio News
San Diego Union

San Jose Mercury Times
Saskatoon Star Phoenix
Schenectady Gazette
Seattle Times
Springfield Union
Toronto Globe and Mail
Tucson Arizona Daily Star
Washington Post

United Kingdom
Daily Telegraph
European
Evening Standard
Guardian
News Chronicle
Sunday Telegraph
Sunday Times
The Times

France
L'Humanité
Le Monde
Libération

Germany
Die Zeit

USSR
Izvestia
Komosolpravda
Moscow News
Pravda

New agencies, as referenced in the Notes, include:
Associated Press
International News Service
Novosti

Reuters
Tass
United Press International

Conference papers, hearings, speeches, dissertations and monographs

Adelman, Kenneth L., 'A World without Nuclear Weapons,' Address before the Woodrow Wilson School of Public and International Affairs at Princeton University, *Department of State Bulletin*, January 1987

Alexander, Dr Charles C., 'Pathway to the Moon,' Paper delivered to the Organization of American Historians, Chicago, 30 April 1967

Atkinson, Joseph Donahue Jr, 'The National Aeronautics and Space Administration Astronaut Recruiting and Selection Process 1959–1978: An Administrative History,' School of Public Affairs, University of Colorado, Denver, 1983

Central Intelligence Agency, 'A Dollar Comparison of Soviet and US Defense Activities,' Washington, DC, February 1976

Central Intelligence Agency, National Intelligence Estimate, 'The Soviet Space Program,' Top Secret, 5 December 1962

Central Intelligence Agency, 'Threats to the Security of the United States,' Top Secret, 28 September 1948

Clifford, Clark, 'American Relations with the Soviet Union: A Report to the President, by the Special Counsel of the President,' Top Secret, Eyes Only, 1946

Clowse, Barbara Barksdale, 'Education as an Instrument of National Security: The Cold War Campaign to Beat the Russians – From Sputnik to the National Defense Education Act of 1958,' PhD, University of North Carolina, 1977

Committee for State Security (KGB) of the USSR, 'Evaluation of the Launch by the Soviet Union of the Artificial Earth Satellite,' Top Secret, limited distribution, Moscow, 1957

Cooper, Mariane Abonyl, 'United States Secondary Information Services in Physical Sciences and Engineering: Evolution and Trends from Sputnik to Nixon,' PhD, Catholic University of America, 1980

Dulles, Allen, 'Statement by the Director of Central Intelligence to the Senate Foreign Relations Committee,' Top Secret, 31 May 1960

Foreign Relations of the United States: 1955–1957, Volume XI, '*Outer Space*'

Foreign Relations of the United States: 1955–1957, Volume XXIV, *'Soviet Union'*

Gaither Committee, Report to the President, 'Deterrence and Survival in the Nuclear Age,' Top Secret, November 1957

Gallagher, Donald Robert, 'A Comparison of Lay Opinion toward Education as Revealed in Selected Popular Magazines in the United States before and after Sputnik,' EdD, Temple University, 1969

Helms, Richard, 'Intelligence in American Society,' Speech given to the Council on Foreign Relations, Washington, DC, 17 April 1967

Holland, Frederick Eugene, 'Changes in Values in Adolescent Societies: Pre-Sputnik and Post-Sputnik Assessments,' EdD, University of California at Los Angeles, 1965

Institute for Strategic Studies, 'The Soviet Union and the NATO Powers – The Military Balance,' London, 1959

LeBlanc, M. Elizabeth, 'The Concept of General Education in Colleges and Universities: 1945–1979,' EdD, Rutgers University, 1980

McQuade, Lawrence, Report by the Assistant Secretary of Defense, 'Where Did the Missile Gap Go?' Top Secret, 30 May 1963

Miller, Steven Edward, 'The Limits of Mutual Restraint: Arms Control and the Strategic Balance,' PhD, Fletcher School of Law and Diplomacy, Tufts University, 1988

Mishin, V. P., 'Roads to Space – The Role of S. P. Korolev,' *Gagarian Scientific Readings on Astronautics*, Moscow, 1981

Mishin, V. P., 'Life Support and Crew Safety of Spacecraft,' *Scientific Readings on Aviation and Space Science*, Moscow, 1979–1980

National Security Council, NSC-68, 'A Report to the National Security Council by the Executive Secretary on United States Objectives and Programs for National Security,' Top Secret, 14 April 1950

Portanova, Peter L., 'The American Space Entrepreneur: A Guide to Strategic Planning,' PhD, Claremont Graduate School, 1988

Rauschenbach, B. V., 'S. P. Korolev and Soviet Rocketry,' Institute of Control Sciences, Moscow, USSR and 28th International Astronautical Congress, Prague, September – October 1977

Rockefeller Brothers Fund, *Prospects for America: The Rockefeller Panel Reports, Report No. II: International Security: The Military Aspect*, Doubleday and Co, New York, 1958

Seamans, Dr Robert, *Oral History*, National Air and Space Museum, 1996

Sigethy, Robert, 'The Air Force Organization for Basic Research 1945–1970,' PhD, The American University, 1980

US Army Ballistic Missile Agency, 'Chronology of the Army Ballistic Missile Agency February 1956 – December 1960,' Redstone Arsenal, Alabama, Secret, September 1961

US Army Ballistic Missile Agency, 'History – 1 July to 31 December 1957,' Redstone Arsenal, Secret, May 1958

US Army Ballistic Missile Agency, 'Historical Monograph – Army Ordinance Satellite Program,' Redstone Arsenal, Secret, November 1958

US Army Missile Command, 'Redstone Arsenal's Pioneering Efforts in Space,' by Dr Kaylene Hughes, Historical Division, Redstone Arsenal, Alabama, December 1990

US Congress, House Committee on Armed Services, 'Investigation of National Defense and Missiles,' 85th Congress, Second Session, Volumes I, II, III, IV

US Department of Defense, 'Report by the Joint Intelligence Committee to the Joint Chiefs of Staff on Implications of Soviet Possession of Atomic Weapons,' Washington, DC, Top Secret, 23 February 1950

US Library of Congress, Legislative Reference Service, 'United States Defense Policies in 1957,' 85th Congress, Second Session, House Document No. 436

US Library of Congress, Legislative Reference Service, 'United States Defense Policies in 1958,' 86th Congress, Second Session, House Document No. 227

US Presidential Papers, including Harry S. Truman, Dwight David Eisenhower and John F. Kennedy (Kennedy papers include US Senate)

US Senate, Committee on Armed Services, Preparedness Investigating Sub-committee, Hearings, 85th Congress, First and Second Sessions, Volumes I, II, III

US Senate, Select Committee to Study Government Operations with Respect to Intelligence Activities, 94th Congress, Second Session, Report 94–755

US Space and Rocket Center, 'Dr Wernher von Braun and the German Rocket Team,' privately printed monograph, 1990

US Vice-Presidential Papers, including Richard M. Nixon and Lyndon B. Johnson (Johnson papers include US Senate)

Van Wormer, James William, 'Sputnik and American Education,' PhD, Michigan State University, 1976

Von Braun, Wernher, 'A Minimum Satellite Vehicle Based on Components Available from Developments of the Army Ordinance Corps,' US Army, Secret

Washington Center of Foreign Policy Research, 'Developments in Military Technology and their Impact on United States Strategy and Foreign Policy,' Study No. 8, Johns Hopkins University, Baltimore, 1959

Williams, Robert Edward Jr, 'The Evolution of Disarmament and Arms Control Thought 1945–1963,' PhD, University of Virginia, 1987

Miscellaneous

Various contributors to the Sixth Scientific Readings on Cosmonautics took place in Moscow from 11 January through 15, 1982. The 190 papers that were delivered can be found at the Soviet Academy of Sciences under the title 'Letatelnyye Apparaty, Proyektir I Konstruktsii, Trudy Shestykh Nauch Chteniy Po Kosmonavt, Posvyashchen Pamyati Vydayushch Sovets Uchenykh-Pionerov Osvoyen Kosmiches Prostr.'

Unpublished sources

Include the private notes of V. E. Luppo, Moscow, 1957; Dr M. Tikhonravov, Moscow, 1957; some papers of the Communist Party of the USSR; some papers from the Foreign Ministry of the USSR; and one diary from a confidential source in Moscow.

Index

International Council of Scientific
Unions (ICSU), 90
International Geophysical Year
(IGY), 90
Inverchapel, Lord, fund request by,
13
'Iron Curtain', origin of term, 8
Israel
role in Allies' Egypt dilemma, 112
Sinai Peninsula attack by, 116
Izvestia, 207
Adjoubei's nepotism and, 311

Jackson, CD, 254
Jackson, Senator Henry 'Scoop', 186
Japanese Astronautical Society, 286
Jefferson, Thomas, 47
Jet Propulsion Laboratory, 139, 278
Johnson, Clarence 'Kelly', U-2
designer, 88-9
Johnson, Jake, 40
Johnson, Lyndon,
Eisenhower's defense
management, 266-7
Kennedy's running mate, 324
on space technology, 299
Sputnik response, 184
Joint Intelligence Committee
(JIC), 247-8
on translating Russian texts,
279-80
Soviet risk report, 19-21
Jones, Sir Harold Spencer, on moon
landings, 287
Juarez, 134
Jupiter-C, 141
satellite launch success, 282-3
Jupiter, successful testing of, 233

Kaganovich, demotion of, 158-60
Kaiser, Henry J, 42
Kaliningrad, 152-3

Kamchatka Peninsula, R-7 crash
into, 164
Kapitza, Pyotr Leonidovich, 156-8
Sputnik mastermind possibility,
190
Kapustin Yar, 145
Karpenko, AG, 91
Kefauver, Estes, 45
Keldish, Mstislav, 92
Korolev supporter, 156, 158
Kellogg, William, 40
Kennan, George
Cold War negotiation wish, 295
'Long Telegram' of, 9-10, 15
Kennedy Space Center *see* Florida
Missile Testing Range
Kennedy, Jacqueline, 48-9
Kennedy, John Fitzgerald
birth of, 41
election of, 324-6
Khrushchev, response to, 330-1
military build up of, 327
moon race, 303
KGB
reorganization of, 217-18
trailing von Braun, 161
US satellite and rocket plans, 292
Khrushchev, Nikita Sergeivich
background and rise of, 31-8
'Big Four' summit, 73-8
British visit, 107-109
Cold War blame by, 64-5
coup attempt against, 158-9
domestic policy, 298-9
Egypt war involvement, 116-7
Eisenhower betrayal of, 319-21
Eisenhower bonding with, 312-14
House of Lords, impressions
of, 109
Kennedy, Cuban crisis letter to,
329-30
Kennedy, response to, 327